CRITICAL ACCLAIM FOR

WINES of CALIFORNIA

"Two of the coolest guys on the planet . . . one of the coolest wine regions out there. . . . It is your encyclopedia to California."

—TRACY BURN, *Wine with Me*, Fox Business

"A comprehensive guide to this exciting and ever-changing region—from the history and geography to the current trends and new crop of winemakers to watch."

—*Wine Enthusiast*

"The ultimate guide to the world of wine in California. . . . The duo's newest venture includes descriptive coverage of all California wine regions and variety vineyards equipped with specific tasting notes, addresses, phone numbers and websites. They've also included telling interviews with key winemakers. . . . Not to be missed!"

—*USA Today Travel*

"Big in size and ambition. . . . A very accessible, leisurely, well-written guide, geared to a broad audience."

—*Newsday*

"Until Mike DeSimone and Jeff Jenssen decided to tackle the great state, no book had come close to covering all of California's wine regions. . . . What you read in the pages of *Wines of California* is the honest and highly-informed descriptions of two very passionate wine experts. . . . *Wines of California* is a must-have book for anyone who wants to get serious about, and have fun with, California wines."

—*HuffPost Taste*

"You'll find no one more agreeable with whom to explore the vineyards of California and their exciting wines."

—OZ CLARKE, wine writer and broadcaster, author of *Oz Clarke's Pocket Wine Guide* and *The History of Wine in 100 Bottles*

"An easy-to-understand foundation and overview of the regions, grapes, and notable producers. . . . Each regional category offers a synopsis of its geography and viticulture, with supporting facts and stats delivered in a straightforward manner. . . . The authors give short profiles of important wineries—from benchmarks to newcomers—with a tasting note of an illustrative wine or two concluding each vignette."

—*Village Voice*

"A massive undertaking in bringing the ever-changing and massive California wine industry into one book. . . . The book provides a fresh look at hundreds of wineries and their signature wines [and] notable people from trailblazers to iconoclasts. . . . A good and proper introductory guide."

—*WineShout*

"Organized by region from north to south, *Wines of California* offers short entries on selected wineries, highlighting some of their best efforts. A starting point for exploring the world of California wines."

—*Library Journal*

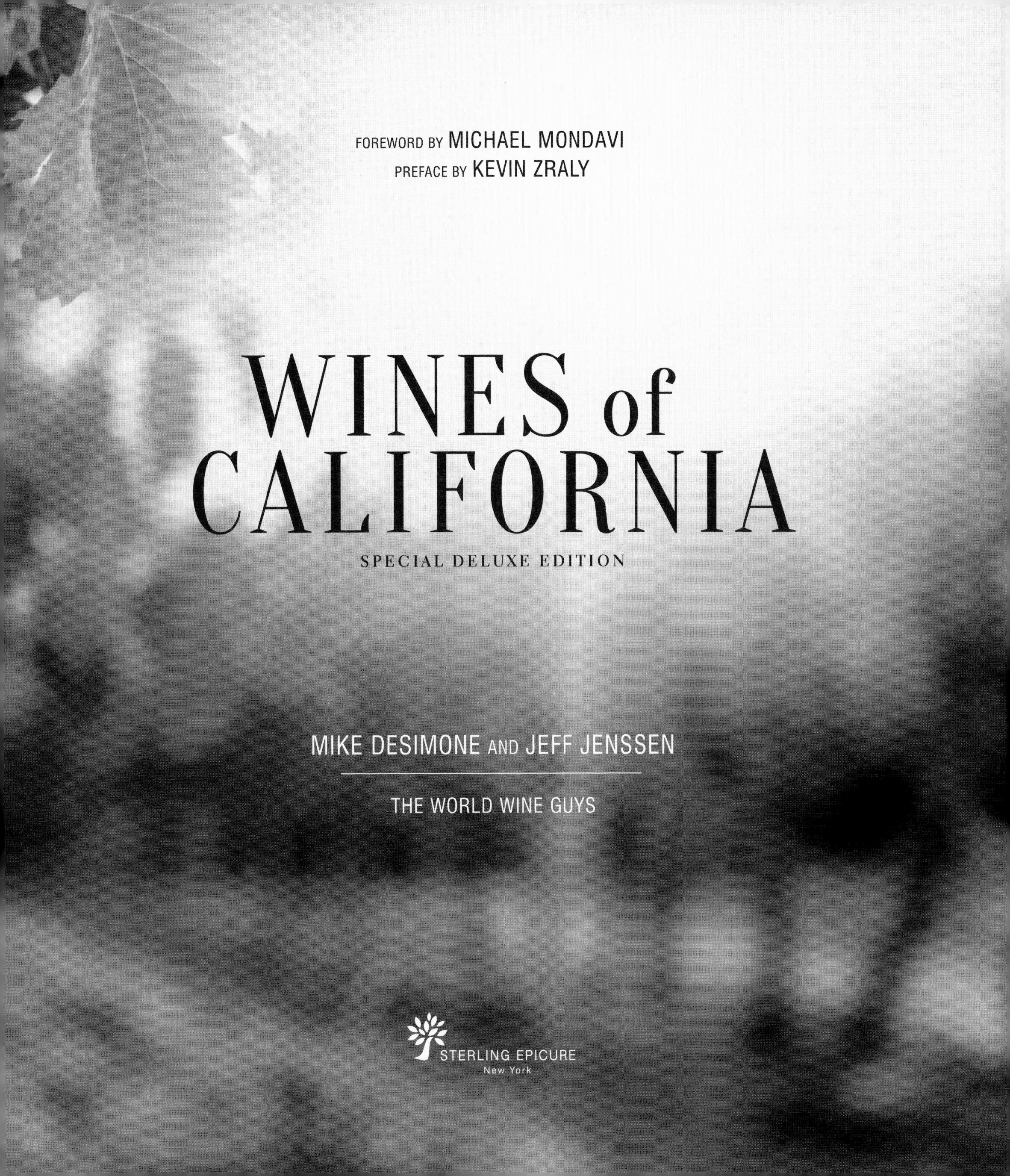

FOREWORD BY MICHAEL MONDAVI

PREFACE BY KEVIN ZRALY

WINES of CALIFORNIA

SPECIAL DELUXE EDITION

MIKE DESIMONE AND JEFF JENSSEN

THE WORLD WINE GUYS

STERLING EPICURE
New York

STERLING EPICURE
New York

An Imprint of Sterling Publishing
1166 Avenue of the Americas
New York, NY 10036

STERLING EPICURE is a trademark of Sterling Publishing Co., Inc.
The distinctive Sterling logo is a registered trademark of Sterling Publishing Co., Inc.

This special deluxe edition published 2015
Originally published in 2014 by Sterling Publishing Co., Inc.

Additional information courtesy The Wine Institute and the US Department of Agriculture.

A complete list of picture credits appears on page 270.

ISBN 978-1-4549-1782-3

Distributed in Canada by Sterling Publishing
c/o Canadian Manda Group, 664 Annette Street
Toronto, Ontario, M6S 2C8 Canada
Distributed in the United Kingdom by GMC Distribution Services
Castle Place, 166 High Street, Lewes, East Sussex, BN7 1XU, England
Distributed in Australia by Capricorn Link (Australia) Pty. Ltd.
P.O. Box 704, Windsor, NSW 2756, Australia

Design by Amy Trombat
Maps by Philip Buchanan and Susan Walsh

For information about custom editions, special sales, and premium and corporate purchases, please contact Sterling Special Sales at 800-805-5489 or specialsales@sterlingpublishing.com.

Manufactured in Canada

2 4 6 8 10 9 7 5 3 1

www.sterlingpublishing.com

TO ALL THE FAMILIES OF WINEMAKERS AND GRAPE GROWERS IN CALIFORNIA, PAST, PRESENT, AND FUTURE, AND TO OUR MANY FRIENDS IN THE WONDERFUL WORLD OF WINE

CONTENTS

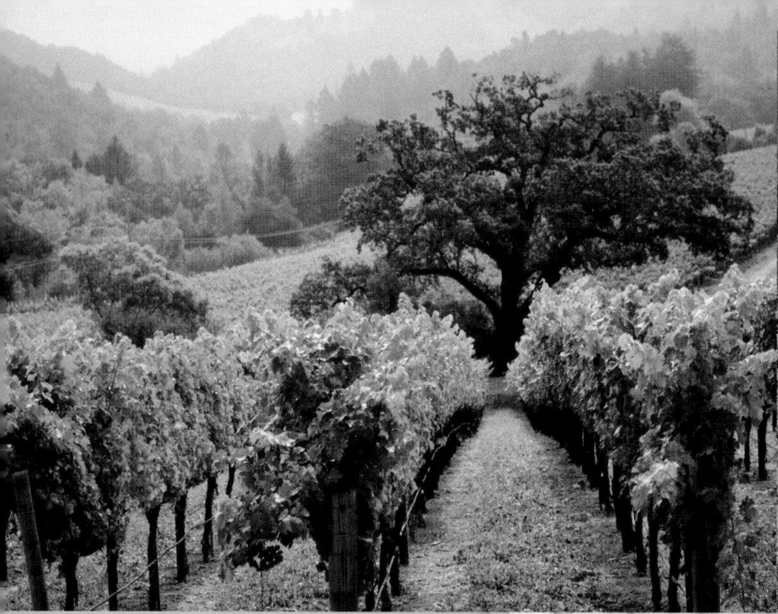

CALIFORNIA COUNTIES AND MAJOR GROWING REGIONS

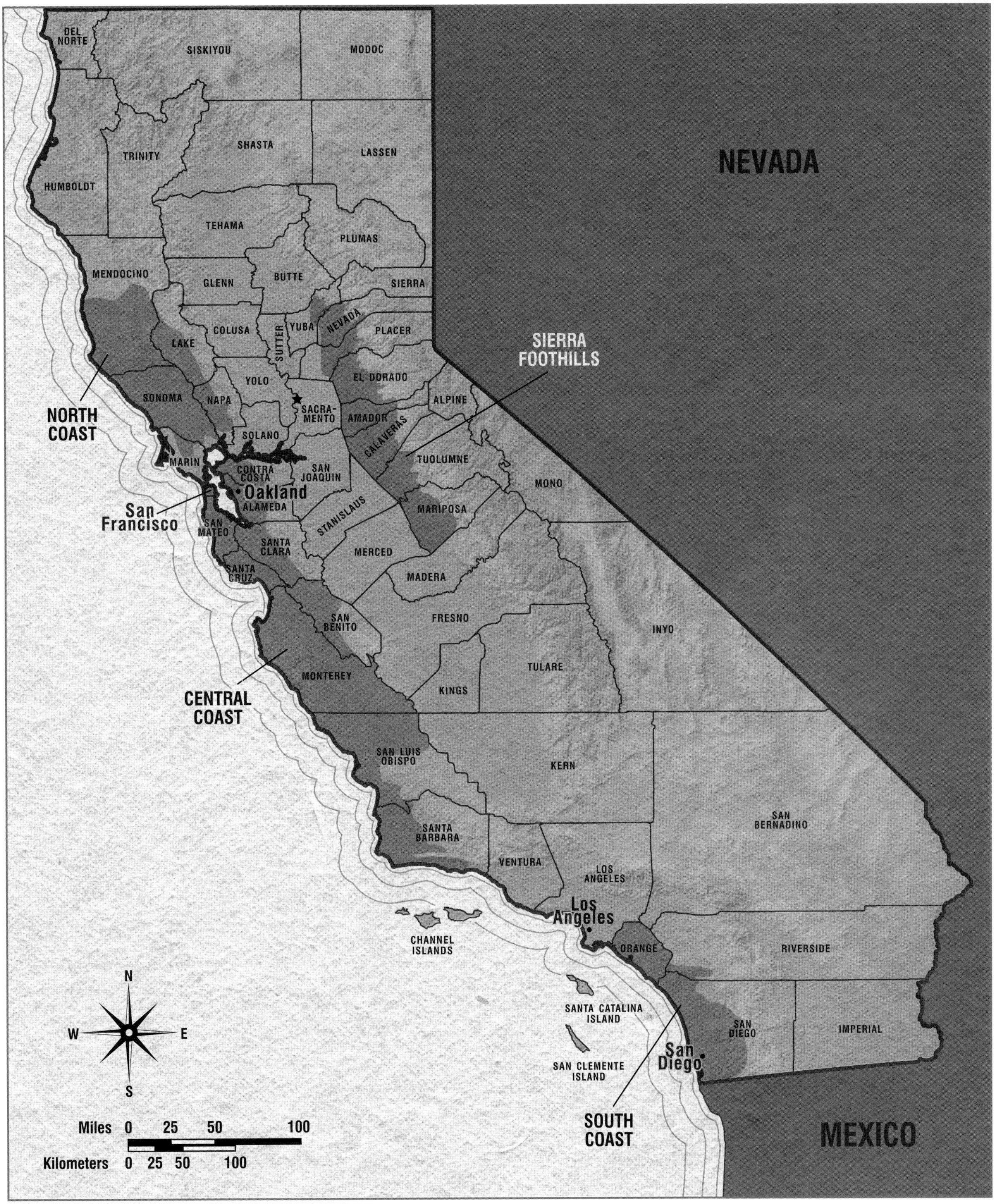

NEVADA
MEXICO
DEL NORTE
SISKIYOU
MODOC
TRINITY
SHASTA
LASSEN
HUMBOLDT
TEHAMA
PLUMAS
MENDOCINO
GLENN
BUTTE
SIERRA
COLUSA
SUTTER
YUBA
NEVADA
PLACER
LAKE
YOLO
EL DORADO
SONOMA
NAPA
SACRA-MENTO
AMADOR
ALPINE
SOLANO
CALAVERAS
TUOLUMNE
MARIN
CONTRA COSTA
SAN JOAQUIN
MONO
Oakland
ALAMEDA
STANISLAUS
MARIPOSA
San Francisco
SAN MATEO
SANTA CLARA
MERCED
SANTA CRUZ
MADERA
SAN BENITO
FRESNO
INYO
TULARE
MONTEREY
KINGS
SAN LUIS OBISPO
KERN
SAN BERNADINO
SANTA BARBARA
VENTURA
LOS ANGELES
Los Angeles
CHANNEL ISLANDS
ORANGE
RIVERSIDE
SANTA CATALINA ISLAND
SAN DIEGO
IMPERIAL
San Diego
SAN CLEMENTE ISLAND
NORTH COAST
SIERRA FOOTHILLS
CENTRAL COAST
SOUTH COAST
N
W
E
S
Miles 0 25 50 100
Kilometers 0 25 50 100

FOREWORD

I've had the pleasure of knowing Jeff and Mike for many years and have constantly been impressed with their love of food, wine, travel, culture, history, and storytelling, so when they asked if I would consider writing a foreword for *Wines of California*, I jumped at the chance.

While countless books have crossed my desk over the decades, it was the depth of study they were prepared to undertake—not only on wine and wineries in California (everyone's favorite cornerstone), but also the history of food, culture, community, and the arts—that impressed me the most. I feel that this information has been missing in recent times for books of this kind.

Born and raised in the Napa Valley and in the wine industry, I felt that I was quite knowledgeable on the history of California wines, but through their words, Mike and Jeff made the early pioneers come alive and taught me much of the wonderful detail I had either forgotten or never learned.

The flow of the book is ingenious, starting with the history of California music, the geography, the geology, the way the mission fathers developed the wine industry—all of it is a wonderful history lesson in itself. The extensive research on the California pioneers, from Father Junípero Serra, to Charles Krug, Karl Wente, and so many others, is a joy to read and an integral part of the history that has shaped California's vibrant wine industry today.

This work is also a testament to the amazing American spirit and creativity. The impact of phylloxera in the early 1900s, then World War I, and Prohibition in 1919 did not break the spirit of the California wine pioneers. They were, and remain, a true inspiration.

Also, the history of many of the innovations that we take for granted today is beautifully documented. From the development of improved sanitation to the reduced oxidation of wines to the adaptation of cold stabilization, the book clearly explains so many techniques that now are widely used. In fact, during the late '50s and early '60s during my formative years at Charles Krug Winery, I vividly remember the flavor differences in the wines being made before and after the implementation of cold fermentation. It was wonderful to be reminded of those times of innovation, change, and the quest to constantly improve on what had gone before.

Mike and Jeff also have succeeded in making the many wine regions of California accessible. The personalities and styles of the wine regions are captured in the detailed descriptions of the wineries. I think you will appreciate the clarity they bring to the importance of place in the wines produced.

For the last 25 years, I have used English author Hugh Johnson's *World Guide to Wines* as my reference book on wines, families, and producers, and I think Mike and Jeff have accomplished this for California. With the rapid changes and development over the last ten years, *Wines of California* provides accurate and timely information on the people, the families, and the regions of California.

Although Jeff and Mike's original objective may have been to create a book brimming with history, colorful stories, and educational nuances, this work also serves as a great reference book for everyone who wants to learn about California wines and visit the many regions that are covered in this comprehensive guide.

"In His or Her Own Words" showcase many of the pioneers and great winemakers of California and their personal insights—the conversation is an absolutely wonderful foray into the many visionaries, personalities, and people who comprise our diverse and dynamic industry.

I know you will look forward to reading and enjoying this book as well as keeping it nearby for reference. Please enjoy.

MICHAEL MONDAVI

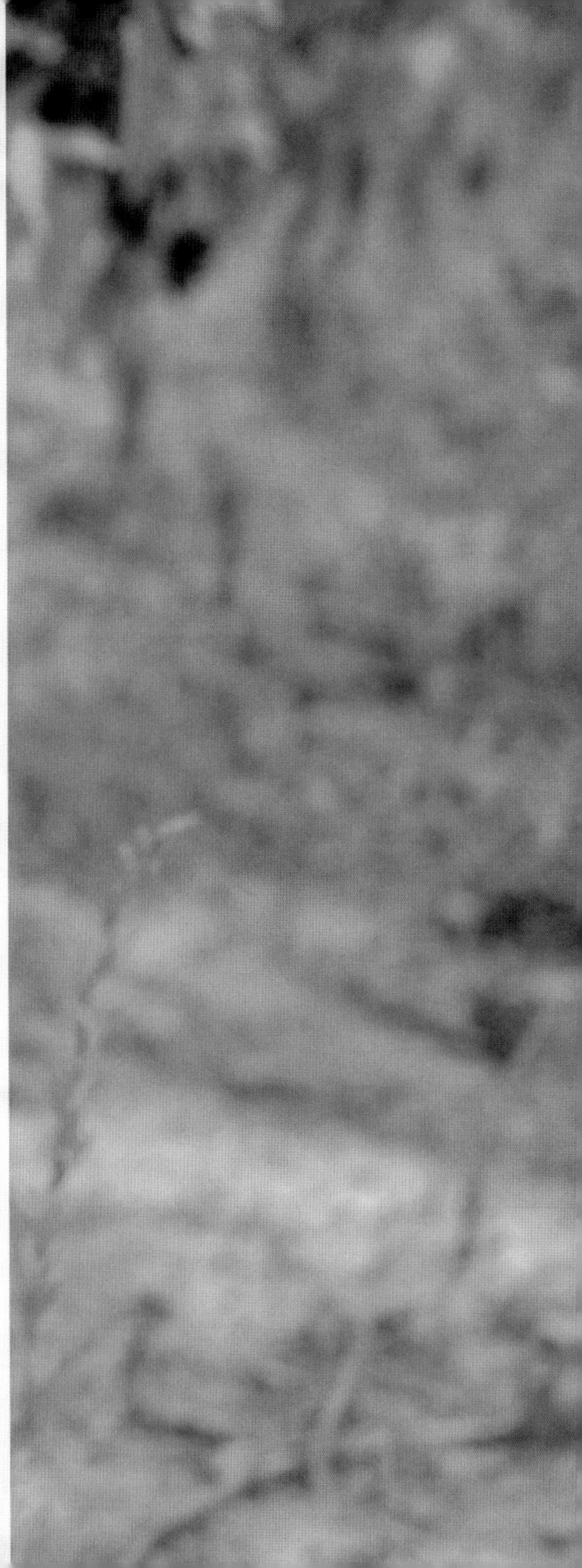

PREFACE

Mike DeSimone and Jeff Jenssen truly are movers and shakers in the world of wine. I know I can breathe easy any time I invite them to step in as guest speakers at the Windows on the World Wine School or for my master classes. I often say that if we compare wine educators and writers to doctors, I am a general practitioner, but when I need expertise in a particular area, I refer to a specialist. This is where folks like Mike and Jeff come in: they put in the long hours crafting *Wines of California* (just as they did on their prior title, *Wines of the Southern Hemisphere*), homing in on the state that is now the fourth largest producer of wine in the entire world. I have long felt that the time for a new book on California has come, and these two gentlemen have finally done it.

In 1970, there were only around 240 wineries in the state of California, and today there are more than 3,700. Beyond the exponential growth in the number of wineries itself, the entire culture of winemaking has changed and continues to change. Winemaking in California is a constantly moving target; it was in its infancy when I first visited wine regions there in the early 1970s, and today it remains in its formative years and has not yet begun to peak.

The two words *fun* and *exciting* don't often come to mind when considering wine writing or wine tastings, yet those are exactly the words I and many of my peers and friends use when talking about Mike and Jeff. Each half of this duo has been blessed with the abilities to both speak and write well. They are engaging and enjoyable speakers as well as prolific writers. By combining history, culture, personality, and intimate knowledge of their subject with the necessary facts and figures, they have turned what in other hands could be a dry book of statistics and listings into a compelling read.

The ability to take what we normally do in a wine tasting or master class and put that into words on paper is extremely difficult, and yet it appears that Mike and Jeff are able to do this effortlessly. I cannot imagine the number of hours they spent traveling to and from California, tasting wines, compiling all the information, and then putting it all together in such a comprehensive yet easy-to-read volume. It is quite obvious that they have done the requisite legwork. Not only have they incorporated the timeline of wine in the state, they also have focused on the particularities of the varied wine regions and brought to life the personalities of dozens of major players. In other words, they have successfully brought the story of the entire culture of wine in California to life.

The authors have a great respect for the past and for the "founding fathers" of California wine. They also have chosen to include stories of the second and third generations of many great California wine families through the series of interviews titled "In His or Her Own Words." Many of their subjects are old friends of mine, and it makes me happy to see the story of California wine, especially that of the late twentieth and early twenty-first centuries, told through their eyes. Mike and Jeff have generously opened the pages of their book to winemakers and winery owners, allowing each to give his or her unique outlook on winemaking in California. Collectively, these interviews add another dimension to the story of California wine.

The first time I visited California in 1972 you could count the number of wine-country restaurants on one hand. Then, simultaneously, the United States grew to become the number one consumer of wine in the world, with much of that wine coming from California, and the popularity of the farm-to-table movement took off. The result has been a renewed interest in food and an enormous number of restaurant choices in all the wine regions of California. Naturally, many of these establishments offer locally grown specialties paired with wines from the immediate area. The inclusion of recipes from winery kitchens and wine country restaurants in this tome gives great insight into what is going on in the California food movement today, and also serves as a travel guide to the best meals when you visit these regions yourself. This keeps the culture of wine in perspective—wine is meant to be enjoyed, not drunk in a vacuum.

The way we view wine has changed in the past 40 years. California wine used to just be described as white or red, and then we moved on to calling those same wines (however incorrectly) Chablis or Burgundy. People then started to request wine from a few specific wineries, and then they began seeking out bottles first from Napa and then Sonoma. As wine drinkers became more sophisticated, they looked for particular vineyard names on labels, and then they got savvy in terms of AVAs. Although many writers have glossed over the regions of California beyond Napa and Sonoma, Mike and Jeff have been both inclusive and forward thinking by delving into the other less popularized regions of California and discussing them in depth.

These two seasoned wine professionals have brought us an up-to-date, modern look at what is happening in one of the most exciting wine regions in the world, and they have done it with style. As much as I have enjoyed reading *Wines of California*, I look forward to the next edition, as a testament to the innovation and tenacity of the grape growers and wine-makers of California.

KEVIN ZRALY

CALIFORNIA
1
CALIFORNIA REPUBLIC

INTRODUCTION

California looms large in the collective psyche. It has been mythologized through popular music, starting with "California Here I Come," written for Broadway in 1921 and popularized by Al Jolson in 1924. That tune launched numerous television and movie characters and countless people to a better life or at least an unforgettable time in the Golden State.

Impressions of California pepper the playlists of oldies, easy listening, and classic rock stations, including the Beach Boys' "California Girls," the Mamas and the Papas' "California Dreamin'," the Eagles' "Hotel California," Albert Hammond's "It Never Rains in Southern California," Led Zeppelin's "Going to California," and the Red Hot Chili Peppers' "Californication." Younger music lovers may be inclined to play Phantom Planet's "California," Katy Perry's "California Gurls," Rihanna's "California King Bed," or Train's "California 37," but whether your favorite California song was first bought on vinyl or streamed online, one of these iconic tunes has buzzed through your head, conjuring sandy beaches, sleek convertibles, and beautiful sun-kissed people.

California has been legendary since the mid-sixteenth century, when the first Spanish explorers arrived. The word *California* comes from a 1510 Spanish novel, *Las Sergas de Esplandián* (*The Adventures of Esplandián*) by Garci Rodríguez de Montalvo, which describes an island ruled by beautiful Amazon warriors. Rodríguez based the name on the Spanish word *califa*, itself based on the Arabic word for ruler or leader. Even before its boundaries or interior was known, California captured the imagination of those who set out to explore and conquer it. The most populous US state first appeared on a map in 1562 as an island, and in those days before mechanical transportation it might just as well have been one.

The features that make it perfect for those wishing to live the dream—bright, sunny days ideal for driving with the car top down and refreshing, low-humidity evenings—also make it unequaled for cultivating the fruit of the vine. Ample sunshine provides exemplary conditions for ripening, and 800 miles of coastline provide fog and breezes essential to promoting the retention of acidity, a necessary component in a balanced glass. Inland valleys receive similar cooling action from nearby rivers and lakes.

Spanish missionaries planted the first grapes, but California as a grape-growing state is a melting pot as diverse as the United States itself; viticulturists worldwide bring their hometown varieties to the state's varied soils, from Covelo in the north to Ramona Valley in the south. Many wine drinkers think of California as the home of high-alcohol Cabernet Sauvignon and buttery Chardonnay (or worse, the home of White Zin), but the different varietals, from Albariño to Zinfandel, and the array of styles astound all who look more closely.

At present, the state has 130 federally approved American Viticultural Areas, or AVAs, with petitions on file for several more. The state consists of four major regions: North Coast AVA, Central Coast AVA, South Coast AVA, and the Central Valley, which isn't an AVA. These break down further into multiple AVAs.

California is the top wine-producing region in the United States, responsible for 90 percent of the wine made in the country. It boasts 3,800 bonded wineries, an increase of 2,100 in the last decade, and 4,600 grape growers. Its 163,695 square miles contain 546,000 acres of wine grapes, and in 2012 just over four million tons of grapes destined for a glass were harvested. Over 207 million cases of California wine were sold in the US market that year, representing a total retail value of $22 billion, with an additional $1.43 billion of US wine, 90 percent from California, exported to a growing roster of nations around the world. Perhaps the most startling fact about the California wine industry is that, as our friend Kevin Zraly mentioned, it's the world's fourth largest producer of wine by volume, behind France, Italy, and Spain.

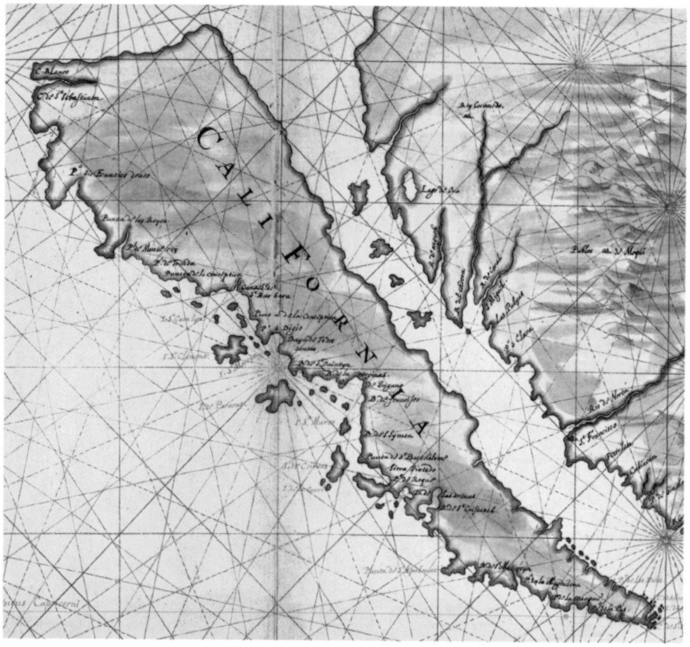

California's first vineyard was planted by a Jesuit missionary at Mission San Bruno in 1683, though historians believe the grapes weren't harvested and no wine was made there. Father Junípero Serra, also a Jesuit and known today as the father of California wine, established a more successful vineyard in 1779 at Mission San Diego de Alcala in the Province of the Californias in the viceroyalty of New Spain. He built a rudimentary winery onsite a year later. Before his death in 1784, he had founded eight other missions, most with their own vineyards. The first—and for many years the only—grape grown here was the Mission grape, known in Chile as Pais and in Argentina as Criolla Chica.

The cultivation of European grapes, *Vitis vinifera*, came to North America about two hundred years later than to South America, although by the same route: In the entourages of the conquistadors came Catholic priests who planted vines and made wine for Mass and the table. It's worth noting the similarity in latitudes in the opposing hemispheres. Mendoza, Argentina, and Santiago, Chile, sit at 32.89 South and 33.45 South, and San Diego lies at 32.71 North. But more than just analogous latitudes and shared origins connect the grape-growing regions of California to Chile and Argentina. The major influence that moved production from a by-product of Holy Communion to a highly quaffable beverage was the introduction of French grape varieties and the pioneering efforts of French and other European viticulturists and enologists.

Jean-Louis Vignes, a winemaker, distiller, and cooper, planted the first non-Mission vines near Los Angeles in 1833. Born near Bordeaux, Vignes didn't like the quality of wine made with available stock, so he sent for Cabernet Franc and Sauvignon Blanc cuttings. He's thought to be the first Californian to age his wines in barrels he made of wood from his land in the San Bernardino Mountains. Within about 10 years, he was shipping wine north to Santa Barbara, Monterey, and San Francisco, and by 1850 he was producing upward of 150,000 bottles annually. People from other nations, notably Italy and Germany, have made their mark on the California wine industry, but the French influence continues today through the efforts of winemakers, consultants, and owners such as Jean-Charles Boisset, Stephane Derenoncourt, Philippe Melka, Christian Moueix, Michel Rolland, and Pierre Seillan.

James Marshall discovered gold at Sutter's Mill in Coloma, near Sacramento, in January 1848. Word spread quickly, and soon more than 300,000 people from around the world headed to California. The site lies in El Dorado ("the Golden") County in the Sierra Foothills AVA. The first known grapes in the Sierra Foothills were planted during the Gold Rush, but the more lasting effect of the geological discovery was California's first major population increase, particularly San Francisco and the Bay Area. The age of California dreamin' had begun.

San Francisco increased from about 200 residents to over 36,000 between 1846 and 1852, and, after the Mexican-American War, California became a state in 1850 as part of a legislative package that also involved the territories of Texas, New Mexico, and Utah. Steamships were plying the seas, bringing people from China and South America, and by 1869 railroads stretched across the continent. As towns and cities grew, European immigrants, newly arrived or previously settled elsewhere, set out for California to purchase inexpensive land, establish farms, and provide produce, meat, and dairy to the ever-increasing population.

A Spanish priest holds the title of Father of California Wine, and a Hungarian "count" holds the same for California viticulture. Over several years, Agoston Haraszthy, founder of Buena Vista Winery (owned today by Jean-Charles Boisset), imported cuttings from more than 150 of Europe's great vineyards. After growing grapes near San Francisco, he settled on a small vineyard near Sonoma in 1856. He transplanted some of the French varieties that he had planted near the city and hired as his winemaker Prussian immigrant Charles Krug, who in 1861 founded his eponymous winery in Napa Valley, owned today by Peter Mondavi and his family. Krug had worked for John Patchett, who planted a Napa vineyard in 1854 and opened the first winery there in 1858.

By 1857 Haraszthy had begun construction on a stone winery complete with the latest equipment and underground cellars. He ultimately owned more than 5,000 acres, including many vineyards. In addition to his pioneering efforts in Sonoma, Haraszthy authored a groundbreaking document in 1858. His 19-page "Report on Grapes and Wine of California" is the first written study of vineyard practices and winemaking in the United States.

Many fifth- or sixth-generation grape growers descend from Italians or Germans who started by raising melons, peaches, or dairy cows before some enterprising forebear planted grapes. Karl Wente, a German immigrant who learned from Charles Krug, started his own winery in 1883 and entered the grape-growing avant-garde in Livermore Valley with his purchase of 48 acres. Jacob Beringer, another Krug protégé, bought land in Napa Valley with his brother Frederick in 1875 and founded their winery, the oldest continually operated winery in Napa Valley, a year later. The histories of every winemaking region and many individual wineries teem with the names of farmers and winemakers whose heirs continue their legacy today.

As railroad tracks connected the Eastern Seaboard to the Pacific, the phylloxera insect was ravaging Europe, causing farmers from Spain, France, Italy, and Croatia to abandon their vineyards and seek their fortunes overseas. Many headed to North America, South America, and Australasia to ply their trade, spreading European practices worldwide. With its wide stretches of farmland, growing population, and near-mythic status, California became the North American destination of choice. By the beginning of the twentieth century, California had a maturing winemaking industry. California wines had begun to win awards in international competitions, including Captain Gustave Niebaum's Inglenook Wine, the first Bordeaux-style wine in the United States, which took gold at the World's Fair in Paris in 1889. That same year, Livermore Valley's Cresta Blanca won two gold medals at the Paris Exposition, including Best of Show, thanks to pioneering grower Charles Wetmore. A thriving export business also had begun that saw California wine shipped to Australia, Britain, Germany, and Latin America.

Phylloxera decimated the vineyards of Europe, then the temperance movement nearly destroyed winemaking in America, Australia, and New Zealand. The Eighteenth Amendment to the US Constitution, known as the National Prohibition Act or the Volstead Act (after Andrew Volstead, chair of the House Judiciary Committee), took effect on January 17, 1920. This nationwide ban on the production, sale, or transportation of alcoholic beverages remained in effect until ratification of the Twenty-First Amendment on December 5, 1933. For the first and only time, the country repealed an amendment to the Constitution.

But wine remained legal for religious purposes, and other spirits were legal for medicinal purposes as prescribed by a doctor. These loopholes allowed a handful of wineries to operate during the 13-year dry reign of Prohibition. As such, several Sonoma and Napa wineries lay claim to the title of oldest continually operating winery in the country. Another provision of the Volstead law allowed for the head of each household to "make 200 gallons of non-intoxicating cider and fruit juice each year," so much of California's grape production traveled by rail to winemakers across the country who may or may not have consumed their allotted gallons under their own roofs.

Italian immigrants Cesare Mondavi and his wife, Rosa, already had shown their entrepreneurial prowess by opening a grocery store, saloon, and boardinghouse in Minnesota. There they began making wine with grapes from California. But the Mondavis saw California's promise even during Prohibition. They brought their family, including sons Robert and Peter, to Lodi, California, where they began buying grapes and shipping them nationwide to others interested in making wine in their own homes.

Before Prohibition, more than 2,500 wineries operated across America, but by 1933 fewer than 100 remained. California accounted for more than 700 wineries as of 1920, and it took until well into the 1980s before the same number was operating again. From 1933 into the 1960s, fortified wines gained a stronghold in the domestic market. Made with brandy or grain alcohol, which retains a high sugar level and an alcohol level of 20 percent, fortified wines were taxed at the same levels as wine. This regulation made them less expensive than hard liquor, thus offering more bang for the buck for those drinking more for the alcohol content.

Beaulieu Vineyards' André Tchelistcheff and Brother Timothy, a member of the Christian Brothers order and a science teacher turned winemaker, figure strongly in California's post-Prohibition resurgence. Beaulieu's founder, George de Latour, met Tchelistcheff at the French National Agronomy Institute in

1938 and invited him to Napa as his chief winemaker. Among the first California winemakers to age wine in French oak barrels, Tchelistcheff focused on high-quality Cabernet Sauvignon. He also made important advances in the understanding and implementation of now-common techniques, such as vineyard frost protection, malolactic fermentation, and cold fermentation (first introduced to California by Peter Mondavi Sr.). Tchelistcheff proved instrumental in developing vineyard sites in Carneros and other regions. He stayed at Beaulieu until retiring in 1973, after which he consulted for high-profile wineries in Napa, Sonoma, and the Pacific Northwest. Many prominent winemakers in the business since the 1960s and '70s name Tchelistcheff among their most important mentors or influences.

Brother Timothy first worked as a wine chemist at the Christian Brothers' Mont La Salle Winery in 1935. After Prohibition, the order decided to produce wine commercially, and Brother Timothy became the face of the nationally popular brand. His role at Christian Brothers continued until his retirement in 1989, when the winery was sold.

In 1955, the University of California at Davis acquired 40 acres in Oakville, Napa Valley, for research and education. Three years later, Wickson Hall, the Department of Viticulture and Enology's current home, was built. Many of today's luminary winemakers and vineyard managers graduated from UC Davis, which had a strong hand in training those who revitalized California's wine industry from the 1960s onward. By the late 1960s—a generation after World War II veterans came home with a taste for French and Italian wine and at the same time that Julia Child was introducing French cuisine to American palates—dry wine finally became more popular than sweet, fortified wine, prompting a revolution.

Ernest and Julio Gallo founded their winery in 1933, almost immediately after the repeal of Prohibition, using money borrowed from Ernest's mother-in-law, Theresa Franzia, and pamphlets from UC Davis that they found in a public library in Modesto. By 1960, Gallo was the largest wine brand in the country, a position it has held firmly since. In addition to the entry-level labels that fueled its growth, the Gallo family today produces many mid- to high-level brands, including the Gallo Signature Series, Frei Brothers, William Hill Estate, Louis M. Martini, and MacMurray Ranch.

Robert Mondavi left his father's Charles Krug winery in 1965 to establish the first large, purpose-built winery in Napa Valley since the start of Prohibition. Mondavi was among the first Californians to identify varietal names, such as Cabernet Sauvignon and Chardonnay, on bottle labels. A new gold rush in Napa was beginning, prompting a growth spurt in the number of new wineries and a meteoric rise in quality. In 1965, only 232 wineries operated in the state, a number that has grown more than 15-fold in the half century since.

Into the 1970s, the popularity of California wine was growing nationwide, but its reputation in the global market ranged from nonexistent to negative. French wine still reigned supreme. Then the Judgment of Paris took place on May 24, 1976. Steven Spurrier, then a wine merchant living in Paris, organized the famous wine competition. He set up a blind tasting pitting top California Chardonnay against the best Burgundian whites, and highly rated California Cabernet Sauvignon against the finest reds from Bordeaux. A strong proponent of French wine, Spurrier, it's said, expected the French wines to win. The eleven judges tasted each wine and rated it on a scale of 20 points, ranking them from high to low. The scores of Spurrier and his American colleague at l'Académie du Vin, Patricia Gallagher, weren't included in the averages, leaving the final judging to the nine French winemakers, sommeliers, winery owners, and restaurateurs.

The French press first ignored and then spurned the results, so it's fortunate that *Time* magazine's George M. Taber attended the event and shared the results with the rest of the world. The top white wine was Chateau Montelena Chardonnay 1973 from Calistoga in Napa Valley, made by Mike Grgich, who had yet to establish his own winery. Chateau Montelena beat Joseph Drouhin Beaune Clos des Mouches 1973, Ramonet-Prudhon Batard-Montrachet 1973, and Domaine Leflaive Puligny-Montrachet Les Pucelles 1972. The winning red wine was Stag's Leap Wine Cellars Cabernet Sauvignon 1973, which conquered esteemed wines such as Château Mouton-Rothschild, Château Montrose, and Château Haut-Brion.

The Judgment of Paris landed a definitive triumph not just for the individual wines but for the entire California industry. As word slowly spread, California wines grew in stature nationwide and around the world. Today more than 20 million tourists visit California wine regions annually, spending $2.1 billion each year. Tour through Napa, Sonoma, Paso Robles, or Santa Barbara today, and you're as likely to see tourists from as far away as Japan, Australia, and France as you are to see day-trippers from nearby cities.

Of the more than $1.4 billion in US wine shipped around the world in 2012, 90 percent was grown and produced in California. The largest foreign market is the European Union, especially Britain, France, Spain, and Italy. The largest individual export country is Canada, followed by the U.K., Japan, China, Vietnam, Mexico, and South Korea. In 2012, America became the largest wine-consuming nation in the world by volume, and 58 percent of that volume came from California.

The vast array of wine from California is staggering, from the infamous "Two-Buck Chuck," Bronco Wine Company's private label Charles Shaw wines for Trader Joe's (which retails for $2.49 in its home state), to cult-status wines available only to the lucky few for upward of $500 on release. The Golden State truly has something for everyone who likes wine.

Off-dry Moscato is the fastest-growing category in America. Pinot Noir from the extreme Sonoma Coast is the favorite of a small but enthusiastic group of international oenophiles, and Silicon Valley's captains of industry are still stockpiling allocation-only Napa Valley Cabernet Sauvignon. Chardonnay is California's most widely planted wine grape as well as the most popular varietal in the United States. Next in line is Cabernet Sauvignon (no surprise), the state's most widely planted red grape. Other important varieties are, in descending order of total acreage, Zinfandel, Merlot, Pinot Noir, Syrah, Sauvignon Blanc, Pinot Grigio, and Riesling.

Strictly a New World designation, "Meritage" refers to a blend using at least two accepted Bordeaux varietals: Cabernet Sauvignon, Merlot, Cabernet Franc, Petit Verdot, Malbec, or Carménère, with no more than 90 percent of one of those varietals in the blend. White Meritage blends must include two or more of Sauvignon Blanc, Sémillon, or Muscadelle de Bordelais, with the same percentage rule. The name "Meritage" (rhymes with heritage) is licensed by the Meritage Alliance, founded in Napa Valley in 1988 by a handful of members but now counting more than 250 wineries in its ranks.

California's wine-labeling laws generally align with US labeling laws but in a few instances hold producers to a higher standard. For example, US wine labeled with a vintage year must contain 85 percent wine from grapes harvested that year. If the label lists a more specific AVA, such as Napa or Oakville, the bottle must contain at least 95 percent wine from the stated year. California law also stipulates that 100 percent of the grapes in wine labeled "California" come from within the state's borders. Wines labeled with single-varietal names, such as Pinot Noir or Sauvignon Blanc, must contain at least 75 percent of the stated variety, and if a single-vineyard designation is given, at least 95 percent of the grapes had to come from that vineyard.

Wine labels also must include the bottler and location. If a label reads "produced and bottled by," the company that bottled the wine fermented at least 75 percent of it. If it simply reads "bottled by," that winery bottled the wine, but another entity may have grown, crushed, fermented, and aged the product. Alcohol content is mandatory on wine labels, with a margin of error of plus or minus 1.5 percent. For wines with more than 14 percent alcohol, there is no margin of error or tolerance. For fortified wines, which have an alcohol content between 14 and 21 percent, the margin of error is 1 percent.

THE GRAPES

An estimated 546,000 acres of wine grapes were growing in California in 2012. The US Department of Agriculture tracks the total acreage, by county, of 69 of the most populous grape varieties. In addition to the Chardonnay, Cabernet Sauvignon, Zinfandel, and other common grapes, it also tracks the smaller coverage of grapes beloved by winemakers and oenophiles, such as Aglianico, Carménère, Counoise, and Pinotage. Bottlings of these are small, but winery tasting rooms and sommeliers at fine restaurants feature many top-quality examples. At the opposite end of the continuum lie Rubired and Ruby Cabernet, which grow on thousands of acres but hardly merit discussion because it's hard to find a high-quality wine made from either.

Scanning statistical data isn't anyone's idea of a good time, but the Department of Agriculture's breakdown by county spotlights rising stars in the wine world. For example, Albariño: Total acreage in the state amounts to a mere 180 acres. That output is minuscule, but in 2004 only 28 total acres were growing in the state. That the highest current concentration—55 acres—lies in San Luis Obispo County, home to Paso Robles, itself a rising star, tells us that this is a grape to watch.

WHITE GRAPES

ALBARIÑO

Small in quantity but big on flavor, Albariño comes from Spain's Rias Baixas region. (French monks reportedly brought it to Spain in the twelfth century.) Some winemakers bottle it under its Portuguese name, Alvarinho. It covers 180 acres across the state, particularly in San Luis Obispo, Monterey, Napa, and Yolo counties, where it has found a home in the Clarksburg AVA. The grape thrives in hot, sunny days bracketed by foggy mornings and cool nights, and its citrus, tropical fruit, and stone fruit flavors and aromatic floral notes shine through with a minimum of oak or none at all.

CHARDONNAY

Despite cries in recent years of "ABC!" (Anything but Chardonnay!), consumers can't get enough of this French transplant. Much of the backlash had to do with the high-alcohol, overoaked style that overwhelmed wine shops around the country than with the natural qualities of the grape itself. The top choice among American wine drinkers as well as the most prolific variety in the state, covering 95,074 acres, Chardonnay ranges across styles and price points from "cheap and cheery" to expensive, rare, and ageworthy. Its lemon and Granny Smith apple flavors work equally well in crisp, steel-fermented bottlings; a buttery, well-oaked style; and sparkling wine. Colder temperatures coax the mineral notes of Chardonnay to the fore, whereas vines growing on warm valley floors yield grapes with more prominent tropical fruit flavors. It grows throughout the state—notably in Monterey (16,882 acres), Sonoma (15,255 acres), San Joaquin (14,410 acres), and Napa (7,165 acres) counties—and plays an important role in Champagne-style sparkling wine.

CHENIN BLANC

This Loire Valley native, which most wine drinkers know as the most popular variety from South Africa, also thrives in California's rich soils. A total of 6,090 acres grow across the state, with the highest concentrations in Fresno and Madera counties. Smaller acreages thrive in Yolo, San Luis Obispo, and Santa Barbara counties, with a high concentration of standout bottlings coming from the Santa Ynez Valley. The grapes ripen late in the season, so they're among the last to be picked each year. Rich minerality and racy acidity complement flavors of pear and apple.

FRENCH COLOMBARD

Also known simply as Colombard, this workhorse grape lent acidity and citrus flavors to inexpensive bottles before consumer demand for single-varietal whites took off in the 1980s. It was once the most extensively grown grape in California, thriving on more than 90,000 acres as recently as the late 1980s. Still grown on 22,487, it's starting to appear in single-varietal bottlings by innovative producers such as Jean-Charles Boisset of Buena Vista Winery. Expect flavors of peach, apricot, and citrus rind with light floral touches. It's also used in the production of brandy in California, as it is in France, where much of it is distilled into Cognac and Armagnac.

GEWÜRZTRAMINER

This northern Italian native known to wine drinkers through the wines of Germany and Alsace has a bright acidity and floral notes, most distinctively that of rose petal. An aromatic white, it covers 1,752 acres, predominantly in Monterey, Mendocino, Santa Barbara, and Sonoma. It thrives in cool-weather regions, and the finest versions feature little to no oak.

GRENACHE BLANC

There's not a lot of Grenache Blanc in California—just 267 acres—but its proliferation in Santa Barbara and San Luis Obispo counties, both known for their Rhône blends, hints at its primary use. It's related closely to Garnacha, which originated in Spain and spread to southern France. Primarily blended with Roussanne but increasingly vinified on its own by daring winemakers, Grenache Blanc features citrus flavors and herbal notes.

MARSANNE

A small-production grape with a big reputation, this Rhône valley variety grows on only 114 acres and is found mainly in blends, but it's an increasingly important player in Santa Barbara, San Louis Obispo/Paso Robles, Monterey, and Sonoma. Marsanne's zesty acidity enhances its rich flavors of peach, jasmine, and a dusting of Christmas spice. Single-varietal bottlings are hard to find, but if you do, bring home at least one.

MUSCAT

For winemaking purposes Muscat is classified as a white grape, but its color ranges from pale green to pink to reddish brown or almost black on the vine. Experts believe that all *Vitis vinifera* grapes descend from Muscat of Alexandria, which originated in North Africa, where the Ancient Egyptians vinified it. Known for its large, oval, pale amber berries, it's the most prominent Muscat variety in California, at 4,180 acres. Next comes Muscat Blanc, officially Muscat à Petit Grains, in reference to its small berries, which covers 2,293 acres. The third most promulgated variety in the state is Muscat Hamburg, which is considered a red grape because of its dark color. Also called Black Muscat, it grows on 661 acres. Orange Muscat, named for its aroma rather than color, totals 329. It's often used on its own or blended in small amounts as a dessert wine. Muscat grapes generally are blended and made into off-dry or sweet wines noted for their aromas and flavors of orange, peach, apricot, honey, and flowers. With the growing popularity of sweet wines, it will be interesting to see the increase in acreage and production in the coming years.

PINOT GRIGIO / PINOT GRIS

It's practically two grapes in one, going by both its Italian and its Alsatian name, depending on winemaker preference and style. An aromatic white that varies on the vine from bluish-gray to light brownish-pink, it takes its name from the pinecone-like clusters that its grapes form and the French word for *gray*. The primary flavors are apple, lemon, and pear with light floral notes and crisp minerality. Pinot Grigio tends toward a lighter, fruitier style, and wines labeled Pinot Gris are often fuller and riper with more pronounced spice notes. It grows on 12,866 acres of California farmland. About one-third of that (4,148 acres) lies in San Luis Obispo, while conspicuous concentrations accumulate in Monterey, Yolo, Sacramento, and Fresno counties. There's not a lot of Pinot Gris in Sonoma (475 acres), compared to other areas, but quite a few higher-end Pinot Gris bottlings are being produced there.

RIESLING

Officially called White Riesling by the Department of Agriculture, this German native now calls 4,452 California acres home, almost half of that in Monterey and the balance distributed throughout the state. It's made in dry, off-dry, and sweet styles, but Riesling's high acidity offers a nice foil for its powerful fruit and floral flavors. Its bulblike green-yellow berries, sometimes tinged with purple, do best in cold-weather areas, where significant diurnal temperature variation preserves its acidity. German immigrants such as Charles Krug and Jacob and Frederick Beringer originally grew the once popular grape. Though its popularity waned, California Riesling is experiencing a comeback as consumer tastes shift toward aromatic whites. In 2004 only 2,121 acres were growing in the state, a number that has more than doubled since.

ROUSSANNE

Native to the Rhône Valley, Roussanne grapes ripen into a deep brown color with an orange red–tinge, known in French as *roux*. Its 324 acres barely register on the scale, but Roussanne's clear-cut flavors of pear and honeysuckle and luscious floral aroma shine in white blends and the rare single-varietal bottling, particularly in San Luis Obispo, Santa Barbara, Napa, Sonoma, and Monterey. Roussanne is blended most frequently with Marsanne and Viognier, bringing its floral and herbal notes and fine-edged acidity into the mix.

SAUVIGNON BLANC

Now cultivated worldwide, Sauvignon Blanc most likely originated in France, where it's most at home in Bordeaux and the Loire Valley. Its name derives from the French for "wild" (*sauvage*) and "white" (*blanc*). The second most widely planted white grape in California, it grows on 15,407 acres. Its flavor varies from crisp and clean with strong tropical fruit and citrus flavors to more structured and elegant, especially when grown in colder climates or judiciously tamed with oak. Stronger notes of asparagus, freshly cut grass, and green bell pepper often emerge as well, adding to its wild reputation. Also known as Fumé Blanc—a name credited to Robert Mondavi in the late 1960s—the largest concentration of Sauvignon Blanc vines grow in Napa (2,736 acres) and Sonoma (2,553 acres). San Joaquin, Lake, Monterey, Mendocino, San Luis Obispo, and Santa Barbara counties also host significant acreages. Its rising popularity may tie to consumer trends toward fresh white wines paired with spicy Mexican, Central American, and Pacific Rim cuisines.

VIOGNIER

Grown on 3,001 acres, Viognier has a highly aromatic, perfumed nose and flavors of apricot, peach, honey, and soft spice. It has moved far beyond the Rhône Valley to become a favorite among winemakers and consumers alike. Often vinified on its own, it's also blended with Marsanne and Roussanne, its hometown companions. Almost a third of California's Viognier grows in San Joaquin County, the home of Lodi, and large contingents concentrate in Santa Barbara, Sonoma, San Luis Obispo, and Yolo counties. Its graceful flavors and intense acidity nicely complement seafood and richly spiced dishes.

RED GRAPES

ALICANTE BOUSCHET

This hearty red-fleshed grape was planted heavily throughout California during Prohibition—some 40,000 acres in the 1930s—because, once harvested, it survived the long cross-country trip by rail to home winemakers back east. Easy to maintain and offering high yields, it also was widely planted across France, Spain, and Portugal in the years after the phylloxera epidemic. It's a cross between Petit Bouschet and Grenache created in 1866 by Henry Bouschet, who sought to create a durable, deep red grape. Currently cultivated on 1,091 acres, it grows mostly in inland counties. Much of it is used for blending, often with Zinfandel, but Ridge Vineyards and Francis Ford Coppola Winery make single-varietal versions.

BARBERA

Far from its home in Italy's Piedmont, Barbera was first vinified in California at the end of the nineteenth century. It served as a mainstay of the Italian Swiss Colony winery's red blends at that time, and although it fell out of favor following Prohibition, plantings remain fairly high at 6,328 acres. Its forceful flavors of blackberry, cherry, and blueberry and accents of spice and vanilla (accreted during barrel aging) form the backbone of many bottles of "red table wine" and some single-varietal versions as well. The first wave of Italian immigrants in California used Barbera widely, and a new generation of winemakers is making high-quality interpretations as a nod to the state's winemaking history and in many cases to their own heritage. More than two-thirds of the crop grows in El Dorado County, with another 15 percent in Madera County.

CABERNET FRANC

One of the parents of Cabernet Sauvignon, Cabernet Franc is most at home in Bordeaux-style blends, which may be called Meritage in California. Noted for its assertive, peppery character, Cabernet Franc also has flavors of cherry, cassis, violet, and earth. It's cultivated on 3,429 acres, with over one-third in Napa, which is no surprise given the number of high-profile (and high-priced) reds produced there—many labeled Cabernet Sauvignon but vinified with the addition of other grapes. Sonoma and Santa Barbara also grow significant amounts. A lot of single-varietal Cabernet Franc is coming out of Sonoma, much of it available only at tasting rooms or direct from the winery.

CABERNET SAUVIGNON

This French offspring of Cabernet Franc and Sauvignon Blanc has become one of the most widely cultivated grapes in the world. It's the second most widely grown grape in California and the most populous red grape, found on 80,630 acres. Almost a quarter of that number thrives in Napa. It's also planted widely in San Joaquin (11,595 acres), Sonoma (11,480 acres), and San Luis Obispo (10,114 acres) counties. "Cali Cab" has become a category unto itself both domestically and in many parts of the world. Like Chardonnay, it covers the spectrum of prices and styles, from entry level and easy to find to hyperscarce and stratospherically priced. One reason that Cabernet Sauvignon receives high scores from critics, which further increases prices, is that its rich tannic structure makes it built to age, so collectors can amass these wines now and pull them out later for special occasions. Oak aging, which adds flavors of vanilla, caramel, butterscotch, and spice, enhances the general profile of black cherry, cassis, plum, violet, and pencil lead. Despite a reputation for being high-alcohol, overoaked fruit bombs, many well-produced California Cabs exhibit remarkable restraint and balance across the price spectrum.

CARIGNANE

A large, dark, round grape that grows in tight clusters, Carignane, or Carignan, hails from Spain (where it's called Cariñena and Mazuelo) and rose to prominence as the most widely planted variety in the Rhône Valley. It grows on 2,558 acres in California and often is blended anonymously into red table wine. As a single variety, it offers bright flavors of red cherry and nutmeg, and in blends it adds strong acidity, healthy tannins, and dark red color. Almost half of it grows in Madera County, but healthy plantings also appear in San Joaquin, Mendocino, and Sonoma.

GRENACHE

Purportedly the most widely grown red grape on the planet, Grenache—or Garnacha in its native Spain—works equally well on its own or in a blend. It flourishes in hot, dry climates, and its thin-skinned, medium purple berries are low in tannin, producing wines perfect for drinking when young. Flavors include raspberry, strawberry, honeysuckle, and light spice. Grenache grows on 6,020 acres in California, with more than half of that divided between Fresno and Madera counties. It was long used throughout the state to make inexpensive, easy-drinking reds and rosés, but its cultivation and vinification have been championed by the Rhône Rangers, a group dedicated to the promotion of Rhône-style wines. Respectable planting occurs in both San Luis Obispo and Santa Barbara, which makes sense to those who know these two areas as hotbeds of Rhône-style winemaking. Grenache is often blended with Syrah and Mourvèdre in what are increasingly called GSM blends.

MALBEC

Originally from France, where it's mainly blended with other grapes, especially in Bordeaux, Malbec made a big name for itself in Argentina. (It's now being marketed as a single variety in the Cahors region of France, the grape's original home, where it has grown for centuries.) Malbec is remarkably dark in color both on the vine and in the glass, and its flavors of black cherry, plum, chocolate, violet, and licorice are equally at home on their own or in an ensemble. It grows on 2,689 acres, although around a third of that is nonbearing, meaning the vines aren't old enough to produce wineworthy grapes. Napa and Sonoma boasts decent chunks of acreage, but more than half of San Joaquin County's 665 acres contain nonbearing vines.

Given the growth in the state as a whole—the total has doubled since 2004—this is another variety to watch.

MERLOT

Despite the disparagement that California Merlot received in the movie *Sideways*, it prospers here on 45,689 acres. Like its blending partner and archrival, Cabernet Sauvignon, it grows in every county in the state. Its smooth tannins and bright flavors of black cherry and blueberry, often backed by a touch of mint or eucalyptus, lighten the tannins in Cabernet-based blends and add freshness in the glass. Because of its softer tannic structure, Merlot doesn't require as much aging as other varieties and can be brought to market earlier. Merlot takes its name from the French word for blackbird (*merle*) due to its deep bluish-purple color. That color carries over into the glass, where Merlot may range from intense black cherry to inky purple. Stylistically, Merlot can run from young, fruity, and fresh to deep and rich, depending on growing conditions, winemaker technique, and length of aging. San Joaquin has the most Merlot (7,818 acres), but there 's plenty to go around: 5,975 acres in Napa, 5,778 in Sonoma, 5,424 in Monterey, and 4,143 in San Luis Obispo.

MISSION

Known as Pais in Chile and Criolla Chica in Argentina, this is the grape that started it all, long before California was even a state. First brought by Spanish missionaries, it was the only variety initially and then the most highly propagated until the arrival of French, German, and Italian grapes. Some 643 acres of Mission still grow here, mainly in the center of the state. The first wines made from Mission would be considered barely drinkable today. A style of fortified wine known as Angelica uses Mission as its primary variety and is still produced elegantly by a small number of producers.

MOURVÈDRE

Officially called Mataro (one of its Spanish names) for statistical purposes in California, Mourvèdre is an essential component in the GSM (Grenache Syrah Mourvèdre) blends, to which it adds a necessary dose of ageworthy tannins. It grows on 954 acres, with a strong showing in San Luis Obispo County and Santa Barbara. Large pockets also grow in Contra Costa County on the northern Central Coast, near San Francisco and Oakland, and in Madera County, where traditionally it was used in fortified dessert wines. Mourvèdre is noted for flavors of mixed berries, spice, and anise. It can also have strong elements of earth or even green notes that can be tamed by a talented winemaker.

PETIT VERDOT

Most commonly used in small quantities in Bordeaux-style blends, Petit Verdot is also crafted into single-varietal bottlings available at many California winery tasting rooms. It adds color, tannins, and a marked violet flavor and aroma when blended with other grapes. The name means "small green" in French, highlighting that the berries may not ripen properly if weather conditions are less than perfect at the beginning of the growing season. When fully ripened, Petit Verdot grapes are small and look nearly black. It grows on 2,228 acres in California, with the largest proliferation in Napa. High concentrations also grow in Santa Barbara, San Luis Obispo, and Sonoma.

PETITE SIRAH

Known in France and Australia as Durif, its original name, Petite Sirah first came to California in the late nineteenth century. It has been used in sweet fortified wines and also to add color and tannins to entry-level red blends, but this offspring of Peloursin and Syrah is striking out on its own in high-quality dry wines made throughout the state. "Petite" refers to the size of the grapes on the vine, but the wine they make is big on flavor, with strong notes of plum and blueberry and hints of spice and mint. A high level of tannins contributes to its excellent aging potential. It grows on 8,637 acres across all of California, an increase of more than 30 percent since 2004. San Joaquin County has 2,001 acres, and relatively large plantings grow in San Luis Obispo, Napa, and Sonoma. The surge in both acreage and popularity no doubt has resulted from the efforts of PS I Love You, an advocacy group for Petite Sirah growers and producers.

PINOT NOIR

Named for its pinecone-like clusters of grapes and the French word for black (*noir*), Pinot Noir tends to appear cherry to medium garnet in color in the glass. The famed red grape of Burgundy now grows all over the world, but the best versions come from cool climates. The extreme west Sonoma Coast is producing a large amount of high-quality, small-batch Pinot Noir. The variety offers flavors of cherry, chocolate, coffee, light spice, and orange zest. Aging in barrel and bottle adds flavors of vanilla and Mediterranean herbs. It's cultivated on 39,610 acres, about a third of that in Sonoma, with smaller but still substantial acreages in Monterey and Santa Barbara. Some of the increased attention to Pinot Noir comes from the movie *Sideways*, but its popularity follows the general trend toward lighter, higher-acid, food-friendly wines. Pinot Noir is also used in Champagne-style sparkling wines, particularly from the Anderson Valley and Carneros.

SANGIOVESE

The famous grape of Tuscany gets its name from the Latin *sanguis Jovis*, or "blood of Jove." Brought by Italian immigrants, it has been grown in California since about 1880. It's planted in amounts large and small in every region in the state, covering 1,894 acres, with the majority in Sonoma and Napa. It's usually seen as a single variety but sometimes is blended with Cabernet Sauvignon, Merlot, or Cabernet Franc, "Super Tuscan"–style. Young Sangiovese tastes of black plum, tart cherry, strawberry, and orange peel; age brings desirable secondary flavors of earth, tar, or truffles. It also makes lovely rosé.

SYRAH

Syrah's numbers are as strong in California as its rich, fruity flavor. Called Shiraz in Australia, the grape name's definitive origin remains a mystery. This Rhône Valley transplant covers 18,798 acres and is found both on its own and in GSM or other red blends. In the New World, Syrah is a big, powerful wine, with flavors of plum, black cherry, cassis, anise, black pepper, and leather. It's also made in a more elegant style, with an emphasis on the savory notes of Mediterranean herbs and earth. San Luis Obispo County has the highest concentration, and it also grows in large numbers include San Joaquin, Sonoma, Madera, Monterey, and Santa Barbara counties. California Syrah makes a luscious rosé that features the refreshing qualities of white wine and the rich mouthfeel of a red.

TEMPRANILLO

A native of Spain, Tempranillo is an up-and-coming winemaker favorite in California. In the past it was used to make inexpensive table wine here, but today it's being produced as a single variety in both fresh and more heavily oaked styles. Its name comes from *temprano*, the Spanish word for "early," identifying that it ripens early in the season. It has a deep garnet color and flavors of cassis, cherry, plum, mocha, and cigar box. Of the 925 acres on which it grows, 178 are in Fresno County and 164 in San Luis Obispo County.

ZINFANDEL

Zinfandel is a pure California success story. The third most prolific grape in California, it covers 49,136 acres and grows throughout the state. The largest plantings lie in San Joaquin County, with 18,999 acres. Sonoma trails, a distant second, with 5,358. A lot of Zinfandel is made into inexpensive pale rosé or blush wine misleadingly labeled "White Zinfandel," but true Zinfandel is inky purple in color, offering rich flavors of raspberry, blackberry, licorice, and black pepper. Cooler-climate versions can be more restrained, with hints of herbal notes or green pepper. Its high sugar content means that it's easy to make high-alcohol Zinfandel, but the trend is toward a more elegant, lower-alcohol style. Zinfandel is related closely to the Italian Primitivo and Croatian Plavac Mali grapes and has been said to be genetically identical to the Croatian grape Crljenak Kastelanski. Many old-vine Zinfandel vineyards include plantings of other varieties such as Carignan, Petite Sirah, and Alicante Bouschet, sometimes called "mixed blacks," that were accidentally included in field blends in the past and are blended in intentionally now. Zinfandel Advocates and Producers, a group dedicated to the study and celebration of this flavorful grape, has played a strong part in Zinfandel's transition toward a fine-wine variety.

ONE

MENDOCINO COUNTY AND LAKE COUNTY

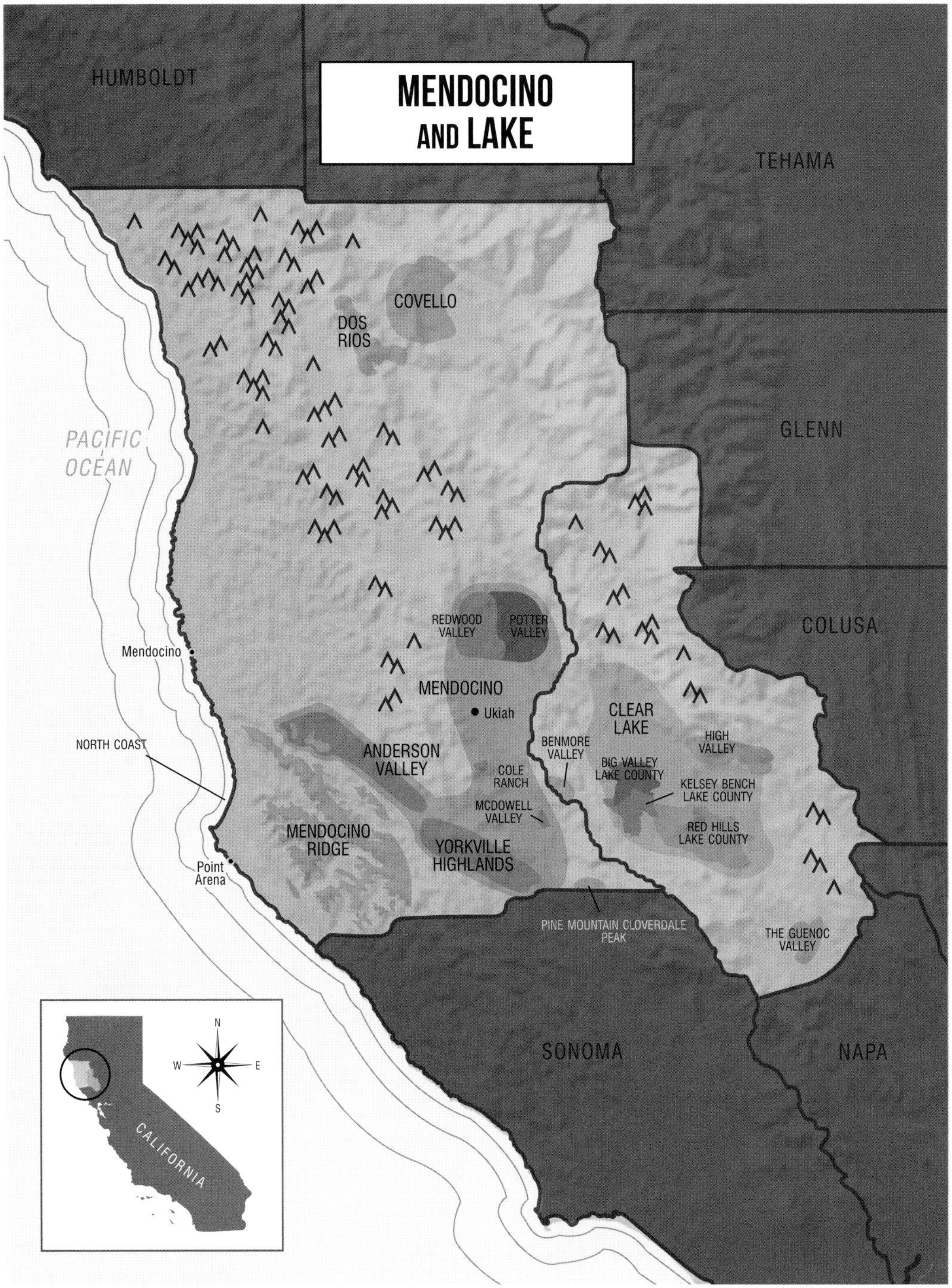
MENDOCINO AND LAKE
HUMBOLDT
TEHAMA
GLENN
COLUSA
PACIFIC OCEAN
COVELLO
DOS RIOS
REDWOOD VALLEY
POTTER VALLEY
Mendocino
MENDOCINO
Ukiah
CLEAR LAKE
NORTH COAST
ANDERSON VALLEY
BENMORE VALLEY
HIGH VALLEY
BIG VALLEY LAKE COUNTY
COLE RANCH
KELSEY BENCH LAKE COUNTY
MCDOWELL VALLEY
RED HILLS LAKE COUNTY
MENDOCINO RIDGE
YORKVILLE HIGHLANDS
Point Arena
PINE MOUNTAIN CLOVERDALE PEAK
THE GUENOC VALLEY
SONOMA
NAPA
N
W
E
S
CALIFORNIA

In Northern California, hikers, mountain bikers, and sailors enjoy the pristine surroundings of statuesque redwoods that shade ferns, orchids, and moss along the weather-beaten Pacific coast. To the west, Mendocino County is 60 percent redwood forest, and Lake County, to the east, boasts the largest lake in the state and one of the oldest lakes on the continent.

The northernmost wine-growing regions in the North Coast AVA, Mendocino County and Lake County sit side by side, each just north of higher-profile neighbors Sonoma and Napa. Established in October 1983, the North Coast AVA has a total area of 3,008,000 acres (4,700 square miles), and these four regions contains the state's highest concentration of wineries. Both Mendocino and Lake counties trace their winemaking histories to the Gold Rush days, and large corporate wineries have used both counties extensively for the past 40-odd years as grape-growing centers for entry-level bottlings. Both are entering a golden age of winemaking as young winemakers—many the descendants of area wine industry pioneers—are striking out on their own and making high-quality, small-batch wines. Although they share many features, including latitude, Mendocino and Lake stand worlds apart in terms of geography, climate, soils, and top grape varieties.

MENDOCINO

The Mayacamas mountain range forms the natural border between Mendocino and Lake counties. The largest AVA in the county is called simply Mendocino, and this and its largest sub-AVA, Anderson Valley, form an angled V, with Mendocino in the east and Anderson Valley in the west. Farther west is the Mendocino Ridge AVA, noted for its high-elevation plantings.

Russian River, which runs parallel to Highway 101 and flows into Sonoma, traverses the large north-to-south portion of the Mendocino AVA. The Navarro River starts in the Coastal Mountain Range and flows northwest, through the top portion of Anderson Valley, and into the Pacific about 10 miles south of the city of Mendocino.

The Mendocino AVA encompasses 275,200 acres, of which 16,700 are planted with grapes. The majority of wineries here are family-owned, and many of Mendocino's winemakers can trace their roots to the founding families of the 1850s. This multigenerational stewardship of the land and the 1970s influx of back-to-nature types have lead to a regional commitment to protect the earth and to farm using natural practices. Notably, 28 percent of the vineyards here are certified organic or biodynamic, and almost all the boutique and midsize wineries in the region use green and sustainable vineyard practices. A significant number also use solar power, and one winery relies completely on the sun for all of its energy needs. Fish Friendly Farming is growing in popularity, with more and more vineyard owners and wineries enrolling in the certification program each year. Frey Brothers, the first organic winery in the United States, was founded here in 1980; Frey was also the first producer of certified biodynamic wine. The largest certified organic grower in the state, Fetzer Vineyards, is also here, as is the nation's largest producer of wines from organically grown grapes, Bonterra. One-third of California's total organic wine grape acreage lies in Mendocino County, which also has the highest percentage of certified organic vineyards in the state and the country.

There are 343 growers and over 90 wineries in Mendocino County. Chardonnay is the top variety, growing on 4,660 acres, followed by 2,430 acres of Cabernet Sauvignon and 2,251 of Pinot Noir. In addition to smaller acres of Zinfandel, Merlot, and Syrah, many vineyards are growing Petite Sirah, Carignane, and Barbera, and some of those plantings date back to the early twentieth century. Other white varieties grown here are Sauvignon Blanc, Gewürztraminer, Viognier, and Chenin Blanc. White grapes tend to do well in the alluvial soils along the Russian and Navarro rivers, while reds thrive in the higher-elevation benchlands.

Two small AVAs lie within Mendocino County, north of the Mendocino AVA: Dos Rios and Covelo. Established in November 2005, Dos Rios consists of 15,500 acres. Spanish for "two rivers," it lies between the Eel River and one of its forks. It's noted for its rocky soils and steep slopes, but only one winery operates within its boundaries. To the northeast, Covelo, established in March 2006, contains 38,000 acres on mainly flat terrain, and the surrounding mountain peaks protect the region from the effects of the Pacific Ocean.

The Anderson Valley AVA was established in September 1983 and is home to some of the finest Pinot Noir vineyards in the area. Because of its proximity to the ocean, it enjoys cool morning and evening temperatures and fog that helps create the ideal growing conditions for other cold-weather lovers as well, including Gewürztraminer and Riesling. Day-to-night temperature swings during the growing season can vary by as much as 40 to 50 degrees Fahrenheit. Highly sought Anderson Valley Pinot Noir is used in a number of appellation-specific bottlings by a Who's Who of high-profile producers in Napa, Sonoma, and elsewhere in California.

The Yorkville Highlands AVA, southeast of Anderson Valley, received official status in June 1998. Its 40,000 acres straddle Highway 128, and it has the highest concentration of red grapes in the county at 83 percent. Among the varieties grown here, Cabernet Sauvignon is the most abundant, followed by Syrah, Pinot Noir, Merlot, and Chardonnay. About 450 acres are planted, divided among twenty-five family-owned vineyards. Most vineyards sit at between 1,000 and 2,200 feet above sea level, a position that benefits from the cool afternoon Pacific breezes. Cool late-day temperatures prevent overripening, and much colder nighttime temperatures preserve acid balance.

The Mendocino Ridge AVA is the only noncontiguous AVA in the country. Only vineyards planted at elevations of 1,200 feet or higher are considered part of it; lower elevations fall into the Anderson Valley or Mendocino County appellation. The high peaks of Mendocino Ridge poke through the fog, offering continuous sunshine during daylight hours. Established in December 1997 and covering 87,466 acres, Mendocino Ridge hosts just 75 acres of vineyards. Italian pioneers planted the first Zinfandel vineyards here at the end of the nineteenth century, and the Mendocino Ridge AVA is still noted for this variety.

The Redwood Valley AVA achieved recognition in February 1997. Cooler than the broad valley floor of the larger Mendocino AVA, it hosts Cabernet Sauvignon, Zinfandel, Barbera, and Petite Sirah. East of Redwood Valley lies the Potter Valley AVA, which sits more than 200 feet higher than its neighbors. Valley temperatures can soar during the day, but it's downright cold at night. Pinot Noir, Chardonnay, Riesling, and Sauvignon Blanc do well in Potter Valley, which has a total area of 27,500 acres and was established in November 1983.

Consisting of 540 acres, the McDowell Valley AVA sits in the southeast of Mendocino, mainly on benchland with altitudes up to 1,000 feet. Recognized as an AVA in February 1987, it's home to Zinfandel, red Rhône varieties such as Grenache and Syrah, and small amounts of white Rhône varieties.

Across the Russian River lies the even smaller Cole Ranch AVA, established in May 1983, which covers just 150 acres. The smallest AVA in the country, it features 60 acres of Cabernet Sauvignon, Merlot, and Riesling growing between 1,400 and 1,600 feet above sea level.

Mendocino's newest AVA, the Pine Mountain-Cloverdale Peak, became official in November 2011. Its 230 planted vineyard acres are home to mainly red varieties. A portion of the appellation lies in Sonoma County, and it begins at an altitude of 1,600 feet, above the town of Cloverdale, and runs as high as 3,000 feet at the peak of Pine Mountain. Grapes have been grown here since the Gold Rush era, mostly on plots smaller than 30 acres.

Two AVA petitions pending before the Alcohol and Tobacco Tax and Trade Bureau (TTB) are Ukiah Valley and Sanel Valley. The Russian River dominates the former, dividing it roughly in two in a straight line from north to south. The folksy town of Ukiah serves as county seat of Mendocino. Sanel Valley, an alluvial plain just north of Sonoma County, sits astride the Russian River and is home to Sauvignon Blanc, Chardonnay, Merlot, and Cabernet Sauvignon.

The vineyards of Mendocino County lie just a couple of hours north of San Francisco, and wine tourism here is booming. But once you pass Cloverdale, you have a decision to make: Either you can bear left up Highway 128 to savor the delights of the Anderson Valley from Yorkville to Boonville and beyond or keep straight on Highway 101 along the Russian River to enjoy the small-town ambience of Hopland and Ukiah. Either way, you won't be disappointed.

LAKE COUNTY

After the Gold Rush melted into the gold bust, many immigrants who chose to seek their fortune in fields rather than mines turned to the fertile, untouched soils surrounding Clear Lake, the largest lake wholly within California's borders. From the mid-nineteenth century until Prohibition, vineyards flourished in the volcanic or shale soils of hillsides and the alluvial soils of terraces and valleys. Farmers turned their land over to walnuts and fruit trees for a good part of the twentieth century, but once wine industry pioneer Jess Jackson bought a farm here in the 1970s and began growing grapes, a new rush began, bringing a significant number of grape growers to the region, most of whom sold their grapes to large wineries for entry-level California appellation bottlings. About 90 percent of the grapes grown here are still sold to wineries in other areas, but buzz is growing about Lake County wines and the new innovators drawn to the foot of Mount Konocti. Some 8,600 acres of grapes grow in the county—the bulk in the Clear Lake AVA and its sub-AVAs—and 170 grape growers farm there.

Seven AVAs lie within Lake County. The largest, Clear Lake, surrounds the eponymous lake, which takes up half of the AVA's geographic area. Two "older" sub-AVAs within Clear Lake are High Valley, northeast of the lake's midpoint, and Red Hills Lake County on its southern shores. Covering 168,960 acres, the Clear Lake AVA was established in June 1984, and its first two sub-AVAs received official recognition 20 years later: Red Hills Lake County in September 2004 and High Valley in August 2005. High Valley AVA vineyards range from 1,600 to 3,000 feet above sea level, and Red Hills Lake County's vineyards, at the base of the extinct volcano Mount Konocti, run from 1,400 feet to 3,000 feet as well. The Kelsey Bench-Lake County AVA encompasses 9,100 acres, with 900 planted to grapevines, mainly red varieties. There are twenty-seven vineyards here and one winery. The Big Valley-Lake County AVA has 1,800 acres planted to vines, and six wineries and 43 vineyards make their home here.

Although many inland areas in California suffer from extreme daytime heat, the Clear Lake AVA enjoys the lacustrine effect of the large body of water in its midst. The dominant grape variety is Cabernet Sauvignon, planted on 3,300 acres, followed by Sauvignon Blanc on 1,790. Other Bordeaux varieties are also planted here, as are Chardonnay, Petite Sirah, Syrah, Tempranillo, and Zinfandel, and most of the vineyards lie within shouting distance of the lake. More than thirty wineries call Lake County home, mostly small and family-owned, and every major English-language wine magazine has lauded Lake County Cabernet Sauvignon in recent years.

The Benmore Valley AVA, established in November 1991, consists of 1,440 acres but has no wineries within its borders yet. It lies west of the Clear Lake AVA, on the border with Mendocino County. The Guenoc Valley AVA, just north of Napa County, was recognized in December 1981 and sits within the borders of nineteenth-century British actress Lillie Langtry's estate. It's believed to be the first single-proprietor AVA in the nation.

Lake County's tourism options used to be rustic, but the influx of upscale wineries has provided an increasing range of lodging and dining options. In addition to mountain biking, rock climbing, white-water rafting, hiking, sailing, and fishing, locals and tourists alike now include wine tasting on their lists of must-do activities in Lake County.

THE WINERIES

BLACK KITE CELLARS

22686 Greenwood Ridge Road, Philo, CA 95466
(415) 923-0277, www.blackkitecellars.com

Tom Birdsall and Rebecca Green Birdsall were cycling in Burgundy when the idea of owning a winery struck them. In 1995 Rebecca's parents, Donald and Maureen Green, had bought 40 acres of land that now include Kite's Rest Vineyard. In 2004 the family hired Paul Ardzrooni to manage the vineyards and Jeff Gaffner to direct the winemaking. Black Kite Cellars' wines consistently garner high scores from respected wine publications. Recommended bottlings include Black Kite Kite's Rest Vineyard Anderson Valley Pinot Noir and Black Kite Stony Terrace Block Anderson Valley Pinot Noir. They both have a nice touch of spice in the finish.

BONTERRA VINEYARDS

2231 McNab Ranch Road, Ukiah, CA 95482
(707) 462-7814, www.bonterra.com

The concept for Bonterra Vineyards originated in 1990, and the wines were first released in 1992 under the name "Fetzer Organic." In 1994 the name "Bonterra" began appearing on the label, and today they're the leading producer of organically grown wines in California. Head winemaker Bob Blue has been with Fetzer since 1988. Dave Koball has been vineyard director since 1995 and oversees 970 acres of Mendocino County certified organic land—284 of those further certified as biodynamic—and produces 4,400 tons of grapes per year. Together Bob and Dave oversee 110 employees, making this one of California's largest organic wine producers. Bonterra Organic Vineyards Mendocino County Chardonnay and silky Bonterra Organic Vineyards Mendocino County Merlot are two of our suggestions. ❶

BRASSFIELD ESTATE

10915 High Valley Road, Clearlake Oaks, CA 95423
(707) 998-1895, www.brassfieldestate.com

Jerry Brassfield acquired 1,600 acres in 1973 and over the years bought additional land. Brassfield Estate consists of 2,500 acres in the High Valley AVA of Lake County. The estate's vineyards include Monte Sereno, Volcano Ridge, Ridge Top, and High Serenity. David Ramey is the consulting winemaker, with Jason Moulton as associate winemaker. Make sure to try Brassfield Estate Serenity and Brassfield Estate Eruption, they're both delicious blends. ❷

BREGGO CELLARS

11001 County Road 151, Boonville, CA 95415
(707) 895-9589, www.breggo.com

Cliff Lede (page xxx) partnered with the team at Breggo Cellars in the Anderson Valley, and together with winemaker Ryan Hodgins and president Jack Bittner the group is making delicious wine. Look for Breggo Cellars Savoy Vineyard Anderson Valley Chardonnay with delightful stone fruit aromas and Breggo Anderson Valley Riesling.

CEAGO VINEGARDEN

5115 E. Highway 20, Nice, CA 95464
(707) 274-1462, www.ceago.com

Jim Fetzer, past president of Fetzer Vineyards, has created a beautiful biodynamic winery estate and farm on the shores of Clear Lake. From a Native Pomo word, *Ceago* ("shee-ye-ho") means "grass-seed valley," but Fetzer interprets that to mean nurturing respect for the land. Visitors enjoy long walks on Ceago's lakefront pier, and if you're lucky enough to reserve one of the two rooms available for an overnight stay, you may never want to leave. We think you will enjoy Ceago Vinegarden Estate Grown Reserve Lake County Chardonnay with its enticing aromas and full-bodied Ceago Vinegarden Del Lago Syrah.

DALLIANCE WINES

13151 East Highway 20, Clearlake Oaks, CA 95423
(707) 998-9656, www.dalliancewines.com

The owners of Dalliance employed a playful double entendre for the name of their winery. From the French for *un affaire romantique*, the word "dalliance" refers both to playful frolicking and amorous play on the side. What better wine to enjoy on a picnic in the park with someone special than refreshing Dalliance Lake County White Wine or fruit-forward Dalliance Lake County Red Wine? 3

DREW FAMILY CELLARS

P.O. Box 313, Elk, CA 95432
(707) 877-1771, www.drewwines.com

After several years of managing and serving as assistant winemaker for Sonoma vineyards, Jason Drew and his wife, Molly, moved to Australia to study at the University of Adelaide. Eighteen months later they returned with Jason's degree in enology and their newborn son, Owen. Jason began working at Corison Winery before moving to Babcock Vineyards. In 2004 the Drews bought a 26-acre apple orchard in the Mendocino Ridge AVA. Make sure to try elegant Drew Morning Dew Vineyard Anderson Valley Pinot Noir. 4

ELKE VINEYARDS

12351 Highway 128, Boonville, CA 95415
(707) 246 -7045, www.elkevineyards.com

At first, the grapes grown on Mary Elke's land were used in wines made by others, including Au Bon Climat, Far Niente, Mumm, and Roederer, but in 1997 she began producing her own wine. Her winemaker, Matt Evans, lives in New Zealand but comes each year to make Elke's wine. Two of our favorites are crisp and clean Mary Elke Pinot Gris and cherry scented Mary Elke Boonville Barter Pinot Noir. 5

FETZER

12901 Old River Road, Hopland, CA 95449
(707) 744-1250, www.fetzer.com

Barney and Kathleen Fetzer bought 720 acres of land in 1958 and with their sons, Jim and John, produced 2,500 cases of their first commercial red wine in 1968. Over the years the Fetzers acquired additional land, and in 1978 Fetzer was one of the first California wineries to produce white wine made from Chardonnay. Brown-Forman bought their company in 1992, and that year production reached 2.2 million cases. Today, Concha y Toro owns the Fetzer brand, and Dennis Martin, Charlie Gilmore, and Michael Chupp head winemaking. Fetzer makes an array of wines from thirteen varieties. Try the Fetzer Sundial Chardonnay; it's the perfect wine to take to a picnic or a family gathering on the beach. As Barney likes to say, "We'll never disappoint you with our Chardonnay: it's like saying hello to an old friend." 6

12

7

11

18

10
GREENWOOD
RIDGE
VINEYARDS
Tasting Room
OPEN

4

FOURSIGHT WINES

14475 Highway 128, Boonville, CA 95415
(707) 895-2889, www.foursightwines.com

Homer "Twink " Charles, his wife, Margaret, and their son Homer "Norman" settled in Anderson Valley in 1943 to join the lumber trade. They built a small sawmill and bought their current property in 1950, but not until 2001 did subsequent generations plant Charles Vineyard. The family started Foursight Wines in 2006. Two of our recommendations are crisp and clean Foursight Charles Vineyard Sauvignon Blanc and fruit-forward, elegant Foursight Charles Vineyard Clone 05 Pinot Noir. 7

FREY VINEYARDS

14000 Tomki Road, Redwood Valley, CA 95470
(707) 485-5177, www.freywine.com

Paul and Beba Frey met and married while in medical school and settled down to raise a family in Northern California in the early 1960s. Twelve children later, the family decided to plant Cabernet Sauvignon and Riesling and sell grapes to nearby wineries. In 1980 the family bonded the winery and became the first organic winery in the country. In 1996 they became the first producer of Demeter-certified biodynamic wines in North America. Frey Vineyards lies in Mendocino County's Redwood Valley AVA, and all of its wines are made with no added sulfites. We like Frey Organic Mendocino County Petite Sirah and Frey Organic Mendocino County Sangiovese. 8

GOLDENEYE WINERY

9200 Highway 128, Philo, CA 95466
(707) 895-3202, www.goldeneyewinery.com

Looking for a place to plant Pinot Noir, Dan and Margaret Duckhorn found the perfect terroir in the Anderson Valley in 1996. The next year they harvested the first grapes used to make Goldeneye's 375 inaugural cases of wine. Zach Rasmuson became the winemaker and general manager in 2003 and over the last decade has earned the winery a well-regarded reputation in the field of California Pinot Noirs. Goldeneye is one of a few California wineries to have earned the coveted LEED Gold Certification for its environmental practices. We recommend Goldeneye Anderson Valley Estate Grown Gewürztraminer Confluence Vineyard, it has notes of Anjou pear and kumquat, and Goldeneye Anderson Valley Pinot Noir with seductive aromas of mixed berry preserves and ripe red fruits. 9

GREENWOOD RIDGE VINEYARDS

5501 Highway 128, Philo, CA 95466
(707) 895-2002, www.greenwoodridge.com

The Greenwood Ridge tasting room is a sight to see. It was designed by architect Aaron Green, an associate of Frank Lloyd Wright and the father of owner-winemaker Allan Green. Only one fallen redwood—with a diameter of 13 feet—provided all the lumber to build the octagonal structure. The tasting room runs on solar power from roof panels, and the excess energy is diverted back to the grid. Allan Green limits production of his highly rated wines to 2,500 cases per year, and his efforts have garnered international attention from a variety of wine publications. Seek out Greenwood Ridge Vineyards Sauvignon Blanc with aromas of honeydew melon and Greenwood Ridge Pinot Noir with flavors of red fruit and spice. 10

GREGORY GRAHAM WINES

13633 Point Lakeview Road, Lower Lake, CA 95457
(707) 995-3500, www.ggwines.com

Gregory Graham established his own label in 1992 while working at Rombauer Vineyard in Napa Valley, but not until 2004 did he begin producing wine from grapes grown on his own vines. He and his wife, Marianne, now live among those vines. Completed in 2006, their winery has been operating under solar power since 2011. They currently produce 4,500 cases of wine made from varieties that include Sauvignon Blanc, Riesling, Viognier, Chardonnay, Grenache, Pinot Noir, Syrah, Zinfandel, and Cabernet Sauvignon. Gregory Graham Wines Cinder Cone Reserve 2008 was the first blend from the estate, mingling Syrah, Cabernet Sauvignon, and Grenache from Graham's Crimson Hill Vineyard and a touch of Malbec from nearby Red Hills Ranch. Try the current vintage; you won't be disappointed. Or try Gregory Graham Roumiguiere Vineyard Riesling—with bright fruit flavors and a delightful amount of sweetness. This is the perfect wine to pair with hot and spicy Asian cuisine.

HANDLEY CELLARS

3151 Highway 128, Philo, CA 95466
(707) 895-3876, www.handleycellars.com

Milla Handley graduated from the University of California at Davis in 1975 and worked at Chateau St. Jean before moving to the Anderson Valley in 1978. After working at Edmeades Winery, she began making her own Chardonnay in her basement. Today her estate vineyard consists of 12 acres of Pinot Noir, 5 of Gewürztraminer, and 13 of Chardonnay. The vineyard was certified organic by the California Certified Organic Farmers group (CCOF) in 2005. Her team consists of vineyard manager José Jimenez, co-winemaker Kristen Barnhisel, and consultant Bill Oldham. Suggested wines include Handley Cellars Anderson Valley Gewürztraminer with aromas of tropical fruits and crisp Handley Cellars Estate Anderson Valley Chardonnay. 11

HAWK AND HORSE VINEYARDS

13048 Highway 29, Lower Lake, CA 95457
(707) 942-4600, www.hawkandhorsevineyards.com

David Boies bought the historic 900-acre El Roble Grande horse ranch in 1982 and planted vines in 2001. The first vintage, in 2004, received high praise in international competitions. Hawk and Horse actively honors its past: Visitors can see American Saddlebred and American Quarter horses as well as Scottish Highlander cattle grazing the land. The ranch and winery are Demeter biodynamic and CCOF organic certified. Mitch Hawkins manages the vineyard, and Richard Peterson and Tracy Hawkins head winemaking. We recommend Hawk and Horse Vineyards Cabernet Sauvignon with complex aromas of ripe black raspberry, blueberry pie, and freshly ground black pepper. 12

JERIKO ESTATE

12141 Hewlitt and Sturtevant Road, Hopland, CA 95449
(707) 744-1140, www.jerikoestate.com

San Francisco judge J. H. Sturtevant built the original mansion in 1898, and a century later Daniel Fetzer acquired Jeriko Estate. Fetzer immediately replanted the vineyards using techniques he learned as a young man from his Fetzer family ties. He added an estate winery and wine bar in 1999. Jeriko Estate is certified organic by Stellar Certification Services and biodynamic by Demeter. Suggested wines include Jeriko Estate Reserve Syrah with loads of big ripe fruit and a touch of white pepper and Jeriko Estate Dijon Clone Pinot Noir with a classic Burgundian finish.

LANGTRY ESTATE

21000 Butts Canyon Road, Middletown, CA 95461
(707) 995-7521, www.langtryestate.com

Grapes were first planted here in 1854, but not until famed British stage actress Lillie Langtry bought the property in 1888 did Guenoc Valley wines receive any attention. In her time, Langtry was known as the most beautiful woman in the world and courted by Edward, prince of Wales. She bought her 8,000-acre property with Fred Gebhard, a friend and suitor. With 21,349 acres, the Langtry Estate remains one of the largest contiguous private land holdings in California. Many consider its corresponding Guenoc Valley AVA the first single-proprietor appellation. Among the winery's offerings are Langtry Estate Guenoc Lake County Sauvignon Blanc with flavors of mango and white stone fruits, and Langtry Estate Guenoc Lake County Petite Sirah with aromas of violets and lavender. 13

MASÚT VINEYARD AND WINERY

1301 Reeves Canyon Road, Redwood Valley, CA 95470
(707) 485-5466, www.masut.com

Brothers Ben and Jake Fetzer grew up on the Fetzer Home Ranch and learned the winemaking business from the ground up. By the eighth grade, they were making blends of Sangiovese and Cabernet Sauvignon. As third-generation grape growers and winemakers, they farm their 1,500-acre Masút Ranch together and make wines that are capturing the attention of critics and consumers alike. Keep your eye on this winery and their elegant and restrained Estate Pinot Noir.

McFADDEN VINEYARD

13275 Highway 101, Hopland, CA 95449
(707) 744-8463, www.mcfaddenvineyard.com

Guinness McFadden fell in love with Potter Valley, planted 23 acres of vineyards in 1970, and since then has planted 140 more. Over the years he has sold grapes to Beringer, Fetzer, Piper Sonoma, Chateau Montelena, and Robert Mondavi, but he decided to make his own Pinot Gris in 2003. The next year he added Riesling and the year after Sauvignon Blanc, Zinfandel, and Pinot Noir, with Chardonnay following the year after that. McFadden Vineyard is CCOF certified organic and well known for its farm stand that sells beautiful bay leaf wreaths and garlic braids. McFadden also receives credit for his commitment to energy sustainability with his hydroelectric power plant and solar panels. Suggested bottlings include McFadden Old Vine Zinfandel and McFadden Sauvignon Blanc with great aromas of lime rind and orange blossom. 14

PARDUCCI

501 Parducci Road, Ukiah, CA 95482
(707) 463-5357, www.parducci.com

The Parducci family moved from Tuscany to Mendocino and established their eponymous winery in 1932. Considered Mendocino County's oldest winery, it has been producing wine continuously for more than 80 years. Bob Swain has been head winemaker for more than 15 years and crafts wine in the Small Lot Blend and True Grit Reserve collections. Parducci Small Lot Blend Sauvignon Blanc is pale yellow, with aromas of pineapple, guava, and lemon zest. On the palate, it has flavors of ripe melon, Ruby Red grapefruit, and lime with a crisp, clean finish. Parducci Small Lot Blend Pinot Noir is cherry red, with aromas of freshly picked strawberries, ripe red cherries, and dried black cherries with top notes of cigar box and Indian spices. It's fruity on the palate with rich berry flavors shining through before a persistent finish. 15

PAUL DOLAN VINEYARDS

501 Parducci Road, Ukiah, CA 95482
(888) 362-9463, www.pauldolanwine.com

Inspired by Paul Dolan's role as a leading proponent of biodynamic and organic grape farming, these wines exclusively use grapes grown in accordance with those principles. Paul Dolan Vineyard Mendocino County Chardonnay is straw yellow, with aromas of Gala apple, citrus blossom, and vanilla caramel. It's full-bodied with balanced acidity and a persistent finish. Paul Dolan Vineyard Mendocino County Zinfandel is garnet in color, with aromas of blackberry preserves, fresh black raspberry, and freshly ground white pepper. Its flavor is fruit-forward with a touch of spice in the finish. 16

ROEDERER ESTATE

4501 Highway 128, Philo, CA 95466
(707) 895-2288, www.roedererestate.com

Fifth-generation Champagne-born winemaker Jean-Claude Rouzaud selected this 580-acre Anderson Valley parcel in 1982 to continue his family's legacy in California. Under the command of his son Frederic, the estate continues making delicious bubbly using the traditional method. Only grapes grown on the estate are used in the cuvée, and the family uses only 70 percent of the first press and none of the second to craft its high-quality sparkling wines. Roederer Estate L'Ermitage 2004 is one of the estate's Tete de Cuvée wines made only in exceptional years. It's persistent on the palate and wonderfully bubbly with a delightful mousse and aromas of Granny Smith apples and toasted brioche. Roederer Estate Brut NV consists of 60 percent Chardonnay and 40 percent Pinot Noir. It's straw colored, with enticing aromas of green apple, ripe pear, and toasted hazelnut that transfer seamlessly onto the palate. It's refreshing in taste with a nice amount of bubbles. 17

SCHARFFENBERGER CELLARS

8501 Highway 128, Philo, CA 95466
(707) 895-2957, www.scharffenbergercellars.com

John Scharffenberger founded his Anderson Valley winery in 1981. The name later changed to Pacific Echo because of the winery's proximity to the ocean, but since Maisons Marques and Domaines took over in 2004, the name has returned to the original. Known for his highly rated *méthode champenoise* sparkling wines, Tex Sawyer has been the winemaker since 1989. Scharffenberger Cellars Brut Excellence Non Vintage is crafted from two-thirds Chardonnay and one-third Pinot Noir. It's straw colored with an abundance of tiny bubbles and aromas of freshly baked brioche, green apple, and ripe pear. Flavors of fruit mixed with toasted hazelnuts combine nicely before a pleasant finish. 18

SHANNON RIDGE

13888 Point Lakeview Rd., Lower Lake, CA 95457
(707) 994-9656, www.shannonridge.com

Clay and Margarita Shannon grew up in Sonoma and Napa, respectively, and met while working at a winery in the Napa Valley. They began their business by growing grapes for other wineries, but a visit to Clear Lake prompted them to make wine under their own label. On their first vineyard, Terre Vermeille, they planted Sauvignon Blanc, Barbera, Cabernet Sauvignon, and Zinfandel vines. They've solidified their commitment to Lake County by adding additional vineyards and building a home that overlooks them. Shannon Ridge High Elevation Chardonnay is straw yellow, with aromas of honeycomb, white peach, and crème caramel. In the mouth it's creamy with bright fruit flavors and a clean finish. Shannon Ridge Lake County High Elevation Sauvignon Blanc has crisp, clean aromas of tropical fruit that flow seamlessly onto the palate. The finish has a nice level of acidity that makes this a perfect wine to pair with briny shellfish. 19

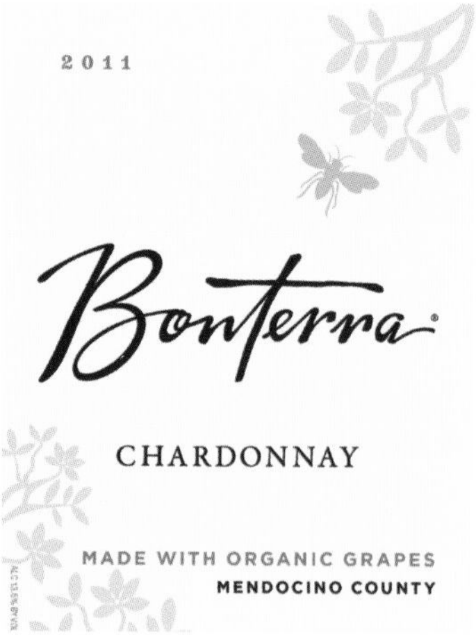

1

2

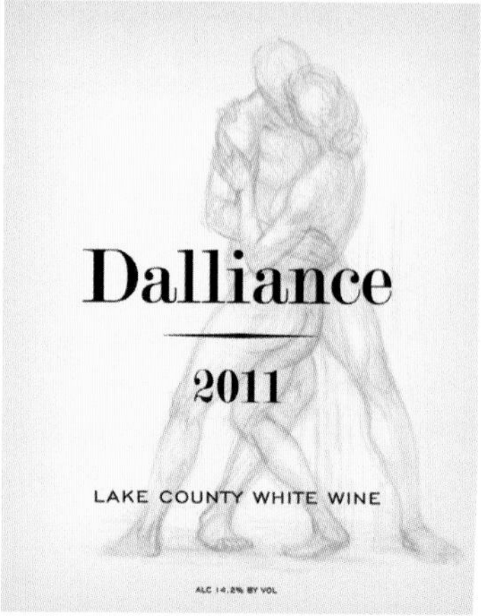

3

9

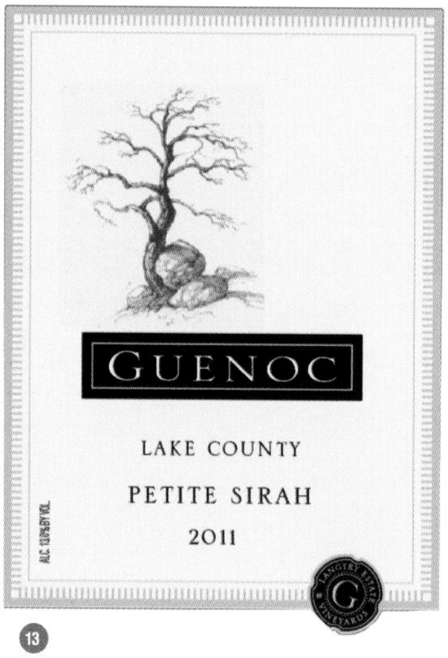

13

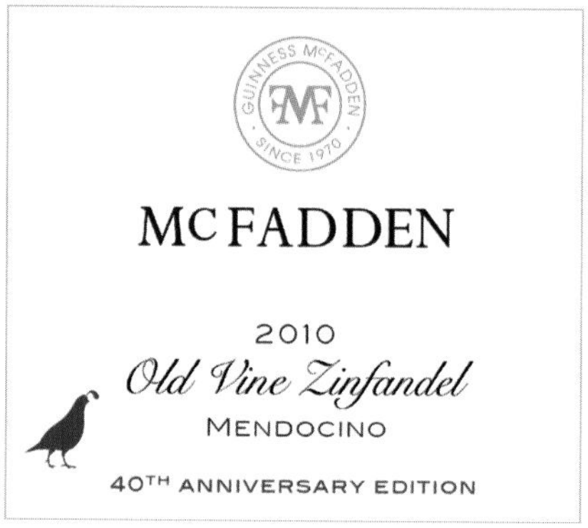

14

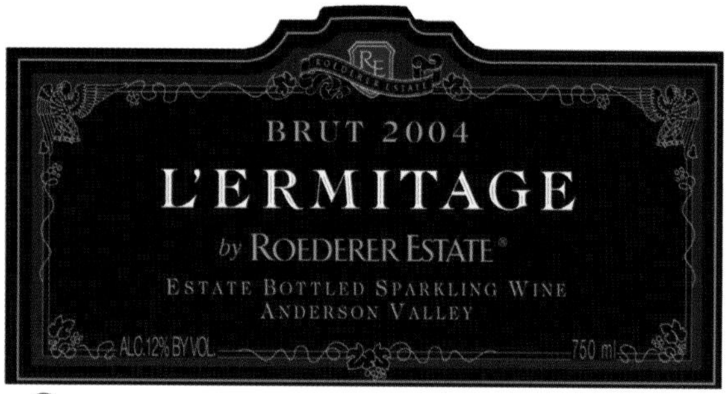

17

19

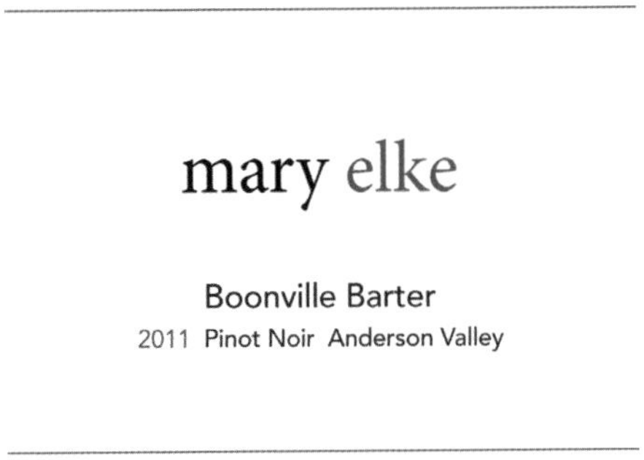
mary elke
Boonville Barter
2011 Pinot Noir Anderson Valley

5

FETZER
THE EARTH FRIENDLY WINERY™
Sundial
CHARDONNAY
CALIFORNIA
2011
PIONEERS IN SUSTAINABILITY
ESTABLISHED IN 1968
14% LESS CARBON EMISSIONS
ALC. 15.0% BY VOLUME

6

Frey
2010
REDWOOD VALLEY
Sangiovese
USDA ORGANIC
organic wine
CONTAINS NO DETECTABLE SULFITES

8

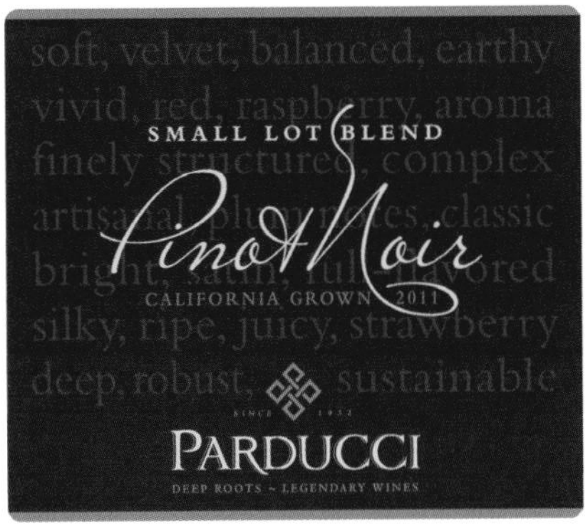
soft, velvet, balanced, earthy
vivid, red, raspberry, aroma
finely structured, complex
artisanal, plum, notes, classic
bright, satin, full flavored
silky, ripe, juicy, strawberry
deep, robust, sustainable
SMALL LOT BLEND
Pinot Noir
CALIFORNIA GROWN 2011
PARDUCCI
DEEP ROOTS ~ LEGENDARY WINES

15

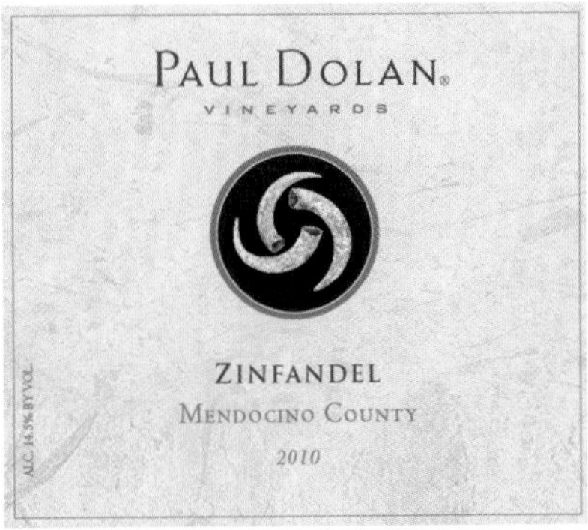
PAUL DOLAN
VINEYARDS
ZINFANDEL
MENDOCINO COUNTY
2010
ALC. 14.5% BY VOL.

16

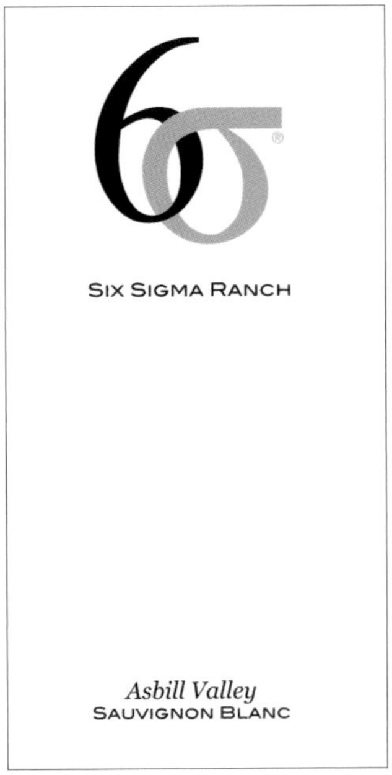
6σ
SIX SIGMA RANCH
Asbill Valley
SAUVIGNON BLANC

20

ZINA HYDE
CUNNINGHAM
RESERVE
MALBEC
NORTH COAST
2009
ALC. 14.5% BY VOL.

21

SIX SIGMA RANCH

13372 Spruce Grove Road, Lower Lake, CA 95457
(707) 994-4068, www.sixsigmaranch.com

In the mid-1800s, twenty families settled the land on which Six Sigma Ranch now sits, each owning a 160-acre parcel. In 1926 Norval Brookins amassed many of those families' holdings, and in 1963 he sold to Bob and Beverly Kleeman, who ran a dude ranch here for a few years. It became a cattle ranch, and in 2000 the present owners, Danish-born Kaj and Else Ahlmann, acquired the property and began making wine. In 2009 they hired winemaker Matt Hughes, whose provenance includes stints at Kendall-Jackson, Verité, and Wildhurst Vineyards. Six Sigma Asbill Valley Sauvignon Blanc is light straw in color, with aromas of white grapefruit, white stone fruit, and tropical fruits. It's crisp and light in the mouth with a pleasantly balanced acidic finish and bracing minerality. Six Sigma Christian's Vineyard Pinot Noir is cherry red, with aromas of black cherry, powdered cocoa, and cranberry juice. It's full in the mouth with ripe fruit flavors and a touch of spice in the finish. 20

STEELE WINES

4350 Thomas Drive at Highway 29, Kelseyville, CA 95451
(707) 279-9475, www.steelewines.com

Jed Steele started as a Napa Valley cellar rat in 1968 before entering UC Davis for a master's in enology. After that he worked at Kendall-Jackson, leaving the same year that production hit the million-cases-per-year mark. In 1991 he started Steele Wines, and he enjoys making small-lot bottlings, many with fewer than 1,000 cases produced. Steele Wines Writer's Block Counoise is garnet in color, with aromas of toasted hazelnut, toasted oat, red fruit, and black plum. It's full bodied on the palate, with dominant fruit flavors that lead to a balanced tannic finish. Steele Wines Viognier is straw colored, with aromas of white stone fruits and dried apricots. It's light and fruity with a crisp, lemon-zesty clean finish.

ZINA HYDE CUNNINGHAM

14077 Highway 123, Boonville, CA 95415
(707) 895-9462, www.zinawinery.com

Zina Hyde Cunningham left Maine in 1849 and traveled cross-country to strike it rich in the Gold Rush. He didn't find a fortune in gold, but what he did find enabled him to purchase a small property in San Francisco, where he became a blacksmith. Tired of city life, he bought a 160-acre ranch in Windsor in 1859 and became a winemaker. In 1865 he began planting vines in Ukiah in Mendocino County. Today, Zina's great-grandson Bill carries on the family tradition in Boonville. Zina Hyde Cunningham Russian River Valley Sauvignon Blanc is straw colored, with light aromas of pineapple, tropical fruit salad, and freshly cut grass. It's soft on the palate with delightful fruit flavors and a pleasant, lightly acidic finish. Zina Hyde Cunningham North Coast Malbec Reserve has aromas of blueberry pie, black raspberry, and a touch of smoked meat. It's silky in the mouth with nice persistence. 21

TWO

SONOMA COUNTY

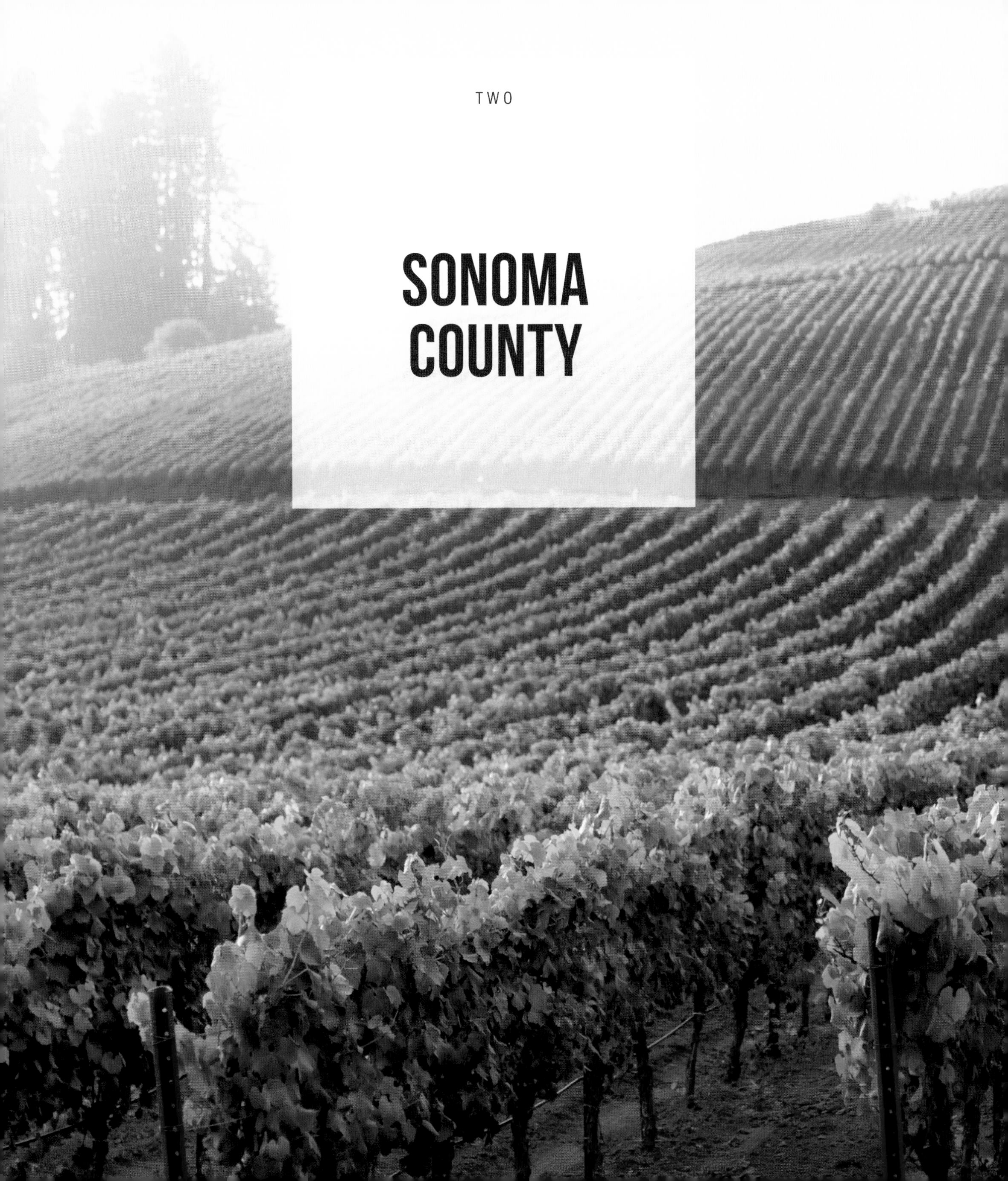

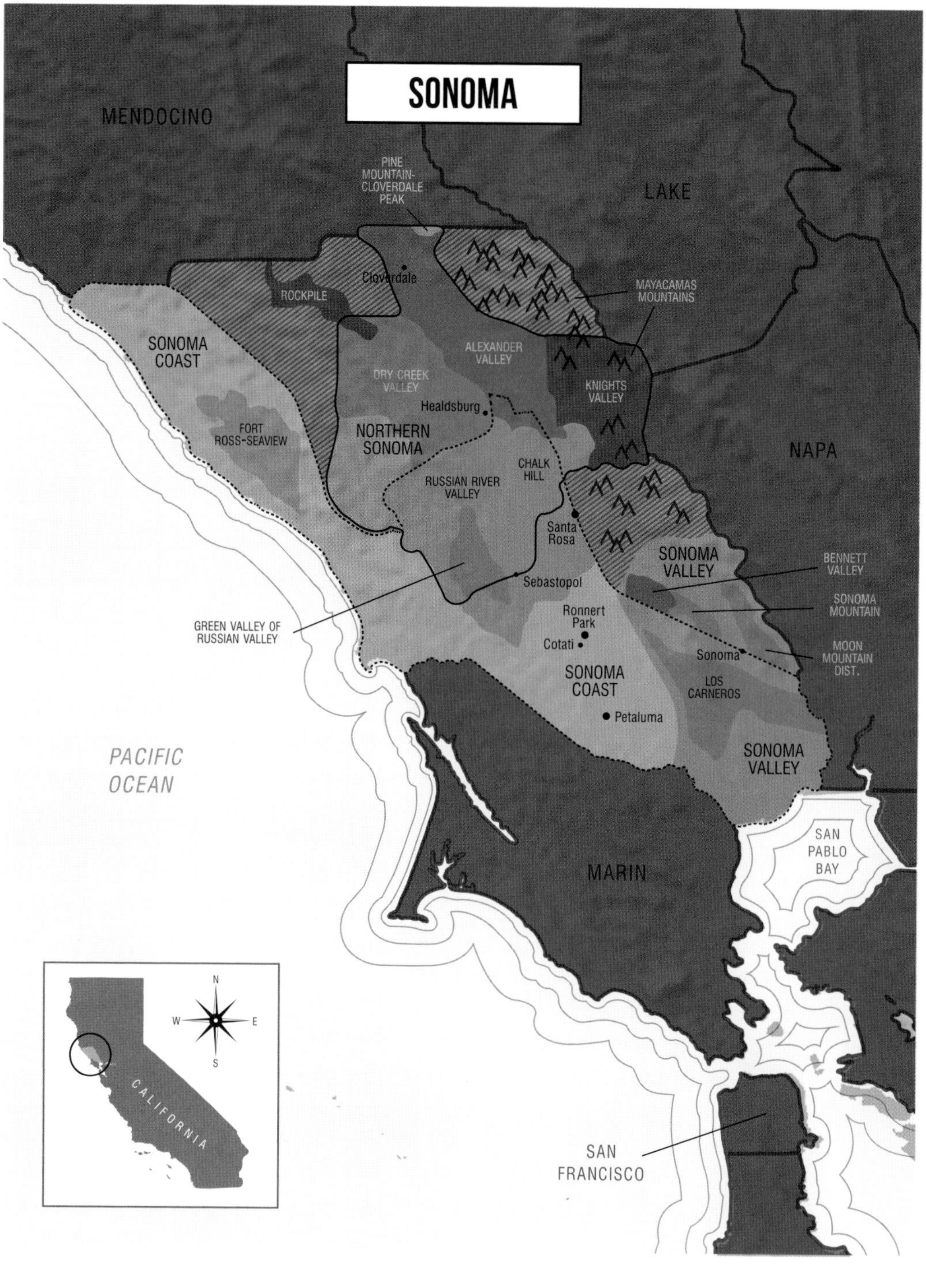
SONOMA
MENDOCINO
LAKE
PINE MOUNTAIN-CLOVERDALE PEAK
Cloverdale
ROCKPILE
MAYACAMAS MOUNTAINS
SONOMA COAST
ALEXANDER VALLEY
DRY CREEK VALLEY
KNIGHTS VALLEY
Healdsburg
FORT ROSS-SEAVIEW
NORTHERN SONOMA
NAPA
CHALK HILL
RUSSIAN RIVER VALLEY
Santa Rosa
SONOMA VALLEY
BENNETT VALLEY
Sebastopol
SONOMA MOUNTAIN
GREEN VALLEY OF RUSSIAN VALLEY
Ronnert Park
Cotati
Sonoma
MOON MOUNTAIN DIST.
SONOMA COAST
LOS CARNEROS
Petaluma
PACIFIC OCEAN
SONOMA VALLEY
SAN PABLO BAY
MARIN
N
W
E
S
CALIFORNIA
SAN FRANCISCO

Sonoma is truly a natural paradise; the isolation of some spots, even now, can only hint at the pristine wilderness that met the area's first European settlers in the early nineteenth century. The county boasts more than 370 wineries and 60,000 acres of grapevines. The laid-back vibe and hands-on methods of winemakers, farmers, and chefs have made this a nearly perfect environment for enjoying the pleasures of the field and vine. Whether you enjoy driving along winding back roads or prefer to flit from tasting room to restaurant to gallery in a Mission- or Gold Rush–era downtown, Sonoma has something to offer.

Sonoma is north of San Francisco and easily reachable from there by car. With sixteen AVAs and dramatically varying topographies and soils, Sonoma County, itself an AVA, is home to wineries ranging from tiny boutique operations to enormous corporate entities. Name a grape variety and someone in Sonoma is growing and vinifying it, although specific subregions are becoming known for particular varieties, blends, and styles. Sonoma County seems to live in the shadow of its neighbor to the east, but the high quality of Sonoma fruit and the role Sonoma's development has played in the simultaneous evolution of Napa indicate that Sonoma may be the wind beneath Napa's wings. In just one example, it's said that George Yount, one of the first to plant vines in Napa Valley and after whom Napa's Yountville is named, planted cuttings acquired from Sonoma County vineyards. In another example, a portion of the grapes that Mike Grgich used in the 1973 Chateau Montelena Chardonnay, which won among white wines in the 1976 Judgment of Paris tasting, came from Sonoma vineyards, including the Bacigalupi Vineyard in the Russian River AVA.

Sonoma Valley was settled 12,000 years ago by native peoples including the Miwok, Wintun, Wappo, Miyakmah, Pomo, Koskiwok, and Patwin tribes. These people gave Sonoma its name, based on a Native word for "many moons." The early inhabitants also named the Mayacamas Mountains, the geographical feature that divides Sonoma from Napa; the name most likely derives from a village called Maiya'kma or from the Miyakmah people themselves.

Since 1542 Sonoma has changed hands several times, with Spain, Russia, Britain, the Mexican Empire, the Republic of Mexico, and the short-lived Republic of California all claiming sovereignty at some point. It finally became part of the United States when California gained statehood in 1850, but Russian trappers had already planted grapes in Sonoma at Fort Ross on the Sonoma Coast in 1812, and in 1823 Spanish missionaries planted grapevines under the direction of Father José Altimira at Mission San Francisco Solano de Sonoma, the last of the Franciscan missions in California and the only one established under the Mexican flag. Ten years after it was built, the Mexican government secularized the Franciscan missions, and Mission San Francisco Solano de Sonoma became a fortified town led by General Mariano Guadalupe Vallejo. This mission-fortress became the center of the city of Sonoma, which was the capital of the California Republic in the summer of 1846. Today, in addition to wine bars, tasting rooms, and restaurants, visitors to Sonoma can tour well-preserved adobe structures near the main plaza that include the mission, the army barracks, and Vallejo's home.

A Hungarian "count," Agoston Haraszthy, sometimes called the Father of California Viticulture, receives credit for bringing the largest collection of European grape varieties to California and to Sonoma County. The founder of Buena Vista Winery (today owned by Jean-Charles Boisset), Haraszthy imported cuttings from more than 150 great European vineyards, originally replanting them near San Francisco but transplanting many of them in 1856 to a small vineyard near Sonoma. He then hired a German immigrant named Charles Krug—who later founded his own winery across the Mayacamas Mountains in St. Helena—and built a stone winery replete with state-of-the-art winemaking equipment and underground cellars.

Franciscan missionaries are credited with first planting grapes and making wine in California, but they used only Mission grapes, and their technique was rudimentary at best, whereas Haraszthy is regarded as the first to have brought a wide array of grapes to Northern California and to have used modern European processes in his winemaking. His vineyard holdings eventually grew to 5,000 acres, including his large family home. Besides his visionary efforts planting grapes in Sonoma, Haraszthy is noted for his 1858 "Report on Grapes and Wine of California," recognized today as the first written study of winemaking and vineyard practices in California and the United States.

Toward the end of the nineteenth century, immigrants from Italy, Germany, and other European countries were planting grapes and making wine in Sonoma, and some of those original wineries exist today. The Gold Rush of 1849 brought many immigrants to California, and when the gold didn't pan out, many bought land and turned their hands to farming. Still more winemakers abandoned fields in their home countries and brought their skills to the New World when phylloxera struck Europe's vineyards shortly thereafter.

German immigrant Jacob Gundlach bought 400 acres in Sonoma in 1858, and three years later he built a winery with his partners. Another German, Charles Bundschu, joined the business in 1868, and today Gundlach Bundschu is considered the oldest family-owned winery in the state. Simi Winery, now owned by Constellation Brands, was established in Healdsburg in 1876 by the Italian brothers and Gold Rushers Pietro and Giuseppe Simi. The Martinelli Winery owes its existence to the teenage Giuseppe Martinelli and Luisa Vellutini, who eloped in 1887, abandoning their native Tuscany for the Russian River Valley. The Sebastiani family's Mission Vineyard was part of the original San Francisco Solano de Sonoma Mission's vineyard. Founded by Samuele Sebastiani in 1904, Sebastiani Winery is now part of the Foley Family Wines portfolio.

By 1920 Sonoma County was home to more than 250 wineries, with grapes growing on 22,000 acres, supplanting Los Angeles as the state's top grape-growing region. Prohibition, the Great Depression, and the two world wars hurt the entire industry, Sonoma included, and though loopholes in the law allowing sacramental or medicinal consumption of wine enabled a handful of wineries to remain open, many vineyards were sold, their land converted to fruit orchards.

By the 1960s Americans were being exposed to different types of international cuisine, especially French and Italian, and were increasing their consumption of wine, with sweet fortified wines gradually giving way to drier, food-friendly wines. In the early 1970s a new wave of vineyard and winery owners began moving into Sonoma County, and by the middle of that decade plantings had returned to pre-1920 levels, with 24,000 acres of vineyards recorded. By the 1980s Sonoma County was transitioning from a center of dairy, grain, and fruit to a place where wine grapes were taking center stage. At the end of that decade wine grapes became Sonoma County's top agricultural crop, and the stage was set for Sonoma to become known as the home of high-quality wine.

Chardonnay grows on a quarter of Sonoma County's grapevines. Used in still and sparkling wines, it's cultivated throughout the region but has an affinity for the Russian River Valley and what's known as the "real" or "extreme" Sonoma Coast. It also does well in the Los Carneros AVA, which straddles Sonoma and Napa counties. Sonoma's next most prolific white variety is Sauvignon Blanc, most prominent in the Russian River Valley, Dry Creek Valley, and Sonoma Coast. Almost every other white variety is grown in Sonoma, including many fine examples of Pinot Gris, Riesling, and Viognier.

The most widely planted red grape in the county is Pinot Noir, which does especially well in Los Carneros (where, like Chardonnay, it is used in still and sparkling wine), the Russian River Valley, and Fort Ross–Seaview. Cabernet Sauvignon is a close second, on 11,480 acres. Although Napa has Cabernet Sauvignon in its DNA, many bottles of top-quality Sonoma Cabernet Sauvignon equal their counterparts from over the Mayacamas Mountains, often at a fraction of the cost. Merlot, vinified on its own or used in Meritage blends, prospers especially in Bennett and Sonoma valleys.

Zinfandel, another widely grown red variety, blankets 5,358 acres of Sonoma vineyards. Syrah is found in the Sonoma Coast, Russian River Valley, and Alexander Valley AVAs. Other red grapes are grown here, including Petite Sirah, Sangiovese, Petit Verdot, Malbec, and even Pinotage.

As of January 1, 2014, all wine produced with grapes from a Sonoma County AVA must include the words "Sonoma County" on the label. For example, a wine made with grapes from the Russian River Valley AVA must be labeled both "Russian River Valley" and "Sonoma County." This conjunctive labeling legislation is intended to both strengthen the image of Sonoma County and increase consumer awareness of Sonoma County's sub-AVAs.

Sonoma County offers many different environments for grape growing. Days are generally cool, with an average daily temperature of 70 to 72 degrees Fahrenheit, and even in high summer the temperature rarely rises above 85 degrees except in northern inland areas, such as the Alexander Valley. Large bodies of water contribute cooling effects: the Pacific Ocean and San Pablo Bay, south of Los Carneros and the Sonoma Coast and Sonoma Valley AVAs, offer late morning fog and cooling breezes. The Russian River enters the Alexander Valley from the north, then veers west, through the Russian River Valley, Green Valley, and Sonoma Coast AVAs before coursing into the Pacific, providing a natural break in the hills to pull Pacific fog inland and north.

ALEXANDER VALLEY AVA

Established in June 1988, Alexander Valley covers 32,536 acres. Named for Cyrus Alexander, a homesteader and farmer who planted grapes there in the 1840s, the valley was known more for prunes and other orchard fruit than for wine grapes until recently. It's home to more than two hundred grape growers and more than forty wineries.

The Pacific Ocean provides cooling maritime breezes and fog, which rolls in at night and flows up the Russian River. Altitudes vary from 200 to 2,000 feet above sea level. Soil types are alluvial with gravel and silt characteristics, and at higher elevations volcanic ash soils prevail. Grapes are grown on more than 15,000 acres here, and although Pacific breezes and fog help cool the fruit during the day, this inland region is known for a fully ripened, warmer-weather style of wine, as opposed to the AVAs closer to the coast. The top variety in the Alexander Valley is Cabernet Sauvignon, grown on more than 6,000 acres. Merlot also thrives here, as does Zinfandel, including a significant quantity of old-vine vineyards. The top white variety is Chardonnay, planted on more than 2,000 acres.

BENNETT VALLEY AVA

Gaining official recognition in December 2003, Bennett Valley is home to a little more than 650 acres of grapevines. It overlaps the Sonoma Valley and Sonoma Coast appellations. Cradled by three mountain peaks, Bennett Valley varies in elevation from 250 to more than 1,800 feet, and cool coastal breezes and morning fog bless its well-drained volcanic rock soils. Almost forty small family vineyards, most fewer than 20 acres, share space among gentle slopes, and only four wineries lie within the AVA, only one open to the public. Merlot, Syrah, and Sauvignon Blanc are Bennett Valley's standout varieties.

CHALK HILL AVA

Chalk Hill's five wineries all lie on the western slopes of the Mayacamas. Named for its volcanic ash chalk-colored soils, it first received AVA status in 1983, amended in 1988. Chardonnay and Sauvignon Blanc thrive here, as does Cabernet Sauvignon. Because of the high elevation, Chalk Hill's vineyards avoid the fog that rolls up along the Russian River, so this AVA is generally warmer than the larger Russian River Valley AVA.

DRY CREEK VALLEY AVA

Dry Creek Valley, established in October 1983, was among the first AVAs in the county, and its grape-growing history reaches back more than 140 years. Italian and other European immigrants gravitated toward its rich farmland shortly after the Gold Rush ended, and by the 1880s there were almost 900 acres of vineyards and nine wineries here. The most widely grown variety, then and now, is Zinfandel, Dry Creek Valley's shining star. Prohibition wasn't kind to Dry Creek Valley, and many vineyards became fruit orchards and fields of grain at that time, but vineyard plantings have increased steadily since the 1970s. Today there are 9,300 acres of vines and more than seventy wineries here. Healdsburg, home to a panoply of tasting rooms and wine-themed restaurants, sits at the southeast corner of the appellation, at its convergence with the Alexander Valley and Russian River Valley AVAs. Soils on the valley floor are primarily well-drained alluvial gravel and sandy loam, while benchland and hillside soils are gravelly clay loam, often tinged with noteworthy streaks of red earth. The most prolific grape varieties here are Cabernet Sauvignon, Zinfandel, Merlot, Chardonnay, and Sauvignon Blanc. Gnarled Zinfandel vines, more than 100 years old, stud numerous vineyards here.

FORT ROSS–SEAVIEW AVA

One of Sonoma County's newest AVAs, Fort Ross–Seaview was granted official status in December 2011. The region features vineyards at heights of 800 to 1,800 feet above sea level, many above the fog line receiving long hours of warm sunshine. The AVA has gained a reputation for its Pinot Noir and Chardonnay, and fine examples of Zinfandel, Syrah, Petite Sirah, and Pinotage grow in its well-drained gravelly loams. White Rhône varieties are planted in small amounts as well and already are showing promise.

Fort Ross was the first site in Sonoma County to be planted with grapes in the early nineteenth century. This Russian stronghold hosted cuttings reportedly brought from Peru and cultivated by Russian fur trappers. Within this area is what many call the "true Sonoma Coast." The Fort Ross Vineyard & Winery offers staggering views of the coast below. Many Pinot Noir producers own vineyards in the Fort Ross–Seaview AVA or source fruit for appellation or vineyard-designate bottlings.

GREEN VALLEY OF RUSSIAN RIVER VALLEY AVA

Established in December 1983 as the Sonoma County Green Valley AVA, this appellation changed its name in 2007 to associate more closely with the famed Russian River Valley. Green Valley is one of the coolest regions in the county because of the breezes and fog that approach via the Petaluma Gap. The AVA features yellow Goldridge soil, a fine sandy loam. Just ten wineries call Green Valley their home, but a stellar roster of wineries either own vineyards or purchase grapes from among the 100 prized vineyards in the AVA. Pinot Noir and Chardonnay are the main grapes here and are vinified in still and sparkling styles. Top-notch Syrah and Gewürztraminer are produced here as well.

KNIGHTS VALLEY AVA

Protected from the cooling Pacific Ocean, Knights Valley, established in November 1983, is the warmest appellation in Sonoma County. Two thousand acres of grapes grow here, and Bordeaux varieties thrive, especially Cabernet Sauvignon, Merlot, and Cabernet Franc, as does Sauvignon Blanc, which, because of the warm climate, takes on a ripe style, with rich nuances of tropical fruit.

LOS CARNEROS AVA

Spanish for "the rams," Los Carneros used to serve as pastureland for grazing sheep. The AVA crosses the border between Sonoma and Napa, so wineries in the western portion may include Sonoma County and Sonoma Valley on their labels, while to the east they may be identified as coming from the Napa Valley AVA as well as Carneros. From the early 1980s, it has been the US vineyard and

winery base of a prominent catalog of European sparkling wine producers, including Moët & Chandon (Chandon), Champagne Taittinger (Domaine Carneros), Freixenet (Gloria Ferrer), Champagne G. H. Mumm (Mumm Napa), and Codorniu (Artesa, previously Codorniu Napa).

Because of its proximity to San Pablo Bay and its east-west orientation, Los Carneros is generally a cold-weather region, but AVAs farther north and west have claimed its former title of "coldest." Both Pinot Noir and Chardonnay have grown here for many years, although a late 1980s phylloxera outbreak necessitated major replanting. Both of these varieties are made into still and sparkling wine, and they have been joined recently by sizable plantings of Merlot and Syrah.

MOON MOUNTAIN AVA

The newest AVA in the county, Moon Mountain falls within the larger Sonoma Valley AVA. Most vineyards here lie on mountainsides rather than the valley floor, with altitudes ranging from 400 to 2,200 feet above sea level. There are eleven wineries and more than forty vineyards in the AVA, including the historic Monte Rosso vineyard, now owned by E & J Gallo, which was planted in the late nineteenth century.

NORTHERN SONOMA AVA

Established in 1985 and amended in 1986 and 1990, the Northern Sonoma AVA encompasses much of the northern portion of the county and covers 348,000 acres, including all or most of the Alexander Valley, Chalk Hill, Dry Creek Valley, Green Valley of Russian River Valley, Knights Valley, Rockpile, and Russian River Valley AVAs, portions of which also fall into the Sonoma Coast AVA. Wine produced from a mélange of grapes grown within the borders of the Northern Sonoma AVA may be labeled as such, but it's more meaningful for wines to bear the designation of one of the more recognizable AVAs inside its boundaries, such as Russian River Valley or Alexander Valley.

PINE MOUNTAIN–CLOVERDALE PEAK

This small AVA became official in November 2011. Its 4,750 acres are home to 230 planted vineyard acres, mainly red Bordeaux varieties with small amounts of Sauvignon Blanc. It crosses the county border, with a portion of the appellation in Mendocino County. The AVA, above the town of Cloverdale, begins at altitudes of 1,600 feet and runs as high as 3,000 feet at the peak of Pine Mountain. Grapes have been grown here since the Gold Rush era, mostly on plots smaller than 30 acres. There are no wineries.

ROCKPILE AVA

Sheep farmer and local sheriff Tennessee Carter Bishop founded Rockpile Ranch, named for a feature of the landscape, here in 1858. The indigenous Pomo people called it *kabe-chana*, "place with many rocks." Sheriff Bishop reportedly planted vines on his ranch in 1872, and in 1884 Swedish immigrant S. P. Hallengren planted vines nearby as well. Established in 2002, Rockpile AVA can claim only 150 acres planted to grapevines. Elevations run between 900 and 1,900 feet, and vineyards planted above the fog line benefit from long hours of sunlight, making this prime territory for red grapes such as Cabernet Sauvignon, Zinfandel, and Petite Sirah. Hallengren's descendants, the Mauritson family, continue to farm grapes in this high-elevation, rock-strewn region.

RUSSIAN RIVER VALLEY AVA

Russian fur trappers named the valley's river but pulled up stakes in 1841, just before Gold Rush–era settlers, many from Italy, gravitated here. The latter planted fruit trees, grain, and other crops. Gravenstein apples reigned supreme for much of the twentieth century, but wine grapes are the area's current claim to fame.

By the end of the 1870s, more than 7,000 acres of vines were planted in the area, and 500,000 gallons of wine were produced annually. Vineyard acreage declined during Prohibition, but the modern era of Russian River Valley winemaking began in the

1960s, when Bob Sisson, a University of California farm adviser, counseled viticulturists to plant Chardonnay and Pinot Noir. First established in November 1983, the Russian River Valley AVA had an original footprint of 96,000 acres, which expanded in October 2005 to 126,600 and then to its present size of 169,029 acres in November 2011. The larger Sonoma Coast AVA overlaps the region to the south and east and the Northern Sonoma AVA to the north. While the original, northern portion of the AVA is prime real estate for Pinot Noir and Chardonnay, the flatter area added in late 2011 grows vines bearing Zinfandel, Cabernet Sauvignon, and other red Bordeaux varieties.

The Russian River draws Pacific fog inward and provides a cooling action for the region's 15,000 acres of grapes. Westside Road, home to a string of high-profile wineries, is affectionately called the Russian River Gold Coast and the Russian River's Rodeo Drive. The emphasis throughout the AVA is on Pinot Noir and Chardonnay, but a fair amount of Zinfandel, Syrah, Petite Sirah, and Sauvignon Blanc is grown here too.

SONOMA COAST AVA

Established in July 1987, the Sonoma Coast AVA, the largest in the county, covers 480,000 acres. Partially overlapping the Northern Sonoma AVA and containing segments of the Russian River Valley, Green Valley, Los Carneros, and Chalk Hill AVAs, it also has a wholly enclosed sub-AVA, Fort Ross–Seaview, in the northwest. In the lower area of the AVA lies Petaluma, cooled by breezes that come through the Petaluma Gap.

Excluding the sub-AVAs, the Sonoma Coast AVA contains seven wineries and 2,000 planted vineyard acres. It's known for its cool climate, caused by the proximity of the Pacific Ocean and the moderating effects of fog and breezes, but some elevated coastal areas rise too high for fog to reach, allowing warm sunshine to penetrate vineyards for the full length of the day. In 2011, winemakers who produce bottlings from the northwest region of the AVA, with a focus on Pinot Noir, banded together, calling themselves the West Sonoma Coast Vintners. Syrah is making a name for itself here as well.

SONOMA MOUNTAIN AVA

A small AVA within the greater Sonoma Valley AVA, Sonoma Mountain, established in February 1985, is a high-elevation region known for rich Cabernet Sauvignon, Zinfandel, Chardonnay, Sauvignon Blanc, Sémillon, and Pinot Noir. Many vineyards lie at altitudes too high for fog, and fissures within steep mountain slopes provide a variety of microclimates; this is why such a diversity of grape varieties thrive on its 800 planted acres.

SONOMA VALLEY AVA

Known as the Valley of the Moon, Sonoma Valley has been planted with grapes since Franciscan missionaries arrived in 1823. General Vallejo expanded their efforts 11 years later, and Agoston Haraszthy's Buena Vista Winery was founded a few decades later. This AVA contains the Bennett Valley, Moon Mountain, and Sonoma Mountain AVAs as well as a portion of Los Carneros. The southern Sonoma Valley AVA overlaps with the southeastern Sonoma Coast AVA. As a result of its location between mountain ranges, cooling breezes from the Santa Rosa Plain move north-south through the valley, which benefits from cooling influences from San Pablo Bay that move in the opposite direction. The Sonoma Mountains shelter the valley from daytime fog and more direct Pacific Ocean breezes.

Granted formal AVA status in 1981 (amended in 1985 and 1987), the Sonoma Valley AVA is home to 15,000 acres planted to grapevines. A wide array of varieties is cultivated here, from Alicante Bouschet to Zinfandel, the latter grown in a number of vineyards dating back to the 1880s and 1890s on untrellised gnarled vines supported by thick bases. Many vines bearing Alicante Bouschet are eligible for the old-vine designation as well, including some growing alongside Touriga Nacional, Petite Sirah, and other "mixed blacks," almost always in close proximity to same-age Zinfandel vines. Cabernet Sauvignon thrives here as well, particularly in the AVA's northern reaches. Chardonnay, Pinot Noir, and Merlot are also notable varieties. There are 114 wineries and seventy-six tasting rooms here, many ringing the Mission-era Sonoma Plaza.

THE WINERIES

ACORN/ALEGRÍA VINEYARDS

12040 Old Redwood Highway, Healdsburg, CA 95448
(707) 433-6440, www.acornwinery.com

Bill and Betsy Nachbaur purchased the Alegría Vineyard in Russian River Valley in 1990 and began producing their own wines in 1996. They make just 3,000 cases per year, so the Acorn name nods to their diminutive size and the oak aging their wines receive. Acorn specializes in field blends, cofermenting multiple varieties from its 120-year-old vineyard. Bill Nachbaur and Clay Mauritson make the wines. The Acorn Hill and Medley are proprietary vineyard blends, and the "single-varietal" bottlings also include small amounts of other varieties. The Acorn Alegría Vineyards Russian River Valley Zinfandel offers rich fruit flavors with luscious tannins. ❶

ADOBE ROAD WINERY

1995 South McDowell Boulevard, Petaluma, CA 94954
(707) 939-7967, www.adoberoadwines.com

Pro racecar driver Kevin Buckler and his wife, Debra, opened Adobe Road Winery to create quality wines in sync with the local terroir and seasonal rhythms. They opened a new boutique wine facility in 2008, with a tasting room on the historic Sonoma Plaza, and winemaker Michael Scorsone often fields visitors' questions there. The creamy Adobe Road Winery Russian River Valley Bacigalupi Vineyard Chardonnay has aromas of canned peaches and English toffee, and the Adobe Road Winery Sonoma Coast Pinot Noir tastes of dried blueberry and cherry preserves. ❷

ADRIAN FOG

2064 Gravenstein Highway North, Sebastopol, CA 95472
(707) 431-1174, www.adrianfog.com

Winemaker Stewart Dormand and his wife, Jane, started Adrian Fog in the late 1990s. From the outset they have received high marks for their small-lot Pinot Noir. They select cool-climate grapes with an eye on the influence of fog patterns, vine age, sun orientation, and clonal selection. For their most recent vintage, the largest bottling was 330 cases and the smallest was 23. The fruity, long-finishing Adrian Fog Savoy Vineyard Anderson Valley Pinot Noir has fruit-of-the-wood flavors with touches of anisette.

ANABA

60 Bonneau Road, Sonoma, CA 95476
(707) 996-4188, www.anabawines.com

Anaba takes its name from a type of wind that blows warm air up steep slopes, and it's no coincidence that owner John Sweazey was the first in Northern California to install a wind turbine to power the winery's tasting room and offices. Winemaker and director of vineyard operations Jennifer Marion works with Burgundy and Rhône varieties, producing stellar Chardonnay, Pinot Noir, and blends and single-varietal wines using Grenache, Syrah, Mourvèdre, Roussanne, Marsanne, and Viognier. The creamy Anaba Gap's Crown Vineyard Chardonnay boasts bright flavors of pineapple and mango, and the silky Anaba Las Madres Syrah has flavors of blackberry, black pepper, and fennel bulb.

ANAKOTA

4611 Thomas Road, Healdsburg, CA 95448
(707) 433-9000, www.anakota.com

A joint venture between Pierre and Monique Seillan and the Jackson family, Anakota shares winery space with the highly acclaimed Verité. Only two wines are made under the Anakota label, both single-vineyard Cabernet Sauvignon. If you can score one of each from the same vintage, enjoy them side by side and note the subtle effects of terroir. The Anakota Helena Montana Vineyard Knights Valley Cabernet Sauvignon tastes of black cherry and espresso bean with touches of butterscotch and spice. The long-finishing Anakota Helena Dakota Vineyard

Knights Valley Cabernet Sauvignon offers rich flavors of baking spices, vanilla, and bacon with a lift of menthol in the finish. ❸

ARISTA

7015 Westside Road, Healdsburg, CA 95448
(707) 473-0606, www.aristawinery.com

Founded in 2002 by Al and Janis McWilliams and their sons Mark and Ben, Arista augmented its Two Birds and Harper's Rest vineyards on the 36-acre Westside Road property with the purchase of the Martinelli Road Vineyard in April 2012. Winemaker Matt Courtney joined the team in November 2012, and Ulises Valdez directs vineyard management. Simple tastings are available, but visitors are encouraged to book a private feast and wine pairing in the glass-walled dojo of the Japanese gardens. The earthy Arista Toboni Vineyard Russian River Valley Pinot Noir has a cherry palate that leads to black plum enhanced by Mediterranean herb notes and a sprinkle of baking spice. The satiny Arista Bacigalupi Vineyard Russian River Valley Pinot Noir offers a palate of fresh fruit joined by oregano and a hint of rosemary. The Arista Two Birds Estate Vineyard Russian River Valley Pinot Noir tastes of black currant and raspberry.

ARROWOOD VINEYARDS & WINERY

14347 Highway 12, Glen Ellen, CA 95442
(707) 935-2600, www.arrowoodvineyards.com

At Chateau St. Jean, Richard Arrowood made some of the first single-vineyard wines in California. In 1986 he and his wife, Alis, founded Arrowood, releasing their first vintage in 1988. Arrowood now belongs to the Jackson Family Wines portfolio, and Heidi von der Mehden took over winemaking duties in 2010. They focus on Chardonnay and Cabernet Sauvignon but produce Syrah, Malbec, Merlot, and Viognier too. The crisp Arrowood Sonoma County Chardonnay has flavors of peach and Gala apple with notes of vanilla and spice. The Arrowood Reserve Spéciale Sonoma Valley Cabernet Sauvignon tastes of black currant, black cherry, and blackberry. ❹

AUTEUR

P.O. Box 1554, Sonoma, CA 95476
(707) 938-9211, www.auteurwines.com

With his wife and business partner, Laura, winemaker-owner Kenneth Juhasz crafts fine cool-climate Pinot Noir and Chardonnay available to winery club members and lucky residents of the states in which Auteur is distributed. The full-flavored Auteur Durrell Vineyard Chardonnay releases flavors of clementine and peach jam with a splash of citrus on the finish. The Auteur Sonoma Stage Pinot Noir opens with notes of cherry and black plum joined by a touch of coffee, and a dusting of Mediterranean herbs. ❺

BEDROCK WINE CO.

554 Michael Drive, Sonoma, CA 95476
(707) 364-8763, www.bedrockwineco.com

The son of Ravenswood's Joel Peterson, Morgan Twain-Peterson started Bedrock Wine Co. in 2007, joined since by New Yorker friend Chris Cottrell. The Bedrock Wine Co. Heirloom Bedrock Vineyard features flavors of sweet fruit accented by nuances of dried Mediterranean herbs and a whiff of peppermint. The Bedrock Wine Co. Heirloom Compagni Portis gives a nose of stone and tropical fruits. ❻

In his own words

MIKE BENZIGER

In 1973 winemaker Mike Benziger headed west from New York City and began his career working in a wineshop. He took an apprenticeship at a winery in 1978, and today he and his family make delicious, highly rated wines using biodynamic principles.

The day I graduated from college, my girlfriend (my wife now) and I drove to California. At that time we had never been west of Philadelphia. When we got to California, we had no money left. By luck, I got a job in a wineshop. It was my first job out of college. I got bit by the wine bug. I fell in love with wine and never looked back.

At the wineshop I worked in, which was a good one, the best-selling wine in 750 ml was Charles Krug Chenin Blanc and Wente Grey Riesling. California Chardonnay was not on the radar screen. The wine consumer at that time was a very narrow demographic. Then, there might have been several hundred wines available; today, tens of thousands. The wine business exploded. The biggest changes have been globalization, consolidation, expansion of the demographics who enjoy wine, and how ingrained wine and food are in American culture. Of course, there's more. I expect the rate of change to continue to increase.

I have been extremely fortunate to learn much of my farming and winemaking from great mentors. They not only presented me with a great example of what to do but, even more importantly, how to be around nature, grapes, and wine. I can't think of anything more important than traveling the world of wine, food, and general agriculture and maintaining global connections. Without a wider view, you will lose relevance and get messed up quickly. My growing and winemaking philosophy is to invite nature in to do the heavy lifting. When you harmonize with nature, it reveals more of itself. That's its way of showing gratitude. My family's goal and mine is to remain humble, passionate, and curious about nature. We believe rhythm, pattern, and harmony are key tools for the future.

I am very encouraged by the awareness that is now developing with many growers and wineries that many of the things we do to create a healthy environment can have a direct effect on wine quality. We need to think about what kind of land, climate, and environment we will leave our grandchildren. As the Indian Chief Seattle said, "We don't inherit this land from our parents; we borrow it from our children." It took my family some time to figure it out, but nature is now our best partner in growing grapes and producing distinctive wines. We are constantly debating the differences/similarities between what is modern quality and authenticity/honesty.

I personally am focused on Pinot Noir and Bordeaux varieties. What Pinot teaches me I adapt to Cabernet Sauvignon. Our experimenting tends to be focused in the field. I am fascinated with farming out close to the ocean. It's kicked our ass. It will take a few lifetimes to figure it out, but that's fun for me.

BELLA VINEYARDS AND WINERY

9711 West Dry Creek Road, Healdsburg, CA 95448
(707) 473-9171, www.bellawinery.com

Scott and Lynn Adams and their winemakers Michael Dashe, Joe Healy, and Dave Majerus make small batches of Zinfandel, Syrah, and Petite Sirah from their three vineyards. Their Big River Ranch vines in Alexander Valley are more than 100 years old, and their Dry Creek Valley Lily Hill Estate nurtures Zinfandel vines more than 85 years old. The lushly smooth Bella Maple Vineyards Dry Creek Valley Zinfandel has flavors of lush wild raspberry, cassis, espresso, and anise, and the Bella Big River Ranch Zinfandel features full-bodied juicy red and black fruit with a dusting of fresh ground pepper and Christmas baking spices. 7

BENZIGER

1883 London Ranch Road, Glen Ellen, CA 95442
(888) 490-2739, www.benziger.com

All of Benziger's vineyards are certified biodynamic, organic, or sustainable, and the health of the vines shows in the glass. General manager, winegrower, and Tribute winemaker Mike Benziger and his family relocated to Sonoma Mountain in the late 1970s. In the 1990s, after noticing that the earth and vines didn't look as healthy and vibrant as they had, they transitioned to natural farming methods. Their Glen Ellen estate is home not just to grapevines but sheep, cattle, and other fauna that help balance the vineyards. The Wine Group purchased Benziger in June 2015. The Benziger Signaterra San Remo Vineyard Pinot Noir tastes of gingerbread spices that reveal bright cherry pie flavors. The zesty Benziger Tribute has a brambleberry palate enriched by splashes of tart cherry. 8

BEVAN CELLARS

3468 Silverado Trail, St. Helena, CA 95504
(707) 542-0123, www.bevancellars.com

Russell Bevan and Victoria De Crescenzo caught the California wine bug while on vacation and eventually bought a dream home on eight acres in Bennett Valley. Their friend Kal Showket gave them one ton of Cabernet Sauvignon grapes so that they could try their hand, and they were hooked. The full yet light Bevan Cellars Showket Vineyard Bab's Cuvée Cabernet Sauvignon has a palate of dark fruit with a hint of dark chocolate. Bevan Cellars Kick Ranch Sauvignon Blanc Robin's Cuvée smells deliciously of tropical fruits and white peach and in the mouth has great depth and pronounced minerality. 9

BLUE ROCK VINEYARD

Cloverdale, CA 95424
(415) 435-1946, www.bluerockvineyard.com

Settled by Italian immigrants in the 1880s, Blue Rock began life anew when Cheryl and Kenny Kahn purchased its hundred acres, restored the original buildings, and replanted the vineyards to five Bordeaux varieties and a small amount of Syrah. Today they produce 1,800 cases per year, with wine club members getting first crack at new releases, but small amounts of winemakers Kenny Kahn's and Nick Goldschmidt's output make it to wine lists of fine restaurants in about fifteen states. The nuanced Blue Rock Baby Blue has flavors of violet and earth. The Blue Rock Best Barrels Cabernet Sauvignon offers mixed-berry pie flavors with a heady dose of espresso bean and toasted vanilla bean. 10

7

3

10

8

33

29

14

45
KUNDE

28

72

36

70

In his own words

JEAN-CHARLES BOISSET

Burgundy-born Jean-Charles Boisset belongs to numerous wine industry organizations, including the Northern California Young Presidents Organization and La Confrérie des Chevaliers du Tastevin. *Decanter* magazine named him one of the Top 50 Power Brokers in the world of wine, and *Wine Enthusiast* dubbed him "Innovator of the Year." He and wife, Gina Gallo, are active in many charitable organizations, including Feed the Children.

I had the pleasure of growing up in the village of Vougeot in Burgundy, France, where my view was the vineyards of the world-renowned Château du Clos Vougeot. As a child, we played amid the vineyards planted by the Cistercian monks as early as 1110, and my bedroom was literally above the barrel cellar and the winery. In 1981, when I, age 11, and my sister, 14, had the opportunity to accompany my grandparents on a journey to California, we found ourselves discovering the spirit of the Gold Rush state in Monterey, San Francisco, and Sonoma. On the square in Sonoma, the birthplace of the California Republic, they noticed a historical landmark—a winery founded in 1857 named Buena Vista. I'll remember forever discovering the oldest stones of the California wine world—a grand winery estate—the first gravity-flow winery, the first caves, and the foundation of modern viniculture in California.

My grandparents allowed us tastes of those incredible Chardonnays in the hotel room, and I was transfixed—such pure, elegant, and tropical notes that we did not know in Burgundy! I recall the moment I declared to my sister, "Wouldn't it be fun one day to make wine in California?" That dream was realized in 2003 with DeLoach in the Russian River Valley, in 2009 with Raymond in the Napa Valley, and in 2011 when we finally brought Buena Vista Winery, California's first and most historic estate, into our family collection of wineries! We are now the stewards of an incredible winemaking heritage.

We've seen an increase in smaller, more specific *terroirs* that mirror the classical appellation system in France. This in combination with exploring more wine-growing regions has led to our discovery of some unbelievable vineyards and a new generation of world-class wines. As dedicated as we are to our wines, we are equally passionate about the long-term health and vitality of our *terroir*, so we have a particular focus on biodynamic and organic winemaking practices. My family began farming according to biodynamic principles in Burgundy in 1994. Today, Domaine de la Vougeraie is the leading organic and biodynamic domaine in the Côte d'Or with more than 95 acres under cultivation. In California, we began implementing biodynamic farming at DeLoach Vineyards, which was certified organic by CCOF in 2008 and biodynamic by Demeter USA in 2010.

One must have patience, passion, and long-term vision to effect change, especially in this business, where change can only be effected over years. We have always embraced innovation when it serves the quality of the wine, and we are very open to the idea that every wine has its own personality, its own place, and its own time—for some, there is nothing better than to be sealed under a screw cap to preserve the freshness and vibrancy of the wines, and for others, cork is the natural choice. We should expand the conversation to include all the positive alternatives for wine packaging that may help reduce the carbon footprint of the wine world—whether it's the Tetra Pak carton or our Barrel to Barrel!

Our vision today is to hope that our spirit of collaboration and commitment to wine will transcend any divisions . . . that the world will vibrate with a passion and appreciation for the elixir of God and wine's expression of our land and our place, that we can realize our vision that, while oceans may separate us, wine unites us!

BUENA VISTA

18000 Old Winery Road, Sonoma CA, 95476
(800) 926-1266, www.buenavistawinery.com

Founded in 1857 by Agoston Haraszthy de Mokesa, self-proclaimed count, Buena Vista Winery now belongs to the Boisset family portfolio under the guidance of wine-royal Jean-Charles Boisset. Buena Vista has passed through several long periods with no wine production, but the Boissets' 2011 acquisition and 2012 renovation have given it new life. The vibrant Buena Vista Carneros Merlot has vibrant flavors of black cherry, fresh ground pepper, and mace, while the bold Buena Vista Vinicultural Society Sonoma Pinot Noir tastes of blackberries and cherries with touches of caramel. ⓫

THE CALLING

205 Concourse Boulevard, Santa Rosa, CA 95403
(877) 289-9463, www.thecallingwine.com

A collaboration between sports commentator Jim Nantz and Peter Deutsch, CEO of W.J. Deutsch & Sons, the Calling began when Peter complimented Jim on his book about his relationship with his father, who was coping with Alzheimer's disease. The winemaking falls under the direction of Marco DiGiulio, and sales bring attention to the Nantz National Alzheimer Center. The long-finishing Calling Russian River Valley Dutton Ranch Jewell Vineyard Chardonnay tastes of white peach with notes of lemon curd and crème brûlée. The luxurious Calling Russian River Valley Dutton Ranch Pinot Noir features delicious fruit flavors followed by a touch of spice.

CARLISLE

P.O. Box 556, Santa Rosa, CA 95402
(707) 566-7700, www.carlislewinery.com

Carlisle founder Mike Officer fell hard for wine in college, and a few years later he and his wife, Kendall Carlisle Officer, were making five-gallon batches of Zinfandel in their kitchen sink. Carlisle Vineyards & Winery launched in 1998, and winemaker-viticulturist Jay Maddox joined the Officers in 2001. The zesty Carlisle Papa's Block Russian River Valley Syrah has flavors of blackberry, wild raspberry, and a pinch of savory herbs and baking spices, and the Carlisle Carlisle Vineyard Russian River Valley Zinfandel tastes of rich berry and plum, backed by Sichuan pepper and Chinese five spice. ⓬

CAROL SHELTON WINES

3354-B Coffey Lane, Santa Rosa, CA 95403
(707) 575-3441, www.carolshelton.com

Having worked with Andre Tchelistcheff and Robert Mondavi, Carol Shelton and her husband, Mitch Mackenzie, established their own brand in 2000. Currently producing about 5,000 cases annually, Carol makes clever use of her original major at UC Davis—poetry—in the names she gives her wines: Wild Thing Zin, Sweet Caroline, and Karma Zin. The creamy, smooth Carol Shelton Wild Thing Mendocino County Old Vine Zinfandel bursts on the palate with fresh fruit and notes of blackberry and vanilla custard. The polished Carol Shelton 'Xander Zin tastes a bit like a layered fruit dessert, though it's not by any means a sweet wine; flavors of raspberry and cherry predominate before vanilla and chocolate take over, and then a pleasant wave of spice hits. The Carol Shelton Coquille Blanc features rich flavors of white peach, pear, and toasted nuts. ⓭

C. DONATIELLO

320 Center St., Healdsburg, CA 95448
(707) 431-4442, www.cdonatiello.com

Chris Donatiello made his name on the sales and marketing side of the wine and spirits industry and then headed to the Russian River Valley to focus on his eponymous winery, producing small-lot, single-vineyard Pinot Noir and Chardonnay. Donatiello and winemaker Webster Marquez create wines (available online and at their downtown Healdsburg tasting room) that stand as a testament to terroir and the art of viniculture. The C. Donatiello Peters Vineyard Chardonnay puts forward flavors of apple, citrus, and Christmas spice, and the earthy C. Donatiello Russian River Valley Floodgate Old Vines Pinot Noir features tastes of fresh summer berries and a hint of spice.

CHALK HILL ESTATE

10300 Chalk Hill Road, Healdsburg, CA 95448
(707) 657-4837, www.chalkhill.com

Founder Fred Furth was flying his plane over the Russian River in 1972 when he spotted the land that became his vineyard. Bill Foley now owns Chalk Hill Estate, with winemaking handled by Lisa Bishop Forbes, who prefers noninvasive, sustainable practices. The crisp, clean Chalk Hill Estate Sauvignon Musque has flavors of mango, grapefruit, and white stone fruits. The well-balanced Chalk Hill Estate Pinot Noir tastes of red fruits and Chinese black tea. 14

CHARLES HEINTZ VINEYARDS

P.O. Box 238, Occidental, CA 95465
(877) 874-3852, www.heintzvineyards.com

Family-owned since 1912, Heintz Ranch produces quality cool-weather grapes. Its truly artisanal wines—produced for two labels, Heintz and Dutch Bill Creek—appear in fewer than 1,000 cases. The fruit-forward Heintz Sonoma Coast Syrah tastes like summer with a restrained, elegant finish. The Heintz Rosé of Pinot Noir offers ethereal aromas of strawberries and cream that shift seamlessly onto the palate. 15

CHASSEUR

2064 Gravenstein Highway North, Sebastopol, CA 95472
(707) 829-1941, www.chasseurwines.com

French for "hunter," Chasseur launched in 1994. In 2009 Andrew Berge joined winemaker Bill Hunter as assistant winemaker. The winery's 2,700-case annual output includes the Hunter Wine Cellars Chasseur Graton's Choice Chardonnay, which has a mouth-pleasing mashup of stone fruits and citrus with a dusting of spice and grated lemon rind. The subdued palate of the balanced Hunter Wine Cellars Chasseur Russian River Valley Pinot Noir offers black cherry, cassis, baking spices, and chocolate.

CHATEAU ST. JEAN

8555 Sonoma Highway, Kenwood, CA 95452
(707) 833-4134, www.chateaustjean.com

Walking through the main entrance and gardens, you can forget that you're in California for a moment and think you've been transported to a Mediterranean villa, but don't be fooled: Chateau St. Jean embodies the spirit of Sonoma hospitality. Winemaker Margo Van Staaveren oversees the production of Chateau St. Jean's thirty or so wines. The creamy and refreshing Chateau St. Jean Sonoma

County Chardonnay has aromas of pineapple upside-down cake, crisp apple slices, and toasted almonds. The luscious, well-balanced Chateau St. Jean Sonoma County Pinot Noir features a touch of spice and generous fruit flavors. 16

CLINE CELLARS

24737 Arnold Drive, Sonoma, CA 95476
(707) 940-4000, www.clinecellars.com

Fred Cline founded Cline Cellars in Oakley, California, where his mother's father, Valeriano Jacuzzi, had taught him to love the land and to make wine. Fred and his wife, Nancy, moved to the Carneros appellation in 1992, and their vineyards are naturally and sustainably farmed. A circa-1850s farmhouse serves as the tasting room, and the California Mission Museum bears witness to the Spaniards who first brought wine grapes to California. The velvety Cline Cool Climate Sonoma Coast Syrah tastes of blueberry pie and freshly ground black pepper. The Cline Contra Costa County Bridgehead Zinfandel, a restrained powerhouse, features flavors of ripe berries and baking spices joined by smooth white chocolate and a hint of toast.

CLOS DU BOIS

19410 Geyserville Avenue, Geyserville, CA 95441
(800) 222-3189, www.closdubois.com

Founder Frank Woods introduced Clos du Bois's first Chardonnay and Pinot Noir wines in 1974 after traveling throughout France. Today director of winemaking Gary Sitton oversees about 800 acres of vineyards that generate an extensive portfolio of bottlings. The crisp and fruity Clos du Bois North Coast Sauvignon Blanc has a nice touch of minerality in the finish, and the big, bold Clos du Bois North Coast Zinfandel gives flavors of fresh fruit and dark berry conserves with some nice spice in the finish. 17

COBB WINES

18100 Fitzpatrick Lane, Occidental, CA 95465
(707) 799-1073, www.cobbwines.com

Originally a marine biologist, David Cobb first crafted homemade wine in the late 1970s while living and working in Saudi Arabia. He and and his wife, Diane, planted their vineyard in 1989, and their son Ross came aboard in 2001. Together David and Ross focus on small-lot, single-vineyard Pinot Noir from the Sonoma Coast appellation. The dark-fruit Cobb Jack Hill Vineyard Sonoma Coast Pinot Noir has dollops of spice and chocolate and a bright finish, while the elegant and richly nuanced Cobb Coastlands Vineyard Sonoma Coast Pinot Noir features a richly nuanced palate that moves from fruit through mint tea and into Moroccan spice. 18

COPAIN WINES

7800 Eastside Road, Healdsburg, CA 95448
(707) 836-8822, www.copainwines.com

After a two-year apprenticeship under Rhône Valley icon Michel Chapoutier, Wells Guthrie began making classic California-style wines with a nod to the craftsmanship of France. Most of Copain goes to club members, but you can buy bottles at its Russian River Valley winery and tasting room and online. The bright but restrained Copain Les Voisins Syrah tastes of blueberry, blackberry, and lavender.

DAVIS BYNUM WINERY

8075 Westside Rd, Healdsburg, CA 95448
(866) 442-7547, www.davisbynum.com

In 1973, former newspaper reporter Davis Bynum built the first winery on Westside Road in Healdsburg and then, with grapes from neighbor Joe Rochioli's now-acclaimed vineyard, made the purportedly first single-vineyard Russian River Valley Pinot Noir. Today, under the ownership of the Klein family and Rodney Strong Wine Estates, Davis Bynum is known for artisanal Russian River Valley Chardonnay and Pinot Noir. Winemaker Greg Morthole has been with the winery since 2005, becoming head winemaker in 2010. Davis Bynum River West Chardonnay has flavors of Granny Smith apple and Bartlett pear, with a nice dose of butterscotch and a touch of lemon zest, and the velvety Davis Bynum Jane's Vineyard Pinot Noir tastes of cherry vanilla parfait. 19

DEHLINGER

4101 Vine Hill Road, Sebastopol, CA 95472
(707) 823-2378, www.dehlingerwinery.com

Enologist Tom Dehlinger planted 14 acres of vines in 1975. Today, Tom; his wife, Carole; daughters Carmen and Eva; vineyard manager Martin Hedlund; and a small staff create 7,000 cases of estate-bottled Chardonnay, Cabernet Sauvignon, Pinot Noir, and Syrah from what has grown to 45 acres. Most of their wine is set aside for wine club members, but a quarter is available at the winery and on restaurant wine lists. The creamy Dehlinger Winery Estate Russian River Valley Chardonnay has a rich nose of orange marmalade on buttered toast, and Dehlinger Goldridge Russian River Valley Syrah proffers flavors of blackberry and raspberry infused with cocoa, espresso, aniseed, and freshly ground pepper.

DELOACH VINEYARDS

1791 Olivet Road, Santa Rosa, CA 95401
(707) 755-3309, www.deloachvineyards.com

Cecil De Loach, a San Francisco fireman, fell in love with winemaking and planted his first grapes in 1973. The Boisset family of Burgundy, France, took the reins at DeLoach in 2003 after scion Jean-Charles Boisset took a shine to the Russian River Valley, likening Sonoma County to Burgundy in terms of climate and terroir. After the 2004 vintage, the new owners ripped out the existing vineyards and replanted them using biodynamic techniques, and the first wines produced from newly planted stock appeared in 2010. Winemaker Brian Maloney, assisted by Katie Cochrane, works with Chardonnay, Pinot Noir, and Zinfandel grown under the hand of winegrower Eric Pooler. The delightful DeLoach Estate Chardonnay has a caramelized pear tart flavor joined by hints of Mediterranean herbs and jasmine. The DeLoach Estate Collection Pinot Noir tastes of black cherry and raspberry finessed with a full complement of autumn spices. 20

DRY CREEK VINEYARD

3770 Lambert Bridge Road, Healdsburg, CA 95448
(707) 433-1000, www.drycreekvineyard.com

Kim Stare Wallace and her husband, Don Wallace, continue the legacy begun by Kim's father, David Stare, in 1972. A pioneer in many ways, David was an early advocate of sustainable farming in the wine industry. A proponent of Dry Creek Valley's AVA status, David was first to label a wine from this appellation in 1983. The elegant and refreshing Dry Creek Vineyard Dry Creek Valley Sauvignon Blanc features a mélange of grapefruit and lemon-lime sorbet, and on the velvety palate of the Dry Creek Vineyard Heritage Zinfandel blackberry and chocolate are joined by North African spices. 21

DUTTON ESTATE WINERY

8757 Green Valley Road, Sebastopol, CA 95472
(707) 829-9463, www.sebastopolvineyards.com

Joe and Tracy Dutton were both born into farming families, and Joe still manages the 1,300-acre Dutton Ranch founded by his parents. The Duttons' vineyards lie in the Green Valley of the Russian River Valley and Sonoma Coast AVAs. Joe and Tracy bought a Chardonnay vineyard in 1995 close to Dutton Ranch and to Kozlowski Farms, Tracy's family's farm, and their initial release of 1,000 cases of Pinot Noir and Chardonnay was bottled under the Sebastopol Vineyards label. The lush Dutton Estate Russian River Valley Kyndall's Reserve Chardonnay tastes of orange crème brûlée and a hint of clove, while the zesty Dutton Estate Russian River Valley Karmen Isabella Pinot Noir presents rich berry fruit and honeysuckle flavors.

DUTTON GOLDFIELD

3100 Gravenstein Highway North, Sebastopol, CA 95472
(707) 823-3887, www.duttongoldfield.com

The fifth generation to live in this area, Steve Dutton began farming grapes with his father at age five. Dan earned his master's in enology and developed a devotion to Pinot Noir while making wine at La Crema and then Hartford Court. This collaboration between Steve Dutton and Dan Goldfield began in 1998. Most of their fruit comes from Dutton Ranch vineyards in the Green River of the Russian River Valley AVA. Their portfolio includes small amounts of Syrah, Zinfandel, and Pinot Blanc. The Dutton-Goldfield Dutton Ranch Russian River Valley Chardonnay has flavors of tangerine, lemon, and butterscotch, and the Dutton-Goldfield Dutton Ranch Russian River Valley Pinot Noir offers cherry that mingles with vanilla and nice spice notes. 22

ENKIDU

8910 Sonoma Hwy., Kenwood, CA 95452
(707) 833-6100, www.enkiduwines.com

Owner and winemaker Phillip Staehle conceived his winery on the principles embodied by Enkidu, the best friend in *The Epic of Gilgamesh* and the protector of animals and the land. Using naturally farmed grapes and traditional winemaking techniques, Staehle creates balanced and complex wines that appeal to the senses. The lean, mineral-driven Enkidu Tin Cross Vineyard Pine Mountain-Cloverdale Peak Chardonnay features flavors of lemon sorbet and flint, and the rich Enkidu Kick Ranch Sonoma County Syrah offers cherry jam and fresh cherry among dashes of Mediterranean herbs and baking spices.

ENROUTE

P.O. Box 2358, Sebastopol CA 95473
(707) 944-2312, www.enroutewinery.com

Started by Beth, Erik, and Jeremy Nickel, Dirk Hampson, and Larry Maguire, who also own Far Niente, Dolce, and Nickel & Nickel. Winemaker Andrew Delos works under director of winemaking Dirk Hampson. The winery has a sole bottling at this time: EnRoute Les Pommiers Russian River Valley Pinot Noir, named for the apple orchards that grapevines gradually have replaced in the Russian River Valley. It opens gracefully with a punch of raspberry and black cherry. Drink it now, and store it to enjoy later. 23

FERRARI-CARANO VINEYARDS AND WINERY

8761 Dry Creek Road, Healdsburg, CA 95448
(707) 433-6700, www.ferrari-carano.com

Don and Rhonda Carano founded Ferrari-Carano Vineyards and Winery in 1981 after visiting Sonoma County on a wine-buying trip for their Eldorado Hotel and Casino in Reno, Nevada. Ferrari-Carano has been making fine wine since 1985. Steve Domenichelli oversees vineyard management, and winemaker Aaron Piotter produces the reds, while Sarah Quider makes the whites. The bright and complex Ferrari-Carano's Fumé Blanc has fresh fruit flavors that make this a perfect wine as an aperitif or with briny seafood. The full-bodied Ferrari-Carano Merlot features lots of fruit and leaves a lingering impression of dark chocolate.

FLOWERS VINEYARD & WINERY

28500 Seaview Road, Cazadero, CA 95421
(707) 847-3661, flowerswinery.com

Walt and Joan Flowers owned a nursery in Pennsylvania before transferring their lives and passion cross-country. In 1989, they bought 321 acres on the northern Sonoma Coast, and today they have developed a partnership with the Agustin Huneeus family. Head winemaker Jason Jardine's bottlings are available via the Flowers wine club and at fine restaurants and wine shops across the country. The lush, delightful Flowers Sea View Ridge Pinot Noir tastes of grilled wild mushrooms and pancetta on lightly buttered toast.

FOPPIANO VINEYARDS

12707 Old Redwood Highway, Healdsburg, CA 95448
(707) 433-7272, www.foppiano.com

Started by Giovanni Foppiano in 1896, Foppiano Vineyards is one of the oldest family-run wineries in Sonoma. Today, fourth- and fifth-generation family members work side by side in their sustainably farmed Russian River Valley vineyards. Foppiano is known worldwide for its award-winning Petite Sirah. Paul Foppiano directs the vineyards, while Natalie West oversees winemaking. The bright Foppiano Vineyards Estate Bottled Petite Sirah Russian River Valley tastes of blueberry pie, cherry conserves, and a smear of Nutella.

FORT ROSS VINEYARD & WINERY

15725 Meyers Grade Road, Jenner, CA 95450
(707) 847-3460, www.fortrossvineyard.com

Attorney Lester and musician and composer Linda Schwartz met as students at South Africa's University of Cape Town in the 1960s. They moved to California in the mid-1970s, purchasing a large swath of land in the coastal mountains above the old Fort Ross settlement, and began ordering rootstock in 1991, which prompted Linda to study viticulture. Their early vineyard experiments established that the area was perfect for Pinot Noir and Chardonnay, to which they added a small amount of Pinotage in homage to their native country. Their first vintage was 2000, and in 2009 Jeff Pisoni, who also makes wine from his family vineyards in the Santa Lucia Highlands, came aboard as winemaker. Fort Ross Vineyard Symposium Sonoma Coast Pinot Noir has flavors of blackberry, black plum, brioche, and baking spices, and the Fort Ross Vineyard Sonoma Coast Pinot Noir tastes of mixed brambleberries, sage, thyme, and chocolate.

FRANCIS FORD COPPOLA WINERY

300 Via Archimedes, Geyserville, CA 95441
(707) 857-1400, www.franciscoppolawinery.com

Academy Award–winning director, producer, and screenwriter Francis Ford Coppola's eponymous Alexander Valley winery, the former Chateau Souverain, reopened in July 2010 after extensive renovations. Coppola teamed with another Academy Award winner, Dean Tavoularis, to create a family-friendly "wine wonderland" featuring wine-tasting bars, restaurants, a park area, swimming pool, movie gallery, and performing arts pavilion. Francis Ford Coppola Director's Cut Russian River Valley Chardonnay has tropical fruit flavors of ripe peach and Asian pear with a touch of crème brûlée, while the fresh Francis Ford Coppola Director's Sonoma Coast Pinot Noir features mixed red and dark berries and baking spices. 24

FREEMAN VINEYARD & WINERY

1300 Montgomery Road, Sebastopol, CA 95472
(707) 823-6937, www.freemanwinery.com

Ken and Akiko Freeman spent several years searching California for a vineyard from which to make cool-climate Chardonnay and Pinot Noir comparable to wines they loved from Burgundy. They founded Freeman in 2001, collaborating with winemaker Ed Kurtzman, who now works as a consultant with his protégé, Akiko. Total production is 5,000 cases per year. The Freeman Vineyard & Winery Ryo-fu Chardonnay tastes of lightly toasted pineapple and mango sorbet with a hint of creaminess. In the Freeman Vineyard & Winery Akiko's Cuvée Pinot Noir, berry flavors dominate, backed by freshly baked bread and a hint of mushroom and orange zest. 25

FREI BROTHERS RESERVE

3887 Dry Creek Road, Healdsburg CA 95448
(866) 346-3963, www.freibrothers.com

Swiss immigrant Andrew Frei bought part of what is now Dry Creek Valley's Frei Ranch in 1890 and built a winery that produced 20,000 cases of wine per year by 1895. Frei's sons, Walter and Louis, took over in 1903, and in the 1930s Julio Gallo began buying grapes from Frei Ranch. The Gallo family bought Frei Ranch and the winery in the 1970s after the remaining members of the Frei family retired. Viticulturist Jim Collins manages the estate vineyards. The Frei Brothers Reserve Russian River Valley Chardonnay has flavors of apple and spice with vanilla custard notes and a light touch of spice. The invigorating Frei Brothers Reserve Dry Creek Valley Merlot 2010 tastes of raspberry and blackberry, joined by strawberry jam, mocha, and white chocolate.

FROSTWATCH VINEYARD & WINERY

5560 Bennett Valley Road, Santa Rosa, CA 95404
(707) 570 0592, www.frostwatch.com

Owners Brett Raven and Diane Kleineke make small-batch wines from grapes grown mostly in their Bennett Valley Frostwatch Vineyard, a 15-acre site originally planted with Chardonnay, Merlot, and a small amount of Zinfandel. For the last several years, they've been replanting to replace the Merlot with mainly white varieties. Fortunately, they've kept about two acres of Merlot. The understated, nicely balanced Frostwatch Bennett Valley Kismet proffers flavors of grapefruit and pineapple with a pleasant lift of spice, and cherry preserves with a splash of cassis predominate on the palate of the elegant Frostwatch Bennett Valley Pinot Noir.

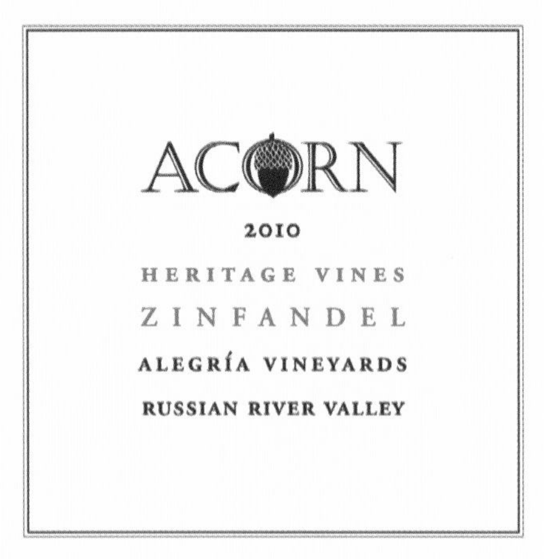
ACORN
2010
HERITAGE VINES
ZINFANDEL
ALEGRÍA VINEYARDS
RUSSIAN RIVER VALLEY

1

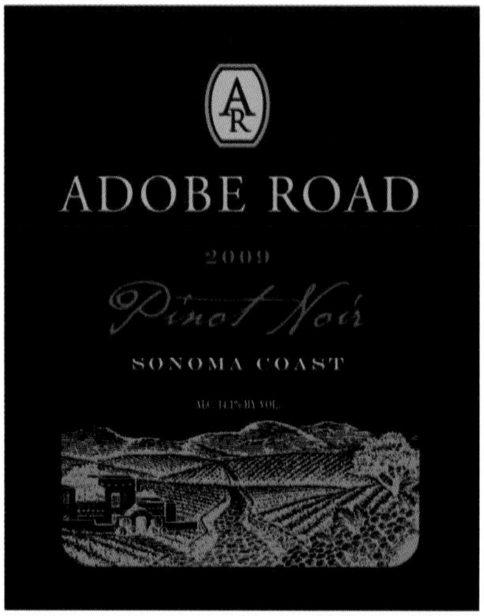
AR
ADOBE ROAD
2009
Pinot Noir
SONOMA COAST

2

RESERVE SPECIALE
ARROWOOD
2007
SONOMA VALLEY
Cabernet Sauvignon
Unfined and Unfiltered
15.5% ALC. BY VOL.

4

CALIFORNIA'S FIRST PREMIUM WINERY
SINCE 1857
Buena Vista
MERLOT
CARNEROS
2010.

11

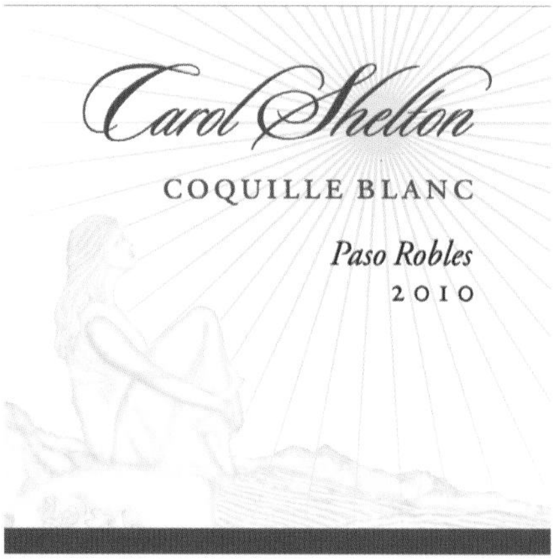
Carol Shelton
COQUILLE BLANC
Paso Robles
2010

13

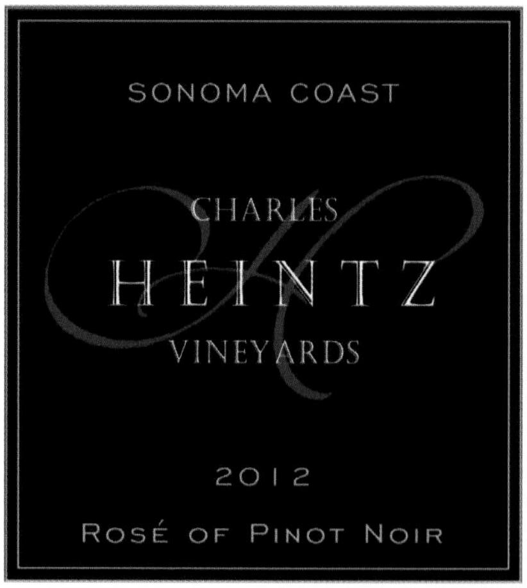
SONOMA COAST
CHARLES
HEINTZ
VINEYARDS
2012
ROSÉ OF PINOT NOIR

15

DAVIS
BYNUM
RUSSIAN RIVER VALLEY
SONOMA COUNTY
Chardonnay
VINTAGE 2011
ALC. 14.5% BY VOL.

19

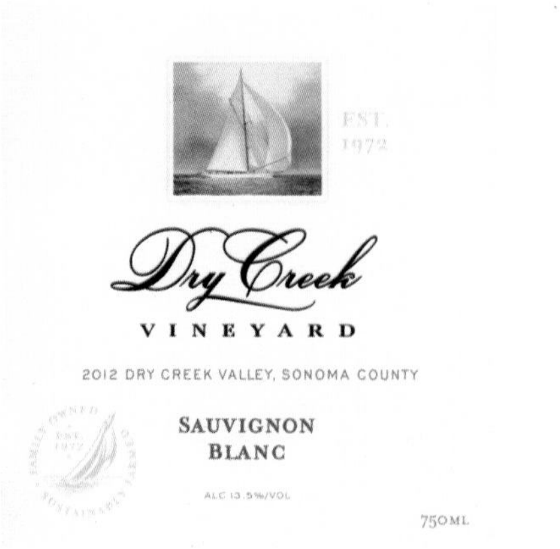
EST. 1972
Dry Creek
VINEYARD
2012 DRY CREEK VALLEY, SONOMA COUNTY
SAUVIGNON
BLANC
750ML

21

DUTTON
Goldfield
CHARDONNAY
DUTTON RANCH
RUSSIAN RIVER VALLEY
2011

22

AUTEUR
Sonoma Stage Vineyard
Pinot Noir
2009
Sonoma Coast

5

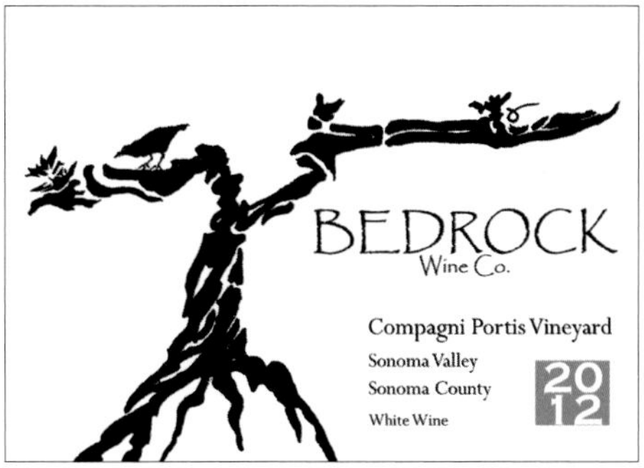
BEDROCK
Wine Co.
Compagni Portis Vineyard
Sonoma Valley
Sonoma County
White Wine
2012

6

KICK RANCH
SAUVIGNON BLANC
Bevan
SONOMA COUNTY
2011
Cellars

9

CHATEAU ST JEAN
SONOMA
Chardonnay
SONOMA COUNTY

16

CLOS DU BOIS
Zinfandel
NORTH COAST 2010

17

2009
COBB
PINOT NOIR
Coastlands Vineyard
SONOMA COAST

18

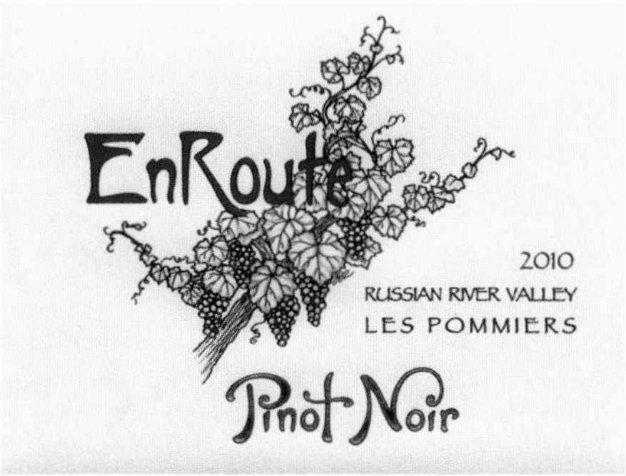
EnRoute
2010
RUSSIAN RIVER VALLEY
LES POMMIERS
Pinot Noir

23

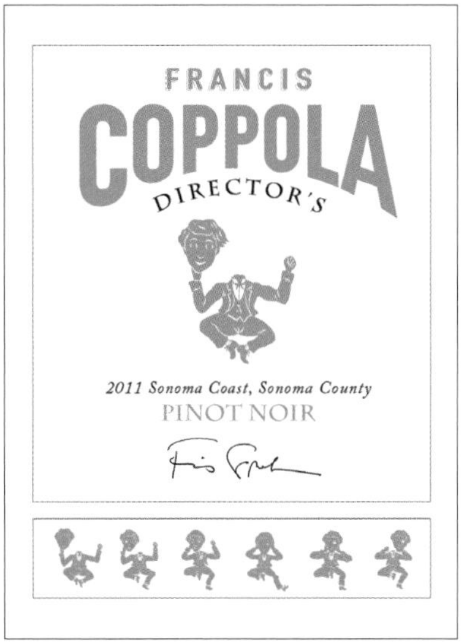
FRANCIS
COPPOLA
DIRECTOR'S
2011 Sonoma Coast, Sonoma County
PINOT NOIR

24

FREEMAN
VINEYARD & WINERY
Ryo-fu
CHARDONNAY
Russian River Valley

25

GLORIA FERRER
FERMENTED IN THIS BOTTLE
MÉTHODE CHAMPENOISE
BLANC DE NOIRS
SONOMA COUNTY SPARKLING WINE

27

GARY FARRELL VINEYARDS & WINERY

10701 Westside Road, Healdsburg, CA 95448
(707) 473-2900, www.garyfarrellwines.com

Gary Farrell launched his eponymous winery in 1982, then sold it in 2004, remaining as winemaker until 2006. In 2011 the winery was sold to Sonoma-based Vincraft Group. Current winemaker Theresa Heredia joined the team after stints at Saintsbury, Joseph Phelps, and Freestone, where she perfected her skill with Chardonnay and Pinot Noir. The bright, textured Gary Farrell Russian River Valley Russian River Selection Chardonnay tastes of pineapple, Fuji apple, honeysuckle, and vanilla pudding with cinnamon. The sprightly Gary Farrell Russian River Valley Russian River Selection Pinot Noir features flavors of cherry and cassis that merge with bread pudding and a sprinkle of orange zest. 26

GLORIA FERRER CAVES & VINEYARDS

23555 Arnold Drive, Sonoma, CA 95476
(707) 933-1917, www.gloriaferrer.com

Barcelona natives José and Gloria Ferrer arrived in Sonoma County in the 1980s, when Carneros had no other sparkling wine producers. Inspired by the Mediterranean climate, the Ferrers realized that this land would be ideal for planting Chardonnay and Pinot Noir. The family has a rich background in sparkling wine production: They're well-known for the Spanish sparkler Freixenet, and their Catalonian homestead, La Freixeneda, dates back to the twelfth century. Gloria Ferrer Caves & Vineyards opened its doors in 1986, and the original 160-acre Carneros ranch has expanded to 335 acres. Executive winemaker Bob Iantosca and head of production Mike Crumly also make still wines. The brightly finishing Gloria Ferrer Blanc de Noirs NV offers rich, zesty flavors of black cherry, lemon zest, and caramel, while the Gloria Ferrer Carneros Cuvée tastes of apple and pear joined by citrus. 27

GUNDLACH BUNDSCHU WINERY

2000 Denmark Street, Sonoma, CA 95476
(707) 938-5277, www.gunbun.com

In 1858, German immigrant Jacob Gundlach purchased 400 acres in Sonoma and named it Rhinefarm in honor of his homeland. Three years later he brought in partners and built a winery. Charles Bundschu joined the business in 1868, and today Gundlach Bundschu is considered the oldest family-owned winery in the state. The original property was divided over the years, but in 1997 the Bundschu family bought a portion of the old Dressel parcel and restored Rhinefarm to a single contiguous estate vineyard. The Gundlach Bundschu Estate Vineyard Sonoma Coast Gewürztraminer has refreshing fruit flavors, crisp acidity, and a touch of austere minerality. The silky, fruit-forward Gundlach Bundschu Estate Vineyard Sonoma Valley Cabernet Franc gives aromas of espresso, blueberry pie, and tobacco leaf.

GUSTAFSON FAMILY VINEYARDS

9100 Stewarts Point Skaggs Springs Road, Geyserville, CA 95441
(707) 433-2371, www.gfvineyard.com

With 20 acres of Zinfandel, Petite Sirah, Syrah, Cabernet Franc, Cabernet Sauvignon, Riesling, and Sauvignon Blanc situated among 250 acres of forest and meadow above Lake Sonoma, Dan Gustafson and his family appear to be sitting on top of the world. Dan, a landscape architect from Minnesota; his wife, Phyllis; and their children work within the natural beauty of this former sheep ranch to create winery grounds that are a favorite spot for locals and visitors alike. Dan got into the world of wine in 2002 and then expanded the property to its current size in 2006. The delicate and complex Gustafson Estate Sauvignon Blanc has citrus and floral flavors joined by a touch of toasted vanilla bean, and the Gustafson Estate Petite Sirah tastes of black cherry, blackberry, and baking spice. 28

HALLECK VINEYARD

3785 Burnside Road, Sebastopol CA 95472
(707) 829-8170, www.halleckvineyard.com

Ross Halleck moved to Sonoma County in 1991 to plant a Pinot Noir vineyard in the Sonoma Coast region. He and wife, Jennifer, planted in 1993, and their first harvest came in 1999. In 2002 they entered their 2001 vintage in the Pinot Noir Summit competition and walked away with the top spot in the United States, setting the stage for successive vintages of highly rated Pinot Noir. Although Ross and Jennifer are no longer married to each other, they continue as business partners, alongside winemaker Rick Davis. The smooth and long-finishing Halleck Three Sons Cuvée Russian River Valley Pinot Noir has flavors of cherry and blackberry heightened by notes of baking spices and freshly ground pepper. The sweet and slightly tart Halleck Hallberg Vineyard Russian River Valley Pinot Noir features underlying flavors of cherry and star anise. 29

HANNA

9280 Highway 128, Healdsburg, CA 95448
(707) 431-4310, www.hannawinery.com

Elias Hanna, a San Francisco cardiac surgeon, bought 12 acres of farmland in the Russian River Valley in the 1970s and began making homemade Chardonnay and Cabernet Sauvignon. In the mid-1980s he hired a winemaker and bought more property. Today his daughter Christine runs a winery that includes 250 acres of vineyards planted on 600 acres. Jeff Hinchliffe has directed winemaking for more than 15 years, and Hanna now has two tasting rooms, one in Alexander Valley and one in Russian River. The smooth Hanna Alexander Valley Cabernet Sauvignon features flavors of black cherry, raspberry, mocha, and vanilla bean. The velvety Hanna Bismark Mountain Vineyard Zinfandel tastes of mixed-berry pie, butterscotch, and a pinch of spice. 30

HARTFORD FAMILY WINERY

8075 Martinelli Road, Forestville, CA 95436
(800) 588-0234, www.hartfordwines.com

Don Hartford and Jennifer Jackson-Hartford released their first vintage in 1996, and current winemaker Jeff Stewart works with Chardonnay, Pinot Noir, and old-vine Zinfandel from some of the finest vineyard sites in Russian River Valley, the Green Valley subappellation, and the Sonoma Coast. The bright Hartford Four Hearts Vineyard Russian River Valley Chardonnay offers an elegant expression of fruit and mineral flavors, and in the luscious Hartford Highwire Vineyard Zinfandel rich berry fruit mingles with violet and anise. 31

HIDDEN RIDGE

110 Camino Oruga, Napa, CA 94558
(707) 481-7021, www.hiddenridgevineyard.com

Couple Casidy Ward and Lynn Hofacket originally bought the Hidden Ridge Vineyard to build and flip a home but ultimately decided that the steep slopes (up to 55 degrees) and elevation (700 to 900 feet) were better suited to grapes than to people. The 60 acres of vines lie on the Sonoma side of Spring Mountain, in the Mayacamas range. They first sold their grapes to other winemakers but made their first small-scale vintage of Cabernet Sauvignon in 2001, eventually growing to today's 3,600 cases per year, crafted by winemakers Tim Milos and Marco DiGiulio. The luscious Hidden Ridge 55% Slope Cabernet Sauvignon offers a mix of fresh berries and fruit compote joined by mocha and Chinese five spice. 32

HIRSCH VINEYARDS

45075 Bohan Dillon Road, Cazadero, CA 95421
(707) 847-3600, www.hirschvineyards.com

Self-described "owner and chief bug" David Hirsch bought his first vineyard plot on the Sonoma Coast in 1978 and planted it with Riesling and Pinot Noir in 1980. He planted 44 more acres between 1990 and 1996 and an additional 25 in the early twenty-first century. Vineyard manager Everardo Robledo has worked with Hirsch for many years and expertly cultivated grapes in this rugged landscape shaped by the San Andreas Fault. Winemaker Ross Cobb's first vintage here was 2010, and the entire team fulfills Hirsch's vision of creating wines that speak to the *terroir* of the extreme Sonoma Coast. In the Hirsch Vineyards San Andreas Fault Sonoma Coast Pinot Noir, rich red fruit mingles with floral, earthy notes. 33

HOOK & LADDER WINERY

2134 Olivet Road, Santa Rosa, CA 95401
(707) 526-2255, www.hookandladderwinery.com

San Francisco firefighter Cecil De Loach and his wife, Christine, bought 24 acres of Russian River Valley old-vine Zinfandel in 1970 and sold grapes to other wineries before founding the successful DeLoach Vineyards. After selling DeLoach in 2003, they started Hook & Ladder, a smaller-scale family-run winery that focuses on estate-grown Russian River Valley fruit. Sons Jason, Michael, and Joshua De Loach are respectively winemaker, president, and head of sales. Their vineyards spread over 375 acres in the Russian River Valley. The crisp Hook & Ladder Russian River Valley Chardonnay has flavors of crisp apple and lemon zest with a smattering of buttered toast, and the lusty-finishing Hook & Ladder Russian River Valley Zinfandel tastes of raspberry, blackberry, a splash of tart cherry, and a ribbon of caramel.

HOP KILN WINERY

6050 Westside Road, Healdsburg, CA 95448
(707) 433-6491, www.hkgwines.com

Named for the historic Walters Ranch Kiln, used for drying hops, Hop Kiln offered its first release in 1976. In 2006, the winery produced the first vintage of its premium brand, HKG. The original kiln building is now the estate's tasting room, which reminds visitors of the California North Coast's importance as a hop-growing region before grapes changed the agricultural landscape. Chuck Mansfield, son of an El Dorado grape grower, became head winemaker in 2007, and vineyard manager David Smith, who came aboard in 2008, is a fifth-generation California farmer. The brightly finishing HKG Russian River Valley Chardonnay has flavors of tropical fruits, apricot, and chopped green herbs, while the HKG Russian River Valley Pinot Noir tastes of black and tart cherry joined by chocolate and dried Mediterranean herbs.

IMAGERY ESTATE WINERY

14335 Highway 12, Glen Ellen, CA 95442
(707) 935-4515, www.imagerywinery.com

After working with his family at their Sonoma winery, Joe Benziger wanted to create his own label, showcasing small-production, single-vineyard wines. While planning, Joe met Bob Nugent, a local artist who designed Joe's first label. Twenty years later, Joe is still handcrafting wines, and Bob curates the Imagery art collection and brings on artists to create the winery's original labels. Imagery's vineyards are Demeter-certified biodynamic, and the Wine Group purchased the company in June 2015. The Imagery Estate Winery Sonoma County Barbera has a palate-pleasing mix of black cherry, blackberry, blueberry, and chocolate-covered espresso beans, while the rich Imagery Estate Winery Sonoma County Tusca Brava features fruit and berry flavors joined by spice and vanilla notes. 34

IRON HORSE VINEYARDS

9786 Ross Station Road, Sebastopol, CA 95472
(707) 887-1507, www.ironhorsevineyards.com

Barry and Audrey Sterling happened upon 300 acres of rolling hills while driving along Ross Station Road in 1976 and bought this beautiful property two weeks later. They took the name from a train that stopped at Ross Station in the early part of the twentieth century, and on the grounds they discovered a weathervane, which became their logo, while building the winery. Forrest Tancer planted the 100 original acres of vines and became the Sterlings' partner in the winery before retiring in 2005. The Sterlings' daughter Joy is now CEO, and her brother Laurence is director of operations. The earthy Iron Horse Thomas Road Pinot Noir tastes intricately of cherry jam, black plum, and vanilla custard, and the opulent Iron Horse Classic Vintage Brut presents flavors of clementine, lemongrass, and almond tart. 35

J. RICKARDS WINERY

24505 Chianti Road, Cloverdale, CA 95425
(707) 758-3441, www.jrwinery.com

Jim Rickards bought a 60-acre ranch in Alexander Valley in 1976, revitalized an old Zinfandel vineyard planted by the Brignole family in 1908, and then branched out into Cabernet Sauvignon. Despite hearing that his land was suitable only as a rock quarry, Jim became a successful grape farmer, and in 2005 he and his wife, Eliza, founded J. Rickards Winery, hiring Blaine Brazil as assistant winemaker in 2011 and specializing in small-lot wines that highlight the varied soils and microclimates of their 45 vineyard acres. With flavors of dark fruits and dark chocolate and a long, rewarding finish, J. Rickards Winery Alexander Valley Five Sisters Blend Cabernet Sauvignon is a strong offering, as is the mouth-pleasing J. Rickards Winery Brignole Vineyard Alexander Valley Old Vine Zinfandel, which tastes of raspberry, black plum, chocolate-covered coffee bean, and clove.

J VINEYARDS & WINERY

11447 Old Redwood Highway, Healdsburg, CA 95448
(888) 594-6326, www.jwine.com

Judy Jordan's father, Tom Jordan, introduced her to the wine business, helping to start her career, and inspiring her sense of entrepreneurship. Judy set out on her own in 1986, leaving the family business behind, and purchased the old Piper Sonoma property, which she christened J Vineyards & Winery. Judy's belief in stewardship of the land has led to sustainable practices in the vineyard and winery. Winemaking falls under the direction of Melissa Stackhouse, and John Erbe directs the vineyards. Gallo acquired the company in March 2015. The crisp J Vineyards Cuvée 20 Russian River Valley Brut NV offers revealing flavors of crisp green apples and pears, orange zest, and a hint of brioche. The J Vineyards Estate Grown Russian River Valley Pinot Noir tastes of cherry cola, smoke, and Mediterranean herbs with a soft but satisfying finish. 36

JACUZZI FAMILY VINEYARDS

24724 Arnold Drive, Sonoma, CA 95476
(707) 931-7575, www.jacuzziwines.com

Fred Cline is a grandson of Valeriano Jacuzzi, whose family founded the water pump, spa, and hot tub business. After starting Cline Cellars in 1982 and then moving it to the Carneros region of Sonoma in 1992, Fred and his wife, Nancy, established Jacuzzi Family Vineyards across the road. Their first Jacuzzi Family Vineyards wine was produced in 1994, and their 18,000-square-foot winery opened in 2007. Charlie Tsegeletos joined as winemaker in 2002. Vineyards in Sonoma-Carneros and the Sonoma Coast are naturally and sustainably farmed. Honoring the family's heritage, Italian grape varieties predominate, including Arneis, Tocai Friulano, Aglianico, Primitivo, and Sangiovese, though Chardonnay, Cabernet Sauvignon, and Merlot are vinified as well. The Jacuzzi Family Vineyards Sonoma Coast Chardonnay has flavors of fresh apple, Seckel pear, and lemon blossom, and the balanced Jacuzzi Family Vineyards Sonoma Coast Sangiovese, tastes of cherry and blackberry, bolstered by a hint of black pepper.

JOHN TYLER WINES

4353 Westside Road, Healdsburg, CA 95448
(707) 473-0115, www.johntylerwines.com

John Tyler Wines is John Bacigalupi and his nephew-by-marriage, Tyler Heck. John's parents-in-law and Tyler's grandparents, Paul and Anna Marie Heck, co-owned Korbel Champagne Cellars. John's family planted one of the Russian River's most well-known vineyards. Bacigalupi Chardonnay was included in Mike Grgich's 1973 Chateau Montelena, the wine that turned the world on its head in the 1976 Judgment of Paris. Today John runs the vineyards, Tyler makes the wine, and John's twin daughters, Katey and Nicole, head the family's marketing efforts. The John Tyler Bacigalupi Vineyard Russian River Valley Zinfandel features flavors of blackberry and black cherry, while the balanced John Tyler Bacigalupi Vineyard Russian River Valley Pinot Noir tastes of dark cherry mingling with oregano, sage, and a pinch of citrus zest.

JORDAN VINEYARD & WINERY

1474 Alexander Valley Road, Healdsburg, CA 95448
(800) 654-1213, www.jordanwinery.com

Tom and Sally Jordan moved to California from Denver and started Jordan Vineyard & Winery in the 1970s. They had flirted with the idea of buying a winery while traveling through France, but their first glass of Napa Cabernet made them realize that they didn't have to cross the ocean to fulfill their dream. Their original purchase was 250 acres in Alexander Valley, and two years later they began construction on a winery, buying 1,300 more acres. In 1976, winemaker Rob Davis, who still holds the winemaking reins, came aboard under the direction of consulting winemaker André Tchelistcheff. The Jordans' son John, born the same day that his parents signed the deed on their first piece of land in Alexander Valley, became CEO in 2005. Only two wines are made here: Chardonnay and Cabernet Sauvignon. The bright and creamy Jordan Russian River Valley Chardonnay offers flavors of Granny Smith apple and white peach with vanilla spice notes. The Jordan Winery Alexander Valley Cabernet Sauvignon features fragrances of cherry, black plum, violet, and spice. 37

JOSEPH SWAN VINEYARDS

2916 Laguna Road, Forestville, CA 95436
(707) 573-3747, www.swanwinery.com

Joe Swan, the son of teetotaler parents from North Dakota, bought a small farm near Forestville in 1967 that included 13 acres of Zinfandel vines. Taking advice from friend and mentor André Tchelistcheff, Swan planted Chardonnay and Pinot Noir. He made his first few vintages in the cellar of the century-old farmhouse that came with the property and built a simple winery in 1974. Current owner and winemaker Rod Berglund became a winemaker in 1979 and married Joe's daughter Lynn in 1986. His first vintage at Swan was 1987, shortly before Joe's untimely passing. The Joseph Swan Vineyards Saralee's Vineyard Russian River Valley Gewürztraminer tastes of ripe summer peach and citrus blossoms mixed with baking spices, while the Joseph Swan Vineyards Trenton Estate Vineyard Russian River Valley Pinot Noir features flavors of black cherry, raspberry, mocha, and orange zest. 38

KAMEN ESTATE WINES

111B East Napa Street, Sonoma, CA 95476
(707) 938-7292, www.kamenwines.com

Robert Mark Kamen sold his first screenplay in 1980, and while celebrating with a hike through the rugged Sonoma Coast, he happened upon a tract of land with awe-inspiring views of San Francisco Bay. Within a week he acquired the 280-acre property, planning to grow Cabernet Sauvignon. He continued a successful screenwriting career while Phil Coturri, an organic viticulture pioneer, oversaw the vineyards. All the grapes were sold to other wineries until 1996, when a fire destroyed half the vines as well as Kamen's home. After replanting Cabernet Sauvignon and adding Syrah and Sauvignon Blanc, Kamen began making estate-grown wine; the first vintage was 1999, and vinification comes under the direction of winemaker Mark Herold. The Kamen Sonoma Valley Cabernet Sauvignon reveals a layered palate of sweet and tart cherry, blueberry, blackberry, toasted almond, baking spices, and lavender. 39

KANZLER VINEYARDS

P.O. Box 1977, Sebastopol, CA 95473
(707) 824-1726, www.kanzler.com

Steve and Lynda Kanzler purchased their vineyard land in 1993; Steve runs the vineyard and winery, and Lynda is CFO. Daughter Melissa Kanzler Grant heads up marketing, while her husband, James Grant, takes care of legal matters. Winemaking falls to Steve and Lynda's son, Alex. The lush Kanzler Vineyards Sonoma Coast Reserve Pinot Noir begins with flavors of cherry and raspberry, opens to cassis and blueberry, and finishes with espresso and vanilla.

KELLER ESTATE WINERY

5875 Lakeville Highway, Petaluma, CA 94954
(707) 765-2117, www.kellerestate.com

While driving the back roads of Sonoma, Arturo and Deborah Keller fell in love with a 650-acre ranch in the Petaluma Gap. They planted their first Chardonnay vineyard in 1989, maintaining a sense of balance and harmony with the natural ecosystem, adding Pinot Noir within a decade. In 2000 they had a gravity-fed winery constructed on the site, where winemaker Alberto Rodriguez works alongside Ana Keller. The Keller Estate La Cruz Vineyard Pinot Gris tastes of peach, pineapple, apricot, and star anise. The Keller Estate La Cruz Vineyard Pinot Noir offers cherry and red raspberry flavors that merge with milk chocolate, orange zest, and soft spice. 40

KENDALL-JACKSON WINE ESTATES

5007 Fulton Road, Fulton, CA 95439
(707) 571-8100, www.kj.com

Jess Jackson was a police officer and attorney before buying a Lakeport, California, fruit and nut orchard in 1974, which he converted to a vineyard. In 1982 he produced the first vintage of Kendall-Jackson Vintner's Reserve Chardonnay, which has

In her own words

BARBARA BANKE

Barbara Banke is the chairwoman and proprietor of Jackson Family Wines and one of the most successful female winery owners in the world. She and her late husband, Jess Jackson, cofounded of the children's charity Sonoma Paradiso Foundation.

I was a passionate consumer of wine and enjoyed wine tasting in Napa and Sonoma. Then I met my husband, Jess Jackson, who had a vineyard and a fledgling winery. I have worked in Tuscany and Saint-Émilion, and that has led to a fascination with Cabernet Franc, both alone and in blends. In Sonoma, Santa Barbara, Monterey, and the Anderson Valley of Mendocino County, Pinot Noirs continue to impress. New clones permit both refined and profound wines. In the Mayacamas Mountains of Sonoma County, mountain vineyards are producing some of the world's best wines in general.

Showcase the best that a vineyard has to offer with balance, complexity, energy, and refinement. If you make something spectacular, you can find a market for it.

become one of the most popular wines in the United States. More than 30 years later Kendall-Jackson is one of the best-known US wineries, with 15,000 acres of California vineyards; Jackson Family Wines owns more than thirty wine brands in total. Jess Jackson died in 2011, but his legacy continues via his wife, Barbara Banke, and five children. The creamy, zesty Kendall-Jackson Grand Reserve Chardonnay combines ripe peach and citrus blossoms flavors with soft custard notes. The Kendall-Jackson Grand Reserve Sonoma County Merlot tastes of black cherry and mocha with a light floral lift. An excellent example of winemaking at Kendall-Jackson is the Kendall-Jackson Stature, which gives rich flavors of fruits of the wood, cherry conserves, hillside herbs, and luscious crème brûlée. 41

KENWOOD VINEYARDS

9592 Sonoma Highway, Kenwood, CA 95452
(707) 833-5891, www.kenwoodvineyards.com

The old Pagani Brothers winery, founded in 1906, came back to life when winemaker Mike Lee, family, and investors bought and refurbished it in 1970. Winemaking still takes place in the original but extensively renovated buildings. Owned by Gary Heck, president of F. Korbel & Brothers, Kenwood produces 500,000 cases per year. The Kenwood Jack London Vineyard Sonoma Mountain Cabernet Sauvignon offers flavors of dark fruit and soothing herbs, while the smooth, brightly finishing Kenwood Vineyards Reserve Russian River Valley Chardonnay tastes of citrus fruit and white peach with notes of vanilla bean and buttered toast. 42

KETCHAM ESTATE

1083 Vine Street, Suite 218, Healdsburg CA 95448
(707) 395-0700, www.ketchamestate.com

After taking early retirement from his computer company and setting up shop importing vintage Italian cars, Mark Ketcham fulfilled a lifelong dream in 2000 by buying a 17-acre Pinot Noir and Chardonnay vineyard in the Russian River Valley. Mark and his wife, Allison, built their home in the middle of the vines, some of which are more than 25 years old. Chardonnay was replanted to Pinot Noir, and Roberto Ordaz oversees the vineyards. The Ketcham Estate Ketcham Vineyard Pinot Noir features flavors of black cherry, Dr. Pepper, and Mediterranean herbs. 43

KISTLER VINEYARDS

4707 Vine Hill Road, Sebastopol, CA 95472
(707) 823-5603, www.kistlervineyards.com

When the Kistler family established their winery in 1978, annual production started at 3,500 cases. Today, under winemaker and vineyard manager Steve Kistler, lab technician and business manager Mark Bixler, and assistant winemaker Jason Kesner, the winery produces 25,000 cases of highly regarded Chardonnay and Pinot Noir annually. The Kistler Vineyard Chardonnay has delightful fruit flavors and light florality, and the Kistler Vineyard Pinot Noir features remarkably balanced soft tannins and a light touch of salinity. 44

KOKOMO WINERY

4791 Dry Creek Road, Healdsburg, CA 95448
(707) 433-0200, www.kokomowines.com

Erik Miller "traded in the soybeans and cornfields" of his hometown, Kokomo, Indiana, for the rugged beauty of Sonoma. He made his first Kokomo vintage in 2004, a Dry Creek Valley Cabernet Sauvignon, and a year later his best friend and college roommate, Josh Bartels, joined him. In 2008 Erik and Josh brought in fourth-generation farmer Randy Peters as their partner. The crisp and creamy Kokomo Peters Vineyard Russian River Valley Chardonnay gives flavors of apple, buttered brioche, and toffee. The Kokomo Dry Creek Valley Zinfandel features a palate dominated by rich fruit with haunting undertones of rosemary, sage, and white pepper.

KOSTA BROWNE

P.O. Box 1555, Sebastopol, CA 95473
(707) 823-7430, www.kostabrowne.com

It's hard to believe that two waiters who pooled their tip money with the dream of making wine one day became founding partners of a highly acclaimed winery, but that's exactly what Dan Kosta and Michael Browne did. The dream began in 1997, and after eight months the pair had enough to buy half a ton of grapes and winemaking equipment. In 2001 they joined forces with Chris Costello and his family, and the three of them remain the guiding hands behind Kosta Browne, acquired by the Vincraft Group in 2009. Michael Browne is executive winemaker, assisted by a team that includes Ryan O'Donnell, Nico Cueva, and Jeremiah Timm. The layered, smoothly finishing Kosta Browne Russian River Valley Pinot Noir 2011 tastes of black cherry and blackberry layered with mocha and cranberry. The delightfully balanced Kosta Browne Sonoma Coast Pinot Noir opens with raspberry and blueberry, followed by a burst of mixed fruit and a touch of savory herbs.

KUNDE FAMILY ESTATE

9825 Sonoma Highway, Kenwood, CA 95452
(707) 833-5501, www.kunde.com

Louis Kunde left Germany for California and in 1904 bought the Wildwood Ranch, the start of what's now the 1,850-acre Kunde Estate in Sonoma Valley. Fourth- and fifth-generation family members continue to farm the land, and winemaker Zach Long's goal is for *terroir* to shine through in each bottle. The full-bodied Kunde Family Estate Sonoma Valley Chardonnay features soft touches of gingerbread spice amid fruit flavors, and the smooth-finishing Kunde Family Estate Sonoma Valley Cabernet Sauvignon tastes of black cherry and pure cocoa. 45

KUTCH WINES

21660 8th Street East, Building A, Suite C, Sonoma, CA 95476
(917) 270-8180, www.kutchwines.com

Heeding Horace Greeley's call to "go west, young man," Jamie Kutch traded in his Wall Street trading desk in 2005 and headed to Sonoma County. Filled with passion and a dream, Kutch worked a harvest at Kosta Browne and began visiting prime vineyard sites on the Sonoma Coast and Anderson Valley to procure the best grapes for his handcrafted, foot-treaded Pinot Noir. Kutch and his wife, Kristen Green, jokingly refer to their tanks, barrels, and fermenters as "our condo," but their quality efforts have met with accolades. The lushly textured Kutch McDougall Ranch Sonoma Coast Pinot Noir tastes of blackberry layered with pine needles and light floral notes. The food-friendly Kutch Falstaff Sonoma Coast Pinot Noir features opulent flavors of blackberry, grapefruit pith, and a touch of forest floor. 46

LA CREMA

235 Healdsburg Avenue, Healdsburg, CA 95448
(800) 314-1762, www.lacrema.com

La Crema was founded in 1979 and became part of Jackson Family Wine Estates in 1993. Elizabeth Grant-Douglas started here in 2001 and became winemaker in 2010. Eric Johannsen and Craig McAllister assist her on the sustainably farmed vineyards. The bright La Crema Monterey Chardonnay tastes of juicy peach pie joined by vanilla bean, and the velvety La Crema Russian River Valley Pinot Noir gives flavors of raspberry, black cherry, chocolate-covered espresso bean, and aniseed. 47

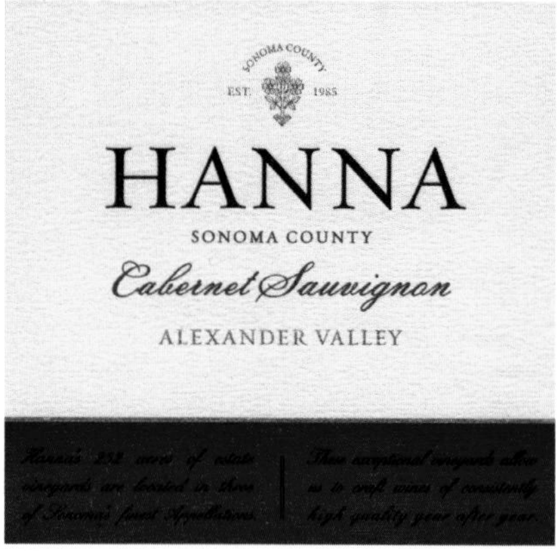

30

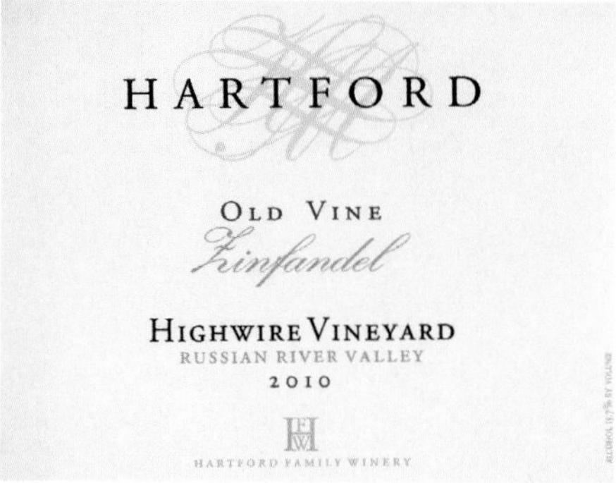

31

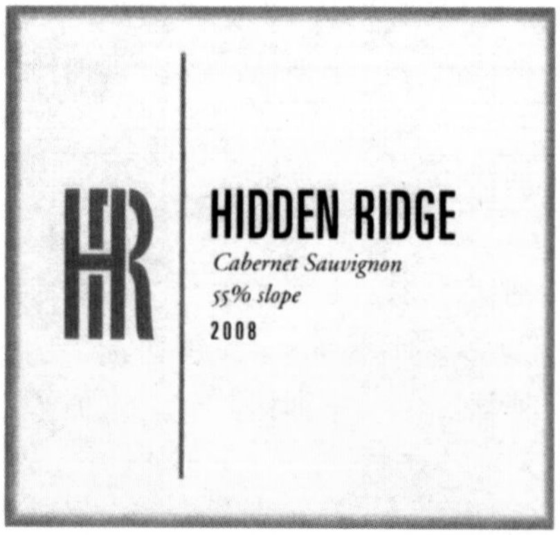

32

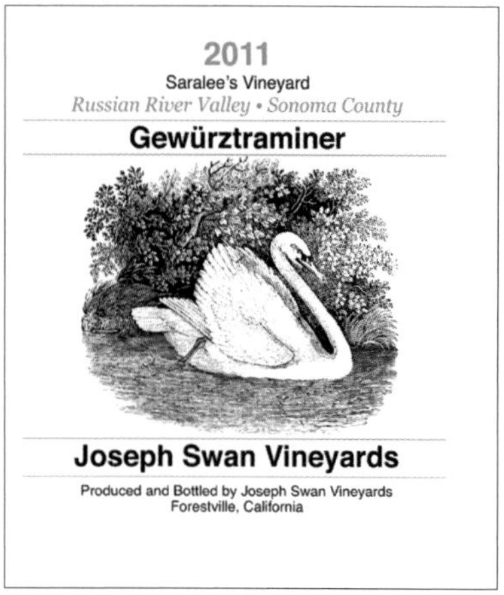

2011
Saralee's Vineyard
Russian River Valley • Sonoma County
Gewürztraminer
Joseph Swan Vineyards
Produced and Bottled by Joseph Swan Vineyards
Forestville, California

38

40

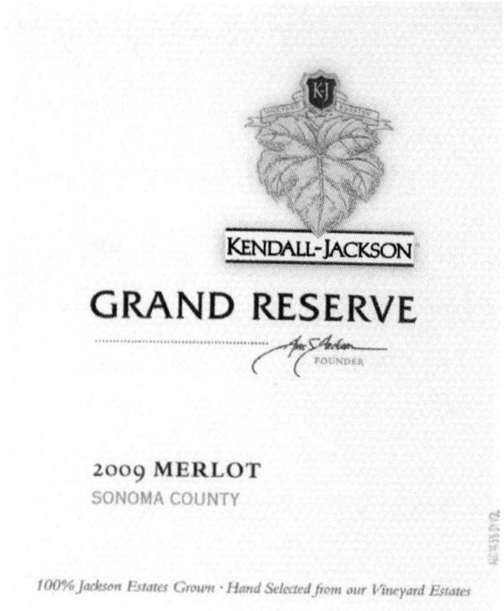

KENDALL-JACKSON
GRAND RESERVE
FOUNDER
2009 MERLOT
SONOMA COUNTY
100% Jackson Estates Grown · Hand Selected from our Vineyard Estates

41

47

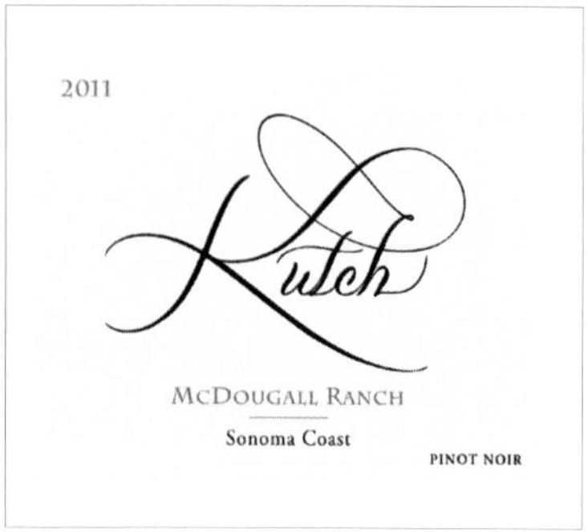

46

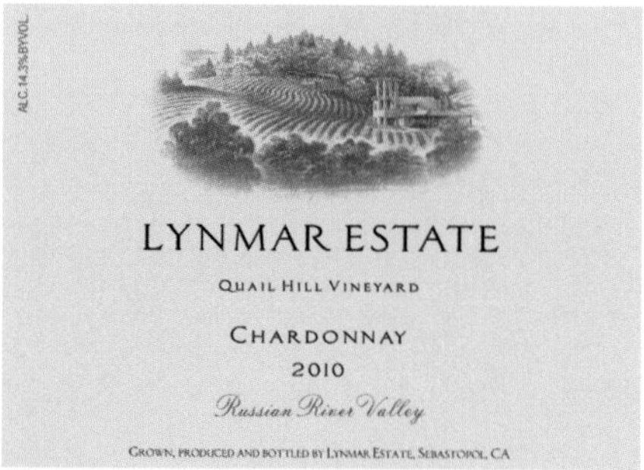

LYNMAR ESTATE
QUAIL HILL VINEYARD
CHARDONNAY
2010
Russian River Valley
GROWN, PRODUCED AND BOTTLED BY LYNMAR ESTATE, SEBASTOPOL, CA

52

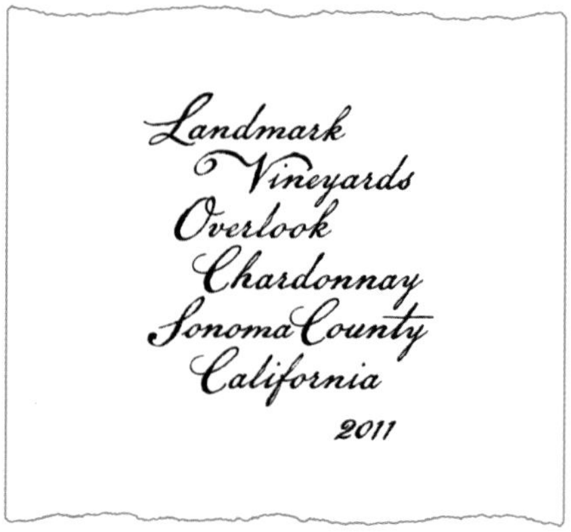

48

34

35

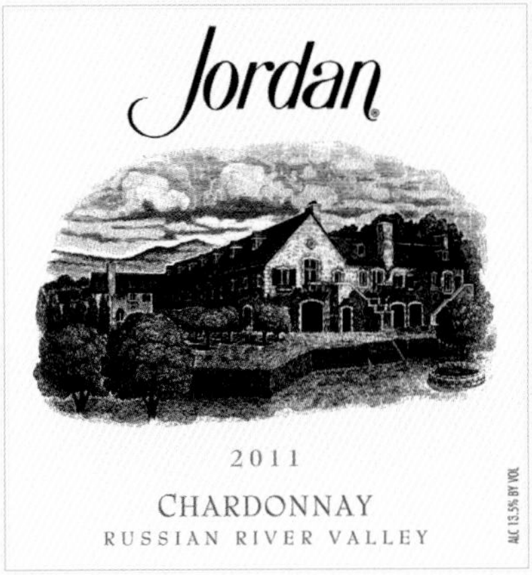

37

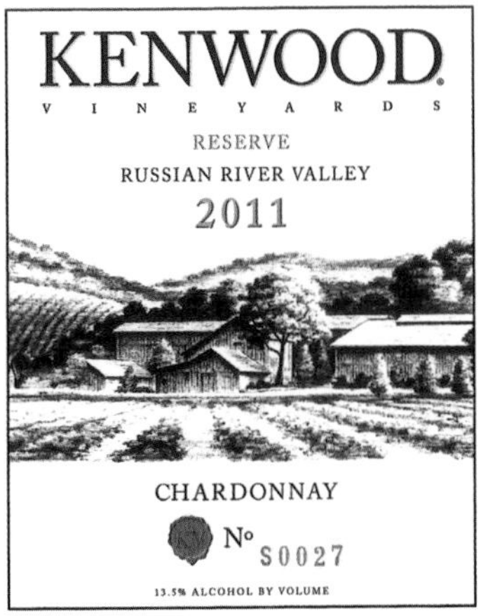

42

43

Kistler
Kistler Vineyard
Sonoma Valley
No.
2009
21960 bottles of this vintage were produced

44

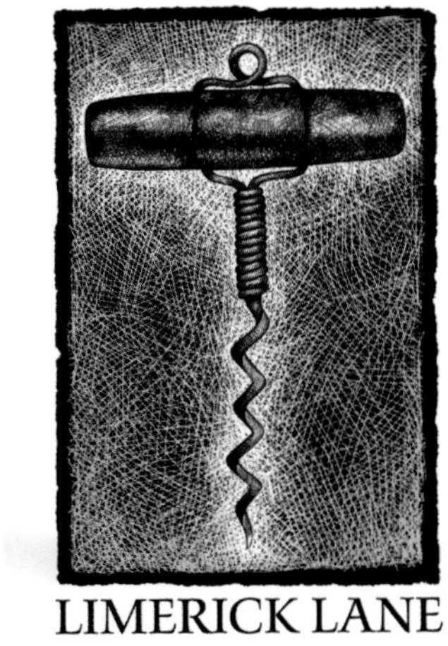

49

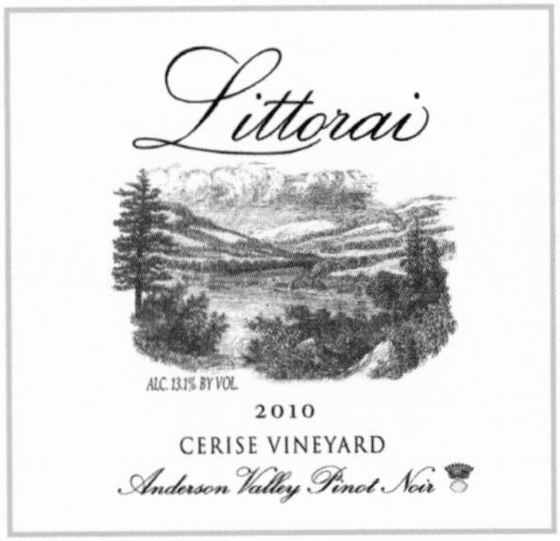

50

51

LANCASTER ESTATE

15001 Chalk Hill Road, Healdsburg, CA 95448
(707) 433-8178, www.lancaster-estate.com

Lancaster Estate was founded in 1995 with a commitment to producing high-quality wines, mainly Cabernet Sauvignon, from grapes grown on the estate's 52 acres in Alexander Valley. Consulting winemaker David Ramey works with winemakers David Drake, who directs the vineyards, and Jesse Katz, who joined Lancaster in 2010. Foley Family Wines has owned the property since 2012. The luscious Lancaster Estate Alexander Valley Cabernet Sauvignon offers flavors of black plum, blackberry, crème brûlée, and dark chocolate, while the bold and invigorating Luscious Estate Alexander Valley Samantha's Sauvignon Blanc proffers pink grapefruit, lychee, and lemongrass flavors.

LANDMARK VINEYARDS

101 Adobe Canyon Road, Kenwood, CA 95452
(707) 833-0053, www.landmarkwine.com

Founded in Windsor in 1974, Landmark moved to the base of Sugarloaf Mountain in Sonoma Valley in 1989. Consulting winemaker Helen Turley came aboard in 1993, later joined by Eric Stern, who retired in 2010. Current winemaker Greg Stach worked alongside Stern for seven years, and his state-of-the-art winery lies amid beautifully landscaped grounds. The rich, crisp Landmark Overlook Sonoma County Chardonnay has rich citrus and tropical fruit flavors that combine with soft spice and crisp minerality. The layered Landmark Kanzler Vineyard Sonoma Coast Pinot Noir gives rich cherry flavors layered with mocha and earth. 48

LEDSON WINERY & VINEYARDS

7335 Highway 12, Kenwood, CA 95409
(707) 537-3810, www.ledson.com

The entrepreneuring son of dairy farmers and cattle ranchers, Steve Ledson was a successful contractor and property developer who in 1989 began construction on a client's home in the middle of a 17-acre Merlot vineyard. When the buyer pulled out, Steve took over the property. Known as The Castle, Ledson's 16,000-square-foot winery was planned as the family home, but Steve decided it was better suited as a winery. Besides the original vineyard, Ledson has 21 acres in Sonoma and another 5,500 in Mendocino County. The Ledson Russian River Valley Sauvignon Blanc features flavors of lemon, lime, and ripe pear enhanced by bracing acidity, and in the Ledson Bertetta Vineyard Russian River Valley "Old Vine" Zinfandel pepper and vanilla custard support full-on berry flavors.

LIMERICK LANE CELLARS

1023 Limerick Lane, Healdsburg CA 95448
(707) 433-9211, www.limericklanewines.com

Limerick Lane, a 30-acre estate south of Healdsburg, was first planted to grapes by the Del Fava family in 1910 and was sold to Mike and Tom Collins in the 1970s. The Collins brothers quickly gained a reputation as a source of prime Zinfandel and Rhône varieties, producing their first estate wines under the Limerick Lane label in 1986. Current owner Jake Bilbro grew up at his family winery, Marietta Cellars. He bought the run-down farm across the road from Limerick Lane in 2007, and he and his wife spent the next two years restoring it. In 2009 Mike Collins offered them the opportunity to buy Limerick Lane Cellars and the Collins Vineyard, and Bilbro and his family now live in the original Del Fava homestead. Bilbro says you can "taste a bit of the limerick" in his wines, which inspired these:

Limerick Lane Block 1910 Russian River Valley Zinfandel

A fresh nose of chocolate and cherry,
With flavors of mocha and berry,
Elegant and restrained,
True perfection attained.
Do we like it much? Yes, we say—very!

Limerick Lane Block 1970 Russian River Valley Zinfandel

A tad lighter than Block 1910,
You can sip it again and again.
Savor fruits of the wood
Amid tannins so good.
It could well replace Proust's madeleine. 49

LITTORAI

788 Gold Ridge Road, Sebastopol, CA 95472
(707) 823-9586, www.littorai.com

The philosophy of *terroir* guides wine production at Littorai, emphasis falling on wine growing as well as winemaking, with additional focus on site selection and vineyard management to create wines with equilibrium and complexity. Ted and Heidi Lemon established Littorai in 1993 and built their winery in 2008. Ted previously made wine at some of the finest estates in Burgundy, and he and Heidi employ sustainable practices in their owned and leased vineyards in the Anderson Valley and Sonoma Coast. The luxurious dark fruit flavors of the Littorai Cerise Vineyard Anderson Valley Pinot Noir intertwine with spice and herb notes into the mineral-driven finish. 50

LONGBOARD VINEYARDS

5 Fitch Street, Healdsburg, CA 95448
(707) 433-3473, www.longboardvineyards.com

Longboard's owner and winemaker, Oded Shakked, was born in Israel, raised around the world, and moved to California to follow his two passions: surfing and wine, both of which require balance, perseverance, and respect for nature. Longboard's lighthearted tasting room is more surf hangout than stuffy wine bar, so even spongers will feel at home. The Longboard Russian River Valley Sauvignon Blanc tastes of lemon-lime sorbet, pear, and passion fruit, and the Longboard Russian River Valley Syrah showcases flavors of brambleberries, aniseed, and mocha. 51

LYNMAR ESTATE

3909 Frei Road, Sebastopol, CA 95472
(707) 829-3374, www.lynmarestate.com

Lynn Fritz bought Quail Hill Ranch in 1980 as a place to relax after traveling the globe as CEO of Fritz Companies. He and his wife, Anisya, moved here in 2008, and they dwell among 70 acres of Pinot Noir, Chardonnay, and a small block of Syrah, all surrounded by abundant gardens. Planted in 1971, their Quail Hill Vineyard harbors some of the oldest vines in the Russian River Valley. Jason Saling heads the vineyard team, and Shane Finley directs winemaking. The Lynmar Estate Quail Hill Vineyard Russian River Valley Chardonnay features mineral, toast, and butterscotch tastes, and the Lynmar Estate Quail Hill Vineyard Russian River Valley Pinot Noir offers strong fruit flavors that intertwine with espresso, Turkish delight, and birch root. 52

MACMURRAY RANCH

3387 Dry Creek Road, Healdsburg, CA 95448
(707) 431-5507, www.macmurrayranch.com

MacMurray Ranch's modern era began when actor Fred MacMurray bought the circa-1850 homestead in 1941 and started raising cattle. The Gallo family owns MacMurray Ranch, but Kate MacMurray continues her father's legacy, and Chris Munsell directs winemaking. The MacMurray Ranch Sonoma Coast Pinot Gris, an aromatic gem, tastes of melon and white peach with recurring notes of spice and citrus blossom. The MacMurray Ranch Winemakers Block Selection Russian River Valley Pinot Noir offers flavors of black cherry, fruits of the wood, and a dash of spice.

MACPHAIL FAMILY WINES

851 Magnolia Drive, Healdsburg, CA 95448
(707) 433-4780, www.macphailwine.com

The energy-efficient MacPhail Family winery, completed in 2008, uses a combination of cutting-edge technology and ecologically friendly innovation, such as solar power and a purpose-built wetland that reclaims winery wastewater. MacPhail crafts small-batch terroir-driven Pinot Noir with fruit from the Sonoma Coast and Anderson Valley appellations, using traditional techniques such as cold maceration and hand punchdowns while avoiding flourishes such as fining and filtration. Maximum production is capped at 5,000 cases by both permit and MacPhail's focus on quality over quantity. With a gratifying finish, MacPhail Pratt Vineyard Sonoma Coast Pinot Noir 2010 offers flavors of dark berries, aniseed, and clove. The MacPhail Ferrington Vineyard Anderson Valley Pinot Noir tastes of black cherry and spice accompanied by raspberry and a touch of Sichuan pepper. 53

MACROSTIE WINERY AND VINEYARDS

21481 8th Street East #25, Sonoma, CA 95476
(707) 996-4480, www.macrostiewinery.com

Steve MacRostie founded his winery in 1987 and released his inaugural Carneros Chardonnay the same year. Five years later he released his first Pinot Noir, but not until 1997 did he partner with Nancy and Tony Lilly and plant vines on his own land. Together the group developed Wildcat Mountain Vineyard and improved on this former pastureland by planting 58 acres of Chardonnay, Pinot Noir, and Syrah. In 2004 Steve shifted focus to the vineyard and to working more closely with his contract growers. Kevin Holt took over winemaking duties and continues Steve's fine legacy of production. The full-bodied MacRostie Winery and Vineyards Sonoma Coast Chardonnay has bright flavors of Anjou pear and stone fruits with a persistent, mineral finish. The pink ripe fruit flavors of the MacRostie Winery and Vineyards Carneros Pinot Noir Rosé taste like summer in a glass. 54

MARCASSIN

3358 River Road, Windsor, CA 95492
(707) 942-5633

Wine Spectator called Helen Turley "the Greatest Winemaker in America," and she has served as consulting winemaker at a Who's Who of notable California wineries. There's a rumored 14-year wait to join the mailing list at Marcassin, the private winery project she founded with her viticulturist husband, John Wetlaufer, in 1993. The wines of Marcassin (French for "young wild boar") were produced at the Martinelli Winery before completion of the Marcassin Winery in 2010. From the 2010 vintage forward, Marcassin has produced only two wines, Chardonnay and Pinot Noir, from its 20-acre Sonoma Coast vineyard. Wines age for five years before release, and prices on the secondary market are often multiples of the original release price. The Marcassin Marcassin Vineyard Sonoma County Chardonnay features rich flavors of tangerine, white peach, and honeysuckle. If you can score a bottle of the 2008 vintage, you will want to drink it immediately, but wait for up to 10 years and your patience will be rewarded.

MARIMAR ESTATE

11400 Graton Road, Sebastopol, CA 95472
(707) 823-4365, www.marimarestate.com

Before starting her eponymous California estate, Marimar Torres worked closely with her family's Spanish wine brand. She settled in California in 1975 and in 1986 began planting her Russian River Valley Don Miguel vineyard, named after her father, which today consists of 30 acres each of Chardonnay and Pinot Noir. Marimar's Doña Margarita vineyard, an homage to her mother, is home to 20 acres of Pinot Noir in the Sonoma Coast AVA. Both vineyards are organically farmed, and all wines are estate grown. Completed in 1992, Marimar Estate's winery was built in a Catalan farmhouse style. The fresh, crisp Marimar Estate Don Miguel Vineyard Russian River Valley Acero Chardonnay tastes of Granny Smith apple and pear with light mineral notes. The palate of the Marimar Estate Don Miguel Vineyard Russian River Valley La Masia Pinot Noir mingles baking spice with freshly picked mushroom. 55

MARTINELLI WINERY

3360 River Road, Windsor, CA 95492
(707) 525-0570, www.martinelliwinery.com

The Martinellis descend from Italian immigrants who came to California in the late nineteenth century and began farming grapes and making wine. Giuseppe Martinelli and his bride, Luisa Vellutini Martinelli, set out from their small Tuscan village in 1887, settling in the Russian River Valley, where they planted Zinfandel and Muscat of Alexandria vines on the 60-degree slope of what is now known as the Jackass Hill Vineyard. The Martinelli Vineyard was born. Giuseppe and Luisa's son Leno farmed the vineyard from the age of twelve in 1918, finally handing over the reins to his son, Lee Sr., in the mid-1990s. In the meantime, Lee and his wife, Carolyn, had taken over family orchards in the Russian River Valley and replaced fruit trees with grapevines. They started the Martinelli Winery in the mid-1970s, converting an old triple-roofed hop barn into a winemaking facility and tasting room. In 1992, Lee and Carolyn met Helen Turley, who served as their head winemaker and then consulting winemaker from 1992 through 2010. Bryan Kvamme, who had worked with Turley since 1997, took over full winemaking duties in 2008. Today third- and fourth-generation family members work side by side growing and producing handcrafted Chardonnay, Pinot Noir, Zinfandel, Syrah, Sauvignon Blanc, and Muscat of Alexandria. The Martinelli Winery Martinelli Road Russian River Valley Chardonnay proffers flavors of lemon curd, Bosc pear, and toffee underscored by striking minerality, while the Martinelli Winery Jackass Vineyard Russian River Valley Zinfandel has raspberry and blueberry flavors that intertwine with baking spices and pepper. 56

MATANZAS CREEK WINERY

6097 Bennett Valley Road, Santa Rosa, CA 95404
(707) 528-6464, www.matanzascreek.com

Bennett Valley's Mediterranean climate comes into sharp focus when encountering Matanzas Creek's luxuriant lavender gardens. Founder Sandra McIver purchased a dairy farm in 1971, added neighboring properties as time passed, planted Merlot and lavender, and started Matanzas Creek Winery in 1997. The estate now falls under the Jackson Family Wines umbrella and specializes in Chardonnay, Sauvignon Blanc, Syrah, and Merlot. The Matanzas Creek Winery Bennett Valley Sauvignon Blanc features flavors of chopped Thai basil and lemongrass. The Matanzas Creek Winery Bennett Valley Merlot proffers luscious cassis, herbal, and spice notes on the palate. 57

MAZZOCCO SONOMA

1400 Lytton Springs Road, Healdsburg, CA 95448
(800) 501-8466, www.mazzocco.com

Ken and Diane Wilson couldn't pass up the opportunity to acquire Mazzocco's Lytton Spring's hilltop vineyards straddling Dry Creek and Alexander Valley, which gave them more room to make their wines and provided the quality fruit they needed to make their single-vineyard-designated Zinfandels. Their winemaker, Antoine Favero, was born in Champagne and raised in Peru before attending UC Davis. The Mazzocco Sonoma Seaton Dry Creek Valley Zinfandel has flavors of black fruit, espresso, mocha, and bittersweet chocolate. The Mazzocco Sonoma Serracino Reserve Dry Creek Valley Zinfandel tastes of wild brambleberry and gives way to cocoa powder.

MEDLOCK AMES

13414 Chalk Hill Road, Healdsburg, CA 95448
(707) 431-8845, www.medlockames.com

Since opening their tasting room just outside Healdsburg as a winery offshoot, owners Chris James and Ames Morison have created a vibe rarely found along wine roads. After 5 p.m., when tasting rooms close, they offer garden-to-glass cocktails in the speakeasy-style Alexander Valley Bar. Their commitment to nature is also apparent in their 56 acres of organic vineyards set among more than 300 acres of meadow and woodlands just up the road. Strong offerings include the vibrant Medlock Ames Bell Mountain Vineyard Alexander Valley Sauvignon Blanc, with its whiff of citrus, melon, and fresh green herbs, and the refreshing Medlock Ames Bell Mountain Vineyard Alexander Valley Cabernet Sauvignon, with a pleasing taste of berries and spice sprinkled with hints of mocha. 58

MERRIAM VINEYARDS

11654 Los Amigos Road, Healdsburg, CA 95448
(707) 433-4032, www.merriamvineyards.com

After specializing in Bordeaux-style red blends from their own Russian River Valley Windacre Vineyard and other local growers, Peter and Diana Merriam expanded their holdings in 2009, planting Pinot Noir and Sauvignon Blanc in their Los Amigos Vineyard. Peter is an avid outdoorsman and Diana loves all things culinary, and their combined passions show in the vineyard and the glass. Winemakers David Herzberg and Margaret Davenport work alongside Peter to create blends and single-varietal bottlings that reflect both the *terroir* and the vintner's craft. The palate of the Merriam Vineyards Russian River Valley Miktos features flavors of fresh and preserved cherry and blackberry.

MERRY EDWARDS WINERY

2959 Gravenstein Highway North, Sebastopol, CA 95472
(707) 823-7466, www.merryedwards.com

Merry Edwards was one of California's first female winemakers; her career started at Mount Eden Vineyards in 1974, and she was the first winemaker at Matanzas Creek Vineyards before becoming a consulting winemaker on multiple projects throughout California and Oregon. She and her husband and business partner, Ken Coopersmith, completed their winery in 2008, after having used other people's facilities since the founding of her eponymous brand in 1997. The winery sits among the vines of the Coopersmith Vineyard, one of five estate-owned vineyards. They use sustainable practices in the winery and vineyards, which grow Sauvignon Blanc, Chardonnay, and Pinot Noir, including a solar power system installed in 2010. The Merry Edwards Olivet Lane Russian River Valley Pinot Noir has fruit flavors joined by luscious fennel, baking spices, and Turkish delight. The Merry Edwards Russian River Valley Sauvignon Blanc features zesty acidity amid flavors of tropical fruits, Bartlett pear, and kiwi. 59

MICHEL-SCHLUMBERGER WINE ESTATES

4155 Wine Creek Road, Healdsburg, CA 95448
(707) 433-7427, www.michelschlumberger.com

The white stucco and terra-cotta visitor center at Michel-Schlumberger bears witness to the history of Spanish California, while the estate-grown Chardonnay, Cabernet Sauvignon, Cabernet Franc, and Merlot pays homage to the European roots of founding partners Jean-Jacques Michel, a native of Switzerland, and Jacques Pierre Schlumberger, whose family has been making wine in Alsace, France, for four centuries. Michel first planted his Dry Creek Valley vineyard in 1979, and he called the estate Domaine Michel. Schlumberger joined him and was winemaker from 1991 until he retired in 2011. Now Bryan Davison directs winemaking along with consulting winemaker Kerry Damskey. Annual output is about 7,000 cases. The Michel-Schlumberger Benchland Wine Estate La Nue Dry Creek Valley Chardonnay tastes of peach, honeysuckle, and green apple. The Michel-Schlumberger Benchland Wine Estate Dry Creek Valley Maison Rouge features flavors of black cherry, cassis, white pepper, and anise.

MONTEMAGGIORE

2355 West Dry Creek Road, Healdsburg, CA 95448
(707) 433-9499, www.montemaggiore.com

Vince and Lise Ciolino—members of a sprawling Italian family with ties to Montemaggiore in southern Italy—keep it simple at their winery, focusing on biodynamically farmed Syrah and olive oil. Vince tends their 10 acres of vines in Dry Creek Valley, and Lise makes Syrah, a Cabernet-Syrah blend, and a small amount of 3 Divas, their white Rhône-style blend. The cherry flavor of Montemaggiore Paolo's Vineyard Syrah coats the tongue in pleasing waves, supported by mocha and spice.

MUELLER WINERY

118 North Street, Healdsburg, CA 95492
(707) 473-8086, www.muellerwine.com

Set among their Russian River Valley vineyards, Bob and Lori Mueller's Cellar Tasting Room offers guests a laid-back, friendly atmosphere and exquisite Pinot Noir. Bob Mueller worked at Foppiano, Charles Krug, and Souverain before striking out on his own in 1991. That year Mueller Winery offered its first vintages of Chardonnay, and Pinot Noir in 1994. The Muellers built their 5,000-case-per-year Windsor winery a decade later. The Mueller Tempi Russian River Valley Pinot Noir has sensuous flavor layers of freshly picked berries saturated with spice and vanilla. If you can wait until the end of the decade to pop the cork, your patience will be rewarded.

MURPHY-GOODE WINERY

20 Matheson Street, Healdsburg, CA 95448
(800) 499-7644, www.murphygoodewinery.com

In 1985 while playing liar's dice, Tim Murphy, Dale Goode, and Dave Ready decided to start making their own wines, starting with Chardonnay and Fumé Blanc. Their labels celebrate their love of a good time: Liar's Dice Zinfandel, All In Claret, and Dealer's Choice Cabernet Sauvignon. David Ready Jr. has been working here since 1997 and took over as winemaker in 2001. Murphy-Goode now belongs to the Jackson Family portfolio. In Murphy-Goode The Fumé North Coast Sauvignon Blanc, tropical fruit flavors mingle with peach and cantaloupe and a hint of smoke. The Murphy-Goode Dealer's Choice Alexander Valley Cabernet Sauvignon presents cherry and smooth vanilla on the tongue, yielding to wild raspberry and sage. 60

MUTT LYNCH

602 Limerick Lane, Healdsburg, CA 95448
(707) 942-6180, www.muttlynchwinery.com

Owners Chris and Brenda Lynch and their rescue greyhound, Patch, offer serious wines behind their fun-loving, dog-centric labels with zany names such as Fou Fou le Blanc, Merlot Over and Play Dead, and Unleashed Chardonnay. Chris and Brenda are also serious about our four-legged friends, donating much time and money each year to animal charities. Their top-of-the-line bottlings bear the MBF designation, shorthand for "Man's Best Friend." The Mutt Lynch MBF Zinfandel has vigorous cherry and blueberry flavors that mingle with pepper and licorice, and the Mutt Lunch MBF Primitivo tastes of raspberry, black cherry, fresh ground pepper, and a dusting of spice. 61

NOVY FAMILY WINES

981 Airway Court, Santa Rosa, CA 95403
(707) 578-3882, www.novyfamilywines.com

The extended Novy family traces their roots to the former Czechoslovakia, where *Novy* means "new." In that spirit, Adam and Dianna Lee, founders of Siduri Wines, created this new label. The pair already had found success with their Siduri Pinot Noir, their first vintage garnering a 90-point rating from Robert Parker. Joining forces with Dianna's family, they started a new brand in 1998 and quickly gained accolades for this project as well. Adam and Dianna share winemaking duties, and Jackson Family Wines bought the company in January 2015. The Novy Keefer Ranch Vineyard Chardonnay tastes of pear and clementine with clean mineral undertones, while the Novy Sonoma County Syrah features fruit flavors that yield to bacon and fennel bulb.

PAPAPIETRO PERRY WINERY

4791 Dry Creek Road, Healdsburg, CA 95448
(707) 433-0422, www.papapietro-perry.com

Owned by two couples with a passion for wine, food, and fun, Papapietro Perry began when Ben Papapietro, a former newspaperman, asked friend Bruce Perry to join him during harvest at another friend's Sonoma County winery in the early 1980s. Shortly thereafter Ben and Bruce were making wine in Ben's garage each fall, a hobby that became a new career for Papapietro and Perry and their wives, Yolanda and Renae. Ben Papapietro heads winemaking, Renae handles sales and marketing, and Yolanda oversees distributor relations. The Papapietro Perry 777 Clones Russian River Valley Pinot Noir has bright cherry flavors enhanced by vanilla and spice, and the Papapietro Perry Leras Family Vineyards Russian River Valley Pinot Noir features sweet cherry augmented by tart cherry with notes of toasted bread.

PAUL HOBBS

3355 Gravenstein Highway North, Sebastopol, CA 95472
(707) 824-9879, www.paulhobbswinery.com

Before starting his own brand, Paul Hobbs made wine and consulted at some of the best-known wineries in California and South America. In addition to his eponymous Sonoma winery, which also produces the CrossBarn label, Hobbs helms Viña Cobos in Argentina and Paul Hobbs Imports, and consults as winemaker with more than twenty wineries around the globe. He founded his namesake winery in 1991 and in 1998 purchased the land in Sebastopol that later became Katherine Lindsey Estate. The first vintage at the Sebastopol winery was 2003. The powerfully elegant Paul Hobbs Ulises Valdez Vineyard Russian River Valley Pinot Noir features rich flavors of black cherry, raspberry conserves, Chinese five-spice powder, and white chocolate, and the Paul Hobbs Beckstoffer To Kalon Vineyard Oakville Napa Valley Cabernet Sauvignon has a complex taste profile of dark berries and mocha with a sensuous finish.

PEAY VINEYARDS

227 Treadway Drive, Cloverdale, CA 95425
(707) 894-8720, www.peayvineyards.com

Not wanting to take his parents' advice and become a lawyer, Nick Peay worked his first harvest in 1988 at Schramsberg, loved it, and took a full-time position at La Jota Vineyards the same year. He coaxed his brother Andy into starting their own winery, and along with Nick's wife, Vanessa, the team at Peay makes some delicious cool-weather varieties. The crisp yet full-bodied Peay Vineyards Estate Chardonnay has a pleasant minerality and salinity, and the Peay Vineyards Sonoma Coast Pinot Noir offers aromas of Indian spice, orange blossom, and black cherry in the complex bouquet. 62

PEDRONCELLI

1220 Canyon Road, Geyserville, CA 95441
(800) 836-3894, www.pedroncelli.com

The fourth generation of Pedroncellis is now old enough to begin working in the vineyards and winery bought by forefather John Pedroncelli Sr. in 1917. His son John Jr. became winemaker in 1945 and continues as head winemaker today, working with assistant winemaker Montse Reece, cellarmaster Polo Cano, and Lance Blakely, who runs the vineyard and winery operations. The Pedroncelli tasting room is said to be the oldest in Dry Creek Valley. The Pedroncelli Vintage Selection Dry Creek Valley Sonoma County Chardonnay offers a palate of Granny Smith apple, jasmine, and lemon zest, and the Pedroncelli Bushnell Vineyard Dry Creek Valley Sonoma County Zinfandel features rich flavors of blackberry, black cherry, and plum. 63

PETER MICHAEL WINERY

12400 Ida Clayton Road, Calistoga, CA 94515
(707) 942-3200, www.petermichaelwinery.com

The Michael family's "100-by-100" plan envisions 100 percent family ownership of their winery and vineyards for at least 100 years. Sir Peter and Lady Michael, known to friends as Pete and Maggie, bought more than 600 acres of land in Knights Valley in 1982. They planted red Bordeaux varieties, and when their first wineworthy crop came to fruition in 1987, they brought in Helen Turley, the first in a list of prominent winemakers, to craft their first vintage. Succeeding his brother Luc, current winemaker Nicolas Morlet has stood at the helm since 2005.

Sir Peter has passed the torch to his son Paul Michael, who, along with his wife, Emily, upholds his parents' ideals. The Peter Michael Winery Les Pavots Single Vineyard Estate Cabernet Blend has multihued flavors of cassis, black cherry, black pepper, and anise. The Peter Michael Winery La Carrière Single Vineyard Estate Chardonnay tastes pleasingly of fresh peach and lemon sorbet. 64

PORTALUPI

107 North Street, Healdsburg, CA 95448
(707) 395-0960, www.portalupiwine.com

Husband-and-wife team Jane Portalupi and Tim Borges first met as children, worked in different areas of the industry for years, and started Portalupi in 2002. You can find them behind the counter of their welcoming Healdsburg tasting room sharing their love of wine. Their Old World–style, half-gallon jug of Vaso di Marina blends Zinfandel, Cabernet Franc, and Petite Sirah in honor of Jane's grandmother. The crisp, clean Portalupi Bianco has a palate of grapefruit, guava, and freesia, and the Portalupi Dry Creek Valley Zinfandel offers flavors of raspberry, pepper, and spice.

55

71

64

74

20

26

39

12

57

In his own words

JOEL PETERSON

Called the "Godfather of World-Class California Zinfandels," Joel Peterson began his career as an immunology researcher and cofounded Ravenswood Winery in 1976. He is a founding member of Zinfandel Advocates and Producers (ZAP) and past president of the Sonoma Valley Vintners and Growers Alliance.

My parents discovered wine in 1951 and became early foodies. That of course meant that they were also heavily involved in the developing Bay Area wine culture. By the 1970s I was living in Berkeley doing some wine writing, store consulting, and tasting extensively. It was during the era of the food revolution: Chez Panisse, Pig by the Tail, Peet's Coffee, The Cheese Board were all new, exciting, and singular in their focus on food. Wine was very much intertwined with this. I met Joe Swan at a tasting at the Vintners Club and began working on a part-time basis with him late in 1972, learning the nuts and bolts of winemaking. By 1976 I felt that I could make my own wine and thus made the first 427 cases of Zinfandel for what became Ravenswood.

The understanding of wine chemistry and wine technology was virtually nonexistent when I began drinking wine. We have better barrels, more international understanding of wine style, and an overall quality improvement of wine in general. One of the exciting changes is the return to California's roots and reinvestigation of winemaking style and viticulture by a number of young California winemakers. They have focused on understanding viticulture, taking lessons from California's historic vineyards, and in the process have maintained and enhanced some of California's most historic vineyards and also have made some very exciting wines along the way.

While I have focused, primarily because of market imperatives on varietal wines, on Zinfandel, I have been experimenting with California field blends and attempting to understand the interrelationships between different grape varieties: how they are planted in vineyards and how they influence one another when combined in the winemaking process. There is no doubt that a winemaker needs to make wines that he feels are reflective of his personality and of the character of the grape and place of which he is working. On the other hand, no winemaker works in a vacuum. By the very nature of being human, a winemaker is influenced by the social fabric around him. Consumers, sommeliers, wine writers, and indeed his own family all have some influence on how he perceives the wine that he makes. Ultimately, though, a winemaker, to be influential in the market, needs to make wines that he believes in.

QUIVIRA VINEYARDS

4900 West Dry Creek Road, Healdsburg, CA 95448
(707) 431-8333, www.quivirawine.com

The mythical kingdom of Quivira, its legendary streets paved in gold, first appeared on European maps in the sixteenth century, referring to what is now Sonoma County. Henry and Holly Wendt founded Quivira in 1981, and Pete and Terri Knight took the reins in 2006. Pete and Terri use biodynamic and organic farming techniques and, with expert winemaker Hugh Chappelle, continue Holly and Henry's vision of protecting the environment and creating better wine through natural vineyard management. The Quivira Vineyards and Winery Fig Tree Vineyard Dry Creek Valley Sonoma County Sauvignon Blanc offers flavors of Granny Smith apple, passion fruit, lemon, and chopped herbs. The Quivira Vineyards and Winery Dry Creek Valley Sonoma County Zinfandel tastes of raspberry, blueberry, and Damson plum backed by Christmas spices and vanilla. 65

RAMEY WINE CELLARS

25 Healdsburg Avenue, Healdsburg, CA 95448
(707) 433-0870, www.rameywine.com

David Ramey belongings to a short list of pioneers who bolstered the quality and profile of California wine. He founded his eponymous winery with his wife, Anne, in 1996. Using traditional techniques and fruit from throughout Napa and Sonoma, they craft highly sought Cabernet blends, Chardonnay, and Syrah. The delicate yet complex Ramey Platt Vineyard Sonoma Coast Chardonnay has flavors of peach, caramelized pineapple, pear compote, Asian spice, and vanilla. The Ramey Rodgers Creek Vineyard Sonoma Coast Syrah offers pleasing berry flavors melding with chocolate-covered espresso bean, smoked pork, and Christmas spice. Drink it now, or age it for up to 12 years. 66

RAVENSWOOD

18701 Gehricke Road, Sonoma, CA 95476
(707) 938-1960, www.ravenswoodwinery.com

More than just a winemaker, Ravenswood founder Joel Peterson is a veritable historian of the California wine industry and all the major players of the last 40 years. With his first vintage of Ravenswood in 1976, the microbiologist-turned-winemaker became one of those major players himself. Although Ravenswood is now corporately owned, Peterson still involves himself in every step from the vineyard to marketing. The Ravenswood Single Vineyard Designate Barricia Sonoma Valley Zinfandel offers berry flavors with notes of tobacco and potent spice, while the smooth, fruity Ravenswood Single Vineyard Designate Belloni Russian River Valley Zinfandel has flavors of plums, blackberry, cassis, anise, and dark chocolate.

RAYMOND BURR VINEYARDS

8339 West Dry Creek Road, Healdsburg, CA 95448
(707) 433-4365, www.raymondburrvineyards.com

The magnetic star of *Perry Mason* (1957–1966) and *Ironside* (1967–1975) on TV, Raymond Burr met his partner, Robert Benevides, an actor and producer, on the set of *Perry Mason*, and the two shared a life that included an orchid business, a cattle and coconut ranch on their private island, and a vineyard and winery. Benevides bought the Dry Creek Valley farm in 1976, and their first grapevines, bearing Cabernet Sauvignon, Chardonnay, and Portuguese varieties, were planted in 1986. The first vintage was produced in 1990 and released in 1995. Burr died in 1993, but Benevides continues the vineyard and winery they began together with Phyllis Zouzounis as winemaker. The creamy, mouth-pleasing Raymond Burr Vineyards Sonoma County Chardonnay features flavors of clementine, lemon curd, and vanilla bean, and the invigorating Raymond Burr Vineyards Quartet tastes of mixed berries, spice, and vanilla.

J. ROCHIOLI VINEYARDS & WINERY

6192 Westside Road, Healdsburg, CA 95448
(707) 433-2305, www.rochioliwinery.com

Joe Rochioli Sr. bought this land, which previously he had farmed, in 1938. Today his family, including Joe Jr., carries on the tradition of highly praised site-specific wines. The Rochioli vineyards border Westside Road—often called the Rodeo Drive of Sonoma—each of them planted to a single clone of Pinot Noir and Chardonnay, and there's a five-year wait on the mailing list for single-vineyard releases. The rest of us can enjoy their estate-grown Sauvignon Blanc, Pinot Noir, and Chardonnay. The Rochioli Estate Grown Russian River Valley Sauvignon Blanc has zippy flavors of grapefruit and lemon, with touches of cut green herbs, bright acidity, and a lasting finish. The smooth-finishing Rochioli Estate Grown Russian River Valley Pinot Noir tastes richly of cherry vanilla with a lift of spice. 67

RODNEY STRONG VINEYARDS

11455 Old Redwood Highway, Healdsburg, CA 95448
(707) 431-1533, www.rodneystrong.com

After retiring from careers as professional dancers in 1959, Rodney Strong and his bride, Charlotte Ann Winson, moved to Northern California, bought a century-old boardinghouse, and began making wine. They made their first vintages with purchased juice, but within three years Rod planted the first Chardonnay in what is now the Chalk Hill AVA, and in 1968 he planted Pinot Noir in the Russian River Valley. In 1970 he built the Russian River Valley winery, which has become a tasting room and cellar. In 1979 Rick Sayre joined as winemaker, and 10 years later Tom Klein, whose family has been farming in California since the early twentieth century, bought Rodney Strong Vineyards. The vineyard has implemented sustainable practices, and in 2003 a large solar power grid was installed. In 2009, Rodney Strong became the first carbon-neutral winery in Sonoma County. Rick directs winemaking, with David Ramey as consulting winemaker, and Greg Morthole works on the Reserve and Single Vineyard wines. The Rodney Strong Reserve Russian River Valley Pinot Noir tastes of black cherry, blackberry, and crème brûlée with notes of Chinese five-spice and vanilla bean. The Rodney Strong Rockaway Single Vineyard Alexander Valley Cabernet Sauvignon gives luscious fruit and vanilla flavors accented by a touch of spice and black pepper.

RUSSIAN HILL ESTATE

4525 Slusser Road, Windsor, CA 95492
(707) 575-9428, www.russianhillestate.com

Edward Gomez and Ellen Mack, husband-and-wife physicians, founded Russian Hill Estate in 1997. Ed's nephew Patrick Melley directs winemaking, working with fruit from their Tara Vineyard and from sites owned by noted grape growers and winemakers. The Russian Hill Estate Vineyards Russian River Valley Syrah has aromas of black currant liqueur, lavender, and cranberry, and the Russian Hill Tara Vineyard Russian River Valley Pinot Noir tastes of ripe black plum, birch root, and cinnamon stick. 68

ST. FRANCIS WINERY

100 Pythian Road, Santa Rosa, CA 95409
(707) 538-9463, www.stfranciswine.com

Joe and Emma Martin purchased the 100-acre Behler Ranch in 1971, selling their output to other producers until 1979, when they built the St. Francis Winery. Its name and distinctive Mission-style bell tower acknowledge both the patron saint of animals and nature and the pioneering Franciscan priests who planted grapes in California. Katie Madigan succeeded original winemaker Tom Mackey in 2012. The St. Francis Sonoma County Merlot tastes of cherry and mocha joined by blueberry and mixed spice, and the St. Francis Sonoma County Old Vines Zinfandel offers flavors of cherry pie, black raspberry, butterscotch, and cracked black pepper.

SAXON BROWN WINES

255 West Napa Street, Sonoma, CA 95476
(707) 939-9530, www.saxonbrown.com

Owner and winemaker Jeff Gaffner founded Saxon Brown in 1997, naming it after the female protagonist in Jack London's *Valley of the Moon*, set in the Sonoma Valley. Gaffner limits Saxon Brown's annual production to fewer than 2,500 cases. The Saxon Brown Sonoma Coast Parmelee-Hill Owl Box Block Syrah has full-on fruit flavors, and the Saxon Brown Sonoma Coast Durell Vineyard Hayfield Block Pinot Noir features lasting flavors of fruit and spice with a complex finish.

SBRAGIA FAMILY VINEYARDS

9990 Dry Creek Road, Geyserville, CA 95441
(707) 473-2992, www.sbragia.com

In 1904, winemaker Ed Sbragia's grandfather arrived from Tuscany and worked at the Italian Swiss Colony Winery. Born and raised in Dry Creek Valley, Sbragia created wines for Beringer for 32 years before he and his wife, Jane, acquired the old Lake Sonoma Winery in 2006. Ed and son Adam make the wine, and Adam's wife, Cathy, handles hospitality. Ed and Jane's youngest son, Kevin, works in the cellar during harvest, and Jane and daughter Gina help out in the tasting room. The Sbragia Family Vineyards Dry Creek Valley Home Ranch Chardonnay has flavors of lemon, citrus blossom, vanilla, and light spice. The Sbragia Family Vineyards Dry Creek Valley Gino's Vineyard Zinfandel features wild blackberry and raspberry flavors with touches of pepper and spice. 69

SCHUG CARNEROS ESTATE WINERY

602 Bonneau Road, Sonoma, CA 95476
(707) 939-9363, www.schugwinery.com

Walter and wife Gertrud Schug grew up in the winemaking business in Germany, and in 1961 they headed to California. Walter worked at E & J Gallo before moving to Joseph Phelps. There he made one of the first varietal Syrahs in the United States and one of the first modern California Bordeaux-style blends, Insignia. Walter and Gertrud bought 50 acres in Sonoma and started Schug in 1989. Their three children have taken part in the business, and today son Axel is CEO, with his wife, Kristine, serving as winery chef. Michael Cox now heads winemaking, but Walter holds the title of winemaker emeritus. The Schug Sonoma Coast Chardonnay tastes cleanly of ripe stone fruits with a hint of ginger and nutmeg, and the Schug Heritage Reserve Sonoma Valley Cabernet Sauvignon has succulent berry, chocolate, and spice flavors. 70

SEBASTIANI

389 Fourth Street East, Sonoma, CA 95476
(707) 933-3230, www.sebastiani.com

Tuscan stonemason Samuele Sebastiani established his winery in 1904. It remained open during Prohibition by making sacramental and medicinal wine, but Samuele also canned fruit to keep his workers employed. Samuele's son August continued his father's legacy from 1944 until 1980, and August's daughter Mary Ann oversaw a major winery and hospitality center renovation in 2001. As president and CEO, Mary Ann directed Sebastiani toward small-lot artisanal winemaking, adding cultural programs to the lineup of visitor experiences and remaining until the sale and transition to the Foley Family Wines portfolio in 2008. Winemaking continues under Mark Lyon, who has been with the winery since 1978. The Sebastiani Cherryblock Sonoma Valley Cabernet Sauvignon offers flavors of fresh berries and berry confit with notes of espresso, anisette, and cranberry. The Sebastiani Patrick's Vineyard Carneros Chardonnay tastes of white peach, nectarine, and almond paste. 71

SEGHESIO FAMILY VINEYARDS

700 Grove Street, Healdsburg, CA 95448
(707) 433-3579, www.seghesio.com

After leaving Italy for California and working with the Rossi family, Edoardo Seghesio planted his first Alexander Valley Zinfandel vineyard in 1895. His family still farms 300 acres of Zinfandel and Italian varietals throughout the Dry Creek, Alexander, and Russian River valleys. Great-grandson Ted Seghesio is head winemaker, and Ted's brother David directs operations. Their uncle Pete is chief grape grower; their brother-in-law Jim Neumiller manages the vineyards; and Jim's son Ned handles grower relations. Today they form part of the Crimson Wine Group. The Seghesio Home Ranch Alexander Valley Zinfandel features flavors of wild fruits of the wood and light vanilla enhanced by soft cinnamon and toast. 72

SIDURI WINES

981 Airport Court, Suites E & F, Santa Rosa, CA 95403
(707) 578-3882, www.siduri.com

Self-described wine geeks Adam and Dianna Lee met while working at Neiman Marcus in Texas—Dianna in fine foods and Adam in wine—and headed to California to immerse themselves in the wine industry, starting Siduri in 1994 and naming it for the Babylonian goddess who holds the wine of eternal life. One night, they heard that Robert Parker was staying in Napa, so they left a bottle at his hotel. Parker gave them 90 points in *Wine Advocate*, and Siduri Wines became an overnight sensation. Adam is winemaker alongside cellarmaster and assistant winemaker Ryan Zepaltas, and Jackson Family Wines bought the company in January 2015. The powerful yet elegant Siduri Russian River Valley Pinot Noir gives fruit on the palate with touches of soft chocolate, vanilla, and citrus zest. The Siduri Rosella's Vineyard Pinot Noir offers black cherry, aniseed, and violets in a sophisticated play of tannins and acidity.

SIMI WINERY

16275 Healdsburg Avenue, Healdsburg, CA 95448
(800) 746-4880, www.simiwinery.com

Brothers Giuseppe and Pietro Simi produced their first wines in 1876, and 14 years later made their first vintage at the winery on Healdsburg Avenue that still bears the family name. Both brothers died young in 1904, and Giuseppe's 18-year-old daughter Isabelle took over. Simi weathered Prohibition by selling vineyards and providing pharmacies with wine for people with prescriptions. A year after Prohibition ended, Isabelle Simi built a tasting room from a 25,000-gallon wine barrel and positioned it so that it could be seen from the road. She continued to run the business until retiring in 1970, when she sold Simi to grape grower Russell Green. In 1973 Maryann Graf, the first woman to graduate from an American university with a degree in enology, became head winemaker. Zelma Long succeeded Graf in 1979 and later became president and CEO. LVMH bought the winery in 1982, and over the next 10 years Simi added to its vineyard holdings in the Alexander and Russian River valleys. A new hospitality center replaced Isabelle's wooden tasting room in 1990, and Simi became part of Constellation Brands' wine empire in 1999. Winemaking continues under the direction of Susan Lueker, who joined Simi in 2000. The Simi Russian River Valley Pinot Gris has a palate of citrus fruit, peach, and white flowers with a touch of spice; the Simi Alexander Valley Chardonnay features fruit flavors alongside toasted brioche and vanilla; and the long-finishing Simi Alexander Valley Landslide Vineyard Cabernet Sauvignon tastes of blackberry and blueberry giving way to violet and slate notes. 73

SONOMA-CUTRER WINERY

4401 Slusser Road, Windsor, CA 95492
(707) 528-1181, www.sonomacutrer.com

Founder Brice Cutrer Jones's commitment to quality from vineyard to bottle has helped make Sonoma-Cutrer Chardonnay one of the most recognized brands among US wine consumers. From its 1973 start as a grape-growing company through the establishment of a winery focusing on estate-grown Chardonnay and several ownership changes culminating with current parent Brown-Forman, that emphasis has remained. Winemaker Mick Schroeter works with estate-grown fruit from six large vineyards in the Russian River Valley, Sonoma Coast, and Chalk Hill appellations to produce Chardonnay and Pinot Noir. In Sonoma-Cutrer Vineyards Russian River Ranches Sonoma Coast Estate Bottled Chardonnay, apple flavors meld with citrus fruits, and vanilla bean. 74

STEPHEN & WALKER TRUST WINERY

243 Healdsburg Avenue, Healdsburg, CA 95448
(707) 431-8749, www.trustwine.com

Owner-winemakers Tony Stephen and Nancy Walker continue to hold other winemaking, sales, and consulting positions in the industry. Most of their outside projects are larger in scale, but their experience and knowledge show through in their own handcrafted wines. The Stephen & Walker Green Valley of Russian River Valley Sauvignon Blanc featuers lush flavors of lime, guava, mango, and orange blossom, and the Stephen & Walker Dry Creek Valley Petite Sirah tastes of blackberry, cherry cola, and crème brûlée.

STONESTREET

7111 Highway 128, Healdsburg, CA 95448
(707) 433-9463, www.stonestreetwines.com

Jess Stonestreet Jackson purchased the former Zellerbach Winery in 1989 and renamed it after his family. His Alexander Mountain estate lies in the Mayacamas Mountains, high above the Alexander Valley floor. More than 5,000 acres of rugged landscape nurture 800 acres of grapevines, tended by a team headed by Tony Viramontes and Gabriel Valencia, and South Africa native Graham Weerts heads winemaking. The Stonestreet Gravel Bench Alexander Mountain Estate Chardonnay presents a green apple palate balanced by toasted nuts and vanilla. The Stonestreet Alexander Mountain Estate Bear Point Cabernet Sauvignon exhibits flavors of blueberry and cassis, flecked by notes of tobacco and citrus blossom. 75

STUHLMULLER VINEYARDS

4951 West Soda Rock Lane, Healdsburg, CA 95448
(707) 431-7745, www.stuhlmullervineyards.com

Roger and Carmen Stuhlmuller acquired their 150-acre Alexander Valley property in 1982 and, along with son Fritz, built a small artisanal winery in 1996. When they needed more room a few years later, they renovated a historic barn on the property to accommodate small-batch fermentation. Leo Hansen has been winemaker since 2004, and Stuhlmuller Vineyards produces 6,000 cases a year. The crisp, clean Stuhmuller Vineyards Alexander Valley Estate Chardonnay tastes of lemon curd, brown baking spices, and toasted hazelnut, and the Stuhmuller Vineyards Alexander Valley Estate Zinfandel offers flavors of black raspberry sorbet, brown spices, and black plum.

SUACCI CARCIERE WINES

P.O. Box 2317, Sebastopol, CA 95473
(707) 829-3283, www.suaccicarciere.com

The Suacci and Carciere families have been friends for more than 25 years. Both have Italian backgrounds and grandfathers who made homemade wine, so in 2001 they planted a vineyard and sold the grapes. In their fifth year, they kept the grapes and made their own highly acclaimed wine. Suacci Carciere wines are artisanally made by Ryan Zepaltas, a well-respected and highly sought winemaker. The creamy Suacci Carciere Suacci Vineyard Pinot Noir has aromas of hickory smoke, dried Mediterranean herbs, and red fruit preserves, and the full, rich, crisp Suacci Carciere Heintz Vineyard Chardonnay tastes of lemon blossom and lemon curd with a touch of minerality.

macphail

53

MacRostie
Winery and Vineyards
Chardonnay
SONOMA COAST
2011

54

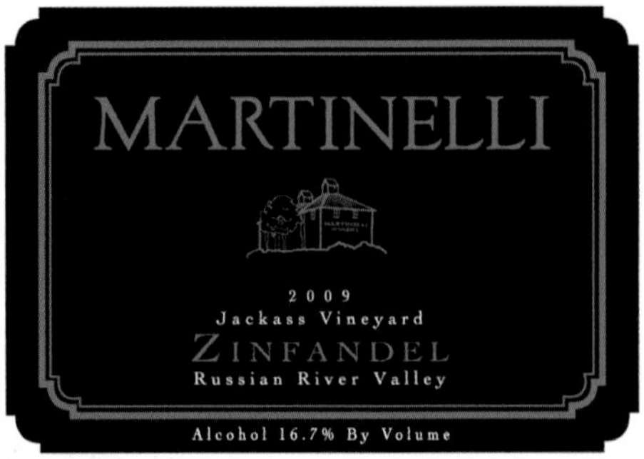
MARTINELLI
2009
Jackass Vineyard
ZINFANDEL
Russian River Valley
Alcohol 16.7% By Volume

56

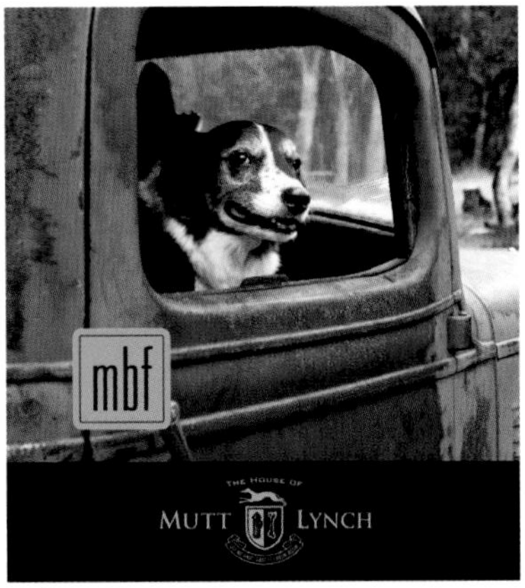
mbf
MUTT
LYNCH

61

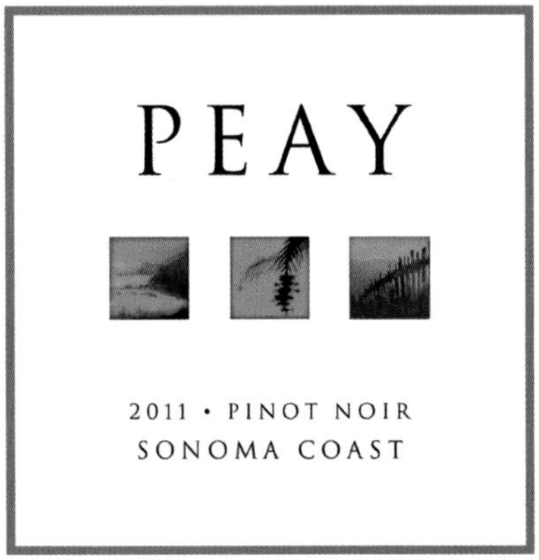
PEAY
2011 • PINOT NOIR
SONOMA COAST

62

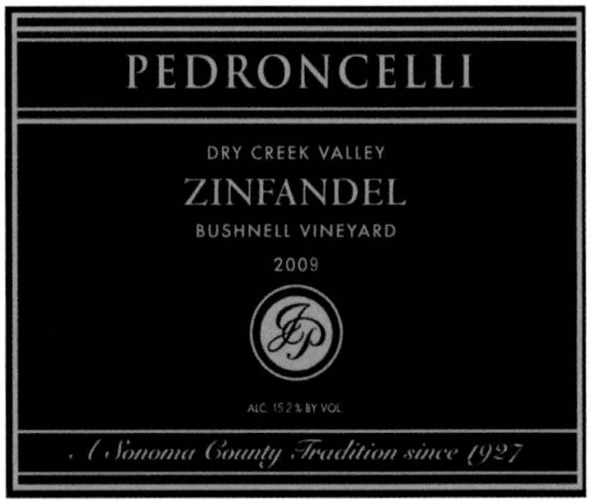
PEDRONCELLI
DRY CREEK VALLEY
ZINFANDEL
BUSHNELL VINEYARD
2009
A Sonoma County Tradition since 1927

63

RUSSIAN HILL
2009
SYRAH
RUSSIAN RIVER VALLEY
ESTATE VINEYARDS
ESTATE GROWN
FAMILY OWNED

68

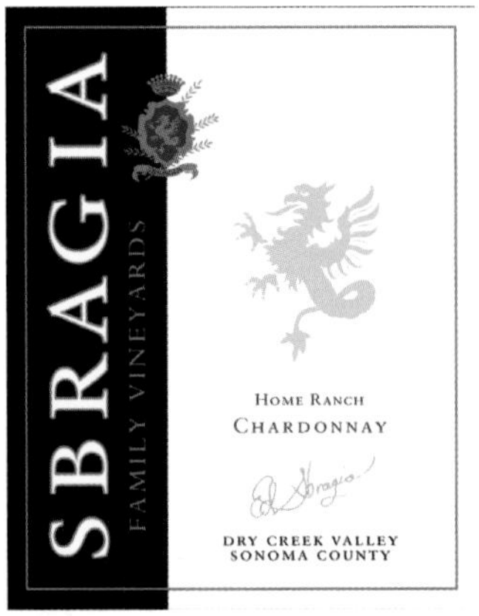
SBRAGIA
FAMILY VINEYARDS
Home Ranch
Chardonnay
DRY CREEK VALLEY
SONOMA COUNTY

69

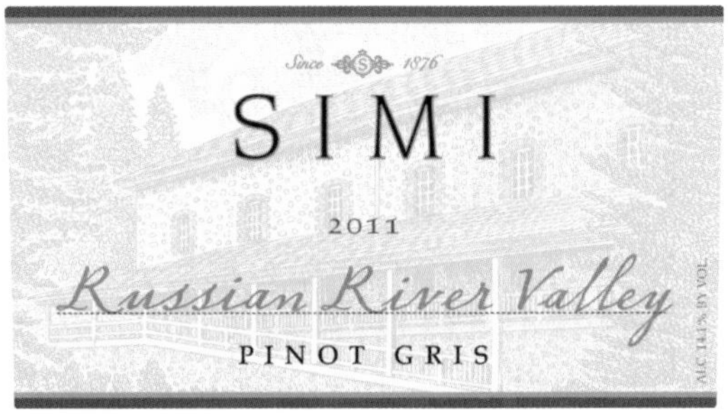
Since 1876
SIMI
2011
Russian River Valley
PINOT GRIS

73

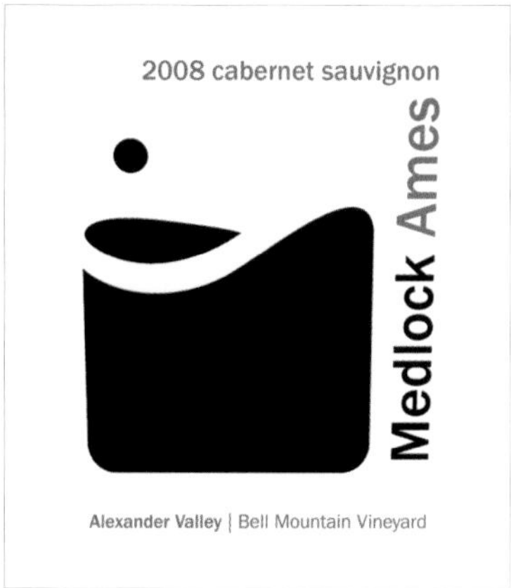

2008 cabernet sauvignon
Medlock Ames
Alexander Valley | Bell Mountain Vineyard

58

59

60

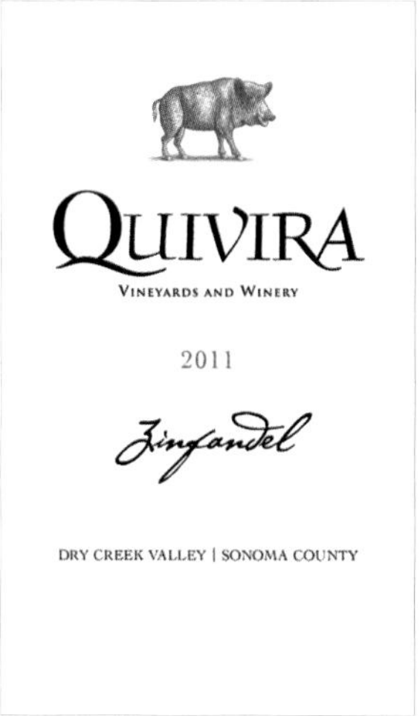

65

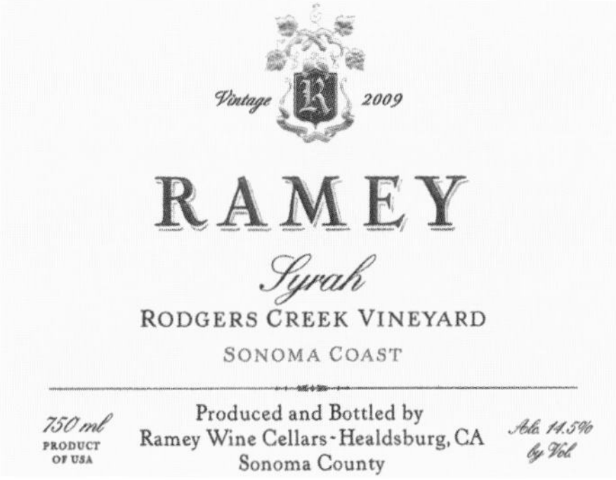

66

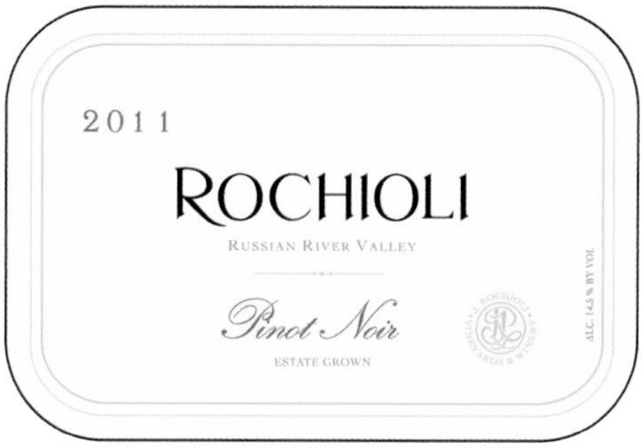

67

75

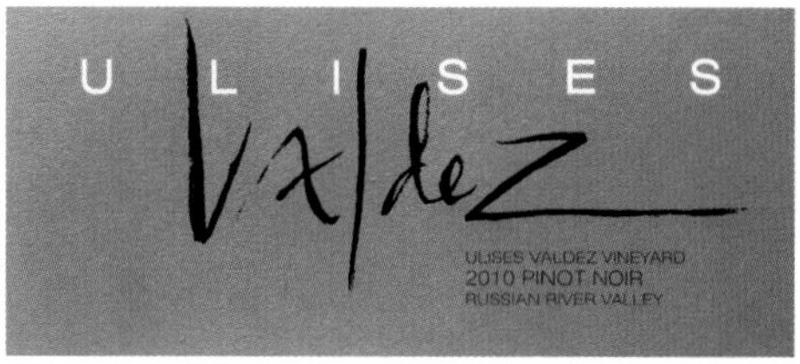

76

77

78

In his own words

PIERRE SEILLAN

French-born Pierre Seillan began his wine career in his family's vineyards in Gascony. He later moved on to Château de Targé in the Loire Valley and then seven châteaux in Bordeaux before accepting Jess Jackson's invitation to make Vérité wine in California.

I learned very early how to be a servant of the soil, to help identify and express the message of the soil. I started in Gascony, then I was a trainee developing vineyards in Temecula in 1976. I worked in Saumur-Champigny with Cabernet Franc and managed several châteaux across the different regions of Bordeaux before discovering the diversity of Sonoma. All of this experience helped me develop my micro-cru philosophy and learn about different *terroirs*.

My philosophy is that of micro-crus, working with small parcels of vineyards that each have a unique *terroir*, keeping them separate during harvest and through fermentation and barrel aging to let each develop its own message of that particular micro-cru. Using the micro-crus of the best oak forests for my barrels, selecting the best places in twelve to fifteen forests to source trees that will help the complexity of the grapes, and the micro-crus of the cork, to find all of the best places for these to grow, and to find a synergy between all of them. The goal of my winemaking philosophy is to capture the message of the soils to get the signature of the wine!

I have seen a lot of changes with newer technologies in the vineyards and in the cellar. We now have a grape-sorting table with a Vision computer, we have temperature-controlled tanks, we have mechanical harvesters. When I started out back in France we did not have all of this technology; a lot was done by hand, and we had concrete and wooden tanks. I am excited to see that Sonoma is starting to become a star of California; the diversity of the *terroir* and the proximity to the Pacific Ocean make it one of the best places in the world to make wine.

SUNCÉ WINERY

1839 Olivet Road, Santa Rosa, CA 95401
(707) 526-9463, www.suncewinery.com

Frane and Janae Franicevic purchased a four-acre horse ranch in 1998 and called it Suncé, "sunshine" in Serbo-Croatian, after their newborn daughter. Suncé Winery began with Pinot Noir and established itself as a "small, ultrapremium winery" producing wine from small lots of rare varieties of grapes. The crisp, fruity Suncé Malvasia Bianca features flavors of lemon curd and custard with a crisp, fruity finish, and the fruit-forward Suncé RRV Cattich Vineyard Zinfandel is balanced and restrained.

TEN ACRE

9711 West Dry Creek Road, Healdsburg, CA 95448
(707) 473-4418, www.tenacrewinery.com

Scott and Lynn Adams put down roots in the Russian River Valley by acquiring their first vineyard in 1995. Within four years they opened Bella Vineyards and Wine Caves in Dry Creek, and in 2008 they established another microwinery specializing in Chardonnay and Pinot Noir from the Russian River Valley and the Sonoma Coast. They named it Ten Acre after the bucolic spread they share with their grapevines and two children. Charlie Chenowith, whose family has been farming in Sonoma for more than 150 years, manages the vineyards, and Michael Zardo, who has worked at Pisoni, heads winemaking. The Ten Acre Green Acre Hills Sangiacomo Sonoma Coast Chardonnay offers flavors of guava, apple cobbler, candied lemon rind, and butterscotch. The Ten Acre Cummings Vineyard Russian River Valley Pinot Noir tastes richly of blackcherry, raspberry, crème brûlée, and gingerbread spice.

VALDEZ FAMILY WINERY

113 Mill Street, Healdsburg, CA 95448
(707) 433-3710, www.valdezfamilywinery.com

Ulises Valdez's success story begins when he crossed the Mexico-California border in 1985 and found work in Sonoma's Dry Creek Valley. After years of experience as a vineyard manager in partnership with Jack Florence Jr., he gained US citizenship in 1996. Valdez bought Florence's share of the company in 2003, changing the name to Valdez & Sons Vineyard Management Inc., and Florence now manages the Valdez Family Winery. The fruit-forward Valdez Family Winery Ulises Valdez Rockpile Botticelli Vineyard Zinfandel proffers aromas of black plum, black pepper, and black raspberry, while the restrained and elegant Valdez Family Winery Ulises Valdez Vineyard Russian River Valley Pinot Noir has a nose of dried black cherry, red cherry conserves, and Christmas baking spices. 76

VERITÉ

4611 Thomas Road, Healdsburg, CA 95448
(707) 433-9000, www.veritewines.com

Pierre Seillan first came to Sonoma in 1998 at the invitation of Jess Jackson, who wanted to make a California Merlot to rival that of Bordeaux. Seillan has worked with Merlot and Cabernet Franc for more than 40 years, first at his family's estate in Armagnac and eventually as the technical director at seven Bordeaux châteaux. Verité began in 1998 as a joint effort between Seillan and Jackson Family Wines. The fruit comes from small vineyard blocks that Seillan calls "micro-crus." Seillan's first vintage (1998), simply called Verité, is still fresh and young in the glass, filled with gorgeous flavors of plum, cassis, black cherry, mint, and black pepper. Verité La Joie, a truly beautiful wine, unfolds on the palate with lush blackberry, black currants, and espresso bean. Verité La Muse tastes of black cherry, blackberry, mocha, and fennel.

WILLIAMS SELYEM

7227 Westside Road, Healdsburg, CA 95448
(707) 433-6425, www.williamsselyem.com

Burt Williams and Ed Selyem produced the first of many award-winning vintages of Pinot Noir in 1981, and in 1998 wine club customer number 2,080—John and Kathe Dyson, who also owned Millbrook Winery in New York State and vineyards on California's Central Coast—bought the winery from its founders. Winemaker and general manager Bob Cabral was also a wine club member—customer number 576. A fourth-generation California grape grower, Cabral was making wine long before Burt Williams introduced him to John and Kathe in 1998 and recommended that Bob replace him as winemaker. In 1998 John and Kathe bought the Drake orchard on the Russian River in Guerneville, planting it to various Pinot Noir clones. The smooth-finishing Williams Selyem Russian River Valley Pinot Noir has flavors of black and tart cherries, aniseed, and birch root. 77

WOODENHEAD VINTNERS

5700 River Road, Santa Rosa, CA 95401
(707) 887-2703, www.woodenheadwine.com

Contractor-turned-vintner Nikolai Stez started making homemade garage wines in 1986. He partnered with Zina Bower, who handles the bookkeeping and management sides of the business, and together they are responsible for the delicious small-batch wines from Woodenhead Vintners. The Woodenhead Russian River Bertoli Zinfandel features flavors of black cherry, black raspberry, and aromatic brown spices, including a whiff of clove. 78

THREE

NAPA VALLEY

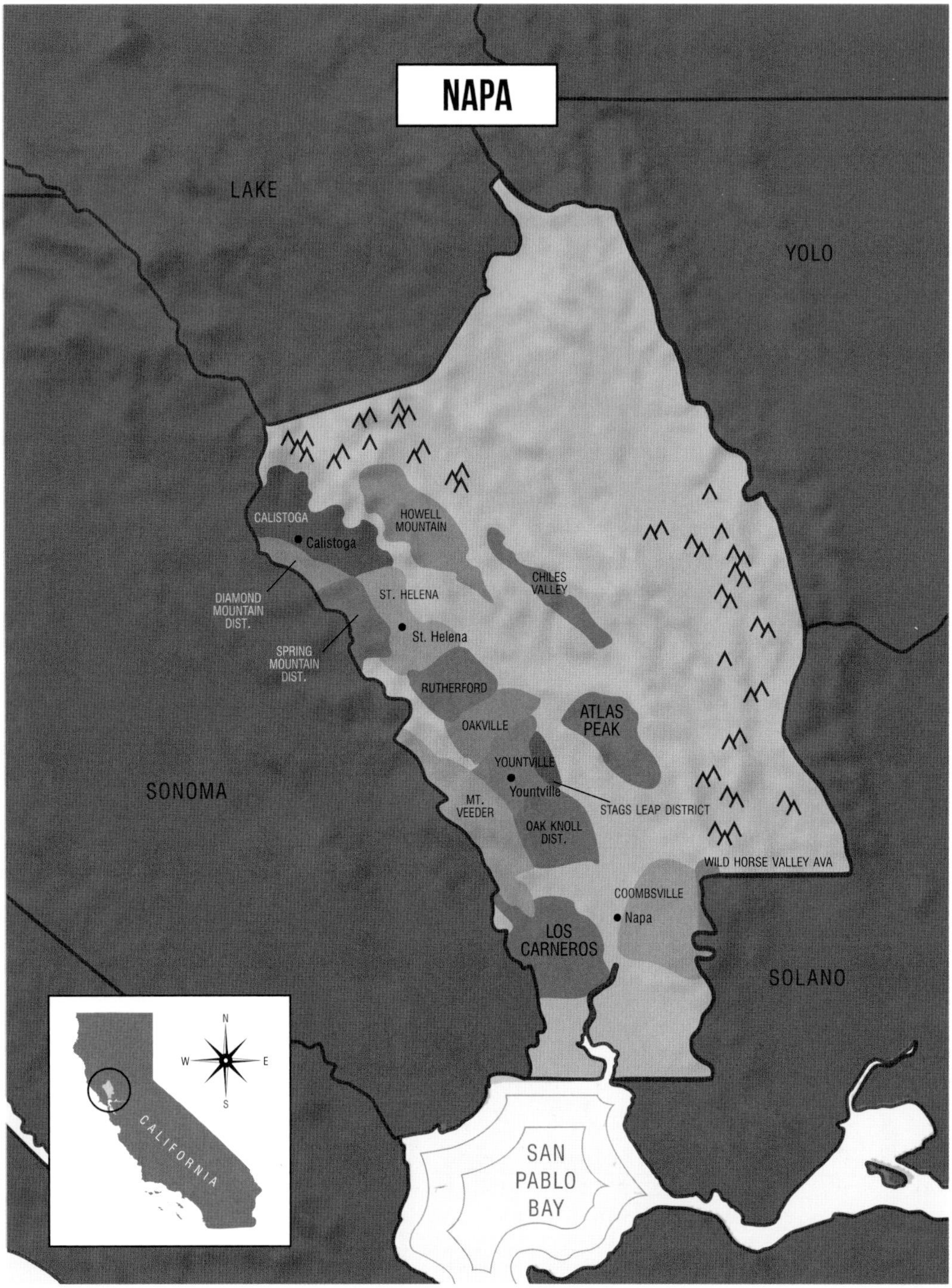
NAPA
LAKE
YOLO
CALISTOGA
Calistoga
HOWELL MOUNTAIN
DIAMOND MOUNTAIN DIST.
ST. HELENA
St. Helena
CHILES VALLEY
SPRING MOUNTAIN DIST.
RUTHERFORD
ATLAS PEAK
OAKVILLE
YOUNTVILLE
Yountville
STAGS LEAP DISTRICT
SONOMA
MT. VEEDER
OAK KNOLL DIST.
WILD HORSE VALLEY AVA
COOMBSVILLE
Napa
LOS CARNEROS
SOLANO
N
W
E
S
CALIFORNIA
SAN PABLO BAY

Although grape growing here dates back to 1839, Napa's preeminence among wine regions emerged in 1976 with the Judgment of Paris, the blind tasting that pitted California Chardonnay and Cabernet Sauvignon against their counterparts from Burgundy and Bordeaux. To the shock of the nine French evaluators, California wine took top honors in both the white and red categories. Though it produces only 4 percent of California wine, it put the state onto the global wine map.

Grape growing took off in Napa County after the Gold Rush, especially the 1860s and 1870s, as immigrants from Europe who had come to the United States to seek their fortunes planted the same crops as in the old country. John Patchett planted winemaking vineyards here in 1860 and hired Prussian immigrant Charles Krug to make wine using a cider press. In 1861 Krug opened his own winery, still in operation. Jacob Schram planted what's considered the first hillside vineyard in Napa in 1862, establishing Schramsberg Winery that same year. Another German immigrant, Jacob Beringer, bought land in Napa Valley in 1875 with his brother Frederick and founded the Beringer Winery. Owned today by Treasury Wine Estates, Beringer is said to be the oldest continually operating winery in Napa Valley.

By the end of the nineteenth century Napa Valley winemaking was thriving. Captain Gustave Niebaum's Inglenook Wine, reportedly the first Bordeaux-style wine in the United States, took gold at the Paris World's Fair in 1889. That year, 140 wineries were operating in Napa, with almost 16,000 acres of planted grapes. But within a few years phylloxera attacked transplanted European rootstock, and by 1900 only 2,000 acres of grapevines remained. Before the vineyards could be restored, World War I, Prohibition, and the Great Depression left Napa Valley in total disrepair.

André Tchelistcheff helped restore Napa's vineyards and reputation after Prohibition by coming from France to become head winemaker for George de Latour, founder of Beaulieu Vineyards. Tchelistcheff focused on high-quality Cabernet Sauvignon and reportedly introduced to California the practice of aging wine in small French oak barrels. He made important advances in cold fermentation, frost protection, and malolactic fermentation as well and was instrumental in the development of vineyard sites in Carneros and other California regions. He retired in 1973, but many prominent winemakers list Tchelistcheff among their most important influences in the business.

Robert Mondavi left his family's Charles Krug winery in 1965 and with son Michael established the first large purpose-built winery in Napa Valley since the start of Prohibition. He was also among the first to label wines with varietal names rather than European wine regions. American wine drinkers were developing more sophisticated palates, preferring dry and food-friendly varieties, prompting a surge in the number of new wineries. Quality also improved dramatically. By the time of the Judgment of Paris, there were more than fifty wineries in Napa Valley. The stage was set for Napa to become the premier wine region in the United States.

Napa is flat in the south and rises as you head north. Nearby San Pablo Bay and its sea-level estuaries cool the southern end of the valley. The mountains to the east and west reach as high as 2,500 feet, and the valley floor rises more or less steadily toward the 4,000-foot Mount St. Helena in the north. Napa River runs north to south, and Lake Berryessa, a man-made reservoir, lies to the east.

Summers are usually hot and dry, with a minimum of rainfall. During the day, rising hot air draws in cool air from the Pacific Ocean, producing fog that protects the grapes from the sun. With the cooling influence of San Pablo Bay, the temperature variation from south to north can range as much as 10 to 15 degrees Fahrenheit in summer, and day-to-night temperature swings can vary by 40 degrees. Napa Valley's sixteen sub-AVAs provide a variety of soil types, slopes, elevations, and orientations that subtly influence the finished wine.

The union of tradition and innovation here produces the best-quality wines. Viticulturists here were among the first to use NASA satellite technology to survey vineyard sites to achieve the best possible layout, but vineyards still are tended and harvested by hand and wine is crafted in small quantities, often measured by the single barrel. The University of California at Davis maintains a 40-acre experimental vineyard and research facility in Napa Valley's Oakville AVA, analyzing the effects of industry innovation.

Covering almost all of Napa County, Napa Valley was the first recognized AVA in California, established in February 1981. The Napa Valley AVA, about the same size as Burgundy's Côte d'Or, hosts 45,000 acres of vines of Cabernet Sauvignon, Chardonnay, Merlot, Pinot Noir, and Sauvignon Blanc. More than sixty varieties grow in sixteen AVAs, and more than 450 wineries thrive here, the majority family owned and relatively small.

Napa Valley Cabernet Sauvignon accounts for about one-quarter of all the Cabernet Sauvignon in the state. Next comes Chardonnay, with additional acreage in the Los Carneros AVA. Merlot is the third most cultivated variety, followed by Pinot Noir, Sauvignon Blanc, Zinfandel, and Petite Sirah. Where Cabernet Sauvignon and Merlot grow, the other Bordeaux grapes follow, among them Cabernet Franc, Petit Verdot, and Malbec. These last three are used in Bordeaux-style or Meritage blends and are bottled as single varieties as well.

The smaller appellations in Napa Valley vary from the 2,700-acre Stags Leap District to the 15,000-acre Mount Veeder AVA. Downtown Napa has twenty tasting rooms, forty hotels and inns, and seventy restaurants, all within walking distance of the revitalized waterfront. The Oxbow Market offers artisanal products, freshly prepared food, and local produce. The Silverado Trail offers vineyard views, while each of the valley's towns features style and charm, from Yountville's Michelin-starred restaurants to the spas and mud baths of Calistoga.

ATLAS PEAK AVA

First planted with grapevines in 1870, Atlas Peak received AVA status in 1992, taking its name from the region's highest point. Vineyards vary from 760 to more than 2,600 feet above sea level, accessible only via two roads leading from foothills near the valley floor. The shallow, well-drained soils tend to be rocky and volcanic, often with strong tones of red basalt. There are ten wineries and about as many growers in the AVA, and more than eighty wineries throughout Napa Valley bottle wine under the appellation. The superstar variety is Cabernet Sauvignon, but other reds do well here: Cabernet Franc, Malbec, Petit Verdot, Sangiovese, Syrah, and Zinfandel. Chardonnay, Sauvignon Blanc, and white Rhône varieties are also cultivated.

CALISTOGA AVA

The area gets its name from hot springs enthusiast Samuel Brannan, who set out to make this town the Saratoga Springs of California, combining the names to create "Calistoga." Wine grapes were reportedly first planted here in 1852, and Alfred L. Tubbs founded Chateau Montelena in 1882. Current winemaker Bo Barrett and his late father, Jim, fiercely pressed for establishment of the AVA, which took place in 2010.

It's the northernmost AVA in the valley, and unlike most AVAs farther south, most of Calistoga's vines are cultivated on hillsides and slopes, with elevations from 300 to 1,200 feet above sea level. Calistoga enjoys cool Pacific air that enters Napa Valley through gaps in the northwestern hills. Temperature variation in summer can swing as much as 60 degrees Fahrenheit, reaching 100 during the day and plummeting into the 40s after sunset. As expected in an area dominated by hot springs, soils are volcanic. Red grapes dominate here, primarily Cabernet Sauvignon, Petite Sirah, and Zinfandel. As elsewhere in Napa Valley, growth is rising: Close to thirty wineries operate within the AVA now, up from just thirteen 25 years ago. An absence of fast-food restaurants and the nearby narrowing of Highway 29 to a two-lane road have allowed Calistoga to retain its small-town feel.

CHILES VALLEY AVA

Joseph Ballinger Chiles received an area land grant from Mexico in 1841, and grapes have been grown here since Swiss immigrants arrived in the 1880s; some vineyards even date to that era. This long, narrow AVA in the Vaca Mountain Range, granted AVA status in April 1999, is home to vineyards planted at altitudes of 600 to 1,200 feet above sea level. Red varieties predominate, primarily Zinfandel, Cabernet Sauvignon, and Cabernet Franc, with plantings of Chardonnay and Sauvignon Blanc as well. Its inland location thwarts the cooling effects of the Pacific Ocean, so elevation causes day-to-night temperature variations. There are seven wineries within its borders.

COOMBSVILLE AVA

In the foothills of the Vaca Mountains, in a small valley south of Atlas Peak, Coombsville has a reputation for Cabernet Sauvignon and other Bordeaux reds, which grow in warm hillside vineyards. San Pablo Bay moderates summer temperatures, and Chardonnay, Pinot Noir, and Syrah do well in cooler locations. Most of the forty vineyards and growers are at elevations between 100 and 500 feet, but some rise as high as 1,000 feet above sea level. The soils teem with the volcanic detritus of Mount George. Coombsville received AVA status in 2011.

DIAMOND MOUNTAIN DISTRICT AVA

Grapes have been grown here since the early 1860s, when Jacob Schram, founder of Schramsberg, planted his first vines, and the Diamond Mountain District AVA was established in 2001. Most vines are planted at altitudes of 400 to 2,200 feet. High elevations, beyond the reach of daytime fog, aid in cooling ripening grapes after the sun goes down. Granular soils with a powdery consistency bear witness to ancient volcanic activity. There are ten wineries in the AVA, which is best known for Cabernet Sauvignon and Cabernet Franc, though cold-weather whites are planted here as well.

HOWELL MOUNTAIN AVA

Named for Isaac Howell, who arrived in 1847, Howell Mountain's grape-growing history stretches back to the 1880s, when Jean Brun and Jean V. Chaix planted vineyards and opened a winery here. They won a bronze medal at the Paris Exhibition of 1889, and their original winery is the renovated home of Ladera Vineyards. In addition to the wineries here, an A-list of other Napa wineries buys fruit from the AVA, bottled with the Howell Mountain designation.

The first sub-AVA within Napa Valley, Howell Mountain received its formal designation in January 1984 and has almost fifty wineries. Vineyard elevations range from 600 to 2,600 feet, with the majority planted between 1,400 and 2,200 feet, some offering commanding views of St. Helena. Vineyards planted in well-drained volcanic soils sit mainly above the fog line, benefiting from full-day sun that aids in ripening and sugar development. Cool nights counter the hot days, preserving acid balance in the Cabernet Sauvignon (Howell Mountain's standout variety), Sauvignon Blanc, Merlot, Zinfandel, and Viognier.

LOS CARNEROS AVA

Sometimes simply called Carneros, the name of this appellation is Spanish for "the rams," a reference to the region's former role as pastureland. It straddles Napa and Sonoma counties, so wines in the eastern portion may be identified as from the Napa Valley AVA as well as Carneros, and in the west, bottles from Carneros may be labeled with the Sonoma County and Sonoma Valley appellations. Since the early 1980s onward—the AVA established in 1983—it has been the American vineyard and winery base of prominent European sparkling wine producers, including Moët & Chandon, Champagne Taittinger, Freixenet, Champagne G.H. Mumm, and Codorniu. Today twenty-two wineries operate here.

Its proximity to San Pablo Bay and its east-west orientation make Los Carneros generally a cold-weather region, though the coldest AVAs lie farther north and west, in Sonoma County. Both Pinot Noir and Chardonnay grow here. A phylloxera outbreak in

the late 1980s necessitated major replanting, but both varieties are made into still and sparkling wines, and they recently have been joined by sizable plantings of Merlot and Syrah.

MOUNT VEEDER AVA

This region takes its name from Peter Veeder, a German Presbyterian minister who lived here in the 1860s. Captain Stelman Wing purportedly produced the first wine made from Mount Veeder grapes in 1864, and his legacy lives on in the Wing Canyon Vineyard. German immigrants made the area home throughout the 1880s and 1890s, and by the start of the twentieth century twenty vineyards and six wineries dotted the slopes of Mount Veeder. After Prohibition the first new wineries in the area appeared in the 1950s and 1960s. The first Petit Verdot in Napa Valley was reportedly planted here in 1975, and the first Napa Valley vineyard featuring all five Bordeaux varieties purportedly was planted on Mount Veeder as well. The AVA was established in March 1990.

Today Mount Veeder, the largest sub-AVA in Napa Valley, has almost twenty-five wineries and twenty growers. Planted elevations range from 500 to 2,400 feet above sea level. Most soils are shallow clay seabed with excellent drainage. Sitting at high elevations yet cooled by San Pablo Bay, the slopes of Mount Veeder don't suffer from excessive daytime heat, providing for a long, slow ripening season. Cabernet Sauvignon is the preeminent variety, but almost twenty varieties grow here, with considerable plantings of Malbec, Merlot, Cabernet Franc, and Petit Verdot, as well as Chardonnay, Syrah, and Viognier.

OAK KNOLL DISTRICT OF NAPA VALLEY AVA

Established in 2004, the Oak Knoll District of Napa Valley AVA, has a dozen wineries. Valley floor vineyards lie at sea level, and the highest elevations rise to 800 feet. Soils at lower elevations are alluvial, primarily gravel and loam, whereas coarse volcanic soils prevail at higher elevations. Nearby San Pablo Bay cools Oak Knoll, and early morning fog provides a counterpoint to hot summer days. Cabernet Sauvignon is the champion of the region both in acreage and in reputation, although Merlot, Chardonnay, Pinot Noir, Sauvignon Blanc, and Riesling also do well here.

OAKVILLE AVA

H. W. Crabb planted the first vineyard in Oakville in 1868, and UC Davis's Oakville Experimental Vineyard is here. The most densely planted of any Napa Valley appellation, Oakville spans the valley floor. Its population of seventy people soars daily as visitors experience the AVA's wineries and vineyards. Elevations range from sea level to 500 feet.

Established in 1993, Oakville has two main soils: a mix of sandy loam and clay and a mix of sedimentary sand and gravel. Both offer good drainage. Daytime is hot through the growing season, but breezes and fog temper the heat early and late in the day. Forty wineries and sixty growers operate here, and Cabernet Sauvignon, the backbone of Napa Valley, reigns supreme. But Oakville is also known for Sauvignon Blanc and Chardonnay and for other Bordeaux reds, especially Merlot and Cabernet Franc.

RUTHERFORD AVA

Inglenook, the oldest Rutherford winery, was founded in 1879, and the oldest continuously bonded winery, Beaulieu Vineyard, opened its doors in 1900. Nearly three quarters of the grapes grown in Rutherford, granted AVA status in 1993, are Cabernet Sauvignon, followed by Merlot and Cabernet Franc. White varieties include Sauvignon Blanc and Chardonnay. Vineyard elevations range from 172 feet to 500 feet above sea level. The deep, alluvial soils have gravel, sand, and loam components and good drainage. Rutherford has forty-eight wineries and seventy-seven vineyard owners. The grapes spend much of their days in direct sunlight. Diurnal temperature variations set in swiftly, though, and temperatures may drop 12 degrees Fahrenheit just minutes after sunset and continue to drop into the night.

ST. HELENA AVA

Shaped like a pear, St. Helena achieved AVA status in 1995, but its winemaking past dates to 1861 and the founding of Charles Krug's winery. By 1880 more than a hundred people were producing wine in this area named for Mount St. Helena. Other wineries surviving from that era are Spottswoode Estate (originally called Kraft Winery), founded in 1882; Freemark Abbey, also established under another name in 1886; and Beringer Vineyards, established the same year.

Vineyards range in elevation from 100 to 700 feet. Summer days are mostly warm, and temperatures can approach 100 degrees Fahrenheit. Soils in the west and center are sedimentary, with compositions of gravel and clay, whereas those on the east side are volcanic. There are fifty wineries and thirty growers in the St. Helena AVA. Cabernet Sauvignon is the top variety, followed by Sauvignon Blanc, Merlot, and Cabernet Franc.

The small city of St. Helena has some of the finest restaurants and cafés in the valley. The imposing West Coast campus of the Culinary Institute of America is also here, as is the famed Meadowood Resort.

SPRING MOUNTAIN DISTRICT AVA

The first recorded grape growing occurred here, in the 25-acre La Perla Vineyard, in 1874. The Beringer brothers planted vines on Spring Mountain in the mid-1880s, and a few years later Frenchman Fortune Chevalier built a winery and began growing vines on 25 acres. Around the same time, San Francisco businessman Tiburcio Parrott started Miravalle. Today three of these original vineyards—Miravalle, La Perla, and Chevalier—are part of Spring Mountain Vineyard.

Named for the many springs and streams that run through its terrain, Spring Mountain receives more rainfall than any other area in Napa Valley. Vineyard altitudes begin at 600 feet and climb to 2,600 feet. Maritime breezes from the Pacific keep it cool. Most vineyards lie above the fog line, so mornings on east-facing slopes can run quite warm. Soils are alluvial at lower elevations and closest to the valley floor, transitioning to sedimentary heading westward and moving upward, with volcanic soils in the higher, more westerly vineyards.

There are thirty wineries here; the most frequently planted variety is Cabernet Sauvignon, followed by Chardonnay, Merlot, and Riesling. Spring Mountain District gained AVA recognition in 1993.

STAGS LEAP DISTRICT AVA

This AVA has no apostrophe in its name, though two similarly named wineries in its boundaries do. Grapes have been grown here since the mid-nineteenth century, and the area's first winery, Occidental Winery (now Regusci Winery), was built in 1878. Horace Chase founded Stags' Leap in 1893. By the end of that century, it was bottling 40,000 gallons of wine a year—before phylloxera and Prohibition took their toll, that is. (Today Treasury Wine Estates owns it.) In the early 1960s, Nathan Fay planted 70 acres of Cabernet Sauvignon near the Silverado Trail, and in 1976 a Stag's Leap Wine Cellars Cabernet Sauvignon took first place at the Judgment of Paris, catapulting the region's reputation into the stratosphere. AVA status came in February 1989.

Home to twenty wineries, the Stags Leap District AVA vineyards lie at or near sea level, rising to 500 feet as they head eastward. Stags Leap is planted with mostly red Bordeaux varieties, with the district's largest plantings Cabernet Sauvignon and Merlot, followed by Sauvignon Blanc. Chardonnay and Sangiovese are grown as well.

WILD HORSE VALLEY AVA

Vineyards in the small Wild Horse Valley AVA range in elevation from 400 to 1,500 feet, and soils are volcanic with red pigmentation, typical of basalt. Granted official status in 1988, Wild Horse Valley AVA has one winery, and its best varieties to date are Cabernet Sauvignon and Sangiovese, which benefit from hot days tempered by the cooling effects of nearby Suisun and San Pablo bays.

YOUNTVILLE AVA

Originally called Yount Mill, Yountville is named for George Calvert Yount, who planted the first commercial vineyard in Napa Valley in 1836. Today downtown Yountville boasts a population of about 3,000 and four Michelin-starred restaurants. As such, it's said to have the highest ratio of Michelin stars per square mile of any town or city in the world. Yountville achieved AVA recognition in 1999.

The lowest lying of any appellation in Napa County, Yountville has vineyards that start at 20 feet above sea level and rise to 200. Soils are volcanic in the east; alluvial and sedimentary, with areas of sandy loam, gravel-based loam, and clay in the west. San Pablo Bay generates cool air currents that move north throughout the day. Cabernet Sauvignon, Merlot, and Cabernet Franc lead the pack, but Malbec and Petit Verdot are cultivated as well, as are Zinfandel, Syrah, Petite Sirah, Chardonnay, and Sauvignon Blanc.

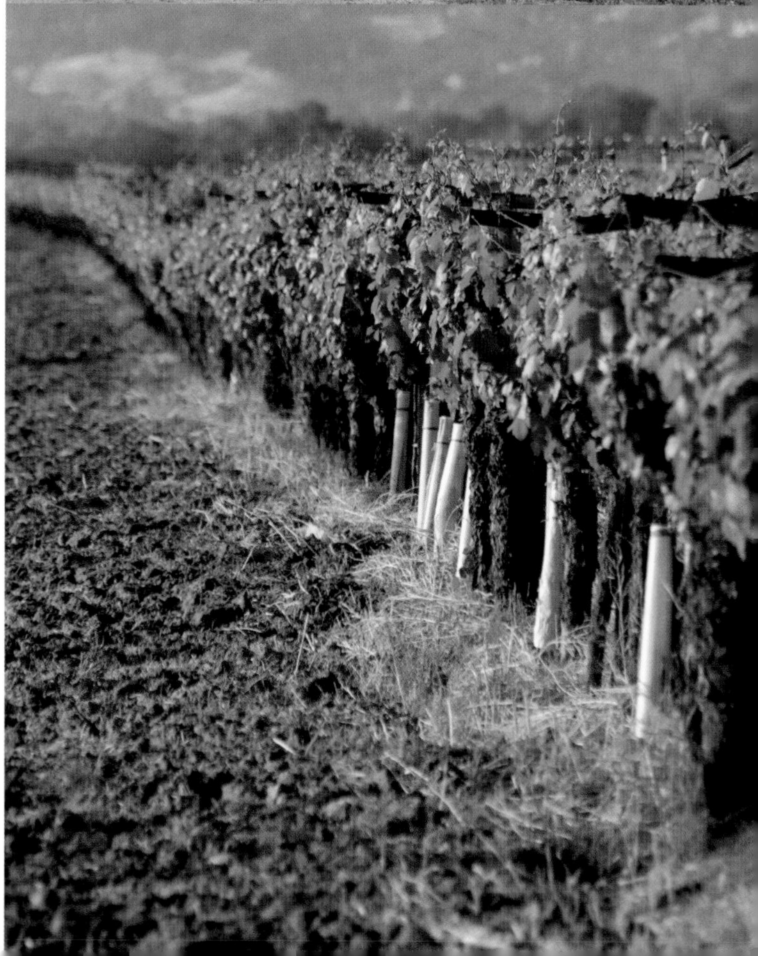

THE WINERIES

ACACIA VINEYARDS

2750 Las Amigas Road, Napa, CA 94559
(707) 226-9991, www.acaciavineyard.com

Started in 1979 by Mike Richmond and Larry Brooks, Acacia was one of the first California wineries to designate its Pinot Noir by vineyard. The estate consists of 150 acres planted with Chardonnay and Pinot Noir. Senior winemaker Matthew Glynn's experience in New Zealand and France influences the style of the vineyard's wines. The crisp, clean Acacia Vineyard Chardonnay Carneros offers flavors of caramelized apples and toasted cashews, and the full-flavored Acacia Vineyard Estate Pinot Noir Carneros Lone Tree Vineyard tastes of ripe sour cherry and cherry jam.

ANCIEN

P.O. Box 10667, Napa, CA 94581
(707) 255-3908, www.ancienwines.com

Ken Bernards worked his first harvest in 1986 in Oregon and then went on to work at Truchard Vineyards. In 1998 he began making Pinot Noir, Chardonnay, and Pinot Gris under his own Ancien label. Ken's experimental style has taken him around the world and prompted him to import whole grapes from France to vinify in California. Ancien has long-term contracts with ten family-owned vineyards in eight appellations, including Morey St. Denis in Burgundy. Ancien Carneros Sangiacomo Vineyard Pinot Gris has pronounced citrus flavors and a clean lingering finish. The bright, refreshing Ancien Sta. Rita Hills Fiddlestix Vineyard Pinot Noir presents notes of orange zest and ripe black cherry.

ANDERSON'S CONN VALLEY VINEYARDS

680 Rossi Road, St. Helena, CA 94574
(707) 963-8600, www.connvalleyvineyards.com

The Anderson family has owned and operated Anderson's Conn Valley Vineyards since 1983. Their Conn Valley estate consists of 40 acres just south of Howell Mountain. They're well-known for their Bordeaux-style blends as well as crisp, clean Chardonnay that doesn't undergo malolactic fermentation. Their Conn Valley Vineyards Napa Valley Chardonnay proffers aromas of white stone fruits and fresh pineapple; the Conn Creek Napa Valley St. Helena Holystone Vineyard Cabernet Sauvignon tastes of dried herbs and dark cocoa powder in the finish; and the Conn Creek Napa Valley Anthology blend offers flavors of dark berries and a touch of creamy vanilla.

ANTICA NAPA VALLEY

3700 Soda Canyon Road, Napa, CA 94558
(707) 265-8866, www.anticanapavalley.com

Piero Antinori first visited Napa Valley in 1966 and returned from Italy 20 years later as part owner in a joint venture with France's Bollinger and England's Whitbread companies. In 1993 he bought out his partners, and in 2006 he named the estate Antica, the Italian word for "ancient" and a combination of "Antinori" and "California." The name symbolizes the family's long-term commitment to making fine wines. The richly flavored Antica Napa Valley Chardonnay tastes of pear, and Antica Napa Valley Pinot Noir has a touch of freshly ground black pepper and baking spices underlying rich fruit flavors. ❶

ARAUJO ESTATE

2155 Pickett Road, Calistoga, CA 94515
(707) 942-6061, www.araujoestatewines.com

In the northeast corner of Napa Valley, Araujo Estate consists of 38 acres of the Eislele Vineyard, established more than 120 years ago and replanted with Cabernet Sauvignon in 1964. Bart and Daphne Araujo took over in 1990 and sold the estate to the Pinault family of Bordeaux's Château Latour in 2013. Wine consultant Michel Rolland joined the team in 2000, and Araujo produces estate-grown wines. The Araujo Estate Eisele Vineyard Napa Valley Cabernet Sauvignon has flavors of sweet stone fruits and a long, luxurious finish, while the Araujo Estate Eisele Vineyard Napa Valley Syrah offers flavors of Asian spice, dried ginger, and bitter chocolate.

ARIETTA

3468 Silverado Trail, St. Helena, CA 94574
(707) 963-5918, www.ariettawine.com

Noted wine auctioneer Fritz Hatton added the title of vintner to his repertoire in 1998. He and wife, Caren, partnered initially with John and Maggy Kongsgaard but assumed sole ownership in 2005. Current winemaker Andy Erickson has been with them since then. The names of the wines reflect the Hattons' passion for music. The Arietta portfolio includes four reds—Quartet, Cabernet Sauvignon, Variation One, and H Block Hudson—as well as one white, On the White Keys. The elegant Arietta Quartet has ripe fruit notes, and the Arietta on the White Keys offers flavors of caramelized pineapple and tropical fruits.

ARTESA VINEYARDS & WINERY

1345 Henry Road, Napa, CA 94559
(707) 224-1668, www.artesawinery.com

Artesa began as Codorniu Napa in 1991 to make quality sparkling wine by the Champenoise method. The owners, the Ravento family from Spain, changed the name to Artesa Vineyards & Winery in 1997. Mark Beringer headed winemaking until recently and the current team crafts wines made from Cabernet Sauvignon, Merlot, Chardonnay, Pinot Noir, Pinot Blanc, and Cabernet Franc as well as limited-release wines from Albariño and Tempranillo. The Artesa Vineyards & Winery Artisan Series Cabernet Sauvignon exhibits aromas of black plums and black currants, and the Artesa Vineyards & Winery Carneros Pinot Noir offers notes of fresh red cherry and dried black cherry.

AUGUST BRIGGS WINERY

1307 Lincoln Avenue, Calistoga, CA 94515
(707) 942-4912, www.augustbriggswines.com

August "Joe" Briggs founded his winery in 1995, sourcing some of the best grapes in Napa Valley to make his small-batch artisanal wines. He and wife, Sally, handed control of the winery to their nephew and co-winemaker Jesse Inman as well as other longtime employees in 2011, making it employee-owned. The team also makes boutique wines for racecar driver Jeff Gordon. The August Briggs Carneros Leveroni Vineyard Chardonnay offers flavors of apple, melon, and creamy lemon curd, and the August Briggs Napa Valley Old Vines Zinfandel has fruit flavors accented with espresso bean and chocolate. 2

6

1

34

59

24

29

40

69

21
CUVAISON
TASTING ROOM

15

B CELLARS

400 Silverado Trail, Calistoga, CA 94515
(707) 709-8787, www.bcellars.com

Jim Borsack and Duffy Keys founded B (for "Brix") Cellars in 2003, and Kirk Venge directs winemaking. The B Cellars Caldwell's Kreuzer Canyon Syrah offers flavors of black raspberry and black currant, and the crisp B Cellars Blend 23 proffers a pineapple aroma and lemon curd flavor.

BACIO DIVINO CELLARS

P.O. Box 131, Rutherford, CA 94573
(707) 942-8101, www.baciodivino.com

Claus Janzen began his love affair with wine while working during ski season in Switzerland's Berner Oberland. After moving his family from Winnipeg to Napa, he made his first vintage of Bacio Divino Sangiovese in 1993. Claus; wife, Diane; son Kyle; winemaker, Kirk Venge; and vineyard manager, David Bartolucci, make wines under five labels: Bacio Divino, Pazzo, Vagabond, Janzen, and Lucie. The Janzen Beckstoffer Missouri Hopper Vineyard Napa Valley Cabernet Sauvignon offers aromas of ripe black cherries, black currants, and cherry vanilla. 3

BARNETT VINEYARDS

4070 Spring Mountain Road, St. Helena, CA 94574
(707) 963-7075, www.barnettvineyards.com

Hal and Fiona Barnett purchased this property in 1983, producing 100 cases of wine in 1989. Today total production is around 6,000 cases, about half dedicated to Cabernet Sauvignon. They also produce small amounts of single-vineyard Chardonnay, Pinot Noir, and Merlot with fruit sourced from other appellations. The estate vineyards grow Cabernet Sauvignon, Cabernet Franc, and Merlot and are farmed by hand because of the steep grades at the top of Spring Mountain. The Barnett Vineyards Spring Mountain Cabernet Sauvignon offers aromas of black currants and black plums, and the Barnett Vineyards Rattlesnake Hill Cabernet Sauvignon has rich notes of black fruits and baking spices. Enjoy the latter now, or age it for 10 to 15 years.

BEAULIEU VINEYARD

1960 St. Helena Highway, Rutherford, CA 94573
(707) 967-5233, www.bvwines.com

Georges de Latour's wife, Fernande, unwittingly named the property in 1900 when she uttered the words *"beau lieu,"* meaning beautiful place. They set out to create Napa Valley wines equal in quality to those of their French homeland. Since then, Beaulieu Vineyard, one of Napa's historic wineries, has been making quality wines. (It survived Prohibition by making sacramental wine.) In 1938, de Latour traveled to France and returned with André Tchelistcheff, who revolutionized winemaking practices for Beaulieu and the whole valley. By the 1940s the White House was serving Beaulieu wines at major events. The Georges de Latour Private Reserve Cabernet Sauvignon offers aromas of black cherry, black plum, and candied violet and the Beaulieu Vineyard Maestro Collection Cabernet Sauvignon and Syrah Blend has flavors of black raspberry and black pepper with a touch of white chocolate in the finish.

BENESSERE VINEYARDS

1010 Big Tree Road, St. Helena, CA 94574
(707) 963-5853, www.benesserevineyards.com

The Benish family bought this property in 1994 to make Italian-style wines. The estate plantings include Zinfandel, Syrah, Merlot, Cabernet Sauvignon, Sangiovese, Moscato di Canelli, and Sagrantino. Grapes sourced from neighbors go into Benessere's Aglianico and Pinot Grigio. Leo Martinez directs winemaking along with wine consultant Alberto Antonini. The light, crisp Benessere Napa Valley Carneros Pinot Grigio is perfect alone or with fresh seafood. The Benessere Napa Valley Sagrantino offers notes of black plums, cassis, and black raspberries.

BERINGER

2000 Main Street, St. Helena, CA 94574
(707) 967-4412, www.beringer.com

Jacob Beringer's brother Frederick emigrated from Mainz, Germany, to New York and wrote letters to his younger brother detailing the exciting opportunities in the New World. Succumbing to his older brother's wishes, Jacob crossed the Atlantic in 1868. Not impressed with New York City, Jacob ended up in Napa Valley in 1870, and Frederick followed suit. The brothers bought land in 1875 and founded Beringer Winery in 1876. Frederick built a replica of his family home, and today the seventeen-room Rhine House mansion hosts Beringer's reserve and library tastings. Jacob's house, Hudson House, is home to the Beringer Vineyards Culinary Arts Center.

One of the oldest continuously operating wineries in the Napa Valley, the estate is listed on the National Register of Historic Places. Treasury Wine Estates bought Beringer in 2011, and in April 2015 Mark Beringer, great-great-grandson of founder Jacob, became the chief winemaker, replacing Laurie Hook, who took on the role of winemaker emerita. The Beringer Napa Valley Private Reserve Chardonnay has aromas of caramelized pineapple and toasted almonds, and the Beringer Napa Valley Private Reserve Cabernet Sauvignon offers heady aromas of rich, ripe dark fruits.

BLACKBIRD VINEYARDS

1330 Oak Knoll Avenue, Napa, CA 94558
(707) 252-4444, www.blackbirdvineyards.com

Before Michael Polenske bought Blackbird Vineyards and began making wine under his own label in 2003, many of the Merlot grapes grown here went into wines made by other wineries. The Blackbird Vineyards Arise proffers aromas of ripe black cherry and black plum, and the Blackbird Vineyards Arriviste Rosé has pronounced flavors of freshly picked summer fruits. 4

BLACK STALLION WINERY

4089 Silverado Trail, Napa, CA 94558
(707) 253-1400, www.blackstallionwinery.com

Sitting on the historic Silverado Horseman's Center property, Black Stallion winery came under the stewardship of the Indelicato Family in 2010. Visitors can see the thirty-six original horse stalls and witness wine production in the former indoor horse track. The estate vineyards surrounding the winery are planted to three different Cabernet Sauvignon clones, and you can taste Black Stallion wines at the large round tasting bar or sit on the landscaped outdoor terrace. The Black Stallion Winery Bucephalus Red Blend has flavors of deep, dark ripe fruits and a touch of vanilla, while the Black Stallion Winery Napa Valley Merlot offers flavors of black plum, ripe red cherries, and dark chocolate. 5

BOND ESTATES

P.O. Box 426, Oakville, CA 94562
(707) 944-9445, www.bondestates.com

The team at Bond Estates crafts wines from five Napa Valley vineyards—Melbury, Quella, St. Eden, Vecina, and Pluribus—which share a commitment to producing the best expressions of *terroir* in winemaking. The team consists of proprietor H. William Harlan of Harlan Estates, winemaker Cory Empting, vineyard manager Mary Maher, and director of winegrowing Robert Levy. The Bond Melbury Napa Valley offers aromas of freshly picked black cherries, red plums, and red cherries, and the Bond Vecina Napa Valley presents a nose of red fruits laced with a whiff of peppermint. 6

In his own words

MARK BERINGER

Mark Beringer is a fifth-generation Napa Valley winemaker. The great-great-grandson of Jacob Beringer, Mark was vice president of production and winemaking at Artesa Vineyards and Winery at the time of this interview but became chief winemaker at Beringer in April 2015.

My great-great-grandfather cofounded Beringer Vineyards in 1876, and the wine business has been in my family for generations. I began my training early working in my parents' wine store, went on to work in my uncle's winery doing various cellar jobs, and then after studying enology at California State University, Fresno, joined Glen Ellen Winery, then Duckhorn Vineyards, before coming to work at Artesa in 2009.

The biggest change to me has been the shift from family-owned-and-operated wineries to the consolidation of brands that has created mammoth companies that produce huge volumes of wines. I am excited to see that there is never a shortage of new brands being developed. Even as old brands get consolidated away, new fledgling brands emerge on the market. I am lucky to work for an international company with its roots in Spain, so I do get to travel and work with our other winemakers in Europe and Argentina. Working alongside my international counterparts, I have learned the value of a well-balanced wine that pairs well with many types of food. Wine is an integral part of the daily meals in Europe, something that is evolving and gaining momentum in the United States.

With so many wonderful winery properties in both Napa and Sonoma it is a challenge to establish a point of differentiation from wineries. Also, we seem to be challenged every vintage by Mother Nature. Climate change has made things much less predictable in the last 10 years or so, and weather events seem to be more extreme than before. It has even been suggested that our area may no longer be able to grow such premium grapes due to the shift in climate. Another challenge worth mentioning is limitations to direct shipping due to state laws and regulations.

The philosophy of winemaking at Artesa is to always be true to the place where the grapes were grown. The wine should always overdeliver in the glass and have the potential to be enjoyed with food or without. We use a variety of both traditional and modern techniques to create our wines. The modern ones allow us to control temperature, avoid contamination, and lower our risks. The traditional ones allow us to make wines that are true to their place and express their *terroir.* We avoid any technique that is designed to manipulate the wine's flavor. Fermentations are conducted in both stainless-steel and wood vessels, with many types of yeast, and with different temperatures. These techniques create a palate of component wines with a variety of aromas and flavors. We then step into the artistic realm of winemaking as we create blends from the dozens of separate lots we created during the year. Blending is the time when a winemaker is truly able to express his or her artistic side and form the finished wine into the masterpiece they have envisioned from the day the grapes were harvested.

A winemaker can make the best wines, but it hardly matters if nobody wants to buy them. However, I also feel that wines should never be forced into a mold that has been created by a marketing ideal and should always reflect where they came from. I also really enjoy drinking wines from all over the world, like the Scala Dei wines from Priorat, Spain. It fascinates me to see that there can be so many differences in what seems to be such a simple ancient beverage.

BOUCHAINE VINEYARD

1075 Buchli Station Road, Napa, CA 94559
(707) 252-9065, www.bouchaine.com

Early settler Boon Fly first planted vines here in the 1800s. Italian immigrant Johnny Garetto bought the property in 1927 and opened the area's first tasting room, selling to Beringer in 1951. When Gerret and Tatiana Copeland took over in 1981, they extensively renovated the original structures and hired current general manager and winemaker Michael Richmond. The Bouchaine Estate Napa Valley–Carneros Chardonnay has a generous mouthfeel, with a light touch of vanilla, and the velvety Bouchaine Copeland Estate Napa Valley Carneros Pinot Noir offers notes of fresh red cherries and dried black cherries. 7

BRYANT FAMILY VINEYARD

1567 Sage Canyon Road, St. Helena, CA 94574
(707) 963-0483, www.bryantwines.com

Art collector and CEO of the Bryant Group, Donald L. Bryant Jr. bought this property in 1985 and recognized its potential for grape growing. Helen Turley was the first winemaker, and the first vintage release was in 1992. Other luminary winemakers have included Philippe Melka, Mark Aubert, and Helen Keplinger. Wine consultant Michel Rolland has been with the winery since 2002 and works closely with head winemaker Todd Alexander. The Bryant Family Vineyard Cabernet Sauvignon offers bold yet restrained dark fruit flavors, and the fruit-forward Bryant Family Vineyard Bettina, named for Donald's wife, offers aromas of ripe dark fruits and black plums. 8

BUCCELLA

P.O. Box 11, Yountville, CA 94599
(707) 944-1000, www.buccella.com

Founders Bill and Alicia Deem still have the cork from the bottle of Gaja they shared on their first date. It reminds them every day that dreams really do come true. "Buccella" means "mouthful" in Latin and evokes the spirit of their big, bold wines. The Buccella Napa Valley Cabernet Sauvignon, offering aromas of cherry liqueur and blueberry pie, drinks nicely now and will continue to do so through the next 10 to 12 years. 9

BURGESS CELLARS

1108 Deer Park Road, St. Helena, CA 94574
(707) 963-4766, www.burgesscellars.com

After traveling Europe in the 1960s, Tom Burgess bought a small winery and called Napa Valley home in 1972. His wines are produced from grapes sourced from two vineyards on Howell Mountain and Triere Vineyard in the Oak Knoll District. Winemaking has fallen under the direction of Bill Sorenson since the winery's inception. The Burgess Cellars Estate Vineyards Reserve Napa Valley offers a mouthful of fruit flavors with a touch of black pepper, and the Burgess Cellars Estate Napa Valley Cabernet Sauvignon has aromas of toasted vanilla and black cherry.

CADE ESTATE WINERY

360 Howell Mountain Road South, Angwin, CA 94508
(707) 945-1220, www.cadewinery.com

Founded in 2005 by John Conover, Gordon Getty, and Gavin Newsom, Cade Estate Winery, the first gold-certified Leadership in Energy and Environmental Design (LEED) winery in the Napa Valley, is a sister winery to PlumpJack. The estate's name comes from a Shakespearean term for barrels used to transport Bordeaux wine from France to England, and the estate consists of 21 acres planted with Cabernet Sauvignon and Merlot vines. The Cade Winery Napa Valley Sauvignon Blanc has flavors of lemon confit and green apple, and the Cade Winery Cuvée Cabernet Sauvignon Napa Valley offers flavors of black raspberry, mocha, and cherry vanilla ice cream.

In his own words

PETER MONDAVI SR.

A wine world legend, Peter Mondavi Sr., son of Cesare and Rosa, attended Stanford University, graduated in 1938, and studied cold fermentation at the University of California at Berkeley. He receives credit for many innovations used in the California winemaking process, including cold fermentation and sterile filtration.

Having grown up in the grape-growing area of Lodi and being Italian, it was a natural business for my father and mother and we children. When Prohibition was repealed, it was a question of learning the production along with the sale of wine. I researched cold fermentation of white grape juice at the University of California at Berkeley. This maintained the fruity character of the white juice. Upon my graduation from Stanford in 1937, I did laboratory work and assisted the winemaker at Woodbridge Winery for about two years, after which time I was employed as assistant winemaker at Acampo Winery and Distillery until 1942, when I was drafted into the Army for World War II. I was released from the Army in 1946 and was soon employed as winemaker at Charles Krug Winery, which my father purchased in 1943. My brother, Robert, was the general manager.

I was the first person in Napa Valley to purchase and use French oak barrels in 1963. The ambassador to France, who owned a boutique winery in Sonoma County (Hanzell), was the first person in Sonoma County to use French oak barrels; that is where I had the opportunity to taste Chardonnay aged in French oak. Up until that time I had high hopes about the quality of French oak barrels for all wines but was hesitant at the cost of $35 per barrel. The tasting of Chardonnay in Sonoma County convinced me of the quality regardless of the price.

Over these past 10 to 15 years the economy improved and wineries, especially the boutique wineries, concentrated on soils best suited for the Bordeaux varieties, which were the most respected varieties. With the improved economy the wealthy wine enthusiasts could afford to establish boutique wineries for the expensive hillside mountain vineyards, which were found to have excellent soil for the desired Bordeaux grape varieties. Napa Valley has great soil and climate conditions overall, but the mountain vineyards have proved to be the best for the Bordeaux varieties along with certain valley areas. The improved economy has been a major factor in the relocating of vineyards in the hills. We ourselves have gradually developed hillside vineyards. It's an expensive operation, but the quality warrants the expense. Hillside and mountain vineyards are very expensive but have their place, while the valley vineyards offer quality at a more reasonable price. This presents a good balance for us. We hope to add a few more mountain vineyards as our business warrants it. I keep saying one has to enjoy wine in spite of its many challenges. But if you love it, it's well worth it.

CAIN VINEYARD AND WINERY

3800 Langtry Road, St. Helena, CA 94574
(707) 963-1616, www.cainfive.com

Joyce and Jerry Cain bought more than 500 acres of the historic McCormick Ranch in 1980 and planted Cabernet Franc, Merlot, Malbec, Petit Verdot, and Cabernet Sauvignon. Their first vintage was 1985, and the next year they partnered with Nancy and Jim Meadlock, who have run the day-to-day business since the Cains' 1991 retirement. Christopher Howell makes the wines. The Cain Vineyard and Winery Cain Five has aromas of black raspberry and cassis, and the Cain Vineyard and Winery Cain Concept–The Benchland offers notes of black cherry, baking spices, and espresso bean. 10

CAKEBREAD CELLARS

8300 St. Helena Highway, Rutherford, CA 94573
(707) 963-5221, www.cakebread.com

Auto mechanic and photographer Jack Cakebread accepted a commission for Nathan Chroman's 1972 book *The Treasury of American Wines*. Cakebread fell in love with Napa, and he and his wife, Dolores, bought property and began splitting their time between Cakebread's Garage in Oakland and Cakebread Cellars. In 1979 their son Bruce became winemaker. Designed in 1985, the winery expanded in 1995 and 2007. The Cakebread Cellars Dancing Bear Ranch Howell Mountain Napa Valley Cabernet Sauvignon, with flavors of dark fruit, is delightful now and will improve over the next 7 to 10 years. The Cakebread Cellars Napa Valley Cabernet Sauvignon exhibits notes of black fruits, black currant, and black figs. 11

CARDINALE

7600 St. Helena Highway, Oakville, CA 94562
(707) 948-2643, www.cardinale.com

Winemaker Christopher Carpenter makes only one Cabernet Sauvignon each year, using fruit sourced from the higher slopes of Mount Veeder, Howell Mountain, Diamond Mountain, and Spring Mountain. His Cardinale offers generous fruit and dark chocolate flavors; drink it now, or age it for 15 years—you won't be disappointed either way.

CASTELLO DI AMOROSA

4045 North St. Helena Highway, Calistoga, CA 94515
(707) 942-8200, www.castellodiamorosa.com

Owner Dario Sattui began building his dream property, in the style of a medieval Tuscan castle, in 1995 after researching ancient building techniques in Italy. After years of building challenges, Castello di Amorosa opened its doors to the public in 2007. The wines are made with fruit from vines planted between 1994 and 1996. The Castello di Amorosa La Castellana offers pronounced red fruit flavors and a luxurious finish, and the Castello di Amorosa Il Barone Reserve Cabernet Sauvignon, Napa Valley has luscious aromas of black plum, cassis, and fennel bulb. 12

CAYMUS

8700 Conn Creek Road, Rutherford, CA 94573
(707) 963-4204, www.caymus.com

Charlie and Lorna Belle Glos Wagner planned to sell their ranch and move to Australia in 1971 if son Chuck declined their offer to set up a family winery, but Chuck said yes, and Caymus has been producing Cabernet Sauvignon since 1972. Their first vintage produced only 240 cases, but today the family-owned company produces 65,000 cases of wine per year. The Caymus Napa Valley Cabernet Sauvignon has flavors of black plum, ripe black cherries, and cola.

CEJA VINEYARDS

1248 1st Street, Napa, CA 94559
(707) 255-3954, www.cejavineyards.com

Mexican immigrants Pablo and Juanita Ceja and their children pooled their resources and purchased 15 acres of land in 1983. Soon after, they planted Pinot Noir and celebrated their first harvest in 1988. Today the family has three generations in California, owns 113 acres of vines, and produces Pinot Noir, Chardonnay, Syrah, Sauvignon Blanc, Merlot, and Cabernet Sauvignon. The Ceja Carneros Pinot Noir offers flavors of dried cherries and black raspberries, and the Ceja Carneros Merlot has aromas of red plums and dark chocolate. (13)

CHAPPELLET WINERY

1581 Sage Canyon Road, St. Helena, CA 94574
(707) 286-4219, www.chappellet.com

It's generally agreed that Donn and Molly Chappellet were the first to follow André Tchelistcheff's advice and plant vines on Pritchard Hill in 1967. Since 1990, winemaking has fallen under the direction of Phillip Corallo-Titus, who separately ferments and ages different vineyard blocks to achieve the *terroir's* full potential. Chappellet's portfolio includes its famous Cabernet Sauvignon as well as Cabernet Franc, Chenin Blanc, Merlot, and Chardonnay. The Chappellet Pritchard Hill Estate Cabernet Sauvignon proffers notes of black currants, blackberry preserves, red plum, and licorice, and the Chappellet Napa Valley Chardonnay offers flavors of caramelized apples and butter. (14)

CHARLES KRUG

2800 Main Street, St. Helena, CA 94574
(800) 237-0033, www.charleskrug.com

Prussian immigrant Charles Krug, who founded his eponymous winery in 1861, receives credit for first adapting the cider press for winemaking, and his is considered the first commercial winery in Napa Valley. After his death, the winery was sold to James Moffitt, who sold it to Cesare Mondavi in 1943. Today the winery continues under the stewardship of Peter Mondavi Sr. and sons Peter Jr. and Marc. The Charles Krug Vintage Selection Estate Bottled Napa Valley Cabernet Sauvignon exhibits aromas of black currants, cherries, and mocha, and the Charles Krug Carneros Chardonnay has flavors of lemon custard and butterscotch with a bracing finish. (15)

CHATEAU MONTELENA

1429 Tubbs Lane, Calistoga, CA 94515
(707) 942-5105, www.montelena.com

Alfred L. Tubbs purchased 254 acres of land in 1882, planted vines, and built Chateau Montelena, named for its proximity to Mount St. Helena. In 1958 the Tubbs family sold the winery, which soon was sold again. Under the guidance of the late Jim Barrett and his son Bo, the château was modernized and the vineyards replanted. The Chateau Montelena Napa Valley Chardonnay has aromas of lemon-lime and Ruby Red grapefruit juice. The Chateau Montelena Estate Cabernet Sauvignon offers juicy fruit flavors and a touch of spice in the finish. (16)

CHIARELLO FAMILY VINEYARDS

6525 Washington Street, Yountville, CA 94599
(707) 256-0750, www.chiarellovineyards.com

Noted chef and television personality Michael Chiarello makes wine from old Zinfandel and Petite Sirah vines, some planted in the 1890s. The vineyards were restored to good health with the help of Larry Turley and are farmed organically. Chiarello Family concentrates on producing 2,000 cases of wine from estate-grown and single-vineyard fruit. Amigo Bob Cantisano directs vineyard management, and Thomas Rivers Brown has been winemaker since 2000. The Chiarello Family Vineyards Eileen Cabernet Sauvignon has rich aromas of black raspberries and brown baking spices, and the Chiarello Family Vineyards Bambino Cabernet Sauvignon proffers aromas of ripe black plums, black cherries, and black raspberries.

CHIMNEY ROCK WINERY

5350 Silverado Trail, Napa, CA 94558
(707) 257-2641, www.chimneyrock.com

Hack and Stella Wilson bought the 180-acre plot, which included a golf course, and quickly planted vines. Founded in 1980, Chimney Rock Winery brought their love of South African architecture to Napa Valley. Their first vintage was in 1989. The Terlato family has owned Chimney Rock since 2004, and today the estate consists of 119 acres of vines divided into twenty-eight blocks. Terlato vice president of winemaking Doug Fletcher and Chimney Rock winemaker Elizabeth Vianna carry out winemaking duties. The Chimney Rock Cabernet Sauvignon Stags Leap District has notes of cassis, black cherry, and baking spices, and the rich and full-bodied Chimney Rock Sauvignon Gris Stags Leap District offers aromas of guava and mango. 17

CIMAROSSA

1185 Friesen Road, Angwin, CA 94508
(707) 307-3130, www.cimarossa.com

Dino Dina and wife, Corry Dekker, met at a biotech company, and the two maintain their day jobs: Dina at Dynavax and Dekker at Stanford University and as an adviser to the CDC. Their winery name comes from the Italian word for "red hilltop." Mia Klein makes the wines, and the estate has terraced vineyards supplemented with olive trees that produce the estate-made olive oil. The Cimarossa Howell Mountain Riva di Ponente Cabernet Sauvignon has notes of blueberry, black plum, and black cherry, and the Cimarossa Howell Mountain Rian Cabernet Sauvignon offers aromas of dark fruits and anise. 18

In his own words

BO BARRETT

Winemaker Bo Barrett's illustrious career began in 1972 when his family bought the iconic Chateau Montelena and subsequently became known for its award-winning white wine in the Judgment of Paris. He is married to winemaker Heidi Peterson Barrett.

My dad bought Chateau Montelena the same year I graduated high school. I needed money because I was moving to Snowbird to begin my chosen full-time job riding the Snowbird Tram and skiing Utah powder. I needed a source of funds since this was naturally a nonpaying employment, so I went to work in the vineyards. I worked summer and fall at the winery for three or four years to fund my 100-day-a-year skiing job. And then the winemaking got in my blood. I went from Snowbird U to Fresno State in 1976 and have been winemaking full-time ever since.

To make great wine you need the right grape in the right place. The first time you plant a piece of ground it's a crapshoot, then the second planting is usually better, then by the third [time] around we can really fine-tune how to farm that land. Vineyards typically last about 20 years, so since 1972–73 you can do the math. It's been 40 years; so many great vineyards are in the third iteration and better than ever. Heidi and I picked up a piece of bare land close to a Chateau Montelena planting we had kept our eye on for years. It's extremely rocky, and it's the most exciting land I have planted in years.

Winemaking influences the market by making better and better wines, but we need to get paid to stay in business, so we need to make what people will buy, so the market is the final arbiter. Capture sunlight with the land, and put it in a bottle to make people's lives a little better one glass at a time.

CK MONDAVI AND SONS

2800 Main Street, St. Helena, CA 94574
(707) 967-2200, www.ckmondavi.com

Cesare and Rosa Mondavi purchased the Charles Krug winery in 1943 and started CK Mondavi with their sons Peter and Robert. At over a century old, Peter Mondavi Sr. continues to serve as company ambassador, with day-to-day business handled by third-generation sons, Marc and Peter Jr. John Moynier has been winemaker for more than 25 years. The crisp, clean CK Mondavi California Chardonnay has aromas of white stone fruit, and the CK Mondavi California Cabernet Sauvignon offers notes of black raspberry and black plum.

CLIFF LEDE VINEYARDS

1473 Yountville Cross Road, Yountville, CA 94599
(707) 944-8642, www.cliffledevineyards.com

Canadian Cliff Lede started making wine in his mother's basement in his twenties. His 60-acre property is planted to Cabernet Sauvignon, Merlot, Malbec, Petit Verdot, and Cabernet Franc, and his staff includes Chris Tynan as winemaker and Remi Cohen as viticulturist. The Cliff Lede Napa Valley Sauvignon Blanc tastes of tropical fruits. The Cliff Lede Poetry Napa Valley Stags Leap District Cabernet Sauvignon features fruit flavors with Indian spice and dark chocolate.

CLOS DU VAL

5330 Silverado Trail, Napa, CA 94558
(707) 261-5251, www.closduval.com

In 1970 John Goelet hired Bordeaux-raised Bernard Portet to search for land on which to build a wine estate. Their 1972 Cabernet Sauvignon was one of the six California Cabernet Sauvignons entered in the Judgment of Paris. In 1973 Goelet acquired a 178-acre winery property in the Stags Leap District and bought another 180 acres in Carneros. The Clos Du Val Winery Napa Valley Reserve Cabernet Sauvignon opens with luscious fruit intensity followed by flavors of espresso and black plum. The full-bodied Clos Du Val Winery Carneros Reserve Chardonnay offers notes of mango, guava, and pineapple and a clean, crisp finish. 19

CLOS PEGASE

1060 Dunaweal Lane, Calistoga, CA 94515
(707) 942-4981, www.clospegase.com

Jan Shrem made his living in Japan by translating English technical texts into Japanese, falling in love with the country and the woman who became his wife. He studied at the University of Bordeaux, moved to the United States, and enlisted the help of André Tchelistcheff. Jan and his wife, Mitsuko, bought their initial 50-acre estate in Calistoga in 1983. The family later acquired an additional 400 acres in Napa Valley and built a winery designed by architect Michael Graves. Clos Pegase is also well known for its art installations. In 2013, Shrem sold the winery to Vintage Wine Estates, backed by Leslie Rudd, owner of Dean & DeLuca and a fellow Napa Valley vintner. The long-finishing Clos Pegase Cabernet Sauvignon offers aromas of black plum, currant, and black cherry, and the Clos Pegase Mitsuko's Vineyard Pinot Noir has notes of red cherry, dried black cherry, and Christmas baking spices.

COLGIN CELLARS

P.O. Box 254, St. Helena, CA 94574
(707) 963-0999, www.colgincellars.com

With a master of arts from New York University, Ann Barry Colgin started using her talents to make art in the bottle in 1992, and she tirelessly promotes handcrafted, small-production wines. Today Colgin Cellars lies in the Pritchard Hill district and produces only four distinct wines: IX Estate Syrah, IX Estate Napa Valley Red Wine, Tychson Hill Vineyard Cabernet Sauvignon, and Cariad Napa Valley Red Wine. Ann keeps her hand in the art world by consulting with Sotheby's wine department and serving as a charity auctioneer. Her donations of library wine have raised more than $6 million at auction for health-care and art-minded charities. The Colgin Cellars IX Estate Syrah has aromas of black fruits and cured charcuterie, and the silky Colgin Cellars Tychson Hill Cabernet Sauvignon offers notes of anise and a burst of fruit flavors.

CONTINUUM

1677 Sage Canyon Road, St. Helena, CA 94574
(707) 944-8100, www.continuumestate.com

This 172-acre Mondavi property enjoys a privileged location atop Pritchard Hill. Only four varieties are grown on the property: Cabernet Sauvignon, Cabernet Franc, Petit Verdot, and Merlot. Tim Mondavi and his sister Marcia, along with their respective children and other family members, make only one quality wine per year. The big, bold Continuum offers aromas of blackberry, cassis, coffee bean, and anise.

COQUEREL FAMILY WINE ESTATES

3180 Highway 128, Calistoga, CA 94515
(707) 942-4534, www.coquerelwines.com

Clay and Brenda Cockerell visited Napa Valley on their wedding anniversary and fell in love with the region. They purchased grapes in 2004 and 2005 and made small quantities of white wine for family and friends. In 2008 they bought a second parcel of land to make red as well. Today Coquerel makes French-style wines from Petite Sirah, Merlot, Tempranillo, Verdelho, Chardonnay, and Sauvignon Blanc. The big and fruity Coquerel La Petite Sirah has aromas of black raspberry, black plum, and Christmas baking spices, and the crisp, clean Coquerel Verdelho offers aromas of tropical fruit and Ruby Red grapefruit.

CORISON WINERY

987 St. Helena Highway, St. Helena, CA 94574
(707) 963-0826, www.corison.com

Corison Winery is a small family operation. Winemaker Cathy Corison and husband, William Martin, run day-to-day operations and maintain their organically farmed Kronos Vineyard. Cathy's made the first vintage of her Cabernet in 1987. The Corison Cabernet Sauvignon tastes like a mouthful of blueberry pie sprinkled with powdered cocoa. The Corison Kronos Vineyard Cabernet Sauvignon offers fruit flavors with underlying notes of licorice, baking spices, and dark chocolate. [20]

COSENTINO WINERY

7415 St. Helena Highway, Yountville, CA 94599
(707) 921-2809, www.cosentinowinery.com

Established in 1980 and recognized by some historians as one of the first California wines to use the designation "Meritage," Cosentino Winery first made wines under the Cosentino Wine Company and Crystal Valley Cellars labels. Known for its Cabernet Sauvignon, Cabernet Franc, Chardonnay, Merlot, and Meritage wines, Cosentino moved to Yountville in 1990 to be closer to some of the growers with whom it has maintained long-term relationships. The Cosentino Winery Cabernet Sauvignon Napa County exhibits notes of cassis and black raspberry with a rich mouthfeel. The refreshing Cosentino Winery Chardonnay Napa Valley offers aromas of flan, caramelized sugar, and Granny Smith apples.

CUVAISON ESTATE

1221 Duhig Road, Napa, CA 94559
(707) 942-2455, www.cuvaison.com

Established in 1969 with 27 acres of vines in Calistoga, Cuvaison Estate quickly grew to more than 400 acres after its acquisition by the Swiss Schmidheiny family in 1979. In 1998 the family bought the historic Brandlin Ranch on Mount Veeder

In his own words
STÉPHANE DERENONCOURT

Stéphane Derenoncourt began his illustrious career as vineyard help and worked at a variety of French châteaux before becoming a winemaking consultant in 1999. Today he and his company consult for more than ninety wineries around the world, including wineries in France, India, Italy, Lebanon, California, and Virginia. He is considered by many to be one of the world's hottest winemakers, and recently he released his own California label, Derenoncourt California.

I am a self-taught man; I started as a vineyard worker in Fronsac (in the Gironde). At first I was pulling the vine shoots, then I learned to prune. I love pruning; it's giving the vine its shape and strength back for a new vintage. At 23 I got my first cellar job, and soon enough, at La Fleur Cailleau, the owner, Monsieur Barre, gave me free rein. Then I became cellarmaster and vineyard manager at Pavie-Macquin. From a small success to another one, in 1995 Stephan von Neipperg hired me at Canon-la-Gaffelière, and LaMondotte was being born: a 4.3-hectare parcel that did not get the authorization to be reattached to the château, forcing the count to build a cellar on site where its grapes had to be fermented. The *terroir* wine received quickly a phenomenal success and became what we call a "garage wine." I earned recognition. I started consulting in 1999; today we are twelve in the Derenoncourt team.

In California the climate is very sunny and can be hot. You have to preserve the freshness of the fruit to let the identity of the place express itself through the wine. When I first went to Lake County and more particularly to Red Hills, I saw there was something special the soil could give to the vines. Some sites have great potential to make *terroir* wines.

I like to make wines of *terroir* that reveal the identity of a place. There is no technical or rational definition to account for the word, but it starts out as a subsoil, a soil, and an exposure that generate a microclimate. Then the choice of plant material introduced by generations of growers through their experience and history, combined with the type of cultivation that promotes the vine taking firm root to the rock. All of these will draw out the identity of the locality and imprint it on the fruit, thus giving expression to a *terroir*. This could be interpreted as domesticating a place, but we are often reminded to stay humble before the complex work of nature.

and acquired 170 additional acres. Today Cuvaison is known for its state-of-the-art winery that uses solar energy. The velvety Cuvaison Carneros Chardonnay offers aromas of tropical fruits, orange, and lime zest. The Cuvaison Mount Veeder Cabernet Sauvignon has notes of black plums, dark cherry, espresso, and cassis. Drink it now, or age it for a few years. 21

DALLA VALLE VINEYARDS

P.O. Box 329, Oakville, CA 94562
(707) 944-2676, www.dallavallevineyards.com

Gustav and Naoko Dalla Valle acquired what became Dalla Valle Vineyards in 1982. They planted vines at an altitude of 400 feet and then moved on to winemaking. Andy Erickson directs winemaking with consulting enologist Michel Rolland. The Dalla Valle Vineyards Maya offers flavors of dark fruits and bittersweet chocolate; drink it now or in the next 20 years. The big, bold Dalla Valle Vineyards Cabernet Sauvignon has heady aromas of black currant, black plum, and Christmas baking spices. Also drink it now or age it for a decade or two.

DARIOUSH

4240 Silverado Trail, Napa, CA 94558
(707) 257-2345, www.darioush.com

Designed by architects Ardeshir and Roshan Nozari with stone from Persepolis, Darioush Winery welcomes all with Persian hospitality. Founded by Iranian civil engineer turned grocery store mogul Darioush Khaledi in 2004, the winery is known for its Bordeaux-style estate wines. Winemaker Steve Devitt sources grapes from 95 acres of estate-owned vineyards in the Mount Veeder, Oak Knoll, and Napa Valley AVAs. Darioush grows Shiraz, Merlot, Cabernet Sauvignon, Malbec, and Petit Verdot for its single-varietal and red blends as well as Chardonnay and Viognier for its handcrafted whites. The Darioush Duel entices with stone fruit flavors and a fruit-filled finish. The crisp, clean Darioush Signature Napa Valley Viognier has flavors of Granny Smith apples, carambola, and citrus. 22

DEL DOTTO VINEYARDS

1055 Atlas Peak Road, Napa, CA 94558
(707) 963-2134, www.deldottovineyards.com

On vacation in 1988, David and Yolanda Del Dotto fell in love with a historic Frank Lloyd Wright–designed house on 17 acres of land. Two years later, they planted Merlot, Cabernet Sauvignon, Cabernet Franc, and Sangiovese in honor of Dave's Italian heritage. Del Dotto is one of the few Napa Valley wineries making wine in clay amphorae buried in the ground. Visitors enjoy the underground caves and barrel-tasting experience. The crisply finishing Del Dotto Chardonnay has flavors of tropical fruits and almond paste, and the lovely Del Dotto Sonoma Coast Cinghiale Vineyard Pinot Noir has fruit on the palate and top notes of Indian spice and Earl Grey tea.

DERENONCOURT CALIFORNIA

335 West Lane, Angwin, CA 94508
(707) 363-7990, www.derenoncourtca.com

Wine consultant Stéphane Derenoncourt began making wine at Château Pavie-Macquin in Saint-Émilion in the early 1990s. He began producing quality California wine under his own name in 2006 and now owns two wineries, Derenoncourt California and Domaine de l'A in Bordeaux, while consulting for more than sixty wineries around the world. The Derenoncourt Stagecoach Vineyard Napa Valley Merlot offers flavors of ripe red cherries and boysenberries, and the Derenoncourt Meritage Là-Haut Napa Valley tastes of dark cassis berries and juicy black plums and will drink well over the next 15 years. 23

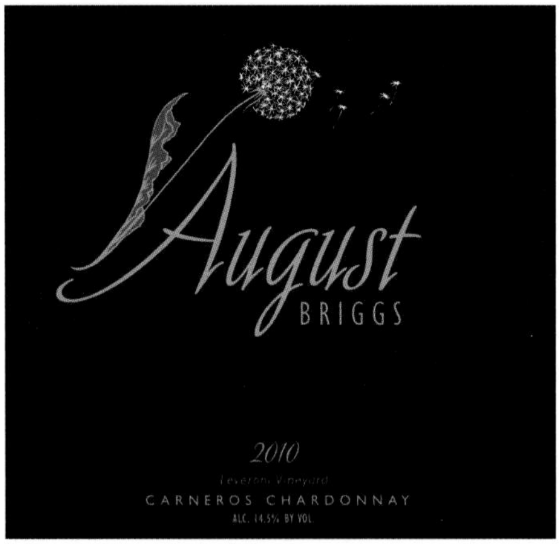
August
BRIGGS
2010
CARNEROS CHARDONNAY

2

janzen

3

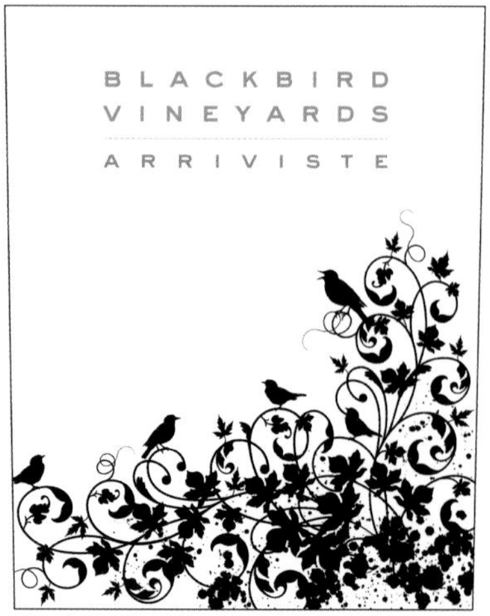
BLACKBIRD
VINEYARDS
ARRIVISTE

4

2009

9

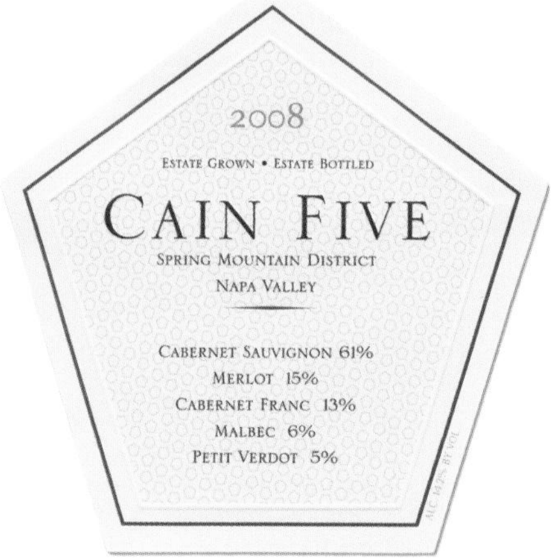
2008
ESTATE GROWN • ESTATE BOTTLED
CAIN FIVE
SPRING MOUNTAIN DISTRICT
NAPA VALLEY
CABERNET SAUVIGNON 61%
MERLOT 15%
CABERNET FRANC 13%
MALBEC 6%
PETIT VERDOT 5%

10

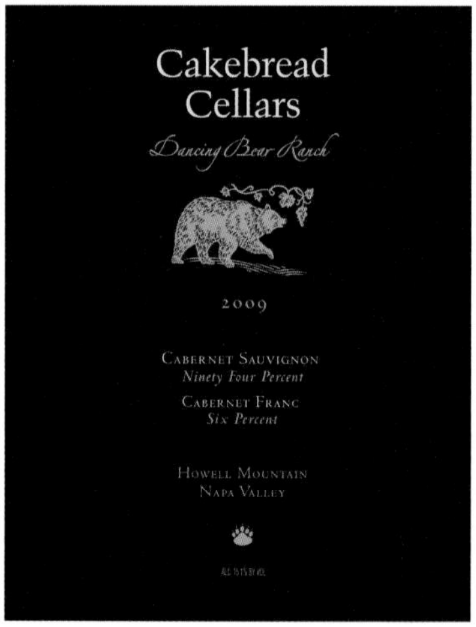
Cakebread
Cellars
Dancing Bear Ranch
2009
CABERNET SAUVIGNON
Ninety Four Percent
CABERNET FRANC
Six Percent
HOWELL MOUNTAIN
NAPA VALLEY

11

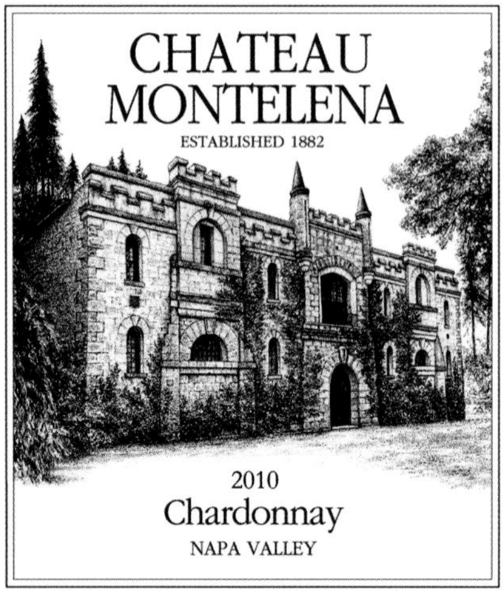
CHATEAU
MONTELENA
ESTABLISHED 1882
2010
Chardonnay
NAPA VALLEY

16

Chimney Rock®
Cabernet Sauvignon
Stags Leap District
Napa Valley
Appellation
ESTATE GROWN

17

Cimarossa
RIVE DI
CIMAROSSA
HOWELL MOUNTAIN
CABERNET SAUVIGNON

18

BLACK STALLION
WINERY
NAPA VALLEY
Merlot
2010
5

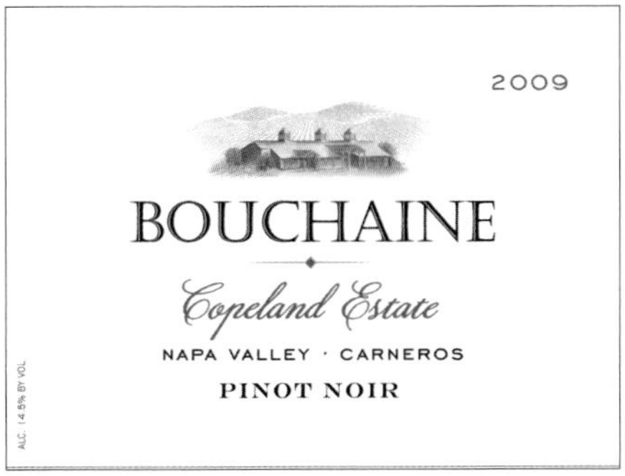
2009
BOUCHAINE
Copeland Estate
NAPA VALLEY · CARNEROS
PINOT NOIR
ALC. 14.5% BY VOL.
7

Proprietor Grown
2009
Bryant Family Vineyard
750 ML
CABERNET SAUVIGNON
NAPA VALLEY
ALC. 15% BY VOL.
8

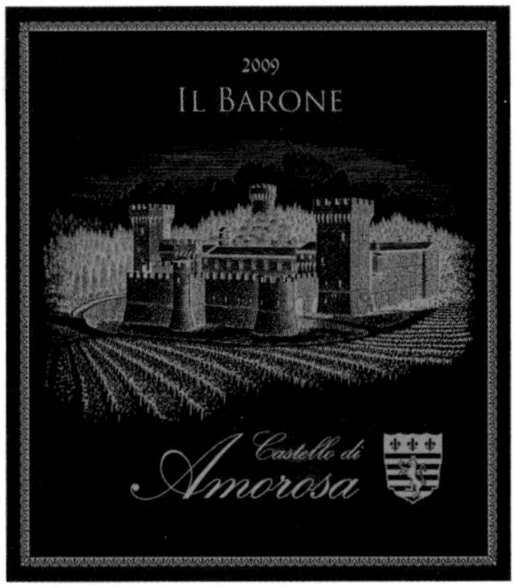
2009
IL BARONE
Castello di
Amorosa
12

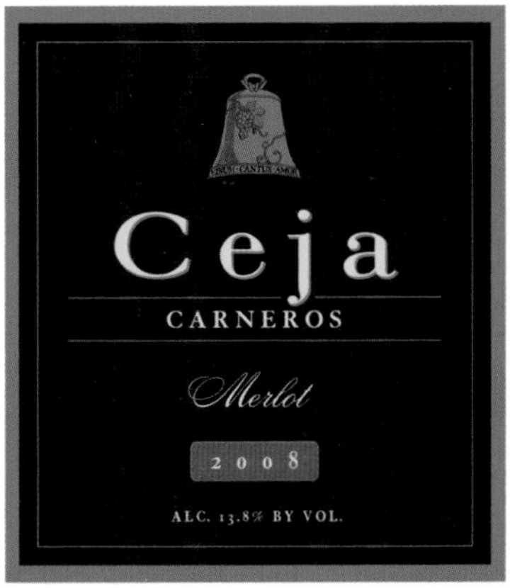
Ceja
CARNEROS
Merlot
2008
ALC. 13.8% BY VOL.
13

CHAPPELLET
Pritchard Hill
NAPA VALLEY 2009
CABERNET SAUVIGNON
14

Clos du Val
NapaValley
CABERNET SAUVIGNON
2008
19

2 0 0 8
CORISON
KRONOS VINEYARD
NAPA VALLEY
CABERNET
SAUVIGNON
ALC 13.8% BY VOL
20

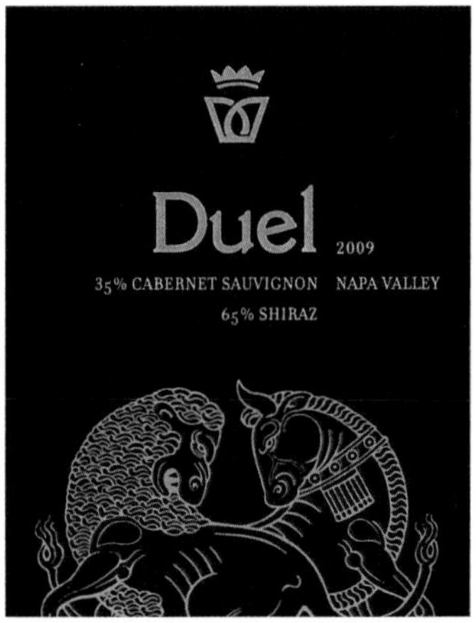
Duel
2009
35% CABERNET SAUVIGNON
NAPA VALLEY
65% SHIRAZ
22

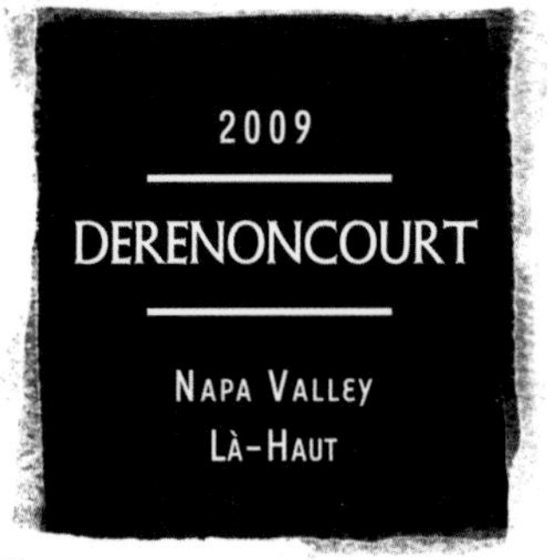
2009
DERENONCOURT
NAPA VALLEY
LÀ-HAUT
23

In her own words

EILEEN CRANE

Eileen Crane is often called America's Doyenne of Sparkling Wine. *The San Francisco Business Times* recognized her as one of the 75 Most Influential Women in Business.

My father had a wine cellar in New Jersey in the 1950s, which was very unusual. When I was about eight years old, he would let me taste a little wine at Sunday dinner. But little girls from New Jersey did not grow up to be winemakers. I assumed that to be a winemaker you needed to grow up in an Italian family in upstate New York, and you certainly were not a woman. So I went on to other jobs, such as social work in Venezuela. I went to the University of Connecticut and obtained a master's degree in nutrition in 1975. I then taught for the university for a couple of years and became very interested in the culinary arts. The CIA [Culinary Institute of America] had started in New Haven, Connecticut, and I knew a great deal about it and the women who had started it. So I took a summer off and went to the CIA for 10 weeks. There I was lucky enough to meet a real-life winemaker through the wine club. He had a book about winemaking from UC Davis, and I was intrigued. Could you study winemaking at Davis?

The first professor of enology at Davis I spoke with discouraged me. He said because I was a woman I would not be able to do the barrel work. He suggested I go to the nutrition department and enroll in a PhD program there. I said thank you, but I was going to be a winemaker. He said, "I don't think so," but he did introduce me to Ann Noble, who was just arriving at Davis. Ann agreed to talk to me amid all of her unopened boxes. She encouraged me to take wine classes at Davis as a concurrent student. I took four months of classes, and then, knowing that it was too early to get a technical job, I took a job as a part-time tour guide at Chandon. By the end of July there was a job in the laboratory, and I was offered it. Six years later, I was hired to build and develop Gloria Ferrer. Then, three years later I accepted the position at Domaine Carneros to once again build and oversee the development of a sparkling wine house. I had no construction background when I took on the Gloria Ferrer job. I had not even done a major home improvement project. What I did do well was to find a good contractor and ask a lot of questions. Both wineries went up on time and within budget. Looking back, even as a child I knew what I wanted to do but could not have conceived that I could make it happen.

One of the biggest changes that I have seen is the evolution of California sparkling wine from nice, clean little wines to wines that hold their own very successfully on the world stage. California sparkling wines have evolved through realization of the importance of cold-climate appellations, the evolution of individual styles, and the overall appreciation by winemakers and owners that we're no longer playing in the minor leagues. Winemaking has become much more sophisticated, and our appellation system has moved into maturity.

When I got to Carneros, there were vast stretches of Pinot Noir clones that were undistinguished. As phylloxera wiped out many of the existing vineyards, replantings were done with smaller-producing, more specialized clones and vineyard selections. Wine growing became much more focused on making the very best wines possible, and we started to see the beginning of highly committed winemakers, wineries, and owners striving to grow the absolutely best Pinot Noir possible.

Domaine Carneros is committed to the Carneros appellation. Within that appellation we are always looking for new great vineyard sites. On occasion we have made Merlot largely because a number of years ago I purchased a small vineyard site that had some extraordinary and healthy Merlot. We couldn't resist seeing what it would do under our tutelage. And just this past year, we brought in a little bit of Pinot Gris for a Blanc de Blancs trial. We are always looking for new, good ideas in clones, varieties, and winemaking. About four years ago we started working on a Pinot Noir made as a white still wine. We call it our Pinot Clair. Domaine Carneros is virtually all estate, and in the next few years we will be 100 percent estate. All of our estate vineyards are certified CCOF organic.

Great winemakers, like great artists, need to have the freedom to create from their gut. It has to be inspired and their authentic inspiration. The first obligation of any wine is to be delicious. I love wines of finesse with the great nose, good body, and a long finish. I view Domaine Carneros wines as Audrey Hepburn in the little black dress. Everything in place, nothing over the top, elegant, and Kiki.

DIAMOND CREEK VINEYARDS

1500 Diamond Mountain Road, Calistoga, CA 94515
(707) 942-6926, www.diamondcreekvineyards.com

Boots Brounstein and her late husband, Al, founded Diamond Creek in 1968 to create California's first exclusively Cabernet Sauvignon estate vineyard. Today Boots, son Phil Ross, and winemaker Phil Steinschriber produce their Cabs on this 80-acre estate (planted approximately 20 acres), which has three distinct soil types: Red Rock Terrace has iron-rich soil; Gravelly Meadow's consists of small pebbles; and Volcanic Hill's is lighter and has more volcanic ash in its composition. The Diamond Creek Red Rock Terrace Napa Valley Cabernet Sauvignon has rich flavors of dark fruits and a silky smooth finish. The luscious Diamond Creek Gravelly Meadow Napa Valley Cabernet Sauvignon has a touch of spice in the finish.

DOMAINE CARNEROS

1240 Duhig Road, Napa, CA 94559
(707) 257-0101, www.domainecarneros.com

With beautiful foyers, a stunning tasting room, and café tables overlooking the vines, the château of Domaine Carneros, owned by the house of Taittinger, feels like France. The crisp and clean Domaine Carneros Brut Cuvée Sparkling has aromas of Granny Smith apples and freshly baked brioche. The Domaine Carneros Cuvée de la Pompadour Brut Rose NV features notes of white peach and freshly sliced strawberries; enjoy it with food or as an aperitif. 24

DOMAINE CHANDON

1 California Drive, Yountville, CA 94599
(888) 242-6366, www.chandon.com

Moët & Chandon was searching for new areas to produce great sparkling wine, and in 1968 the company found sites in Mount Veeder, Carneros, and Yountville. They quickly planted vineyards and released their first sparkling wines in 1976. Tom Tiburzi has been winemaker at Domaine Chandon for more than 20 years, recently assisted by Champagne-born Pauline Lhote. Besides sparkling wines, the house makes still wine from Pinot Noir, Chardonnay, Petit Meunier, and Cabernet Sauvignon varieties. The Chandon Limited Edition Brut Classic has flavors of Anjou pear and Granny Smith apple. The crisp yet fruity Domaine Chandon Carneros Chardonnay offers aromas of white stone fruits and freshly cut apples.

DOMINUS ESTATE

2570 Napa Nook Road, Yountville, CA 94599
(707) 944-8954, www.dominusestate.com

One of Bordeaux's famous sons, Christian Moueix studied at UC Davis in the 1960s, which is when his love of California and the Napa Valley began. He discovered this 124-acre estate in 1981. In 1995 he changed the name to Dominus, the Latin word for "lord," which symbolizes his commitment to the land. Moueix produced wine at Trotanoy, Hosanna, and Magdelaine, among others in Bordeaux, and consulted at Château Pétrus. His love of California *terroir* shines through in the quality of his wines. The velvety Dominus has aromas of dark plums, blackberries, and cedar. 25

In his own words

TOM TIBURZI

Winemaker Tom Tiburzi, the head of Domaine Chandon's sparkling wine program, has been at Chandon for 22 years, and his extensive scientific background and exceptional blending skills have led him to develop an exciting range of sparkling cuvées for the house.

Both of my parents emigrated from Italy, very much Old World, and we made wine at home. I was raised in my family's wine and spirits shops, so the world of wine was a constant. When I went off to college, I had no idea that my path would lead to winemaking. After receiving a degree in environmental studies in biology at UC Berkeley, I dove into algae and bacteria research, but when the group I was working with moved from the Bay Area, I didn't wish to leave. It was 1989, my wife had been working as pastry chef at the restaurant at Domaine Chandon, and harvest was about to start. I thought it would be interesting to work a harvest, and it turns out they had a research position open. I fit right in working with yeast and bacteria in wine and never left, moving from the lab, to staff microbiologist, to assistant winemaker, to associate winemaker, and in 2005 was appointed to sparkling winemaker to head the program.

Domaine Chandon was founded by Moët and Chandon, which was itself founded in 1743. I've had the privilege to receive the knowledge that has been passed down from winemaker to winemaker from their beginnings. It was the blenders of Dom Pérignon that have taught the winemakers at Domaine Chandon. I am the third winemaker in succession at Domaine Chandon, hired by our first winemaker, and have been trained by the same mentors. Domaine Chandon is the only winery I have worked for.

My philosophy in sparkling winemaking is to be true to tradition while leaving room for innovation. When an innovation presents itself, I ask the question, "Would this have been accepted a hundred years ago if available back then?" If yes, then I move forward. One of the biggest challenges is to match supply and demand. When the economy is stable, it is relatively easy to maintain a slow, steady growth rate. But since it takes two to six years, depending on the sparkling wine, to get to market, forecasting how much to make is a challenge during recessions or rapid growth in demand.

Some of the biggest changes have been with the technology used in winemaking, things that make for a more efficient process toward producing wine without flaws. For example, cross-flow filtration with media that lasts for many years has replaced diatomaceous earth filtration, a medium that needs to be mined, shipped to the winery, carefully loaded into the filter to avoid health risk, then hauled off to a dump when spent. Another example is using electrodialysis to cold-stabilize the wine, a very "green" method that is quick and easy on the wine and uses very little energy and resources. This replaces conventional cold stabilization, which takes many days of constant mixing, a lot of electricity to run chillers taking the wine to subzero temperature, producing a slurry of tartaric acid that must be filtered out, then many therms of natural gas to warm the wine back up through heat exchangers. Other changes have been with our knowledge on how to manage tannins so that red wine can be ready to drink sooner, without need for extended bottle aging. Also, we have evolved greater knowledge and new technology toward managing oxygen in the juice before fermentation, making for higher quality.

The supplier industry supporting winemaking has grown to be very competitive; much of the research and development is now done by them, with winemakers reaping the benefits. Only the very biggest wineries now support their own research staff compared to 20 years ago, when many small to medium-size wineries had research enologists or at least staff devoting time to research. The California Enological Research Association (CERA) was very active with wineries doing collaborative research; this still happens, but to a much lesser extent.

The most recent exciting change has been in management of oxygen in juice before fermentation. In sparkling winemaking, we take the grapes directly to press, without crushing. We've known for a long time that a certain amount of oxygen contact with the juice is important for quality, minimizing astringency, and in general improving mouthfeel, with the risk being that too much oxygen could damage fruitfulness. We are now able to measure exactly how much oxygen is needed for each tank of new juice and can finely control the delivery of oxygen to the juice in order to maximize reduction in astringency without losing the fruit aromas and flavors.

I predominantly work with the traditional grapes of Champagne: Chardonnay, Pinot Noir, and Pinot Meunier. Muscat Canelli plays a part in our aromatic sparkling wine when there's a need to push the aroma and flavor toward apricots and peaches. I also work with a small amount of Zinfandel, used for blending with Pinot Noir in our sparkling red wine. For sparkling wine, I need cool growing sites to keep acidity high and extend the growing season. If the growing site is too warm, Chardonnay, Pinot Noir, and Pinot Meunier will achieve the 18–20 Brix sugar level too fast for good flavor development. We need to pick at low sugar because we use second fermentation in the bottle to get bubbles into the wine. This adds alcohol, and if we pick grapes above 20 Brix, then the final alcohol is too high, out of balance. Therefore, cooler areas with direct marine influence are potential new growing sites.

Screw caps are good closures, and the liners available now can dial in exactly the desired level of oxygen egress into the bottle to match the style of wine being produced. These liners are very similar to the ones in the crown caps that we use on our sparkling wines for second fermentation and aging in the bottle. If these alternative closures were available when stoppers were moving away from wooden plugs and oily pieces of cloth, it is my opinion that cork closures would have never been developed. However, there has been a long history of using cork closures, and cork is a great, renewable resource. The issue is that for the masses of normal corks, you can expect about 1 percent to be tainted, and what other product would you allow that rate of flaw, bottles of juice, jugs of milk? However, there has been great innovation with agglomerated cork processing that removes potential taint; we use this type of cork at Domaine Chandon. I am happy to use these taint-free technical corks since they are a sustainable renewable resource.

DUCKHORN VINEYARDS

1000 Lodi Lane, St. Helena, CA 94574
(707) 963-7108, www.duckhorn.com

After extensive travel to Pomerol and Saint-Émilion, Dan and Margaret Duckhorn founded Duckhorn Vineyards in 1976 with a focus on Merlot. Today Duckhorn Vineyards sources fruit from eight estate-owned Napa Valley vineyards as well as from independent growers. Executive winemaker Bill Nancarrow hails from New Zealand and brings a global style to winemaking. Duckhorn makes wine under a variety of labels, including Decoy, Paraduxx, Goldeneye, and Migration. The Duckhorn Vineyards Estate Grown Stout Vineyard Merlot offers subtle flavors of toffee, dark stone fruits, and black raspberry, and the Duckhorn Vineyards Howell Mountain Cabernet Sauvignon has pronounced fruit flavors with nuances of brown baking spices followed by a savory finish. 26

EHLERS ESTATE

3222 Ehlers Lane, St. Helena, CA 94574
(707) 963-5972, www.ehlersestate.com

Bernard Ehlers built the original stone winery here in 1886, and French entrepreneur Jean Leducq founded Ehlers Estate in 1985. The company continues his tradition of philanthropy by donating 100 percent of its profits to the Leducq Foundation, which focuses on cardiovascular research. Under winemaker Kevin Morrisey, Ehlers Estate began producing organic and biodynamic wines in 2005, and in 2008 it received organic certification from California Certified Organic Farmers. Demeter USA gave it biodynamic certification in 2011. The Ehlers Estate 1886 Cabernet Sauvignon has flavors of luscious black fruits and cocoa with an elegant finish. The Ehlers Estate One Twenty over Eighty Cabernet Sauvignon has flavors of black fruits and Christmas baking spices.

In his own words

JON PRIEST

Jon Priest worked at Taz Vineyards in Santa Barbara, Adelaida Cellars in Paso Robles, and Wild Horse with Ken Volk. The winemaker at Etude since 2005, he continues the vision started by founder Tony Soter.

I started as a student of wine, and my study continues to this day. I was fascinated that wine could holistically encompass agriculture, science, art, culture, history, and craftsmanship. It is more than merely a glass of wine—it is the telling of a story of a person or a family and of a place. The more I studied about the history of wine—and the more corks I pulled—the more fascinated I became. I thought that by becoming a winemaker I could help tell a story.

My early winemaking career was as much about my quest for Pinot Noir enlightenment as it was about varietal cross-training. My focus remains on Pinot Noir, Pinot Gris, Pinot Blanc, Chardonnay, and Napa Valley Cab Sauv, and the urge to experiment with something "new" always resides. Just leave it to a Pinot person to interpret experimentation as something other than varieties. We recently planted new Pinot Noir clones and heirloom selections on our estate ranch, with the ambition of broadening the spectrum of our wines.

I have recently had the opportunity to be involved with grapes and wine in Central Otago, New Zealand, and in the Willamette Valley of Oregon. Since Pinot Noir is so much about the place, I hope to gain valuable perspective and understanding from working with the grape in such varying regions and seeing how others approach the variety.

Etude is embarking on a foray into other important Pinot Noir regions. While the Carneros estate will remain our home, our journey will take us south to Sta. Rita Hills and Santa Maria Valley, west to Annapolis on the Sonoma Coast, and north to the Willamette Valley. Every vineyard and vintage has a story to tell, and a winemaker's interpretation is a part of the telling. The beauty of a wine is its nuance and expression: grown in a place and brought forth by the wine grower and winemaker. In that sense, the winemaker crafts the wine to fulfill their intent or persuasion.

ENVY

1170 Tubbs Lane, Calistoga, CA 94515
(707) 942-4677, www.envywines.com

Founded by Richard Carter and Nils Venge, Envy is planted with Cabernet Sauvignon, Sauvignon Blanc, Merlot, and Petite Syrah, and all the estate's wines are produced in a Bordelaise style. Pack lunch, buy a bottle from the tasting room, and have a picnic on Envy's front lawn. Every 40 minutes or so, you'll see Old Faithful geyser across the street. The crisp and refreshing Envy Sauvignon Blanc exhibits aromas of sweet nectarine, and the Envy Bee Bee's Blend delights with flavors of black raspberry, toasted almond, and baking spice.

ETUDE WINES

1250 Cuttings Wharf Road, Napa, CA 94559
(877) 586-9361, www.etudewines.com

Founded by Tony Soter more than 25 years ago, Etude takes its name from the classical musical composition that allows a performer to practice a specific technique over and over. Both Tony and current winemaker Jon Priest believe that concentration on specific technique helps them make better wine. Etude makes wines from Pinot Noir, Cabernet Sauvignon, Pinot Gris, Pinot Blanc, and Merlot varieties. The crisp, clean Etude Carneros Pinot Gris has subtle aromas of white peach and freshly cut green apple, and the velvety Etude Napa Valley Cabernet Sauvignon has aromas of black plum and black raspberry with a top note of caramelized anise. 27

FAMA WINES

No visitor facilities
(415) 250-7505, www.famawines.com

As a girl, Heather Munden wanted to be a lion tamer, but a chance meeting with Robert Mondavi introduced her to the world of wine, and she has made quite a name for herself. After 17 years of making wine for others, she struck out on her own with Fama, establishing herself as a small-batch artisanal winemaker. Her third vintage in 2012 produced only 123 cases of Chardonnay and 25 of her proprietary red blend, The Partners. The crisp, clean Fama Hudson Vineyards Carneros Napa Valley Chardonnay entices with aromas of lemon curd, Granny Smith apples, and Anjou pears. 28

FAR NIENTE

1350 Acacia Drive, Oakville, CA 94562
(707) 944-2861, www.farniente.com

Founded in 1885 by Gold Rush–era entrepreneur John Benson, Far Niente enjoyed a privileged run until Prohibition. The winery lay in disrepair from 1919 until 1979, when Gil Nickel acquired it. Today partners Erik Nickel, Jeremy Nickel, Beth Nickel, Dirk Hampson, and Larry Maguire own it. The robust Far Niente Estate Bottled Napa Valley Chardonnay offers flavors of tropical fruits and buttered toast and a bright, luscious finish. The Far Niente Estate Bottled Napa Valley Oakville Cabernet Sauvignon has flavors of blackberry conserves, clove, and tart cherry preserves. 29

FORMAN VINEYARDS

1501 Big Rock Road, St. Helena, CA 94574
(707) 963-3900, www.formanvineyard.com

Owner Ric Forman purchased his winery in 1978 and began producing Cabernet Sauvignon and Chardonnay in 1983 using traditional French methods. He crafts handmade wines using grapes sourced from the winery site and elsewhere. His red wines ferment in stainless steel and undergo malolactic fermentation in oak barrels; his white wines ferment in oak. The creamy Forman Vineyards Napa Valley Chardonnay has flavors of stone fruits, and the Foreman Vineyards Napa Valley Cabernet Sauvignon offers aromas of black fruit conserves and fruits of the wood.

FRANCISCAN

1178 Galleron Road, St. Helena, CA 94574
(707) 963-7111, www.franciscan.com

In 1972 Justin Meyer and Raymond Duncan planted the original Oakville Estate vines, and Meyer purchased Franciscan in 1975. That year the winery celebrated its first vintage from estate-grown grapes. Winemaker Agustin Huneeus introduced Franciscan's iconic Magnificat in 1985, and two years later winemaker Greg Upton was the first to ferment Napa Valley Chardonnay using wild yeast. Today Janet Myers—credited with creating Franciscan's signature reserve Cabernet Sauvignon, Stylus—directs winemaking. The Franciscan Estate Napa Valley Chardonnay has flavors of tarte Tatin, fresh pear, and lemon curd, and the Franciscan Estate Napa Valley Cabernet Sauvignon proffers flavors of cassis and licorice. 30

FRANK FAMILY VINEYARDS

1091 Larkmead Lane, Calistoga, CA 94515
(707) 942-0859, www.frankfamilyvineyards.com

The Larkmead Winery began humbly in 1884. Refurbished in 1906, it sits on the list of California State Points of Historical Interest and the National Register of Historic Places. Current owners Richard Frank—past president of the Academy of Television Arts and Sciences, chairman of Walt Disney Television, and president of Walt Disney Studios—and Connie Frank produce Cabernet Sauvignon, Chardonnay, Zinfandel, and Sangiovese wines. The Frank Family Vineyards Napa Valley Chardonnay has flavors of homemade applesauce, stone fruits, and cinnamon. The luscious, fruit-filled Frank Family Vineyards Napa Valley Cabernet Sauvignon offers aromas of black cherry preserves. 31

In his own words

MILJENKO "MIKE" GRGICH

Croatian born Miljenko "Mike" Grgich immigrated to the United States in 1958. He is well known in the industry for crafting the 1973 Chateau Montelena Chardonnay that scored higher than the best French Chardonnays at the famous Judgment of Paris. He celebrated 50 years of winemaking in 2008 and was inducted into the Vintners Hall of Fame the same year.

I came to the United States in 1958 to work in wineries. I arrived in California at the age of 34. My first job was at Souverain Cellars, then Christian Brothers, then nine years at Beaulieu Vineyards with André Tchelistcheff and four years with Robert Mondavi. I then joined Chateau Montelena as winemaker and limited partner for five years (1972–1977). At Chateau Montelena I crafted the 1973 Chardonnay that bested the best French Chardonnay at the famous 1976 Paris Tasting. That wine was "the champion" of the Paris Tasting with 132 points, the highest score overall, the best white and red French and California wines. The now-historic 1976 Paris Tasting put Napa Valley on the map as the best wine region of the world, energizing the rest of the world to plant more vines and make better wines.

On Independence Day 1977, Austin Hills and I broke ground in Rutherford to build Grgich Hills Cellar. Since starting Grgich Hills, I continued receiving international awards for my wines and have been recognized for being a leader in sustainable vineyard practices. In 2008 I celebrated 50 years of making wine in California, and the same year I was inducted into the Vintners Hall of Fame. Today all 366 acres of Grgich Hills are certified organic, and the winery has converted to solar power and is completely estate-grown.

In 1996 I opened Grgic Vina Winery in Croatia, producing Plavac Mali, a red wine, and Posip, a white wine, with the goal of helping winemakers in my homeland produce world-class wines from local varieties. I therefore imported French oak barrels for wine aging, set up a modern bottling line, installed air-conditioned storage for aging wines, and brought a rigorous, scientific approach to improve the winemaking. My goal was for Croatian wines to become recognized internationally. I felt great satisfaction when in 1999 a commission of Croatian winemakers selected Grgic Vina 1977 Posi and Grgic Vina 1977 Plavac Mali to represent the Croatian wine industry along with Croatian food to be served for one month in the Delegates Dining Room of the United Nations in New York. I believe that the wines are great messengers to the world of the high quality of Croatian wines. In my style of wines one can detect some European influence, particularly if the tasting takes place in Europe. My world-class wines are food-friendly and crafted for enjoyment.

The Grgich Hills Cellar philosophy was and still is to make "château-quality" wines, consistency in quality, balanced wines with longevity. Following my father's rule, "every day do something just a little better," has guided a long list of advances and innovations at Grgich Hills since it was founded in 1977. Great wine starts in the vineyard, and over the years Grgich Hills has strung together a string of pearls that run through the Napa Valley. Starting with just 18 acres surrounding the winery in Rutherford, we now own and farm five vineyards, with a total of 366 acres. In recognition that all our wines are estate-grown, the winery changed its name to Grgich Hills Estate in 2007.

At Grgich Hills Estate we do not follow somebody else's style—we set the style, and others follow our style. Innovations extend to every area of the winery. We constantly experiment as to how we can maximize the enjoyment of wines, always keeping them "balanced." By having our wine estate-grown, produced, and bottled, my winemaking team and I have total control over the entire process. My nephew, Ivo Jeramaz, who is vice president of vineyards and production, started organically farming the vineyards in 2000. Today every acre is farmed naturally, with no artificial fertilizers, pesticides, or fungicides. Just as my father did in Croatia when I was growing up, we treat the earth as a living organism to maintain a harmonious balance between the vines and the Earth's soil. As part of my belief in sustainable farming, the winery switched to solar power in 2006. As a result, Grgich Hills Estate wines are crafted "from our vineyard to your glass—naturally." In the cellar, Gary Ecklin, chief enologist, has brought in OXOline, an ingenious system for stacking and rotating oak barrels, so that the staff can manage the delicate aging process with even greater care. The winemaking team particularly likes the system for the winery's white wines, which allows the cellar crew to regularly rotate each 60-gallon oak barrel, stirring up the lees and giving the wine additional complexity and body.

FREEMARK ABBEY

3022 St. Helena Highway, St. Helena, CA 94574
(707) 963-9694, www.freemarkabbey.com

Josephine Tychson, one of Napa Valley's first winegrowing women, established Freemark Abbey's original winery in 1889. The current name came about in 1939 by combining the owners' names: Charles Freeman, Markquand Foster, and Abbey Ahern. Seven partners purchased the winery in 1967, and Ted Edwards has been winemaker since 1985. The Freemark Abbey Napa Valley Chardonnay has aromas of lemon curd and Granny Smith apple and vibrant stone fruit flavors. The full-bodied Freemark Abbey Napa Valley Merlot tastes of dried black cherry, mocha, and a hint of black pepper in the finish. 32

FROG'S LEAP

8815 Conn Creek Road, Rutherford, CA 94573
(707) 963-4704, www.frogsleap.com

The historic Adamson Winery, built in 1884, now houses Frog's Leap, which sits among 130 vineyard acres in Rutherford. Renovated in 1994, it's Frog's Leap's permanent home. Winemakers John Williams and Paula Moschetti use Napa Valley Rutherford-grown grapes to make Cabernet Sauvignon, Sauvignon Blanc, Merlot, Zinfandel, and Chardonnay wines. The light, crisp Frog's Leap Napa Valley Rutherford Sauvignon Blanc is perfect with shellfish and seafood. The Frog's Leap Napa Valley Rutherford Cabernet Sauvignon offers aromas of black cherry and black plums leading to restrained dark fruit flavors. Drink it now, or age it for 10 to 15 years. 33

GIRARD WINERY

6795 Washington Street, Yountville, CA 94599
(707) 968-9297, www.girardwinery.com

Current owner Pat Roney began his career as a sommelier at Chicago's Pump Room while attending Northwestern University. Returning to California, he worked for Seagram's and served as president of both Chateau St. Jean and Kunde wineries. In 2000, he purchased Girard, where Texas native Glenn Hugo directs winemaking. The Girard Diamond Mountain Napa Valley Cabernet Sauvignon has strong fruit flavors enhanced by accents of espresso and chocolate. The Girard Petite Sirah Napa Valley offers aromas of mocha, Mediterranean herbs, and black raspberry preserves.

GRACE FAMILY VINEYARDS

1210 Rockland Drive, St. Helena, CA 94574
(707) 963-0808, www.gracefamilyvineyards.com

Dick and Ann Grace left the San Francisco suburbs in the mid-1970s for a better life for themselves and their three children. They fell in love with a fixer-upper Victorian homestead in Napa Valley, planted vine cuttings from a neighbor, and harvested their first vintage in 1978. Today their winery is serene and peaceful, built to resemble Buddhist temples in Nepal. The family also maintains the Grace Family Vineyards Foundation, which donates money to a variety of charitable organizations. The Grace Family Vineyards Napa Valley Cabernet Sauvignon has a bouquet of black cherry, mocha, Christmas baking spices, and Mediterranean herbs.

GRGICH HILLS ESTATE

1829 St. Helena Highway, Rutherford, CA 94573
(800) 532-3057, www.grgich.com

In 1954 Miljenko "Mike" Grgich emigrated from Croatia with ten winemaking books and thirty-two dollars in the soles of his shoes. A few years later he came to Napa Valley, worked at various wineries, and in 1976 learned by telegram that a white wine he'd crafted, Chateau Montelena Chardonnay 1973, won the Judgment of Paris. In 1977, he and partners from the Hill Bros. Coffee Company broke ground on the winery now known as Grgich Hills. The Vintner Hall of Fame inducted Grgich in 2008. The crisp, clean Grgich Hills Estate

Grown Napa Valley Chardonnay offers flavors of pineapple and guava, and the Grgich Hills Estate Grown Miljenko's Old Vines Zinfandel exhibits notes of freshly ground black pepper, dried cherries, and black plums. 34

GROTH VINEYARDS AND WINERY

750 Oakville Cross Road, Oakville, CA 94562
(707) 944-0290, www.grothwines.com

Dennis and Judith Groth set their hearts on buying a Sonoma vineyard and producing Chardonnay wine. But Ren Harris, a Napa grape farmer, persuaded them to drive over the mountain and look at vineyards on the other side. They immediately fell in love with the sea of Cabernet Sauvignon vines in Napa and purchased 121 acres on the Oakville Cross Road in 1981. The next year they purchased 44 acres planted to Chardonnay and Merlot. They completed their winery in 1990 and renovated in 2007. Michael Weis has been winemaker at Groth since 1994, and his philosophy is simple: "Be true to varietal integrity." The Groth Vineyard and Winery Oakville Napa Valley Cabernet Sauvignon has a bouquet and palate of ripe black and red fruit, and the Groth Vineyards and Winery Napa Valley Chardonnay presents notes of pineapple and flavors of tropical fruits. 35

HALL NAPA VALLEY

401 St. Helena Highway S., St. Helena, CA 94574
(707) 967-2626, www.hallwines.com

Craig Hall, founder of the Dallas-based Hall Financial Group, and wife, Kathryn, former ambassador to Austria, founded Hall Napa Valley after acquiring the historic Bergfeld Winery in 2003. In 2005 they unveiled their newly renovated winery, the first in California to achieve LEED-Gold Certification, which assesses environmental impact, water efficiency, decreased energy use, and other parameters. Hall Napa Valley Estate consists of more than 500 acres of Sauvignon Blanc, Cabernet Sauvignon, and Merlot vines. The Hall Napa Valley Kathryn Hall Cabernet Sauvignon offers aromas of freshly baked cherry pie, anise, and Christmas baking spices, while the fruit-driven Hall Napa Valley Napa River Ranch Merlot exhibits flavors of fruit compote.

HARTWELL ESTATE VINEYARDS

5795 Silverado Trail, Napa, CA 94558
(707) 255-4269, www.hartwellvineyards.com

Bob and Blanca Hartwell purchased their estate from Harry See of the See's Candy Company in 1986. They started with a single acre of Cabernet Sauvignon and, using neighbor Dick Grace's facility, produced their first wine in 1990. In 1999 they built their winery and bought another vineyard in Carneros to plant Sauvignon Blanc. The Hartwells blend modern technology with Old World traditions and use a variety of fermenters, including wood tanks and concrete eggs. The Hartwell Estate Merlot offers plum and cherry flavors accented with licorice and dark spices. The crisp, refreshing Hartwell Estate Sauvignon Blanc offers aromas of tropical fruits and citrus.

HEITZ WINE CELLARS

500 Taplin Road, St. Helena, CA 94574
(707) 963-3542, www.heitzcellar.com

Founded by Joe and Alice Heitz in 1961, Heitz is one of a few midcentury Napa wineries to remain independent and family owned. Joe worked with André Tchelistcheff at Beaulieu Vineyards before purchasing this 160-acre ranch in 1964. Today daughter Kathleen Heitz Myers serves as president, and son David Heitz is winemaker. The full-bodied Heitz Wine Cellars Martha's Vineyard Cabernet Sauvignon smells of black plum, blueberry pie, and crushed spearmint leaves. The crisp, clean Heitz Wine Cellars Napa Valley Chardonnay has a nose of Anjou pears and honeydew melon.

HENDRY RANCH WINES

3104 Redwood Road, Napa, CA 94558
(707) 226-8320, www.hendrywines.com

Frederick and John Sigrist first planted what became the Hendry Ranch in 1859, and historians believe it hosted some of the first planted vineyards in the Napa Valley. George and Margaret Hendry moved to Napa Valley in 1939 and bought the land. After extensive replanting in the 1970s, the Hendry family continued selling their grapes to neighboring wineries. In 1992 the first vintage under the Hendry label was produced. The vineyard expanded in 1994 with the purchase of additional land, and today the Hendry Ranch consists of 117 acres divided into 47 vineyard blocks growing ten different varieties, including Cabernet Sauvignon and Pinot Gris. The Hendry Ranch Napa Valley HRW Cabernet Sauvignon offers full-on fruit flavors, and the Hendry Ranch Napa Valley Pinot Gris is crisp and clean, ideal as an aperitif or with raw shellfish.

HESS COLLECTION

4411 Redwood Road, Napa, CA 94558
(707) 255-1144, www.hesscollection.com

Donald Hess acquired his first Mount Veeder vineyard in 1978. Today the Hess Collection owns 704 acres in Napa Valley and 330 in other California AVAs. An arts lover, Hess shares with visitors a curated sampling of some of his favorite pieces and, of course, his wines. The Hess Collection also includes wines made under the Artezin label. The full-bodied Hess Collection 19 Block Cuvée Mount Veeder Napa Valley offers ripe fruit flavors and a touch of vanilla. The crisp, clean Hess Collection Mount Veeder Napa Valley Chardonnay tastes of lemon curd and fruit. The Artezin Mendocino County Zinfandel has aromas of red raspberry, black raspberry, and cracked black pepper, while the Artezin Mendocino County Petite Sirah offers notes of black raspberry and cassis on the palate.

HEWITT VINEYARD

1695 St. Helena Highway, Rutherford CA, 94573
(707) 968-3638, www.hewittvineyard.com

William A. Hewitt, head of the John Deere Company, purchased the estate in 1962, enlisted the assistance of André Tchelistcheff, and replanted the land with Cabernet Sauvignon vines. For many years, Hewitt sold its grapes to other wineries, but in 2001 the estate launched its own label. Tom Rinaldi directs winemaking, and the bold Hewitt Vineyard Estate Cabernet Sauvignon Rutherford has flavors of cassis and dark fruits.

HONIG VINEYARD AND WINERY

850 Rutherford Road, Rutherford, CA 94573
(707) 963-5618, www.honigwine.com

Twenty-two-year-old Michael Honig took over management of his grandfather's ranch in 1984, focusing on getting his wines into high-end restaurants. Over the years, additional family members joined the business, and in 1998 they enlisted the help of winemaker Kristen Belair. The medium-bodied Honig Vineyard and Winery Napa Valley Sauvignon Blanc offers notes of lemon zest and tropical fruits. The Honig Vineyard and Winery Napa Valley Cabernet Sauvignon has aromas of dark fruits and Christmas baking spices with lingering flavors of licorice and spice.

HOURGLASS BLUELINE ESTATE WINES

1104 Adams Street, St. Helena, CA 94574
(707) 968-9332, www.hourglasswines.com

Ned and Marge Smith bought a 6-acre parcel in 1976, planted fruit trees, and watched them wither. After Ned's death, Marge planned to sell the land, but son Jeff brought in soil experts from UC Davis who convinced the family to cultivate vines. In 1992 Jeff planted Cabernet Sauvignon and later released his 1997 vintage. He, his wife, and two other couples subsequently purchased another 41-acre property in 2006 and named it Blueline Vineyard. The Hourglass Blueline Estate Wines Cabernet Franc proffers aromas of violets, Mediterranean herbs, Indian spice, and intense dark berries. 36

HYDE DE VILLAINE HDV WINES

588 Trancas Street, Napa CA, 94558
(707) 251-9121, www.hdvwines.com

Burgundy lovers know the history of Aubert de Villaine, his wines, and his family, but few know that his wife, Pamela Fairbanks de Villaine, is a cousin to the Hyde family of California. HdV is a joint venture between the de Villaine family of Burgundy and the Hyde family of Napa Valley. The wine labels feature the name and coat of arms of "de la Guerra," the family line from which both Pamela and the Hydes descend. The HdV de la Guerra Chardonnay offers white peach and nectarine flavors, and the HdV Californio Syrah tastes of rich dark fruits and cinnamon. Drink it now, or hold it for a few years.

INGLENOOK

1991 St. Helena Highway, Rutherford, CA 94573
(707) 968-1100, www.inglenook.com

Founded in 1879 by Finnish sea captain Gustav Niebaum, Inglenook has had a storied past. After Niebaum's death in 1908, Inglenook thrived from 1939 until the 1960s under Gustav's great-nephew John Daniel Jr. But tough financial times forced Daniel to sell the estate, and over the years a number of owners, including Heublein, Nabisco, and Constellation, divided and managed it. In 1975 Francis Ford Coppola purchased 1,500 acres and named it Niebaum-Coppola and then Rubicon, but the historic winery, trademarked name, and additional 94 acres eluded him until 2011. Inglenook once again is whole. Philippe Bascaules of Château Margaux and consultant Stéphane Derenoncourt carry out winemaking duties. The crisp yet silky Inglenook Blancaneaux offers aromas of citrus, Bartlett pear, and ruby pink grapefruit. The long-finishing Rubicon exhibits fragrances of fresh blueberry, black currant, and dried black cherries. 37

JARVIS ESTATE

2970 Monticello Road, Napa, CA 94558
(707) 255-5280, www.jarviswines.com

When William and Leticia Jarvis moved to Napa Valley, they combined their interest in the performing arts and the art of winemaking. They founded the Jarvis Conservatory, which offers master classes in classical opera, dance, and film. The Jarvis Estate Winery encompasses 1,320 acres, features a 45,000-square-foot underground cave, and uses plantings of Cabernet Franc, Petit Verdot, Merlot, Chardonnay, and Tempranillo in the production of estate-grown wines. The velvety Jarvis Estate Winery Merlot offers flavors of black plum and black currants. Rich and round in the mouth, the Jarvis Estate Winery Finch Hollow Chardonnay has aromas of green apple and top notes of vanilla and English butter toffee. 38

JOEL GOTT WINES

P.O. Box 539, St. Helena, CA 94574
(707) 963-3365, www.gottwines.com

Joel Gott's family has been making wine in California for five generations. He and his brother took over the Calistoga Palisades Market in 1993 and began making wine in 1996. In 1999 he took over management of the iconic Taylor's Refresher in St. Helena, now named Gott's Roadside. The silky-smooth Joel Gott California Alakai has pronounced fruit flavors, and the Joel Gott California Cabernet Sauvignon offers fragrances of black plum, cherry cola, and Mediterranean herbs. 39

JOSEPH CARR

P.O. Box 661, Rutherford, CA 94573
(707) 755-3814, www.josephcarrwine.com

Influenced by the wines of Burgundy and Bordeaux, former sommelier Joseph Carr started his distinctly Californian wine company in 2005. He sources Cabernet Sauvignon and Merlot from vineyards in the Stags Leap District, Oakville, and Rutherford, and in 2010 he joined forces with winemaker Aaron Pott, who studied enology at UC Davis and worked for six years in France before returning to California. His name of his second label, Josh, honors his father. The Joseph Carr Napa County Merlot has rich flavors of red fruits and the Joseph Carr Napa Valley Cabernet Sauvignon tastes of black raspberry, red plums, and candied violets.

JOSEPH PHELPS VINEYARDS

200 Taplin Road, St. Helena, CA 94574
(800) 707-5789, www.josephphelps.com

Looking for a career change, builder Joseph Phelps bought a 600-acre cattle ranch in Spring Valley, planted vines, and then built a winery in 1973. The estate's holdings include the original Spring Valley Home Ranch and property in several other AVAs. Insignia, a Bordeaux-style blend, is Joseph Phelps's flagship wine. Damian Parker, director of winemaking; Napa winemaker Ashley Hepworth; and Philippe Pessereau, director of vineyard operations undertake winemaking. Kelly Fields and Justin Ennis assist the team. Sister winery Freestone Vineyards in Sonoma focuses on wines made from Chardonnay and Pinot Noir. The restrained and elegant Joseph Phelps Insignia Napa Valley Estate offers notes of blueberry pie and freshly picked black raspberries, and the crisp, clean Joseph Phelps Sauvignon Blanc tastes of tropical fruits. (40)

KAPCSÁNDY FAMILY WINERY

1001 State Lane, Yountville, CA 94599
(707) 948-3100, www.kapcsandywines.com

Lou Kapcsándy Sr. fled Hungary during the 1956 Revolution and wound up on the West Coast of the United States, but it wasn't until a 1998 trip to Bordeaux that he and his wife decided to start a winery for their retirement years. In 2000 they acquired the former Beringer Estate State Lane Vineyard and replanted Cabernet Sauvignon and Merlot vines. They completed their current winery in 2005. The Kapcsándy Family Winery Cabernet Sauvignon Grand Vin proffers aromas of anise and juicy red plums. Big and rich, the Kapcsándy Family Winery Roberta's Reserve has notes of ripe black plums and red raspberries.

KONGSGAARD

4375 Atlas Peak Road, Napa, CA 94558
(707) 226-2190, www.kongsgaardwine.com

John Kongsgaard's family has lived in the Napa Valley for five generations. He and wife, Maggy, began planting vines together in 1970, but they didn't launch their eponymous wines until 1996. John, Maggy, and son, Alex handcraft their limited productions wines. The velvety Kongsgaard The Judge Napa Valley Chardonnay has notes of citrus and lemon curd. Big and round, the Kongsgaard Napa Valley Cabernet Sauvignon 2010 offers aromas and tastes of rich red fruits.

KRUPP BROTHERS

3267 Soda Canyon Road, Napa, CA 94558
(707) 226-2215, www.kruppbrothers.com

Physician Jan Krupp purchased 41 acres in 1991 and got his brother Bart involved a few years later. Together they purchased an additional 750 acres and created Krupp Vineyard, Krupp Brothers Vineyard, and Stagecoach Vineyard. The Krupp Brothers Black Bart Stagecoach Vineyard Syrah features seamless notes of black fruits, and the Krupp Brothers Stagecoach M5 Cabernet Sauvignon offers a complex bouquet of cassis, dark chocolate, and black raspberries. 41

KULETO ESTATE

2470 Sage Canyon Road, St. Helena, CA 94574
(707) 302-2209, www.kuletoestate.com

Restaurateur Pat Kuleto acquired 761 acres of eastern Napa Valley's mountainous terrain in 1992 and planted Cabernet Sauvignon, Pinot Noir, Chardonnay, and Sangiovese. He built a 17,000-square-foot gravity-flow winery in 2001. Dave Lattin has directed winemaking since 2002, and Alberto Ochoa handles vineyard management. Bill Foley, owner of Foley Family Wines, bought Kuleto in 2009 and remains at the helm today. The big, bold Kuleto Estate Chardonnay offers aromas of Granny Smith apples and citrus, and the Kuleto Estate Syrah has notes of black plum and violet in the bouquet. Kuleto also makes wines under the Native Son, Frog Prince, and India Ink labels.

LADERA VINEYARDS

150 White Cottage Road South, Angwin, CA 94508
(707) 965-2445, www.laderavineyards.com

Pat and Anne Stotesbery met while attending Stanford and the University of San Francisco and eventually moved to Montana to farm cattle. A trip to Napa Valley changed their lives, and today they are custodians of a circa-1886 stone winery. New Zealander Jade Barrett and consulting winemaker Karen Culler oversee winemaking, and Gabriel Reyes manages the vineyards. The rich and juicy Ladera Vineyards Howell Mountain Cabernet Sauvignon offers aromas of black raspberry, blueberry, and cocoa nibs. The Ladera Vineyards Napa Valley Cabernet Sauvignon has a bouquet of black raspberry, cherry cola, and anise. 42

LAMBORN FAMILY VINEYARDS

1984 Summit Lake Drive, Angwin, CA 94563
(925) 254-0511, www.lamborn.com

After his divorce, Bob Lamborn wanted a change from his career as a private investigator in the San Francisco Bay Area, so in 1971 he convinced his son Mike to buy a plot of Howell Mountain land adjacent to his. The two cleared the land and planting vines, and in 1982 they produced their first 100 cases of wine. In 1996 the Lamborn Family Wine Company brought in winemaker Heidi Barrett, and today production is over 1,000 cases per year. The bold yet luscious Lamborn Family Vineyards Vintage VII Cabernet Sauvignon offers a complex bouquet of dark fruits, black plum, black cherry, and toffee. The fruit-forward Lamborn Family Vineyards Howell Mountain Proprietor Grown Zinfandel The Abundant Vintage has notes of black plums, black raspberry preserves, and freshly ground black pepper. 43

LA SIRENA

3520 Evey Road, Calistoga, CA 94515
(707) 942-1105, www.lasirenawine.com

Celebrated winemaker Heidi Barrett followed her successful winemaking for others by starting her own label, La Sirena. The name La Sirena, the Spanish and Italian word for "mermaid," represents Heidi's love of scuba diving. The big, bold La Sirena Cabernet Sauvignon offers aromas of cherry vanilla ice cream, cassis, and dark plums, and the La Sirena Le Barrettage opens in the mouth with pronounced fruit and spice flavors.

LIPARITA

No visitor facilities
(415) 606-4640, www.liparita.com

W. F. Keyes built the original stone cellar in 1880 atop Howell Mountain, and the wines received international acclaim at the Paris Exposition in 1900 and a gold medal at the St. Louis

Expo in 1904. Spencer Hoopes and winemaker Jason Fisher have dedicated themselves to resurrecting the spirit of Liparita's glorious past. The Liparita Oakville Cabernet Sauvignon has aromas of ripe cherries and red raspberries, and the Liparita V Block Yountville Cabernet Sauvignon offers luscious ripe black fruit aromas and big berry flavors. 44

LOKOYA

7600 St. Helena Highway, Oakville, CA 94558
(707) 948-1968, www.lokoya.com

Named for the indigenous American tribe who lived on Mount Veeder, Lokoya, a boutique winery concentrating on making ultrapremium wines, belongs to the Jackson Family Wine portfolio. Christopher Carpenter heads winemaking. The full-bodied Lokoya Howell Mountain Cabernet Sauvignon has big aromas of blueberry, black raspberry, and licorice.

LONG MEADOW RANCH WINERY

728 Main Street, St. Helena, CA 94574
(707) 963-4555, www.longmeadowranch.com

President Ulysses S. Grant signed the deed for the land now known as Long Meadow Ranch in 1872. It had olive, apple, and wine grape plantings until Prohibition prompted the abandoment of the ranch. In 1989 Ted Hall and his family acquired and began restoring it. Today Ted is president of Long Meadow Ranch and Affiliates, a group of family-owned companies that raise grass-fed beef, make olive oil, and grow organic fruits and vegetables, including the grapes for their wines. The smooth and silky Long Meadow Ranch Winery Napa Valley Sauvignon Blanc offers aromas of tropical fruits and honeydew melon. Big but restrained, the Long Meadow Ranch Winery Cabernet Sauvignon has notes of black raspberries and licorice in the enticing bouquet. Drink it now, or in the next 7 to 10 years. 45

In her own words

HEIDI BARRETT

Winemaker Heidi Peterson Barrett is well known in the world of wine for creating some of California's most notable and highly scoring cult wines, including Grace Family Vineyards, Screaming Eagle, and Dalla Valle Vineyards, to name only a few. She is married to winemaker Bo Barrett.

I grew up in the Napa Valley with a winemaker father and an artist mother. I learned versatility in Australia. I learned balance in Wittenberg, southern Germany, and South Australia, as well as the Barossa Valley. Wine should be simply delicious. Consistency is important too. Any variety can be made well. I just make the best wines I can in a balanced, tasty style and hope people like them.

In her own words

ZELMA LONG

Winemaker and winemaking consultant Zelma Long has made wine with Mike Grgich and Robert Mondavi and eventually became the chief enologist at Robert Mondavi Winery. She was the winemaker at Simi Winery for years and has consulted for Chandon in Argentina, Ruffino in Chianti, and other many other wineries around the world. She now makes wine at Long Vineyards and is a winemaking partner and owner at Vilafonté Wine Estate in South Africa.

In the late 1960s, my in-laws bought and planted to grapes a property in the eastern hills of Napa Valley. The Longs thought they might start a winery from their vineyard holdings. Making wine sounded intriguing to me. I went back to school at UC Davis to study winemaking and grape growing. My master's in enology and viticulture was never completed; at harvest 1970 Mike Grgich called me to work with him at Robert Mondavi Winery. It was an amazing opportunity . . . a beautiful new winery, driven by Robert, the visionary, and Mike Grgich, his enologist, who was so talented. I fell in love with winemaking and never returned to school. After Mike left to become winemaker at Chateau Montelena, I took his place as chief enologist at RMW.

Thanks to Bob Mondavi, I was early on able to travel overseas: in 1973 to Germany, in 1978 with his whole team for three weeks to France and Germany. In 1977 Bob Long and I started Long Vineyards Chardonnay and Riesling. The vineyards were on Pritchard Hill in Napa Valley. This small project continued, produced fine, long-aging Chardonnays. In the early 2000s, his father sold this vineyard and we elected not to continue the wine in the absence of those great old grapes. The heartbreak was that the new owner pulled out the rare and amazing old vines and planted Cabernet . . . of which there is plenty in Napa. I started work as Simi's winemaker in late 1979; Simi soon came to be owned by LVMH. For them I consulted to Ruffino in Italy, to Chandon in Argentina, and with them I traveled to France and Australia for global meetings of their winemakers from around the world. At Simi I built a new cellar, developed Cabernet and Chardonnay vineyards, and brought that wonderful old winery into a vibrant "new" world of California wine. My husband, Phil Freese, and I made Riesling, together with Dr. Monica Christmann, in Germany in 1998, 1999, and 2000, which was an extraordinary insight at making wine at 50 degrees N and its impact on grape and wine flavors. Recently I did a vintage in Bordeaux. I have clients in the Rhône and in Israel, in Oregon and Washington, and in Mendocino. But my deepest and richest overseas work is our South Africa project, Vilafonté, which Phil and I own and run with our South African partner, Mike Ratcliffe. We began in 1997, buying 100 bare acres in the Cape, planting the first tranche of 13 hectares, and making our first wine: two Bordeaux blends, Series C and Series M, for the Vilafonté label in 2003. We are small; we only make wine from our vineyard (which has been expanded) and neither buy nor sell our Cabernet Sauvignon, Merlot, Malbec, and Cabernet Franc grapes. From the start, I regarded traveling and talking to other winemakers and winegrowers, and wine and vine researchers, and tasting their wines as the best training possible, stimulating, and a source of new ideas and insights.

Wine has become part of our American culture. We have learned to grow wine grapes; not just to "produce grapes" . . . resulting in much better wines. The phylloxera problem in the 1990s was expensive but resulted in a major upgrade in the vineyards—better plant material, better planting strategies, better training, all to the benefit of the wines. We are more sensitive to and knowledgeable about our sites and soils, honoring them in the wine growing and winemaking. We are more proficient at selecting the right sites for each grape cultivar we work with. Wine has always been international, but now winemakers travel the world, so ideas, innovations travel quickly. Our wines are more sophisticated . . . more balanced, more harmonious, more flavorful, more delicious. Mike Grgich won the famous (or infamous, if you are French) Paris Tasting in 1976. The New World of wine opened up and challenged the Old World. Both are better for it.

The most important technical changes in the vineyard and winery have been the attention to sustainability, to our carbon footprint, to being sensitive to our vineyard environment, better understanding of soil health, essentially the whole panoply of ways that we can grow and make wine to be gentle with our environment. Everywhere I go in the New World, vineyards are pushing successfully into new sites. Both my parents were born, raised, and educated in eastern Washington, and in my early life it was wheat or sagebrush. I love eastern Washington sites—the Horse Heaven Hills, Red Mountain,

Wahluke Slope, Walla Walla Valley. They are not new but rich both with success and great potential. South Africa, our "second home," is producing internationally significant wines, and vineyards are pushing out from the Cape in every direction. Until 1994 they faced restraints from exploring new sites, and what is happening there now is exciting and energizing.

What I look for in a wine is clarity and purity of expression; a true expression of the *cépage* and its area, but the palate is most important—its harmony, length, balance of components, and length and character in its flavors. That, I believe, is hardest to achieve, and it needs to come from both the vineyard and the winemaking; and the legendary winemakers' wines have these qualities.

Our business is a slow business. The vineyards need time to establish and develop; it takes a year to grow each harvest, then time in the cellar and the bottle. Personally, I love this slow, thoughtful raising of the wine and the fact that we are based in agriculture, our feet in the soil. We take it for granted, but those coming into wine from other industries can be flummoxed by these realities. For the winemaker the challenge is to respond at the best level possible to what Mother Nature provides each harvest, and for the winery owner, to respond to the commercial needs of the business, whatever they may be . . . and both are always changing. Honor the vintage, honor the site, honor the variety. Learn deeply about each, using observation, experience, and science. Make wines by responding to the grapes rather than directing them. Know that grapes and wines are sensitive to their environment; handle them carefully and protect them. Produce beautiful wines, delicious wines, and, if fortunate, occasionally wines that set a benchmark for others. And finally, never stop learning. I landed in one of the most fun, gratifying, and stimulating businesses on earth; at one end it is agriculture—feet in the soil—and the other end, global, and everything fascinating in between.

LONG VINEYARDS

P.O. Box 50, St. Helena, CA 94574
(707) 963-2496, www.longvineyards.com

Formerly married couple Bob and Zelma Long started Long Vineyards in 1977 and produced one of Napa Valley's first barrel-fermented Chardonnays from vines planted in 1967. The family-owned estate winery and vineyards sit on Pritchard Hill, and Long Vineyards produces Chardonnay from estate-grown fruit as well as Cabernet Sauvignon and Sangiovese from fruit sourced from Seghesio Vineyards in Geyserville. Zelma Long, Bob Long, and Sandi Belcher make the wine, and Zelma's husband, Phil Freese, and John Arns manage the vineyards. The Long Vineyards Estate Napa Valley Chardonnay has tantalizing flavors of Granny Smith apple and lemon curd, with a long and lush finish.

LOUIS M. MARTINI WINERY

254 St. Helena Highway, St. Helena, CA 94574
(707) 963-2736, www.louismartini.com

Louis M. Martini emigrated from Genoa in 1899 but returned to Italy a few years later to learn winemaking. In 1922, during Prohibition, he opened LM Martini Grape Products Company, which made wine for the Catholic Church and supplied grape concentrate to home winemakers. He built his eponymous winery in 1933 and passed the baton to son Louis P. Martini in 1954. Today grandson Mike Martini runs the family business under the auspices of the Gallo family. The Louis M. Martini Napa Valley Cabernet Sauvignon offers flavors of ripe fruit, Christmas baking spices, and vanilla in the persistent finish.

In his own words

PHILIPPE MELKA

Born and educated in Bordeaux, Philippe Melka is a winemaker and winemaking consultant. His client list includes Vineyard 29, Quintessa, and Seavey, for which he makes well-regarded and high-scoring wines. He also makes wine under his eponymous label, Melka Wines, with wife, Cherie.

My first position was with Château Haut-Brion in 1990. Following my stint with Haut-Brion, I worked with Dominus sister property Château Pétrus from 1991 until 1994. I then set out traveling, dividing time between soil study and winemaking at world-renowned wineries Badia a Coltibuono in Chianti and Chittering Estate in Australia. After returning to Napa full-time in 1995 and for the past 18 years, I've been working as a winemaking consultant for some of Napa's most highly regarded properties, including Vineyard 29, Hundred Acre, Dana Estates, Gemstone Vineyard, and Lail Vineyards. I have combined Bordeaux's classic winemaking techniques with everything Napa and Sonoma have to offer.

Winemakers are beginning to take more into consideration of the importance of how to handle the grapes upon arrival to the winery; for example, many wineries have incorporated gravity-flow techniques. Additionally, winemaking has become more extreme with longer maceration times and longer barrel aging. Better knowledge of the land and soil types . . . created huge improvement about vineyard plantation with better choices of rootstocks, clones, and density of planting. Also, much better water management with smart irrigation and water monitoring at the winery to minimize usage.

With my family's label, Melka Wines, one challenge is finding vineyard sites that have the ability to express the best combination of New World and Old World. For example, Knights Valley brings a sense of flavors from the New World with the classic *terroir* of Old World grape-growing regions (i.e., clay). I've been working with Cabernet Sauvignon, Merlot, and Cabernet Franc. I recently planted Sauvignon Blanc and Chardonnay in Knights Valley. I will potentially be working with vineyards in Paso Robles and Washington State. Although I don't currently have anything in the works at the time, Languedoc and Sicily have intrigued me as possible areas for vineyard sites.

My winemaking style is to make wines that showcase the purity of fruit and demonstrate finesse while letting the vineyard express itself. I would want people to say that the wines are telling the truth and are not superficial—they are storytellers with regard to the vineyard site, the people behind them, the vintage, and the context.

MARKHAM VINEYARDS

2812 St. Helena Highway North, St. Helena, CA 94574
(707) 963-5292, www.markhamvineyards.com

The Laurent Winery was built in 1879, the fourth oldest continuously operated in Napa Valley. Bruce Markham bought it in 1978, and Markham Vineyards now owns 350 acres of grapevines in Napa Valley. Kimberlee Nicholls directs winemaking. The rich, fruity Markham Vineyards Cellar 1879 Red Blend Napa Valley has notes of black cherry and smoked charcuterie. The soft and elegant Markham Vineyards Merlot offers aromas of rich black fruits and vanilla ice cream. 46

MARSTON FAMILY VINEYARD

3600 White Sulphur Springs Road, St. Helena, CA 94574
(707) 963-8490, www.marstonfamilyvineyard.com

Vines were planted on what is now the Marston Family Vineyard in the mid-1890s. In 1969 Michael and Alexandra Marston took over the property. Today they devote about 50 acres of their 500-acre estate solely to Cabernet Sauvignon and more than 200 acres to natural conservation efforts. The Marston Family Vineyard Spring Mountain District Cabernet Sauvignon offers rich, bold fruit aromas of red raspberries and black plums. 47

MAYACAMAS VINEYARDS

1155 Lokoya Road, Napa, CA 94558
(707) 224-4030, www.mayacamas.com

John Fisher, a German immigrant, sword engraver, and pickle merchant built the original winery in 1889 before founding the Fisher and Sons winemaking company. Robert and Elinor Travers bought Mayacamas Vineyards in 1968. In May 2013, a group including Charles Banks and wife, Ali—former owners of Screaming Eagle and Jonata—bought Mayacamas. The full-bodied Mayacamas Vineyards Cabernet Sauvignon proffers flavors of fresh dark fruits, and the crisp, clean Mayacamas Vineyards Chardonnay tastes of Anjou pear and stone fruits.

MELKA WINES

P.O. Box 82, Oakville, CA 94562
(707) 963-6008, www.melkawines.com

Philippe Melka studied winemaking under some of the world's finest Bordeaux winemakers and eventually chose Napa Valley to hone his craft. Consulting with many well-known wineries, he and wife, Cherie, decided to settle down in the valley, raise a family, and make wines under the Melka name. The big and lush Melka Wines CJ Napa Valley Cabernet Sauvignon tastes of black fruits and lifted Indian spices. The Melka Wines Métisse Napa Valley Jumping Goat Vineyard fills the mouth with luscious fruit and supple tannins.

MERUS WINES

424 Crystal Springs Road, St. Helena, CA 94574
(707) 251-5551, www.meruswines.com

Mark Herold and Erika Gottl began making wine in the two-car garage behind their home; their first vintage was 1998. Bill Foley bought Merus in 2007, and today the winery's offerings are available only to members and select restaurants. The full-bodied Merus Cabernet Sauvignon exhibits notes of black plums and black raspberries with a touch of anise.

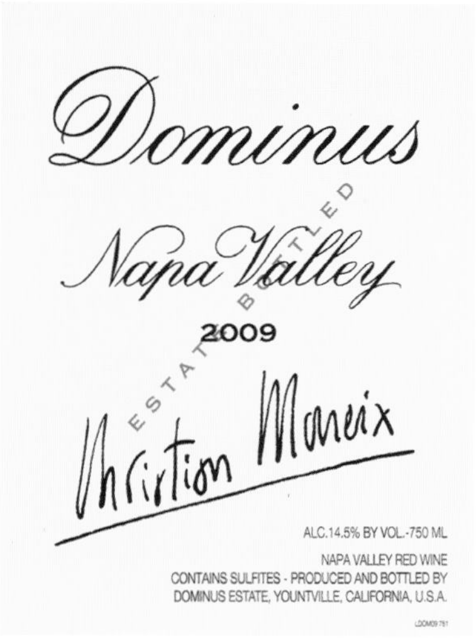

25

26

27

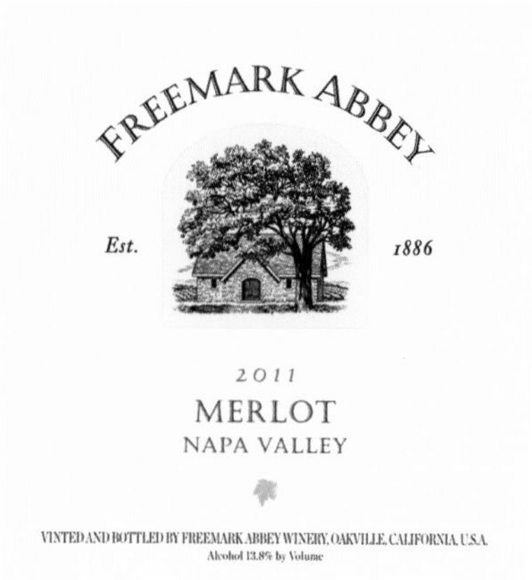

32

33

35

41

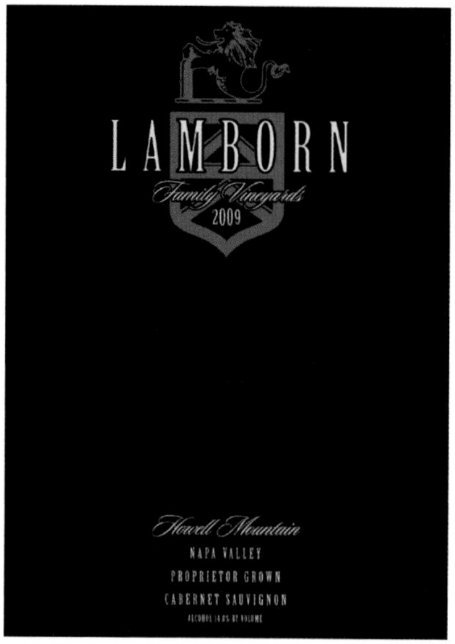

43

44

28

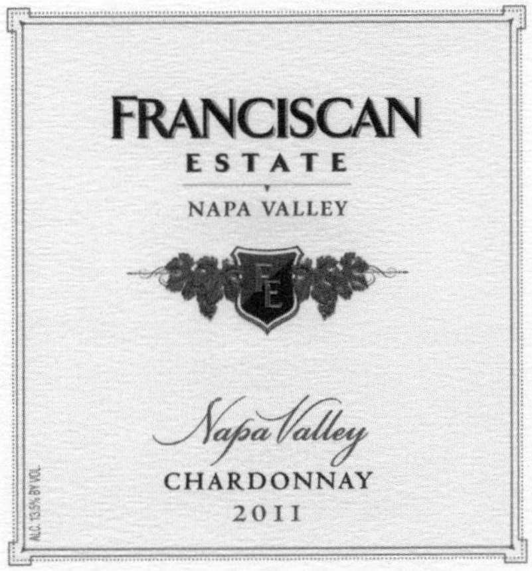

30

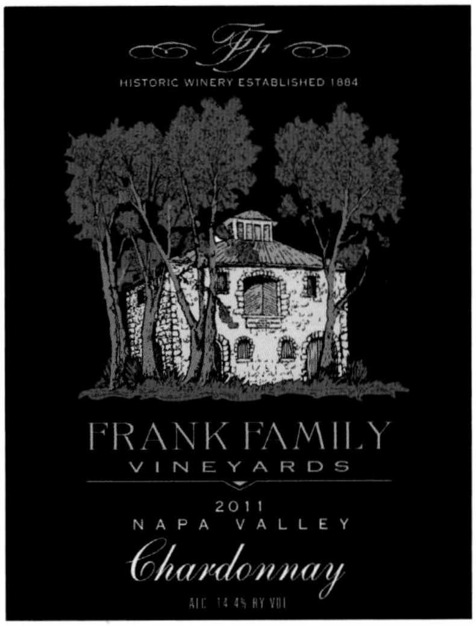

31

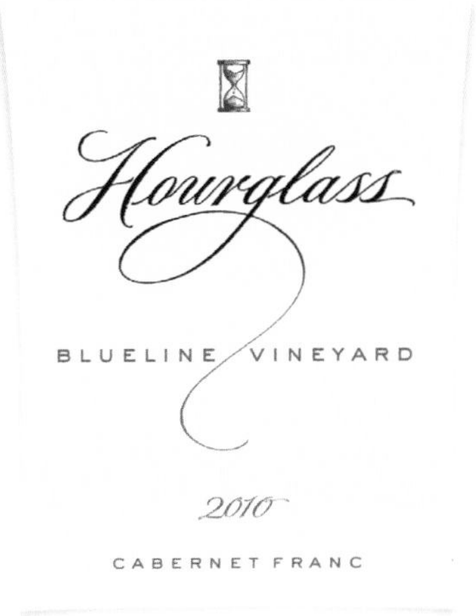

36

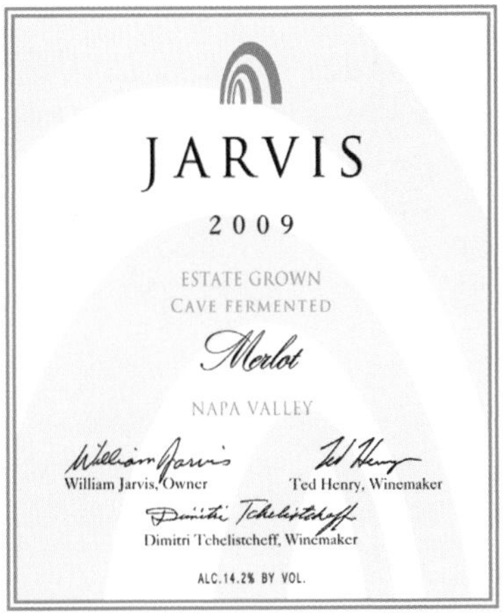

38

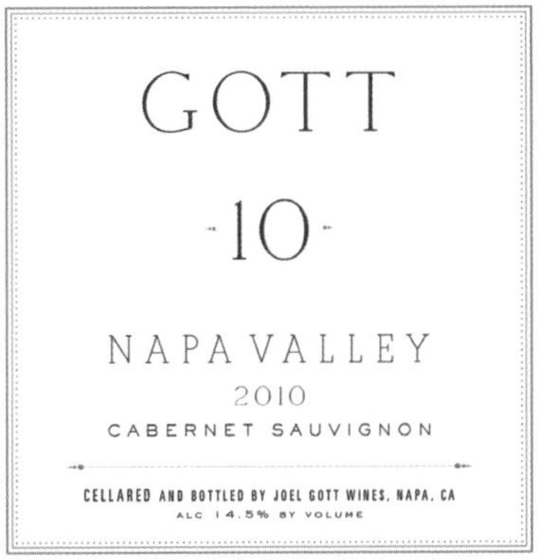

GOTT
10
NAPA VALLEY
2010
CABERNET SAUVIGNON
CELLARED AND BOTTLED BY JOEL GOTT WINES, NAPA, CA
ALC 14.5% BY VOLUME

39

45

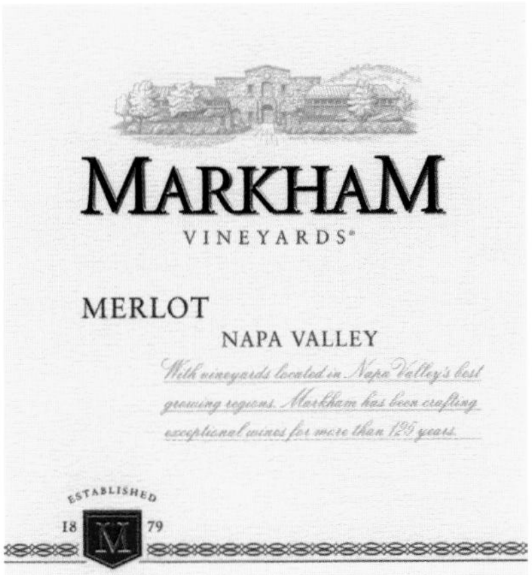

MARKHAM
VINEYARDS®
MERLOT
NAPA VALLEY
With vineyards located in Napa Valley's best growing regions, Markham has been crafting exceptional wines for more than 125 years.
ESTABLISHED
18 M 79

46

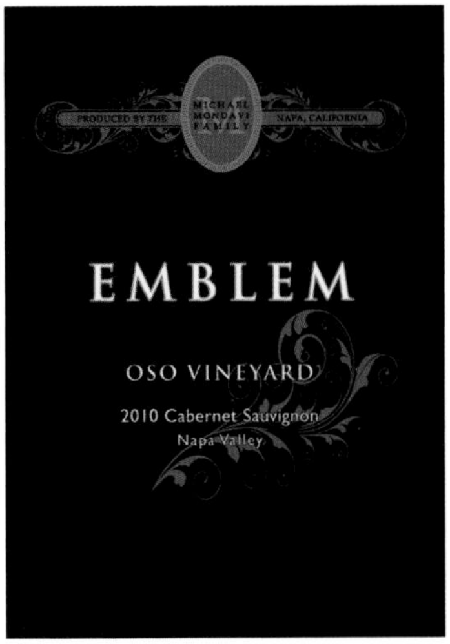

48

In his own words

MICHAEL MONDAVI

Michael Mondavi's career in wine began in 1966 when he cofounded the Robert Mondavi Winery in Napa Valley with his father, Robert Mondavi. Over the years he has taken an active role in the Wine Market Council, Napa Valley Vintners Association, Wine Institute, and Winegrowers of California, among others. He is the founder and "coach" of Folio Fine Wine Partners, a company he established in 2004 with wife, Isabel, and their children, Rob and Dina.

I grew up at the Charles Krug ranch, surrounded by vineyards; the winery was 100 yards from my home. The cellarmaster was my babysitter, and the tanks, barrels, and winemaking equipment were my jungle gym.

Mother Nature is truly the winemaker. The soil and microclimate are the genetic parents, and we are the babysitter, nanny, and teacher. I learned that I was not a winemaker but a wine grower and therefore able to produce wines that communicated the heritage of my family, the soil, and the microclimate where we grow those grapes. You face different challenges as a winemaker than you will as a winery owner. The winemaker's objective is to always produce wine with the personality and style that he or she is passionate about; that may not align entirely with the owner's needs. Managing this is a balance of managing a daily business without losing the wine style and the long-term vision of the company. The beauty of working with my son and daughter is we all share common goals and can make decisions as growers, winemakers, owners, and partners for our collective success.

I've had the pleasure of producing wine with my team in Tuscany in Italy, Languedoc-Roussillon in France, Chile, and Australia, in addition to making wines in Napa, Sonoma, and the Central Coast of California. Each area taught me a different heritage and philosophy of winemaking with techniques that varied from the traditional winemaking techniques practiced in Napa in the '60s and '70s to modern scientific techniques. It opened our eyes to innovation and improved techniques, many of which we are applying today. We are always looking to experiment with soil-microclimate combinations and how they impart different nuances of aroma and flavor to the wines. We have also learned how to better manage our vineyards to ensure we have a long growing season producing wines with moderate sugar and alcohol levels.

In the '60s and '70s, there were really two types of customers: the European immigrants for whom wine was a standard everyday beverage to be enjoyed with a meal and the international traveler or businessperson brought up enjoying wines in Europe or who used prestige wines for entertaining or enjoying at home. Today, the interest in wine and food is beyond our fondest dreams of 40 years ago, and wine is being embraced by everyone from the young Millennial through the thriving baby boomer generations.

The future is the past. Historically, the great wines from Napa in the 1800s were almost exclusively produced from hillside vineyards. From the '60s through the end of the twentieth century, the vast majority of Napa wines were produced in the valley floor. The best wines from Napa Valley will be produced from hillside vineyards. When our family purchased the Animo vineyard in Atlas Peak in the '90s, we knew it had the potential to produce some of the finest Cabernet Sauvignon in the region. We are still only learning the potential of this site, but it is exciting to see what lies ahead.

MICHAEL MONDAVI FAMILY ESTATE

No visitor facilities
Napa, CA 94559
(707) 256-2757, www.michaelmondavifamilyestate.com

Michael Mondavi's grandfather taught him that "all great winemakers must have respect for their soil and make good wine from the ground up," and his winemaking experience includes responsibility for the wines made at Robert Mondavi Winery from 1966 through 1975. His assistants there included winemaking luminaries such as Mike Ggrich, Zelma Long, and Warren Wirniarski. Grapes for Michael's iconic M Cabernet Sauvignon come solely from his Animo Vineyard, from the Italian word for "soul." Winemaking remains a family affair at Michael Mondavi Family Estate: wife, Isabel; son, Rob; and daughter, Dina, all take part. Tony Coltrin assists with winemaking and produces wine under his own label, Oberon. Rob Mondavi Jr.'s label is Spellbound, and he is winemaker for his mother's label, Isabel. Michael, Rob, and Dina all make wine under the Emblem label. The M by Michael Mondavi Cabernet Sauvignon has a luxurious mouthfeel and big yet restrained flavors of dark fruit and spice. The full-bodied Spellbound Petite Sirah offers a bouquet of mint, mocha, black raspberry, and plum. The Emblem Oso Vineyard Cabernet Sauvignon tastes of black fruits complemented by espresso, vanilla bean, and dark chocolate. The crisp, clean Isabel Mondavi Carneros Chardonnay has a nose of Seckel pear and Granny Smith apple. 48

MINER FAMILY WINERY

7850 Silverado Trail, Napa, CA 94558
(707) 944-9500, www.minerwines.com

Dave Miner left the corporate software world in 1993 and he joined Oakville Ranch Vineyards, owned then by his uncle Robert Miner. Dave and wife, Emily, met while working at Oakville Ranch, and in 1999 they married and started the Miner Family Winery. They released their first wine the same year, and they hope that the Miner family legacy will continue with daughters Sophie and Calla. Their flagship Miner Family Winery The Oracle Napa Valley offers aromas of black cherry, black raspberry, and coffee, drinkable now or in the next decade.

MI SUEÑO WINERY

910 Enterprise Way, Napa, CA 94558
(707) 258-6358, www.misuenowinery.com

Rolando Herrera's family emigrated from Mexico when he was young, and he began his wine country career as a dishwasher at Auberge du Soleil. Over the next 20 years he worked his way up at Stag's Leap Wine Cellars, Chateau Potelle, and Paul Hobbs Wine Consulting, eventually opening Mi Sueño, his "dream" winery. It currently lies in an industrial park, but Herrera plans to move it to a large estate winery with rolling vineyards. The Mi Sueño El Llano has aromas of espresso beans, dried cherries, and red plum, and the Mi Sueño Los Carneros Chardonnay offers bright flavors of green apple and lemon curd and a crisp, clean finish. 49

MOUNT VEEDER WINERY

1178 Galleron Road, Napa, CA 94574
(877) 545-4932, www.mtveeder.com

Michael and Arlene Bernstein bought the plum orchard that became the Mount Veeder Winery in the early 1960s. They planted vines and produced their first Cabernet Sauvignon in 1973. Today, Matt Ashby is vineyard manager and Janet Myers is winemaker. The Mount Veeder Winery Cabernet Sauvignon tastes of ripe dark fruits with a hint of chocolate-covered coffee beans. The Mount Veeder Winery Cabernet Franc has aromas of chocolate-covered cherries and black olive tapenade. 50

In his own words

ROB MONDAVI JR.

A fourth-generation California winemaker, Rob Mondavi Jr. and his family founded Folio Fine Wine Partners in 2004, followed by Michael Mondavi Family Estate in 2006. His role as president of winemaking has enabled him to return to his first passion: Today, Rob is the winemaker for Isabel Mondavi, Emblem, Animo, and the family's flagship "M" by Michael Mondavi.

Before I was born in 1971, my father and grandfather were laying the foundation and working tirelessly with the dream of creating the best Napa Valley wines. While bearing the Mondavi name carries a great responsibility, it also offers the opportunity to build upon, and push beyond, what has been done in the past. I was fortunate enough to have worked in our own wineries and vineyards—Robert Mondavi Winery, Vichon, and our joint venture, Opus One, where I worked as one of the opening cellar hands—for many years. While in McLaren Vale, South Australia, I visited twenty different wineries to better understand their fermentation techniques and winemaking philosophy. More recent travels have taken me to Europe, where I have been fortunate enough to meet with some of the best winemakers, including Artadi Viñedos & Vinos in Rioja, Celler Vall Llach in Priorat, and Tuscany's Ornellaia. Each of these wineries has a unique perspective that I wanted to understand, and all were willing to offer their time, knowledge, and mentoring.

The influence of technology has been enormous. With the development of data technology, we are now able to enter, track, and quantify data electronically, giving us better information for the vineyards and winery and helping us craft better wines. Also, the quality and availability of winery equipment that we have today is extraordinary. From destemmers and presses, to tanks and pumps, it helps us to improve the way we manage our winery.

To me, Napa Valley is a winemaker's nirvana. Here we have nearly 50 percent of the world's soil types; we have the diversity of valley floor through to hillside vineyards; and microclimates that vary from hot to very cool. The biggest challenge is climate change. Although overall we are blessed with good vintages, the climate is shifting our seasons, and I believe we have seen more variable climatic conditions over the last decade than we did in the prior 30 to 40 years. These shifts require us to stay nimble in the vineyards and the cellar so we can adapt and shift to make exceptional wines. We have always strived to be great, but today more than ever, there is a new edge, a passion that has people challenging the standard of excellence and raising the bar. When I can taste a sense of place and feel the guiding style of the winemaker, I know I have a special wine.

MUMM NAPA

8445 Silverado Trail, Rutherford, CA 94573
(707) 967-7770, www.mummnapa.com

Champagne house GH Mumm sent attaché Guy Devaux to the United States in 1979 to find suitable land on which to grow traditional Champagne grapes. His search ended in Napa Valley, and in 1986 Mumm Cuvée Napa was established. Devaux died in 1995, but his winemaking spirit continues with winemaker Ludovic Dervin, who had worked at Charles Heidsieck, California's Piper Sonoma, and in South Africa and Greece. The crisp, clean Mumm Napa Blanc de Blancs has aromas of toasted brioche, green apple, and hazelnut. The crisp yet generous Mumm Napa Devaux Ranch features notes of freshly cooked vanilla French toast and lemon curd.

NAPA CELLARS

P.O. Box 248, St. Helena, CA 94574
(707) 963-3104, www.napacellars.com

Since 2007, native Californian Joe Shirley, who left a premed trajectory to earn his master's in enology at UC Davis, has directed winemaking and blending at Napa Cellars, which also makes wines from Sonoma County grapes under the Folie à Deux label. The Napa Cellars Napa Valley Zinfandel tastes of cherry pie and fresh black fruits, and the Napa Cellars Napa Valley Cabernet Sauvignon offers notes of black plum and brown spice. 51

NEWTON VINEYARD

2555 Madrona Avenue, Yountville, CA 94599
(707) 963-9000, www.newtonvineyard.com

Peter Newton and Su Hua bought land on Spring Mountain in 1997 and planted Cabernet Sauvignon, Merlot, Petit Verdot, and Cabernet Franc vines around existing trees to avoid upsetting the landscape's natural balance. Australian Rob Mann directs winemaking, and the winery features a Chinese pagoda representing Su Hua's heritage, a British telephone booth representing Peter's British roots, and Solo Pino, a tall pine tree that graces Newton's wine label. The Newton Vineyard Unfiltered Chardonnay offers a flavor profile of pineapple upside-down cake followed by luscious tropical fruit flavors. The fruity-tasting Newton Vineyard Red Label Cabernet Sauvignon has aromas of black raspberry and red plum. 52

NICKEL & NICKEL

8164 St. Helena Highway, Rutherford, CA 94573
(707) 967-9600, www.nickelandnickel.com

In 1997 the partners at Far Niente decided to produce 100 percent single-varietal, single-vineyard wines. The team acquired the 42-acre John C. Sullenger Vineyard and began construction of a modern winery in the 1880s farmhouse on the property. Nickel & Nickel was born. The Nickel & Nickel Napa Valley Yountville State Ranch Vineyard Cabernet Sauvignon offers aromas of rich berries and Christmas baking spices and flavors of black fruits. The Nickel & Nickel Napa Valley Oakville Branding Iron Vineyard Cabernet Sauvignon has notes of spice and black cherry in the complex bouquet; age it for a few years and you'll enjoy it even more. 53

OAKVILLE RANCH VINEYARDS

7781 Silverado Trail, Napa, CA 94558
(707) 944-9665, www.oakvilleranchwinery.com

England-born Mary MacInnes met Bob Miner while working in Paris. Soon after, the couple married, moved to Napa Valley, and in 1989 acquired the Oakville Ranch. Anne Vawter directs winemaking, and vineyard management falls to Phil Coturri, who maintains both organic and biodynamic practices. The Oakville Ranch Napa Valley Chardonnay has aromas of apple pie and pear compote, with a slight vanilla nuance and a bright finish. The Oakville Ranch Napa Valley Robert's Cabernet Franc features aromas and flavors of fresh blackberries and blueberry pie and pairs well with heavy foods.

OAKVILLE WINERY

7830 St. Helena Highway, Oakville, CA 94562
(866) 422-4818, www.oakvillewinery.com

Established as Brun & Chaix in 1877 and reestablished in 1993, Oakville Winery produces wine in its Bonded Winery #9 Portfolio. The Oakville Winery Napa Valley Cabernet Sauvignon offers aromas of black currant and black raspberry, with rich fruit flavors, drinkable now or over the next 10 years.

OBERON

1285 Dealy Lane,Napa, CA 94559
(707) 256-2757, www.oberonwines.com

Napa-born winemaker Tony Coltrin crafts Oberon wines with the Michael Mondavi Family using Oberon's Sauvignon Blanc, Merlot, and Cabernet Sauvignon varieties. Oberon Napa Valley Cabernet proffers aromas and flavors of black plum, black currant, and black raspberry. The crisp, clean Oberon Napa Valley Sauvignon Blanc has flavors of tropical fruit, Anjou pear, and honeydew melon.

OPUS ONE

7900 St. Helena Highway, Oakville, CA 94562
(707) 944-9442, www.opusonewinery.com

Baron Philippe de Rothschild and Robert Mondavi met in 1970 in Hawaii, later forming a partnership that released wine under the Opus One label. They sold a single case in 1981, with the first commercial release in 1984. Within a year, Opus One became the first American ultrapremium wine, and by 1987 production had grown to 11,000 cases. The winery was completed in 1991, and production grew to 25,000 cases. Baron de Rothschild died in 1988, and his daughter, Baroness Philippine de Rothschild, remained at the helm until her death in 2014. Opus One CEO David Pearson has run the winery since 2004, and Michael Silacci directs winemaking. Rich and full-bodied, Opus One offers luscious dark fruit flavors and top notes of mocha and cherry cola. Drink it now, or age it for a decade. 54

O'SHAUGHNESSY ESTATE WINERY

1150 Friesen Drive, Angwin, CA 94508
(707) 965-2898, www.oshaughnessywinery.com

Minnesota native Betty O'Shaughnessy owned a cooking school in Minneapolis before moving to Oakville in 1990. She met husband, Paul Woolls, at a wine tasting soon thereafter, and today they run O'Shaughnessy Estate Winery. Sean Capiaux serves as president and founding winemaker, aided by winemakers team Aaron Elam and Orlando Preciado. The O'Shaughnessy Estate Winery Howell Mountain Cabernet Sauvignon tastes of blueberry pie and fresh blackberries, while the O'Shaughnessy Estate Winery Mount Veeder Cabernet Sauvignon has flavors of anise, charcuterie, black plums, and black raspberry.

PAHLMEYER WINERY

811 St. Helena Highway South, Suite 202, St. Helena, CA 94574
(707) 255-2321, www.pahlmeyer.com

Jayson Pahlmeyer admits that he likes a bit of international intrigue, and a local legend surrounding the winery has it that one of Pahlmeyer's partners "imported" French vines through Canada. But did those vines cross the border labeled as French or as purchased at UC Davis? Either way, what most people care about today is that Pahlmeyer's wines have a decidedly French flavor profile. Helen Turley held the title of winemaker in 1993, and Kale Anderson continues her legacy today. The smooth and velvety Pahlmeyer Proprietary Red Napa Valley has flavors of dark fruits and a nuance of Indian spice at the finish. The full-bodied Pahlmeyer Napa Valley Chardonnay has citrus flavors with a touch of buttered brioche.

PARADIGM WINERY

1277 Dwyer Road, Oakville, CA 94562
(707) 944-1683, www.paradigmwinery.com

Ren and Marilyn Harris acquired Paradigm Vineyards in 1976. Since their first vintage in 1991, Heidi Peterson Barrett has been winemaker, and her father, Dick Peterson, receives credit for the winery's layout and design. Annual production is around 5,000 cases, which account for about 30 percent of the grapes grown on the estate. The balance of the fruit is sold to neighbors who focus on premium wine. Big and bold yet round on the palate, the Paradigm Winery Napa Valley Oakville Cabernet Sauvignon has aromas of black cherry. The Paradigm Winery Napa Valley Oakville Cabernet Sauvignon offers a touch of spice on the palate and red cherry in the finish.

PARADUXX

7257 Silverado Trail, Napa, CA 94558
(707) 945-0890, www.paraduxx.com

Dan Duckhorn founded Paraduxx in 1994 to allow his winemakers the freedom to work with varieties other than Duckhorn's signature Bordeaux varieties and to make wines to appeal to contemporary tastes and cuisines. The winery opened in 2005 and features a ten-sided fermentation building designed to look like a traditional round barn. The smooth and food-friendly Paraduxx Z Blend Napa Valley Red Wine offers aromas of blueberry pie, black plum, and fresh blackberries. 55

PARALLEL NAPA VALLEY

169 Kreuzer Lane, St. Helena, CA 94559
(707) 255-1294, www.parallelwines.com

Three couples met while skiing in Park City, Utah, in the 1970s and became winemaking partners when they purchased their first vineyard on Maple Lane in Calistoga in 1999. In 2001 they hired Philippe Melka as winemaker, and in 2005 they released their first vintage of Parallel Napa Valley Cabernet Sauvignon 2003 at Deer Valley Ski Resort in their old stomping grounds. The Parallel Napa Valley Cabernet Sauvignon has flavors of sweet red cherry and black raspberry. The Parallel Napa Valley Black Diamonds Cabernet Sauvignon, which plays on the designation for ski trail difficulty, has a bouquet of black plum, dark cherry, and licorice and is round and opulent on the palate. 56

PATZ & HALL

851 Napa Valley Corporate Way, Napa, CA 94558
(707) 265-7700, www.patzhall.com

Started in 1988 by four friends and partners—Donald Patz, James Hall, Heather Patz, and Anne Moses—Patz & Hall sources its grapes from vineyards in Napa Valley, the Sonoma Coast, the Russian River Valley, Mendocino County, and the Santa Lucia Highlands. The full and round Patz & Hall Hyde Vineyard Carneros Chardonnay gives delicious citrus flavors before a long, luscious finish. The Patz & Hall Sonoma Coast Pinot Noir tastes warmly of dried black cherry and red raspberry. 57

PEJU FAMILY ESTATE WINERY

8466 St. Helena Highway, Rutherford, CA 94573
(707) 963-3600, www.peju.com

In 1982 Anthony Peju bought 30 acres of Rutherford vineyards that included Cabernet Sauvignon and French Colombard vines that were more than 60 years old. He and wife, HB, began selling their wine commercially three years later. Tony and HB now own more than 450 acres in the Napa Valley and produce 35,000 cases of estate-grown wines. Visitors to the tasting room can spot HB working in the flower garden and meet the next generation of the Peju family, Lisa and Ariana. The Peju Fifty/Fifty Rutherford Estate Vineyard has dark fruit flavors and a hint of cocoa powder. The Peju Rutherford Estate Vineyard Reserve Cabernet Sauvignon also has notes of dark fruit flavors but with top notes of Indian spice.

70

54

55

42

50

37

67

64

74

65

77

47

52

PHILIP TOGNI VINEYARD

3780 Spring Mountain Road, St. Helena, CA 94574
(707) 963-373, www.philiptognivineyard.com

Philip Togni earned his winemaking degree from the University of Bordeaux and worked at Château Lascombes. He; wife, Birgitta; and daughter, Lisa, have made wines for years. Their first wines, a Sauvignon Blanc and a Cabernet Sauvignon, were bottled in 1983, and today the family concentrates on Bordeaux-style blends made from grapes grown on their 25 acres of Cabernet Sauvignon, Cabernet Franc, Merlot, and Petit Verdot. They limit annual production to 2,000 cases. The Philip Togni Estate Cabernet Sauvignon offers aromas of black plums, dark fruits, and air-dried charcuterie. If you can wait a few years, it only gets better.

PINE RIDGE VINEYARDS

5901 Silverado Trail, Napa, CA 94558
(707) 253-7500, www.pineridgevineyards.com

Gary Andrus founded Pine Ridge in 1978 and planted Cabernet Franc, Cabernet Sauvignon, Malbec, and Petit Verdot. Over time the vineyard grew, and today the estate's 200 acres span five Napa Valley AVAs. Michael Beaulac directs winemaking. The crisp, clean Pine Ridge Chenin Blanc + Viognier offers flavors of white stone fruit, Cavaillon melon, and grapefruit and pairs well with Asian-inspired cuisine. The Pine Ridge Vineyards Napa Valley Cabernet Sauvignon tastes of cherry and blackberry with notes of mocha and crème brûlée. 58

PLUMPJACK WINERY

620 Oakville Cross Road, Oakville, CA 94558
(707) 945-1220, www.plumpjack.com

Gavin Newsom and Gordon Getty founded their winery in 1995, naming it after Shakespeare's character Sir John "PlumpJack" Falstaff, whose famous line about wine consumption, "God help the wicked," echoes Newsom and Getty's sentiments. Known for its Cabernet Sauvignons, the winery and the surrounding 42-acre estate vineyard date back to the 1800s. Today winemaker Aaron Miller bottles approximately half of PlumpJack's reserve wines under screw caps, and PlumpJack Winery is one of the first Napa Valley wineries to use screw caps on super-premium wines. The PlumpJack Oakville Estate Cabernet Sauvignon offers aromas of black raspberry, freshly ground black peppercorns, and dried black cherry with a pleasant top note of peppermint.

PRIDE MOUNTAIN VINEYARDS

4026 Spring Mountain Road, St. Helena, CA 94574
(707) 963-4949, www.pridewines.com

The Summit Ranch once was home to a dilapidated winery that served the entire mountain community. Jim and Carolyn Pride fell in love with it in 1989 and bottled their first vintage in 1991. Because it straddles on the county border, Pride Mountain Vineyards must maintain two separate facilities, one in Sonoma County and one in Napa County. The crush pad has a dividing line down the middle, and some wines are labeled Napa and others are labeled Sonoma. In 1999 the family dug a 23,000-square-foot cave to house approximately 2,400 of its barrels. The crisp, clean Pride Mountain Vineyard Vintner Select Chardonnay has aromas of Granny Smith apple and honeydew melon, and the Pride Mountain Vineyard Syrah has black plum in the bouquet and flavors of cassis and smoked sausage.

QUINTESSA

1601 Silverado Trail South, St. Helena, CA 94574
(707) 967-1601, www.quintessa.com

Chilean-born Agustin Huneeus began his wine career in 1960 as CEO of Concha y Toro. He later worked with Seagram's and Noble Vineyard and was a partner at Franciscan Estates. Today he focuses his energy and talent on Quintessa. His estate consists of 280 acres, 170 under vines, including Cabernet Sauvignon, Merlot, Cabernet Franc, Petit Verdot, and Carménère. The name refers to the property's five hills and microclimates. Son Agustin Jr. helps run the family company in California and Chile. The Quintessa has aromas of black plums, black raspberries, and cassis, with a lush and elegant finish. Drink it now, or store it for a few years. The fruit-finishing Faust Napa Valley Cabernet Sauvignon offers a nose of black raspberry, ripe cherry, and black currant in the bouquet. Also drink it now, or hold it for four to six years. 59

RAYMOND VINEYARDS

849 Zinfandel Lane, St. Helena, CA 94574
(707) 963-3141, www.raymondvineyards.com

Roy Raymond moved to the Napa Valley in 1933, married Martha Jane Beringer a few years later, and worked at her family's winery for more than 35 years before putting his name on a wine label. His first crush was in 1974, and the family continued making wine under its own name for the next 35 years. In 2009 French wine scion Jean-Charles Boisset and his family purchased the property. Stephanie Putnam directs winemaking with Kathy George as assistant winemaker, and Eric Pooler manages the 300 acres of estate-owned vineyards. The full-bodied Raymond Vineyards Generations Napa Valley Cabernet Sauvignon offers aromas of black cherry, Christmas baking spices, and black raspberry. Drink it now, or hold it for up to 12 years for added complexity. The Raymond Vineyards District Collection Napa Valley Calistoga Cabernet Sauvignon features flavors of black cherry and mocha.

In his own words

AGUSTIN F. HUNEEUS JR.

The Huneeus family's holdings, labels, and partnerships include Quintessa, Faust, Illumination, Veramonte, Neyen, Flowers Vineyards and Winery, The Prisoner, and Saldo. Agustin F. Huneeus Jr. (right) has worked in the family business for more than 20 years and continues the family tradition as head of the wine portfolio in America and abroad.

I grew up in the vineyards, visiting wineries, first in Chile and then in Argentina and finally in the Napa Valley, which gives me a unique perspective to think outside the box when we are developing a new blend or harvesting practices. "Wines are a reflection of place," as my father would say. We create wines with a reason for being that represent where the grapes come from. We produce high-quality wines with no compromises or short-cuts. And we own our vineyards, so this means we are in the business of farming. Being at the mercy of Mother Nature is always tough, as the weather can change the outcome of a harvest overnight. One frost can change yields and sugars for an entire vintage. But to make great wine you have to take risks in farming, and that's what we do each year.

In the 20 years I have been in the wine business, I have seen wine go from a niche, unknown product to a mainstream culture where everyone is into wine. It's been great to see Napa become such an important producer of Cabernet in the world and to see the growth of Sonoma Coast Pinot Noirs. If you make wine, chances are you're a wine geek. The greatest results come from winemaking having the ability to influence consumers. Pioneers who led the way, like Robert Mondavi, created wine styles that were new and enticing that had a huge impact on the market. But then with wines like The Prisoner, which started slow, this is now a phenomenon due to the market influencing our winemaking choices.

REYNOLDS FAMILY WINERY

3266 Silverado Trail, Napa, CA 94558
(707) 258-2558, www.reynoldsfamilywinery.com

With his wife's blessing, former dentist Steve Reynolds traded in his chair and drills for construction tools and farm implements in 1994. Steve and Susie bought a 100-year-old chicken ranch, renovated the existing structures, and built new ones. They planted 10 acres of Cabernet Sauvignon in 1996, built a Tuscan-style winery, and produced their first vintage in 1999. The velvety Reynolds Family Winery Persistence has notes of black plum, cassis, and truffle in the bouquet. The Reynolds Family Winery Cabernet Sauvignon offers flavors of black raspberry and black plum.

ROBERT BIALE VINEYARDS

4038 Big Ranch Road, Napa, CA 94558
(707) 257-7555, www.robertbialevineyards.com

Pietro Biale emigrated from Genoa to the Napa Valley and began raising chickens and planting Zinfandel vines in 1937. His son Aldo discreetly sold jugs of homemade Zinfandel wine to help the family through the Depression, using the code words "black chicken." In 1991, Aldo and his son Robert began commercially selling Zinfandel made from Aldo's Vineyard. The current winemaker is Tres Goetting. The Robert Biale Vineyards Napa Valley Black Chicken Zinfandel offers lush fruit flavors, and the fruit-forward Robert Biale Founding Farmers Napa Valley Zinfandel has aromas of blackberry preserves, red plum, and cinnamon.

ROBERT CRAIG WINERY

625 Imperial Way, Napa, CA 94559
(707) 252-2250, www.robertcraigwine.com

Robert Craig started his winery with three partners in 1992 and released his first wine in 1995, but not until 2002 did the Craig family finish their long-awaited winery atop Howell Mountain. The fruit-forward but restrained Robert Craig Affinity Napa Valley Cabernet Sauvignon offers notes of Mediterranean spices and rich dark berries. The Robert Craig Howell Mountain Zinfandel has aromas of dark fruits and is powerful and complex in the mouth. Drink it now, or age it for up to eight years. 60

ROBERT FOLEY VINEYARDS

P.O. Box 847, Angwin, CA 94508
(707) 0965-2669, www.robertfoleyvineyards.com

Bob Foley began making wine in Napa in 1977, bottling his flagship claret in 1998. Today he produces wine on Napa Valley's Howell Mountain, and when he's not at the winery, you might find him performing with his rock group, the Robert Foley Band. The Robert Foley Vineyards Napa Valley Merlot boasts flavors of chocolate, coffee bean, and vanilla. The Robert Foley Vineyards Napa Valley Cabernet Sauvignon is rich with ripe fruit and has aromas of cherry vanilla ice cream topped with dried black cherries and fresh black raspberries. 61

ROBERT MONDAVI WINERY

7801 St. Helena Highway, Oakville, CA 94574
(707) 226-1395, www.robertmondaviwinery.com

When Robert Mondavi walked through To Kalon Vineyard (Greek for "the good"), planted in 1868, he knew it was special and established his eponymous winery here in 1966. A traditionalist who believed that wines should reflect their origins and an innovator who embraced the latest techniques,

Mondavi receives credit for developing Fumé Blanc, his winery's signature wine. Today, visitors can enjoy art installations curated by Robert's widow, Margrit, food and wine tours, and seasonal musical performances in the central courtyard. The Robert Mondavi Winery Napa Valley Reserve Cabernet Sauvignon has aromas of black currant, licorice, and smoked meats and rich fruit flavors. The fruity, crisp, and creamy Robert Mondavi Winery Napa Valley Reserve Fumé Blanc has aromas of citrus, lychee fruit, and dried fragrant herbs.

ROBERT SINSKEY VINEYARDS

6320 Silverado Trail, Napa, CA 94558
(707) 944-9090, www.robertsinskey.com

California-born and New York–educated, Robert Sinskey isn't your typical winemaker and doesn't let not attending winemaking school hold him back. Over the last 20 years he has increased his holdings to more than 200 acres of biodynamic and organic-certified vineyards in Stags Leap, Carneros, and Sonoma Valley. The crisp and refreshing Robert Sinskey Pinot Gris, ideal as an aperitif or paired with light cuisine, tastes of white stone fruits, pear, and citrus. The Robert Sinskey POV offers aromas and flavors of black plums and black cherries. (62)

ROCCA FAMILY VINEYARDS

129 Devlin Road, Napa, CA 94558
(707) 257-8467, www.roccawines.com

Dentist Mary Rocca and physician Eric Grigsby dreamed of reestablishing their childhood connection with farming, so they purchased 21 acres in the Napa Valley and founded Rocca Family Vineyards in 1999. The duo brought in Celia Welch as winemaker and produced their initial bottling in 2000. Mary subsequently purchased the 11-acre Collinetta Vineyard in the Coombsville appellation. Paul Colantuoni is the winemaker today. The Rocca Family Vineyards Estate Collinetta Vineyard Cabernet Sauvignon boasts flavors of black cherry and dark chocolate before a long-lasting finish. The big and fruit-forward Rocca Family Vineyards Vespera smells of cassis, black cherry, and Christmas baking spices. (63)

ROMBAUER WINERY

3522 Silverado Trail North, St. Helena, CA 94574
(800) 622-2206, www.rombauer.com

The Rombauers' ancestors came from the Rheingau region of Germany, but the American branch of the family began its Napa legacy in 1980. The Rombauers have food and wine pairing down to a science, and many of the wines are paired expertly with recipes written by Koerner Rombauer's great-aunt Irma Rombauer, author of the famous cookbook *Joy of Cooking*. The Rombauer Winery Carneros Merlot has aromas of black cherry, red plum, and peppermint, and the Rombauer Winery Carneros Chardonnay, with notes of caramelized peach and melon in the bouquet, is fat and creamy in the mouth.

ROOTS RUN DEEP WINERY

83 Zinfandel Lane, Building C, St. Helena, CA 94574
(707) 945-1045, www.rootsrundeep.com

Mark Albrecht worked for 20 years in the wine business before launching his Roots Run Deep brand. Barry Gnekow directs winemaking. The Roots Run Deep Winery Hypothesis Napa Valley Cabernet Sauvignon boasts flavor notes of rich, ripe black fruits. The Roots Run Deep Winery Educated Guess Napa Valley Cabernet Sauvignon has aromas of black raspberry, dried black cherry, and dark chocolate and a silky-smooth mouthfeel.

ROY ESTATE

Visits only by appointment
(707) 255-4409, www.royestate.com

Both from the East Coast, Charles and Shirley Roy fell in love with Napa Valley and in 1999 purchased Johnny Miller's estate. In 2005 they brought in winemaker Philippe Melka. Generous in the mouth, Roy Estate Cabernet Sauvignon has flavors of black fruits and anise. Drink it now, or store it for up to 15 years. The Roy Estate Proprietary Red Wine boasts fresh fruit flavors and secondary tastes of dark chocolate and mocha.

RUDD WINERY

500 Oakville Cross Road, Oakville, CA 94562
(707) 944-8577, www.ruddwines.com

Leslie Rudd acquired what became his eponumous winery in 1996, and he has been growing Bordeaux varieties there ever since. He expanded the cellar facilities, and today below the property lie more than 20,000 square feet of caves. Patrick Sullivan directs winemaking, and Leslie's wife, Susan, grows organic vegetables in a two-acre garden, created with landscape architect Thomas Hobbs, for the family's Press Restaurant in St. Helena. The Rudd Winery Mount Veeder Sauvignon Blanc offers pronounced peach flavors. Generous in the mouth, Rudd Oakville Estate Red gives fragrances of cassis, espresso, and dark chocolate. Drink it now, or hold it for a decade or so.

RUTHERFORD GROVE WINERY AND VINEYARDS

1673 Highway 29, Rutherford, CA 94573
(707) 963-0544, www.rutherfordgrove.com

Italian immigrant Albino Pestoni planted the vineyards that became Bonded Winery 935 in 1892, and in 1963 his descendants created a composting facility for discarded grape seeds, skins, and stems—the first in the valley. In the mid-1990s the family acquired another small winery and created Rutherford Grove. They now make about 4,000 cases of wine entirely from estate vineyards grown on 60 acres in four different AVAs. The Rutherford Grove Winery and Vineyards Rutherford Estate Cabernet Sauvignon tastes of black fruits and cherry vanilla, with a persistent finish. The Rutherford Grove Winery and Vineyards Pestoni Family Estate Reserve Merlot combines flavors of black cherries, black raspberries, and anise in a luxurious fruity finish. 64

RUTHERFORD HILL

200 Rutherford Hill Road, Rutherford, CA 94573
(707) 963-1871, www.rutherfordhill.com

Anthony Terlato and his sons, Bill and John, bought Rutherford Hill in 1996, and they continue the tradition of making Rutherford Bench Merlot-based wines from its select vineyards. The Rutherford Hill Barrel Select Red Blend has big flavors of black plum and black cherry. Fruity on the palate, Rutherford Hill Merlot has aromas of black raspberry and red plum.

SAINTSBURY

1500 Los Carneros Avenue, Napa, CA 94559
(707) 252-0592, www.saintsbury.com

Richard Ward and David Graves met in 1977 in a beer-brewing class at UC Davis. Both men enjoyed a hearty home brew and shared a passion for Burgundy wines. The next year they roomed together during harvests at Chappellet and Stag's Leap Wine Cellar, and in 1981 they cofounded Saintsbury. Over the years, a few winemakers have passed through their doors, with French-born Jérome Chéry taking the helm in 2004. Voluptuous in the mouth, the Saintsbury Carneros Pinot Noir offers notes of black cherry, fruits of the wood, and ripe red cherry. The rich Saintsbury Carneros Chardonnay has aromas of Anjou pear and Granny Smith apple.

ST. SUPÉRY ESTATE VINEYARDS AND WINERY

8440 St. Helena Highway, Rutherford, CA 94573
(707) 963-4507, www.stsupery.com

Founded in 1982 by French businessman Robert Skalli and his family, St. Supéry began with the 1,531-acre Dollarhide Ranch, which dates back to the late 1800s. The vineyards have more than 500 acres, primarily Sauvignon Blanc and Cabernet Sauvignon, followed by Merlot, Chardonnay, Muscat Canelli, Sémillon, Malbec, Petit Verdot, and Cabernet Franc. Michael Scholz, who earned his enology degree from Roseworthy College in Australia, heads winemaking. The clean, crisp St. Supéry Napa Valley Estate Sauvignon Blanc boasts tropical fruit flavors, and the full-bodied St. Supéry Napa Valley Estate Cabernet Sauvignon has persistent flavors of black fruits and dark cocoa powder. 65

SCHRADER CELLARS

P.O. Box 1004, Calistoga, CA 94515
(707) 942-1540, www.schradercellars.com

Fred Schrader attended Auction Napa Valley in 1988 and was hooked. He soon cofounded Colgin-Schrader Cellars, and in 1998 he started his eponymous Schrader Cellars, where Thomas Brown directs winemaking. The Schrader Cellars CCS Beckstoffer To Kalon Vineyard Cabernet Sauvignon is bold, with aromas of anise, eucalyptus, and ripe dark fruits. Drink it now, or hold it for a decade or so. The Schrader Cellars Beckstoffer To Kalon Vineyard Cabernet Sauvignon has aromas of black currant, Christmas baking spice, dark chocolate, and espresso bean. It's delicious now, but age it for a few years.

SCHRAMSBERG

1400 Schramsberg Road, Calistoga, CA 94515
(707) 942-4558, www.schramsberg.com

Jacob Schram emigrated from Germany in 1826 and eventually came to Napa Valley. The son of a winemaker, he cleared trees and planted vines on the large piece of land he purchased in 1862, and thus Schramsberg began. His production reached 12,000 gallons of wine per year by 1876, and he shipped wine across the country to New York. Schramsberg had numerous owners after Schram's death, but its modern-day incarnation began with its acquisition by Jack and Jamie Davies in 1965. The Schramsberg Blanc de Blancs boasts aromas of tropical fruit, citrus, freshly baked bread, and Granny Smith apple, and the J. Davies Diamond Mountain District Cabernet Sauvignon tastes of ripe sweet black cherry and black raspberry preserves. 66

SCHWEIGER VINEYARDS

4015 Spring Mountain Road, St. Helena, CA 94574
(707) 963-4882, www.schweigervineyards.com

The Schweiger family bought land on Spring Mountain in the early 1960s but didn't plant vines until the early 1980s. At first, they sold grapes to area wineries, including Stags' Leap and Newton, but in 1994 the family created its own label. The new winery was constructed using eco-friendly technology, and solar panels generate all of its electricity. The crisp and refreshing Schweiger Vineyards Sauvignon Blanc has aromas of Granny Smith apples and lemongrass. The Schweiger Vineyards Dedication offers notes of dark ripe berries and is rich but restrained in the mouth. 67

In his own words
MICHAEL TRUJILLO

Winemaker Michael Trujillo began his career in 1982 when he visited a family friend at Sequoia Grove who then offered him a job. Michael learned his winemaking skills and techniques by working closely with some of California's legends, including André Tchelistcheff and Tony Soter.

I took a trip to Napa on college spring break in 1981 and never left. Sequoia Grove founder Jim Allen offered me a job. I learned my craft working with Jim and consulting winemakers André Tchelistcheff and Tony Soter and then later at University of California, Davis, and the Napa Valley School of Cellaring.

Science has played a big role in changing the way we think about farming and the growing of grapes. When I first started in the '80s, conversations about soil and rootstocks were happening, but now these factors are part of everyday life. Napa Valley used to be a hodgepodge of grape varieties, but science has given us a more in-depth view of the best land for the right grapes. We now work in terms of microclimates, soil types, and *terroir*. We're no longer growing Chardonnay in Calistoga because we know it grows better in cooler-climate Carneros. We know what we want to grow and where and how to grow it.

I love to express varietal character and show a wine's true sense of place. You don't need to put too much frosting on the cake, as I like to say about winemaking. I want to make wines that express where they came from, the season they experienced, and the emotion tied to the land. As a winemaker my job is to guide the wine to be an expression of the season and vineyards.

Year in and year out, the biggest challenge for a winemaker is Mother Nature. The weather is unpredictable and creates a waiting game that can put even the most tenured winemaker on edge. It's what keeps us on our toes and challenges us. When it comes to the business of running a winery, the biggest challenges are with the markets, such as grape inflation, energy, and operation costs. This is a big part of the reason why we have made controlling our fruit sources such a priority.

My favorite appellation is Rutherford. Cabernet Sauvignon grown on the Rutherford Bench is the best in all of Napa. Our newest vineyard acquisition, Tonella, is a great piece of Rutherford that our vineyard manager, Steve Allen, replanted to select Cabernet Sauvignon clones that take advantage of the "sweet spot" Napa Valley has for Cabernet. That said, I am curious and am always experimenting with small projects with everything from Tempranillo to Malbec and Rhône varietals. I constantly experiment with fermentations, extractions, and yeast. I enjoy the scientific side of winemaking and embrace any information new technology can give us, but I also firmly believe in the role of intuition. My goal is to make balanced, sexy wines that stand as true expressions of the land. Wines don't have to be huge to have character. If a wine is balanced from first smell to lingering aftertaste, that is what I call art in a glass.

SCIANDRI FAMILY VINEYARDS

50 Kreuse Canyon Drive, Napa, CA 94559
(707) 277-4999, www.sciandrivineyards.com

Descended from Tuscan immigrants, Ron and Roberta Sciandri, Ron Jr., Ryan, and Rebecca and Andy make wine with grapes grown on their Cabernet Sauvignon, Petit Verdot, Cabernet Franc, Malbec, and Merlot vines. Don Baker directs winemaking, Javier Rentoria manages the vineyards, and the family dog, Fudge, a chocolate Labrador, leads the welcome committee. The fruit-forward Sciandri Family Vineyards Napa Valley Coombsville Cabernet Sauvignon boasts aromas of black raspberry and black plum.

SCREAMING EAGLE

P.O. Box 12, Oakville, CA 94562
(707) 944-0749, www.screamingeagle.com

Plenty of people have heard of Screaming Eagle, but the wine is made in such small quantities that it's extremely difficult to source. Founder Jean Phillips hired Heidi Peterson Barrett as Screaming Eagle's first winemaker. Phillips sold the estate in 2006, and today Stan Kroenke owns it. Full and bold, Screaming Eagle has abundant aromas of black raspberry and ripe black currant.

SEAVEY VINEYARD

1310 Conn Valley Road, St. Helena, CA 94574
(707) 963-8339, www.seaveyvineyard.com

In 1979, William and Mary Seavey bought the Franco-Swiss Farming Company estate—planted as a vineyard in the late 1800s but most recently used as a cattle ranch—from a family friend. William worked in San Francisco during the week, and he and the family replanted vines on weekends and during school vacations. Mary died in 2008, but William and the family continue to run the winery. The Seavey Cabernet Sauvignon offers aromas of Indian spice and rich ripe black fruits, with a fruit-filled finish. The crisp and clean Seavey Chardonnay features aromas of white stone fruits and citrus.

SEQUOIA GROVE

8338 St. Helena Highway, Rutherford, CA 94558
(707) 944-2945, www.sequoiagrove.com

Sequoia Grove winery sits on 22 acres of mineral-rich alluvial soils on the Rutherford Bench valley floor, and majestic sequoias surround its 150-year-old barn/tasting room. Director of winemaking Michael Trujillo has been with Sequoia Grove since its start in 1982 and is assisted by winemaker Molly Hill. Together they make wines from 100 percent Napa Valley grapes. Sequoia Grove Winery formed a partnership with the Sequoia Parks Foundation, dedicated to preserving the trees' natural environs, with a percentage of winery sales going to the organization. The Sequoia Grove Napa Valley Cabernet Sauvignon boasts flavors of dark fruit, clove, and dark chocolate, and the Sequoia Grove Cambium tastes of rich ripe fruit, French toast, and dark chocolate. Enjoy it now, or save it for a few years.

SHAFER VINEYARDS

6154 Silverado Trail, Napa, CA 94558
(707) 944-2877, www.shafervineyards.com

Publisher-turned-winery-owner John Shafer purchased a 210-acre estate in Stags Leap District and moved his family to Napa Valley in 1972. Many of the original vines dated back to the 1920s, though, and needed replanting. The current vineyard consists of 50 planted acres. Former winemaker and now winery president Doug Shafer heads the winemaking team with winemaker Elias Fernandez. The Shafer Vineyards Red Shoulder Ranch Chardonnay offers notes of tropical fruits and caramelized pineapple, with extended fruit flavors. The Shafer Vineyards Napa Valley Relentless has ripe fruit on the palate and a complex finish.

SILVERADO VINEYARDS

6121 Silverado Trail, Napa, CA 94558
(707) 259-6617, www.silveradovineyards.com

Diane Disney Miller and her mother first visited the Napa Valley in 1975 to tour two wineries up for sale. As time passed, more vineyard parcels became available, so Diane and husband, Ron, bought one parcel and Diane's mother purchased another. The Millers chose architect Richard Keith to design their winery and Jack Stuart as their first winemaker. Over the years the Millers have purchased additional vineyards in Carneros, Mount George, and Soda Canyon. Jack Stuart retired in 2004, and Jon Emmerich, Elena Franceschi, Fred Hansen, and Rick Thomas now carry out winemaking. The fruit-forward Silverado Vineyards Estate Cabernet Sauvignon has aromas of black plum, Christmas baking spices, and anise, while the Silverado Vineyards Carneros Chardonnay offers notes of lime, lemon curd, and tropical fruits.

SILVER OAK CELLARS

915 Oakville Cross Road, Oakville, CA 94562
(707) 942-7022, www.silveroak.com

Raymond T. Duncan first visited Napa in the late 1960s, buying land here and in Alexander Valley. In 1972 he purchased an old dairy farm in Oakville and planted vines with the help of Justin Meyer. The duo produced their first wine the same year using Alexander Valley fruit, but it wasn't until 1979 that they produced their first Napa Valley Cabernet Sauvignon. Since then Silver Oak has produced two wines each vintage: a Napa Valley Cabernet Sauvignon and an Alexander Valley Cabernet Sauvignon. In 2001 Justin Meyer sold his share of the company to the Duncan family, who built a new winery on the Oakville property in 2008. Big and bold, the Silver Oak Cellars Napa Valley Cabernet Sauvignon has aromas of black raspberry, black plum, and a touch of spice. The velvety Silver Oak Cellars Alexander Valley Cabernet Sauvignon offers flavors of black plum and dark chocolate; drink it now, or keep it for 15 years or so. 68

SMITH-MADRONE VINEYARDS AND WINERY

4022 Spring Mountain Road, St. Helena, CA 94574
(707) 963-2283, www.smithmadrone.com

President Chester Arthur signed the deed for what became Smith-Madrone Vineyards on December 5, 1884, and on December 5, 1933, Prohibition ended. December 5, 2012, marked the milestone release of the winery's first reserve wine, Cooks Flat Reserve, named for George Cook, who first owned the property. Only 2,052 bottles were made, and each is numbered and bears a copy of the 1884 US Land Office deed. The Smith-Madrone Napa Valley Spring Mountain District Cabernet Sauvignon has aromas of cassis and blueberry pie, and the Smith-Madrone Napa Valley Spring Mountain District Chardonnay smells of pear, citrus, and Golden Delicious apple. 69

SNOWDEN VINEYARDS

1478 Railroad Avenue, St. Helena, CA 94574
(707) 963-4292, www.snowdenvineyards.com

Wayne and Virginia Snowden purchased seven acres of vines and six acres of fruit orchards in 1955 and for years sold their grapes to local cooperatives. In 1962 they planted Cabernet Sauvignon vines, and after Wayne's death in 1977 sons Scott and Randy replanted the fruit orchards with more Cabernet Sauvignon. The family continued selling most of their grapes for the next 15 years, but in 1993 they created their own label. The Snowden Vineyards Napa Valley Reserve Cabernet Sauvignon has aromas of red plums and flavors of ripe fruit, and the Snowden Vineyards Lost Vineyard Napa Valley Merlot smells of red fruits and a touch of sweet baking spices. 70

SPRING MOUNTAIN VINEYARD

2805 Spring Mountain Road, St. Helena, CA 94574
(707) 967-4188, www.springmountainvineyard.com

Originally three properties, each with its own winery, Spring Mountain Vineyard includes some of the first vineyards planted by Frederick and Jacob Beringer in 1882. The old Chateau Chevalier property joined the fold in 1993, with La Perla and Miravalle added in 1996. The full-bodied Spring Mountain Vineyard Elivette has aromas of black currant, Chinese five-spice powder, and cherry cola, and the clean, refreshing Spring Mountain Vineyard Estate Sauvignon Blanc smells of kumquat and tropical fruits.

STAG'S LEAP WINE CELLARS

5766 Silverado Trail, Napa, CA 94558
(707) 944-2020, www.cask23.com

Founded in 1970, Stag's Leap Wine Cellars achieved almost immediate success with its S.L.V. Cabernet Sauvignon 1973, rated number one at the Judgment of Paris. Podiatrist-turned-winemaker Nicki Pruss directs winemaking, and Kirk Grace manages the vineyards. Big, fruit-forward, and elegant, the Stag's Leap Wine Cellars Artemis Cabernet Sauvignon has aromas of dark plums and black raspberries. The Stag's Leap Wine Cellars Karia Chardonnay takes its name from the Greek word for "graceful" and offers notes of Anjou pear, Granny Smith apple, and citrus. 71

STAGS' LEAP WINERY

6150 Silverado Trail, Napa, CA 94558
(800) 395-2441, www.stagsleap.com

Not to be confused with the above, Stags' Leap was established in 1893, but modern-day wine production began in 1971 when Carl Doumani purchased the property. Treasury Wine Estates owns it today. The Stags' Leap Winery Petite Sirah has concentrated fruit flavors with nuances of English toffee.

STONY HILL VINEYARD

3331 St. Helena Highway, St. Helena, CA 94574
(707) 963-2636, www.stonyhillvineyard.com

Fred and Eleanor McCrea bought a 160-acre goat farm on Spring Mountain in 1943 and planted Chardonnay vines in 1947. They built a small winery and produced their first Chardonnay wine in 1952. Son Peter and his wife, Willinda, along with their children, Frederick and Sarah, also work at the family business. Mike Chelini heads both winery and vineyard operations. The Stony Hill Vineyard Cabernet Sauvignon tastes of ripe red fruits and a touch of bittersweet chocolate. The luscious Stony Hill Vineyard Chardonnay, with aromas of lemon blossoms and Granny Smith apples, has great fruit flavors and a rich mouthfeel.

STORY BOOK MOUNTAIN VINEYARDS

3835 Highway 128, Calistoga, CA 94515
(707) 942-5282, www.storybookwines.com

In 1976 Jerry and Sigrid Seps bought 90 acres and an abandoned winery built by Adam Grimm in 1883. They replanted Zinfandel vines and released their first wine in 1983. Jerry was a founding member of Zinfandel Advocates and Producers and served as president for the first five years. Sophisticated and elegant in the mouth, the Storybook Mountain Vineyards Estate Reserve Zinfandel has aromas of black raspberry and sweet red fruits.

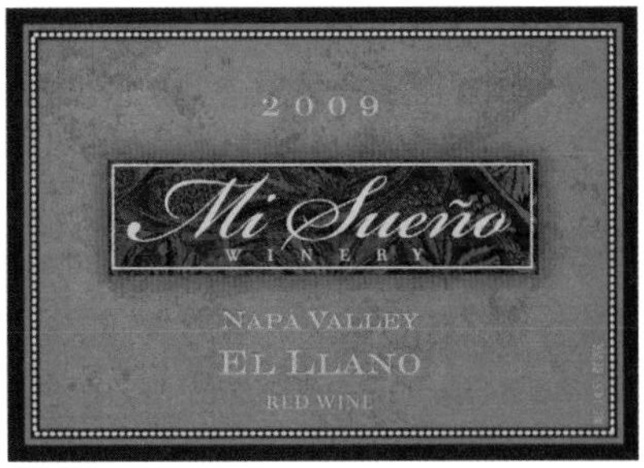

49

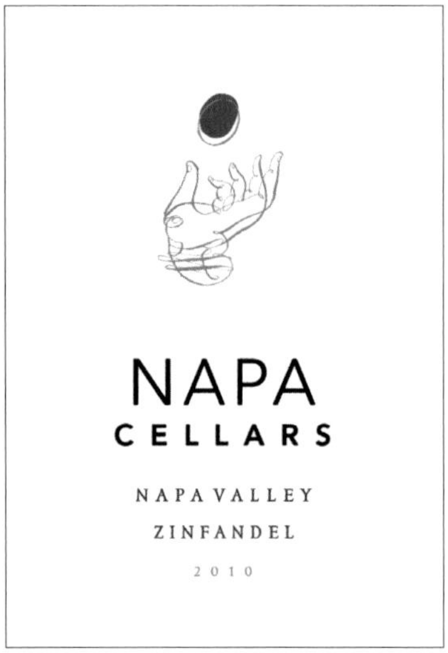

51

53

60

61

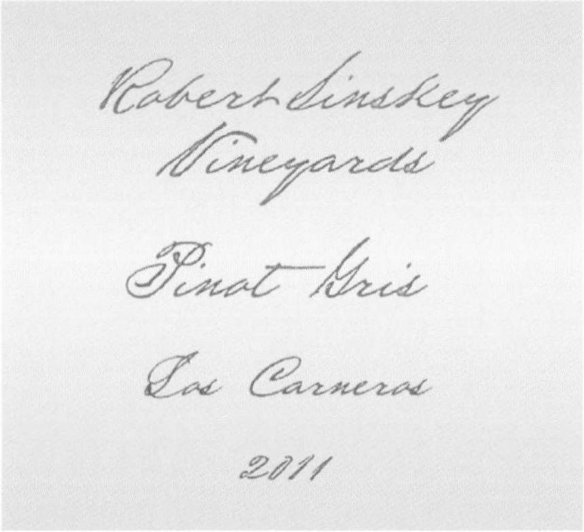

62

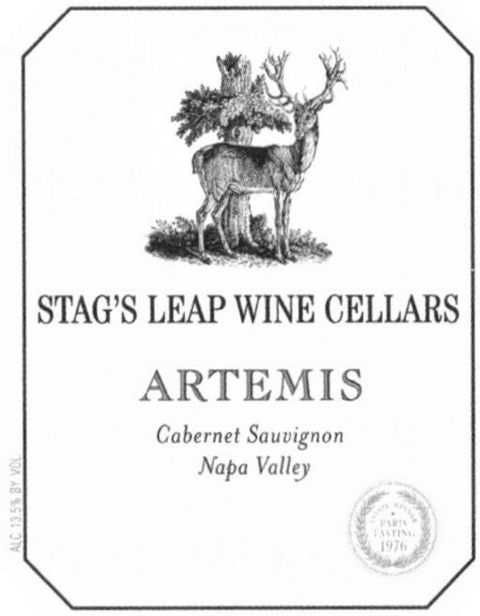

71

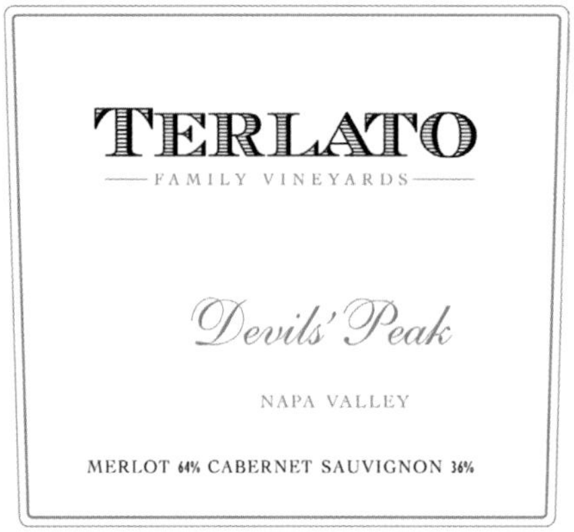

72

73

56

57

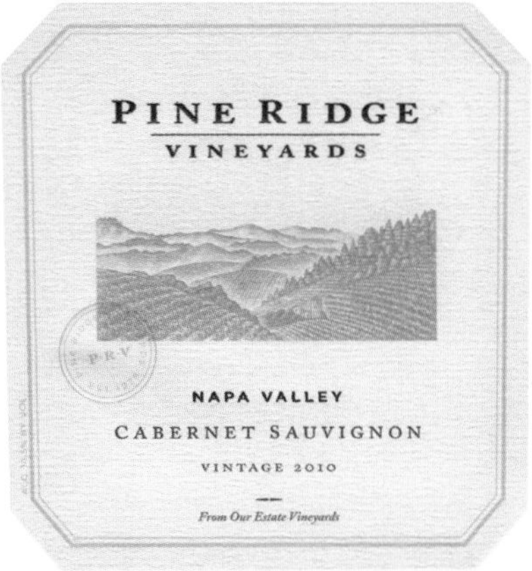

58

63

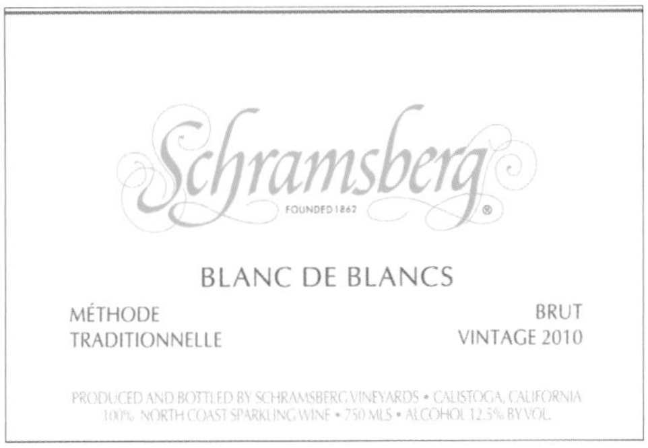

66

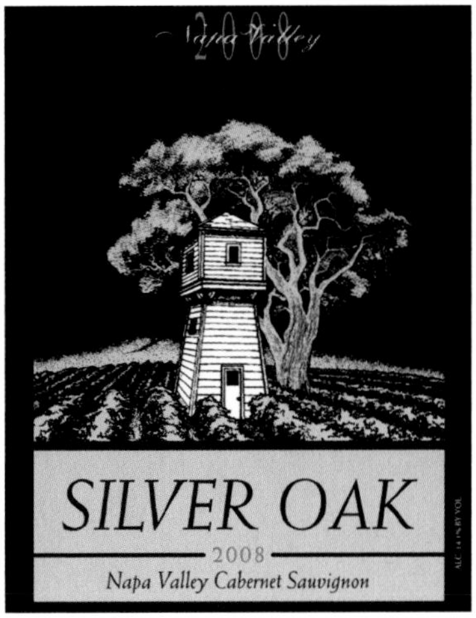

68

75

76

78

TAKEN WINE CO.

PO Box 248, St. Helena, CA 94574
(707) 963-3104, www.takenwine.com

Childhood friends Carlo Trinchero and Josh Phelps were both born to Napa Valley winemaking families. In 2009 they followed a shared dream, created their own label, and thus Taken Wine Co. was born. Their wine names—Available, Complicated, and Taken—reference social media relationship statuses. The Taken Wine Co. Taken Red Blend has flavors of ripe red and black fruits and the Taken Wine Co. Complicated Chardonnay is well balanced with flavors of citrus fruits and white peaches.

TERLATO FAMILY VINEYARDS

200 Rutherford Hill Road, Rutherford, CA 94573
(888) 241-0259, www.terlatovineyards.com

Anthony Terlato was one of the first importers to bring Italian Pinot Grigio into the American market. He has been importing Santa Margarita for years, and it has become one of the industry leaders in the United States. More recently he and sons, Bill and John, decided to become Napa Valley winemakers. The family makes wine under the Terlato Family Wines, Chimney Rock, Sanford, Rutherford Hill, and Alderbrook labels. The crisp-finishing Terlato Family Vineyards Russian River Valley Pinot Grigio has flavors of green apples and peach. The full-bodied Terlato Family Vineyards Devils' Peak Napa Valley smells of freshly baked blueberry pie and tastes of ripe berries. 72

TOR KENWARD WINES

1241 Adams Street, #1045 , St. Helena, CA 94574
(707) 963-3100, www.torwines.com

After working at Beringer Vineyards for 27 is success to the mentorship of Ed Sbragia and Bob Steinhauer, among others, and the help and support of wife, Susan. The Tor Napa Valley Oakville Tierra Roja Vineyard Cabernet Sauvignon has great aromas of rich dark cherries, black raspberry, and black plum, and the Tor Napa Valley Beckstoffer To Kalon Anniversary Cuvée Cabernet Sauvignon, with concentrated aromas of red raspberries, black plums, and smoked meats, is big and bold but maintains restraint and elegance. 73

TREFETHEN FAMILY VINEYARDS

1160 Oak Knoll Avenue, Napa, CA 94558
(866) 895-7696, www.trefethen.com

Gene Trefethen helped plan and build the San Francisco Bay Bridge and the Hoover and Shasta dams. After he retired in 1968, he and wife, Catherine, moved to Napa Valley and bought six contiguous farms and the dilapidated Eschol Winery to create their 600-acre estate. They planned to sell all their grapes, but son John changed their minds when Trefethen's third-vintage 1976 Chardonnay won Best Chardonnay in the World at the 1979 Gault Millau World Wine Olympics in Paris. The Trefethen Family Vineyards Chardonnay has white stone fruit aromas, and the Trefethen Family Vineyards Dragon's Tooth Red Wine features rich flavors of dark fruits and dark chocolate. 74

TRINCHERO NAPA VALLEY FAMILY VINEYARDS

3070 St. Helena Highway, St. Helena, CA 94574
(707) 963-1160, www.trincheronapavalley.com

Mario and Mary Trinchero left New York City for Napa Valley in 1948 and purchased the abandoned Sutter Home Winery. Son Bob crafted the first White Zinfandel in 1972, creating an entirely new category of wine. By 2007 the family had acquired more than 200 acres of Napa vineyards, and in 2009 it released its first estate-grown wines bearing the family name. Fewer than 12,000 cases of Trinchero Napa Valley Family wines are produced. The Trinchero St. Helena Napa Valley Mario's Vineyard Cabernet Sauvignon smells of black cherry and tastes of rich red raspberry and ripe cherry. The velvety Trinchero Napa Valley Meritage offers flavors of fresh berries and mixed-berry preserves. 75

TUCK BECKSTOFFER WINES

807 St. Helena Highway South, St. Helena, CA 94574
(707) 200-4410, www.tbwines.com

The Beckstoffer family moved to Napa Valley in 1975, and from a young age Tuck developed a love of farming. In his teens, he worked in the vineyards of Mendocino and Napa counties, and after college he returned to Napa to work for Beckstoffer Vineyards. He began producing wine under the Tuck Beckstoffer label in 1997. The fruit-forward Tuck Beckstoffer Semper Silver Eagle Vineyard Pinot Noir smells of freshly picked red cherries and red plums with a top note of Christmas baking spices. Juicy and full-bodied, the Tuck Beckstoffer Seventy Five Wine Company The Sum has aromas of anise, smoked meats, and dark fruits. 76

TWOMEY

1183 Dunaweal Lane, Calistoga, CA 94515
(707) 942-7026, www.twomey.com

The Duncan family honored Ray Duncan's mother by naming its winery Twomey, her maiden name. The family makes what they consider their most labor-intensive wine from Merlot grapes here; its sister winery sits on Westside Road in Healdsburg, Sonoma County. The Twomey Single Vineyard Merlot offers aromas of freshly picked black cherries and Christmas baking spices with vibrant flavors of fruit and a touch of cocoa powder.

VIADER ESTATE

1120 Deer Park Road, Deer Park, CA 94576
(707) 963-3816, www.viader.com

Argentine-born Delia Viader established her winery in 1986. She hired family friend Michel Rolland as a consultant in 2006, and her children have joined the family business. Son Alan heads operations and winemaking; his wife, Mariela, directs the culinary program; and daughter Janet oversees marketing and sales. The full-bodied Viader Estate Limited Edition Black Label tastes of black cherry, Chinese tea, and red fruits. Smooth and silky, the Viader Estate Liquid Cashmere's features aromas and flavors of black fruits and dark cocoa powder. Drink it now, or hold it for a few years. 77

VILLA MOUNT EDEN

No visitor facilities
St. Helena, CA 94574
(866) 931-1624, www.villamteden.com

Under George W. Meyers's ownership, Villa Mount Eden became the eleventh bonded winery in Napa in 1881. Meyers planted Riesling and Zinfandel, and the winery was sold in 1913 to Nick Fagiani. The winery changed hands a few times after Prohibition, and in 1969 James and Anne McWilliams bought it. Nils Venge joined as general manager and winemaker in 1974 and handed the baton to Mike McGrath in 1983. The Villa Mount Eden Napa Valley Cabernet Sauvignon has aromas of freshly picked black raspberries and dried black cherries and is rich in the mouth with fruit flavors. 78

VINEYARD 7 & 8

4028 Spring Mountain Road, St. Helena, CA 94574
(707) 963-9425, www.vineyard7and8.com

East Coast–based investment adviser Launny Steffens and wife, Weezie, bought land on Spring Mountain in 1999 and began Vineyard 7 & 8. Only their youngest son, Wesley, lives locally, in Yountville, and he serves as winery manager and assistant winemaker. Winemaker Luc Morlet trained in Bordeaux and Champagne before calling Napa Valley home. The Vineyard 7 & 8 Spring Mountain District Cabernet Sauvignon has aromas of black cherry, blueberry pie, and anise and is big and bold in the mouth with a burst of fruit.

WHITEHALL LANE WINERY AND VINEYARDS

1563 St. Helena Highway, St. Helena, CA 94574
(707) 963-9454, www.whitehalllane.com

San Francisco businessman Tom Leonardini bought Whitehall Lane Winery in 1993, purchasing new winemaking equipment, replanting vineyards, and implementing new barrel-aging protocols. He also scaled down production to focus on four varieties: Merlot, Cabernet Sauvignon, Sauvignon Blanc, and Chardonnay. Unlike Tom's other business ventures, Whitehall Lane is a family affair. He, his wife, and their five children run the winery, and Leonardini hopes that his grandchildren and their children will continue the business for generations. The fruit-forward Whitehall Lane Reserve Cabernet Sauvignon has delightful aromas of black plum and black raspberry. Drink it now, or keep it for a few years.

WISE ACRE VINEYARD

768 Sunnyside Road, St. Helena, CA 94574
(707) 968-9980, www.wiseacrevineyard.com

Founded in 2003 by Kirk and Lynn Grace, with Gary Brookman as winemaker, Wise Acre is one of Napa Valley's smallest commercial vineyard-wineries at just half an acre. In 2005 they planted vines grafted to Bosche Cabernet Sauvignon clones from Kirk's parents' Grace Family Vineyard, and the winery's first release was its 2008 Cabernet Sauvignon. The Wise Acre Vineyard Cabernet, with aromas of dark plums, cassis, and wild herbs, offers fruit flavors that are full and rich.

YAO FAMILY WINES

P.O. Box 111, Napa, CA 94515
(707) 968-7470, www.yaofamilywines.com

Founded by NBA All-Star and Olympian Yao Ming, Yao Family Wines entered the US wine market in 2012 with its 2009 Napa Valley Cabernet Sauvignon and Family Reserve Cabernet Sauvignon. Yao Family Wines sources grapes from Napa Valley vineyards. Tom Hinde directs winemaking, and Larry Bradley is the consulting viticulturist. The Yao Family Wines Yao Ming Napa Valley Cabernet Sauvignon has aromas of lush black fruits and a touch of confectioners' sugar with bright blackberry and strawberry flavors. The smooth and velvety Yao Family Wines Yao Ming Family Reserve Napa Valley Cabernet Sauvignon smells of blackberry and red raspberry.

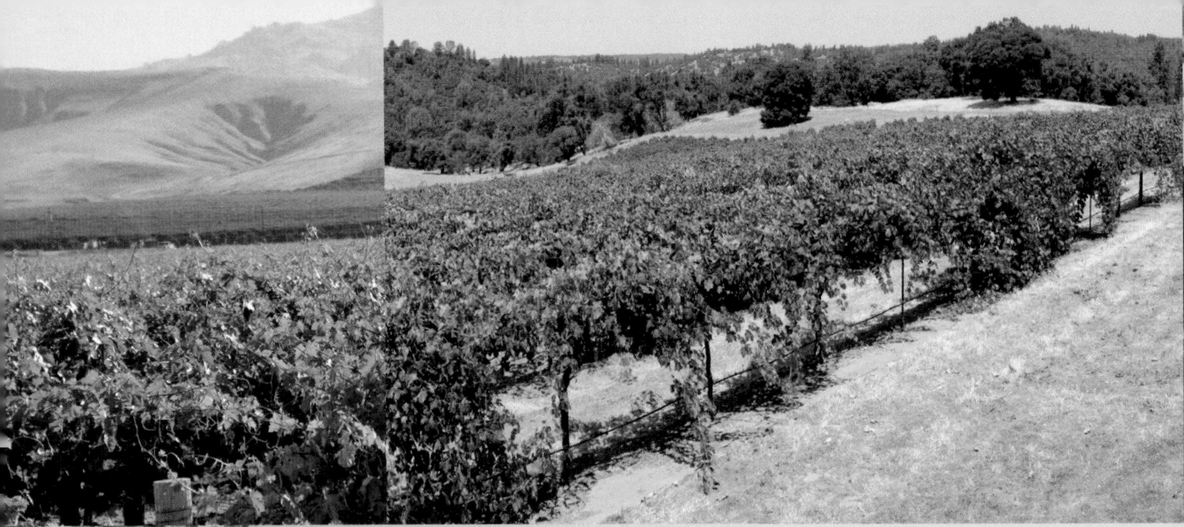

FOUR

SIERRA FOOTHILLS

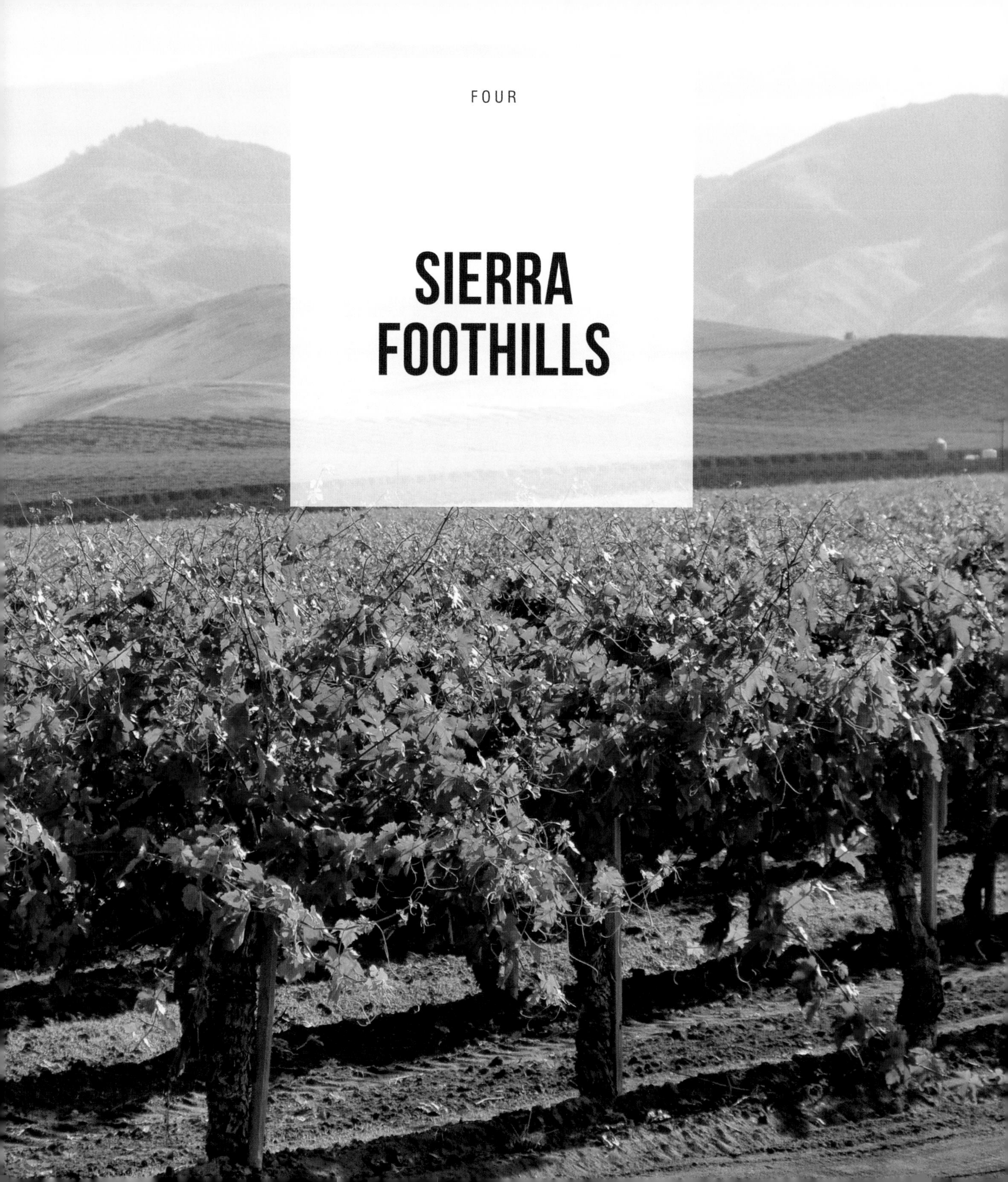

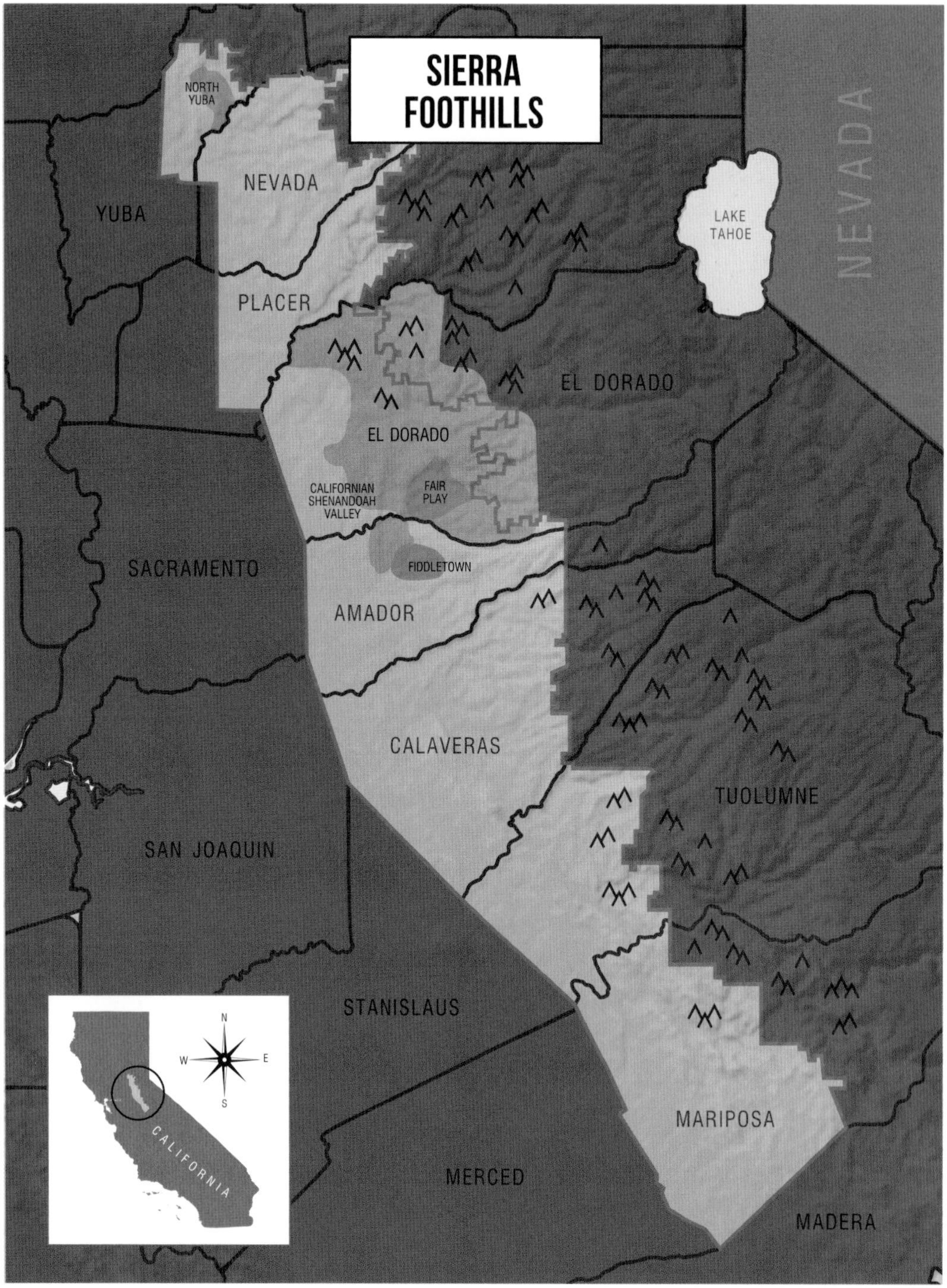
SIERRA FOOTHILLS
NORTH YUBA
NEVADA
YUBA
PLACER
LAKE TAHOE
NEVADA
EL DORADO
EL DORADO
CALIFORNIAN SHENANDOAH VALLEY
FAIR PLAY
FIDDLETOWN
SACRAMENTO
AMADOR
CALAVERAS
TUOLUMNE
SAN JOAQUIN
STANISLAUS
MARIPOSA
MERCED
MADERA
N
W
E
S
CALIFORNIA

James Marshall discovered gold at John Sutter's sawmill in Coloma, California, on January 24, 1848, and soon fortune seekers worldwide made their way into the American West, rapidly boosting the area's population by more than 300,000. Some came with pans, sieves, and pickaxes, others with carefully transported grape cuttings to plant in the mineral-rich soils of the Sierra Foothills. Fifty years later, more than a hundred wineries were operating in the area, but Prohibition later decimated that number. A new wave of winemakers arrived in the 1970s and 1980s, and the number of wineries has surged past the one hundred mark once again.

Coloma lies in what became El Dorado (Spanish for "The Golden") County in the Sierra Foothills AVA. Present-day Coloma is part museum, part ghost town, but among the remnants of the Gold Rush era are some of the oldest Zinfandel vines in the country, dating to the 1860s. The AVA has five sub-AVAs—California Shenandoah Valley, El Dorado, Fair Play, Fiddletown, and North Yuba—and 2.6 million acres, but wine grapes grow on just 5,700 acres because desertlike conditions, infertile soil, extreme elevation, and inaccessible locations make much of the area inhospitable for grape cultivation. Vineyard elevations range from 1,500 to 3,000 feet, and rocky soils offer vines the high stress they need to produce richly flavored grapes.

Zinfandel, king of the region, grows on more than 2,400 acres, a good portion in dry-farmed vineyards dating to the 1860s. Cabernet Sauvignon is second most prolific, followed by Syrah, Chardonnay, Merlot, and Barbera, with a smattering of Sangiovese, one of the first varieties planted by nineteenth-century Italian immigrants. Rhône varieties—Roussanne, Marsanne, Viognier, and Grenache Blanc—are gaining traction as well. More than sixty varieties grow throughout the AVA, and most wineries remain small, family-run affairs.

The largest of the five subregions, El Dorado, established in 1983 and finalized in 1987, lies at elevations between 1,200 and 3,500 feet. Cooling coastal air moderates the summer heat, protecting fragile grapes surviving on minimal groundwater in sandy loams and coarse sandy soils. The Fair Play AVA's vineyards have the highest average elevation in the state: 2,000 to 3,000 feet. Established in 2001 and totaling 36 square miles, it's planted with 350 acres of vines, mainly within ridges between river canyons in some of the deepest, most fertile soils in the region. Vines in the California Shenandoah Valley AVA, established in 1982 and amended in 1987, grow at lower elevations, 500 to 2,000 feet. The Fiddletown AVA, established in 1983 and finalized in 1987, lie at slightly higher elevations. Both sub-AVAs sit in Amador County, where soils consist of sandy clay loam over fragmented granite and volcanic stone. North Yuba in Yuba County, the one noncontiguous sub-AVA, covers 30 square miles and features loam and clay soils with high mineral content.

THE WINERIES

BOEGER WINERY

1709 Carson Road, Placerville, CA 95667
(530) 622-8094, www.boegerwinery.com

Greg Boeger followed in his Swiss-Italian grandfather's footsteps when he purchased a former vineyard site in El Dorado County, planted vines, and opened his winery in 1972. Son Justin recently joined the family tradition, becoming winemaker and giving his father more time to work in the vineyards. The Boeger Winery Sauvignon Blanc has aromas of white stone fruits and flavors of white peach. Big and round on the palate, the Boeger Winery Barbera has aromas of dark cherry, black pepper, and Christmas baking spices. ❶

GROS VENTRE

8054 Fairplay Road, Somerset, CA 95684
(707) 955-5788, www.grosventrecellars.com

Winemaker Chris Pittenger makes Pinot Noir with fruit sourced from the Sonoma Coast, Russian River Valley, and Anderson Valley. Gros Ventre, French for "big belly," was named for his wife, Sarah, during her pregnancy. He makes his wine at Skinner Vineyards and Winery, where he works as winemaker. The Gros Ventre Cerise Vineyard Pinot Noir is bright in the mouth with lovely fruit flavors and an herb-infused savory finish. ❷

HOLLY'S HILL VINEYARDS

3680 Leisure Lane, Placerville, CA 95667
(530) 344-0227, www.hollyshill.com

Tom and Holly Cooper shared their first bottle of Châteauneuf-du-Pape on their honeymoon. Their love of Rhône varieties grew. Holly's Hill Vineyards concentrates on making wine from Grenache, Mourvèdre, Syrah, Counoise, Roussanne, and Viognier grapes, and Josh and Carrie Bendick oversee winemaking. The crisp and balanced Holly's Hill Vineyards Viognier features aromas of clementine, Anjou Pear, and white stone fruits. Fruit-forward and clean, the Holly's Hill Vineyards Grenache Blanc offers notes of lemon-lime and a zing of acidity in the finish. ❸

LAVA CAP WINERY

2221 Fruitridge Road, Placerville, CA 95667
(530) 621-0175, www.lavacap.com

Geologists David and Jeanne Jones and family founded Lava Cap Winery and planted their first vines in 1981. The winery opened in 1986, and today Tom continues the winemaking tradition while brother Charlie manages the vineyards. The Lava Cap Estate Bottled El Dorado Petite Sirah offers a bouquet of black cherry, blackberry, and spice. The full-bodied Lava Cap Estate Bottled El Dorado Barbera has aromas of black raspberry, dark cherry, and vanilla. ❹

MADROÑA VINEYARDS

2560 High Hill Road, Camino, CA 95709
(530) 644-5948, www.madronavineyards.com

Captivated by the charm of the Sierra Nevada, Dick and Leslie Bush planted vineyards here in the 1970s at 3,000 feet. Madroña consists of three family-owned vineyards growing twenty-six varieties of grapes: Madroña Vineyard in Apple Hill and Sumu-Kaw Vineyard and Enye Vineyard in Pleasant Valley. Sons Paul and David and their wives have joined the family business. The fruit-forward Madroña Vineyards Hillside Collection Zinfandel boasts aromas of red raspberry, black raspberry, and cranberry sauce and flavors of sweet cherry. Smooth and silky, the Madroña Hillside Collection Gewürztraminer offers a bouquet of Cavaillon melon, Ruby Red grapefruit, and white stone fruits. 5

MIRAFLORES WINERY

2120 Four Springs Trail, Placerville, CA 95667
(530) 647-8505, www.mirafloreswinery.com

Colombian-born owner Victor Alvarez is a vintner and a practicing pathologist whose love of wine moved him to establish Miraflores in 2003. The tasting room feels like a Mediterranean winery. The Miraflores winery sits on a 254-acre estate, which has 40 acres under vine. Crisp and clean, the Miraflores Pinot Grigio offers notes of citrus and white stone fruit. The fruit-forward Miraflores Estate Zinfandel has aromas of black cherry preserves and cherry vanilla ice cream. 6

MOUNT AUKUM WINERY

6781 Tower Road, Somerset, CA 95684
(530) 620-1675, www.mountaukum.com

Michel Prod'hon, whose winery sits atop Mount Aukum, learned winemaking at a young age in the village of Chaumount in the Champagne region of France. Most of the grapes that go into his artisanal small-batch wines are grown on his estate in the Fair Play AVA. Big and round in the mouth, the Mount Aukum Winery Estate Fair Play El Dorado Sangiovese proffers a bouquet of tart cherry and Mediterranean herbal notes. The Mount Aukum Winery El Dorado Zinfandel is fragrant with dark fruits, anise, blueberry, and clove.

SKINNER VINEYARDS AND WINERY

8054 Fairplay Road, Somerset, CA 95684
(530) 620-2220, www.skinnervineyards.com

Scottish immigrant James Skinner crossed the United States looking for gold and eventually saved enough money to buy land, build a house, and plant vines. By 1861 his wines and distilled brandy had developed a local following. In 2006 Mike and Carey Skinner found a great piece of property on a ridge overlooking the Sierra Nevada and reestablished the Skinner name in the wine business. Today they work with their family and winemaker Chris Pittenger. Clean and crisp, the Skinner Vineyards Seven Generations smells of citrus, tropical fruits, and orange vanilla sherbet. Fruit-forward Skinner Vineyards Grenache offers aromas of red raspberry and freshly picked strawberry. 7

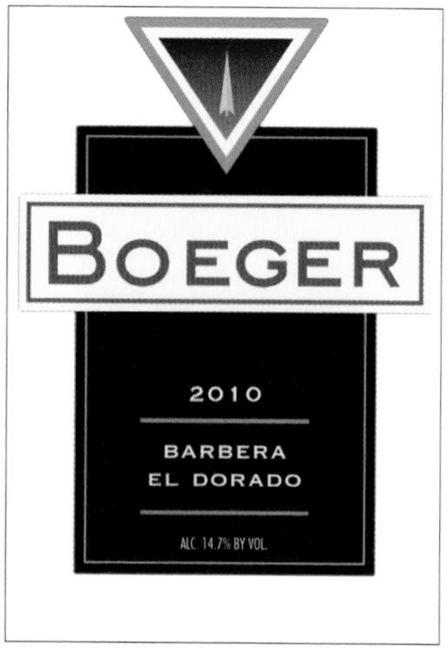
BOEGER
2010
BARBERA
EL DORADO
ALC. 14.7% BY VOL.

1

2011
gros ventre
PINOT NOIR
CERISE VINEYARD
ANDERSON VALLEY

2

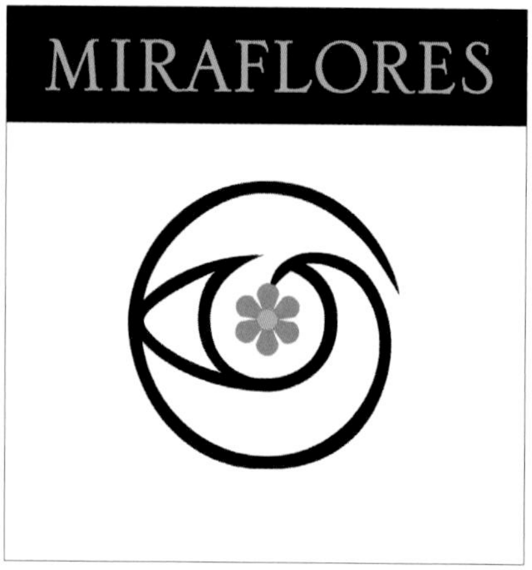
MIRAFLORES

6

—Est. 1970—
TERRA d'ORO
SANGIOVESE

8

HOLLY'S HILL
Vineyards
El Dorado
2012 GRENACHE BLANC
ESTATE

3

MADROÑA
GEWÜRZTRAMINER
El Dorado 2011 Estate Bottled

5

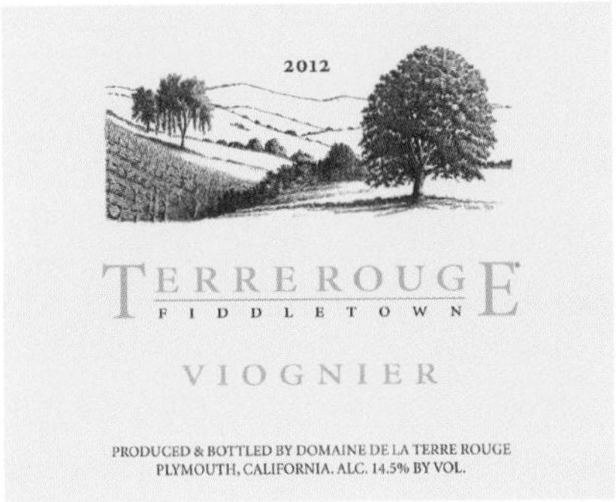
2012
TERRE ROUGE
FIDDLETOWN
VIOGNIER
PRODUCED & BOTTLED BY DOMAINE DE LA TERRE ROUGE
PLYMOUTH, CALIFORNIA. ALC. 14.5% BY VOL.

9

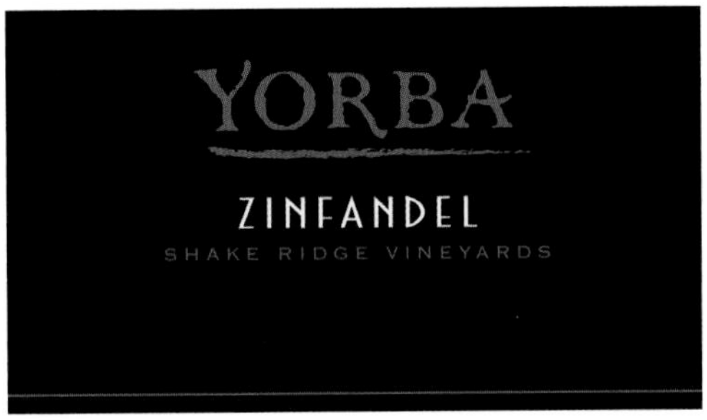
YORBA
ZINFANDEL
SHAKE RIDGE VINEYARDS

10

TERRA D'ORO WINERY

20680 Shenandoah School Road, Plymouth, CA 95669
(209) 245-6942, www.terradorowinery.com

Cary Gott and Walter Field founded the Montevina Winery in 1970, the first to make wine in Amador County after the repeal of Prohibition. Its name has since changed to Terra d'Oro after the gold diggers lured to this "land of gold" in the Sierra Foothills. Today it boasts 400 acres of estate vines, including plantings of Sangiovese, Zinfandel, Barbera, Pinot Grigio, and Moscato. The Terra d'Oro Winery Amador County Sangiovese tastes of Indian spices, black cherry, and cassis, and the Terra d'Oro Winery Amador County Zinfandel offers ripe fruit flavors with notes of black pepper and nutmeg. 8

TERRE ROUGE EASTON WINES

P.O. Box 41, Fiddletown, CA 95629
(209) 245-5415, www.terrerougewines.com

Named (in French) for the region's red earth, Terre Rouge makes wines from Rhône varieties, including Marsanne, Roussanne, Viognier, Mourvèdre, Grenache, and Syrah. Winemaker Bill Easton also makes non-Rhône varieties under his Easton label. Production at Terre Rouge and Easton Wines is small, just 300 to 500 cases of each wine. The Terre Rouge Sierra Foothills Vin Gris d'Amador smells of freshly picked strawberries, red cherry juice, and Christmas baking spices. The Terre Rouge Fiddletown Early Release Viognier has aromas and flavors of white stone fruits and dried apricots. 9

YORBA WINES

51 Hanford Street, Sutter Creek, CA 95685
(209) 267-5055, www.yorbawines.com

The name of the Kraemer family winery honors great-grandmother Angelina Yorba, descended from Spanish settler José Antonio Yorba, who came to California in 1769. The family planted 34 acres of vines at Shake Ridge Vineyards in 2003 and 12 more in 2009. Ann Kraemer manages the vineyards, and Ken Bernards handles winemaking. Voluptuous in the mouth, the Yorba Zinfandel has delightful aromas of dried herbs, red cherries, and black raspberries. The Yorba Syrah offers a bouquet of black raspberry, licorice, and dried Mediterranean herbs, and the fruit flavors pass seamlessly onto the palate. 10

7

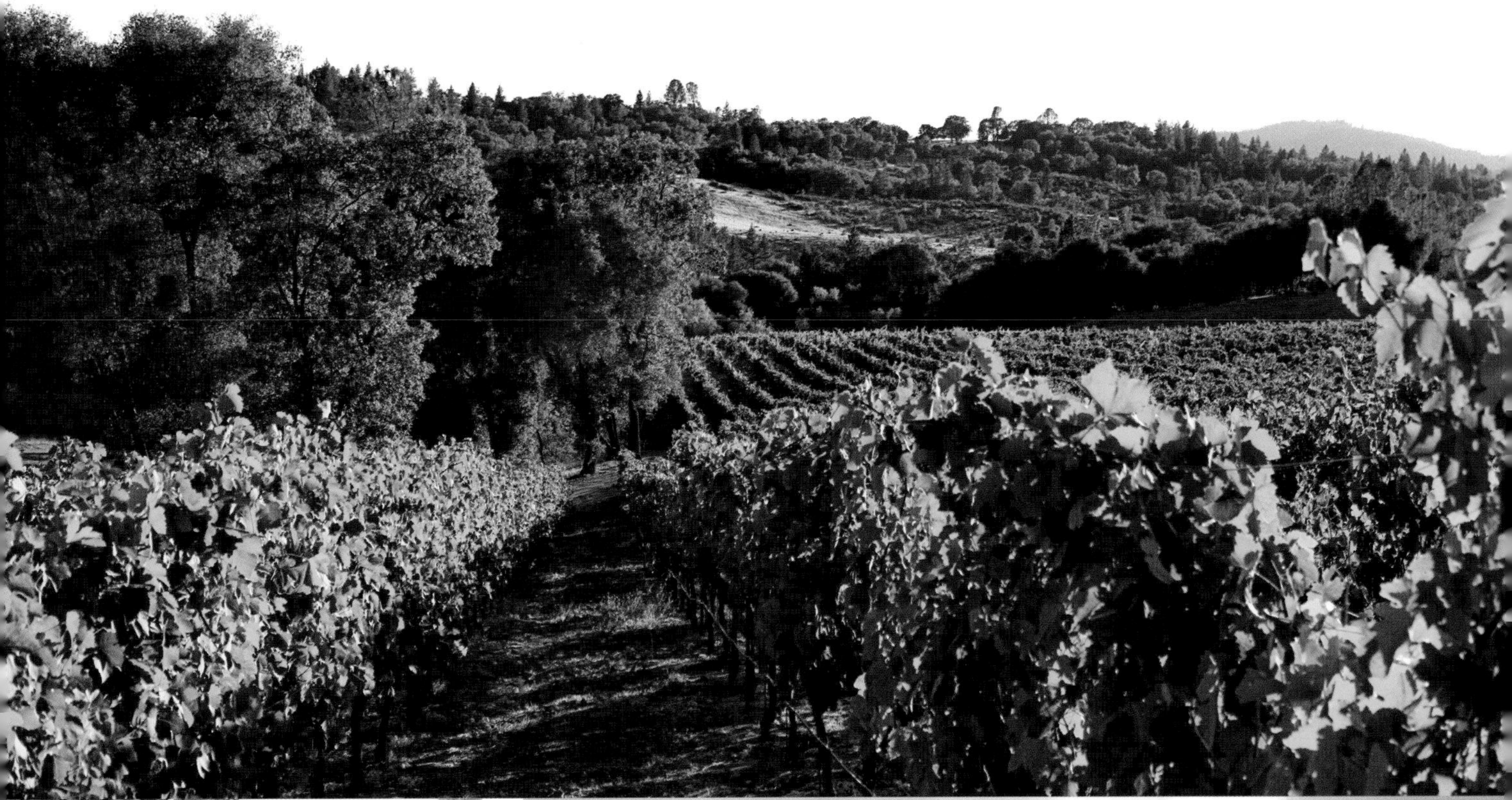

4

FIVE

CENTRAL VALLEY AND THE INLAND COUNTIES

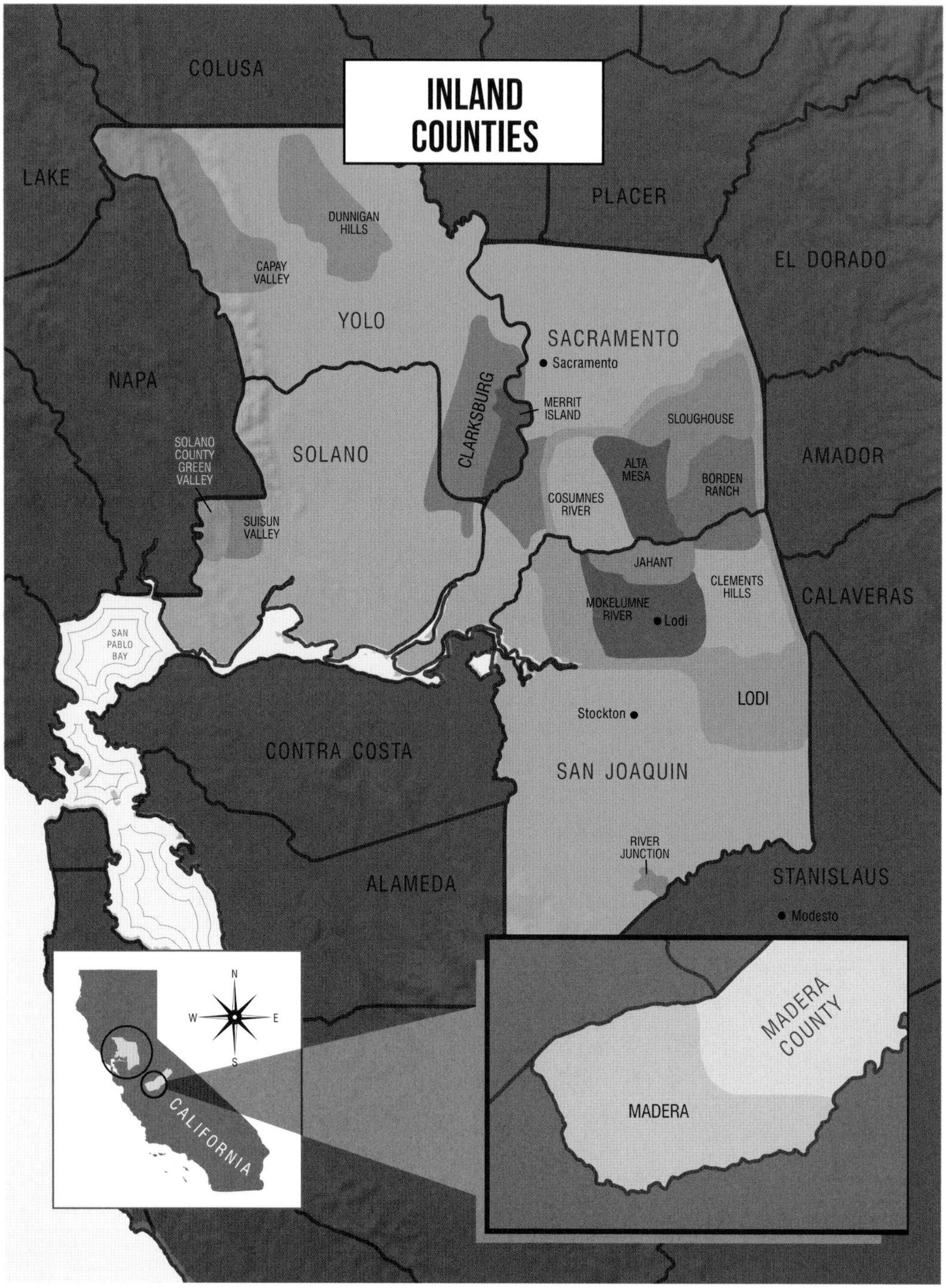
INLAND
COUNTIES
COLUSA
LAKE
PLACER
EL DORADO
DUNNIGAN
HILLS
CAPAY
VALLEY
YOLO
SACRAMENTO
Sacramento
NAPA
MERRIT
ISLAND
CLARKSBURG
SLOUGHOUSE
SOLANO
COUNTY
GREEN
VALLEY
SOLANO
ALTA
MESA
AMADOR
BORDEN
RANCH
COSUMNES
RIVER
SUISUN
VALLEY
JAHANT
CLEMENTS
HILLS
CALAVERAS
MOKELUMNE
RIVER
Lodi
SAN
PABLO
BAY
LODI
Stockton
CONTRA COSTA
SAN JOAQUIN
RIVER
JUNCTION
STANISLAUS
ALAMEDA
Modesto
N
W
E
S
CALIFORNIA
MADERA
COUNTY
MADERA

Central California is the nation's produce stand, home to more than 230 crops, including wine grapes, and the source of the vast majority of the country's vegetables and fruit. Known as the Central Valley, it consists of the San Joaquin and Sacramento valleys and has fertile soils, three hundred days of sunshine per year, and abundant water. Sierra Nevadasnowmelt irrigates vegetable fields, fruit orchards, and vineyards alike.

Grapes were planted throughout central California in the late nineteenth century, after the Gold Rush, and immigrants worked the productive soils of Lodi and Madera, many growing melons and other crops alongside their vineyards. During Prohibition, Italian immigrant Cesare Mondavi relocated his family from Minnesota to Lodi and grew grapes to ship by rail to winemakers back east. After Prohibition, Ernest and Julio Gallo founded their winery in Modesto. In the 1960s and 1970s, as drinking wine became popular in the United States, large-volume wineries such as Gallo and Franzia used Lodi and nonappellation Central Valley grapes for their inexpensive bottles and boxes. Robert Mondavi, who grew up in Lodi, struck out on his own in 1966 and founded his winery in Napa Valley, continuing to use Lodi as a grape source for his entry-level wines.

LODI AND ITS SUB-AVAS

Vitis labrusca grew indiginously in Lodi before Italian and German settlers planted *Vitis vinifera* here in the 1850s; by the 1880s immigrants had planted Alicante, Tokay, and Zinfandel, and today 2,000 acres of old-vine Zinfandel still grow here. Responsible for a third of all California Zinfandel, Lodi also hosts Chardonnay, Cabernet Sauvignon, Merlot, Pinot Grigio, Petite Sirah, Syrah, and Sauvignon Blanc. Boutique wineries work with an intriguing catalog of varieties, including Albariño, Alicante Bouschet, Carignane, Petit Verdot, Sangiovese, Tempranillo, Touriga Nacional, Vermentino, and Viognier. Five large wineries operate here too—Robert Mondavi Woodbridge, Turner Road Vintners, Sutter Home Winery, Bear Creek Winery, and Oak Ridge Winery—alongside nearly eighty small family-owned wineries.

About 750 growers farm 100,000 acres in Lodi AVA, established in March 1986 and amended in 2002, and its sub-AVAs: Alta Mesa, Borden Ranch, Clement Hills, Cosumnes River, Jahant, Mokelumne River, River Junction, and Sloughhouse. The two rivers running through Lodi deposit granitic alluvial soils closest to their shores, and San Francisco Bay offers cool maritime air denied to other inland grape-growing regions.

The AVA of Alta Mesa, Spanish for "high plateau," lies slightly higher than the surrounding areas. Some 10 percent of its 55,400 flat acres of red clay and gravel soils grow vines. It's known primarily for red grapes, notably Zinfandel, Syrah, and Cabernet Sauvignon. The Borden Ranch AVA, covering 70,000 acres, has the widest-ranging altitudes within Lodi, from 73 to 520 feet. Twelve thousand acres of its stone-filled soils, offering good drainage for red varieties, are planted to grapes. The Clements Hills AVA, delineated by the hills and cliffs at the bottom of the Sierra Foothills, also grows mainly red varieties. Warmer and wetter than its neighbors, it has soils that include a loam and clay mixture over granite and volcanic rock. About 25 percent of its 85,400 acres are cultivated with grapevines. Elevations in the Cosumnes River AVA are low—from 5 to 48 feet above sea level—and the cool, wet climate particularly suits white varieties. Grapes grow on 3,500 of its 54,700 acres. Named for its pink Rocklin-Jahant loam soils, Lodi's smallest AVA, Jahant, covers 28,000 acres, a third planted to wine grapes. Proximity to the Mokelumne River and the Sacramento–San Joaquin Delta offers cooling effects. About half of the Mokelumne River AVA, the region's historical center, features grapevines, a much higher percentage than any other Lodi subappellation. Its soils are mainly alluvial, with varying degrees of sand and loam. The majority of old-vine Lodi Zinfandel grows here. River Junction AVA with its fine sandy loam soils is planted mostly to Chardonnay. The Sloughhouse AVA, also in the foothills of the Sierra Nevada, is the warmest of Lodi's subregions. Elevations reach 590 feet above sea level, but of its 78,000 acres fewer than 10 percent are planted to grapes.

CLARKSBURG

Many of the earliest farming families of Clarksburg—named for founder Robert C. Clark, who settled here in 1859—still live here, including the Bogles, who started farming here in the 1850s. Clarksburg covers 64,640 acres, about a third under grapes. Just 20 minutes by car from downtown Sacramento, the Clarksburg AVA was established in February 1984.

Twenty-eight growers and twelve wineries operate in the Clarksburg AVA, and more than thirty-five different varieties of grapes are planted here. Pinot Noir accounts for more than half the red grapes grown in Clarksburg. Noted in the past for red grapes such as Zinfandel, Merlot, and Petite Sirah, this area has an ideal climate for white varieties, in particular Chardonnay, Pinot Grigio, Sauvignon Blanc, and Chenin Blanc, because of the maritime effects from San Francisco Bay and the proximity of the Sacramento River, which runs through Clarksburg and its sub-AVA, 5,000-acre Merritt Island, established in 1987.

SOLANO COUNTY GREEN VALLEY AND SUISUN VALLEY

Suisun Valley and Solano County Green Valley AVAs received recognition a month apart, in December 1982 and January 1983, respectively. With an area of 2,560 acres, Solano County Green Valley enjoys cool afternoon winds and moisture from San Pablo Bay. Suisun Valley, named for the native Suisun people, has 15,360 acres, 3,000 of them with grapevines, and ten wineries. Red varieties such as Cabernet Sauvignon, Zinfandel, Syrah, Petite Sirah, and Pinot Noir grow here, as do Chardonnay, Riesling, Sauvignon Blanc, and white Rhône varieties. Elevations vary from 100 to more than 2,100 feet. The first winery was built in Suisun Valley in the 1860s, and it's the second oldest AVA in the country, established 22 months after Napa Valley.

CAPAY VALLEY AND DUNNIGAN HILLS

Capay Valley, established as an AVA in 2002, covers 102,400 acres, of which fewer than 100 are planted to grapes. The first winery in Yolo County was founded here in 1860, and it was the owner of Capay Valley Winery, the biggest winery in the AVA, who petitioned for official appellation recognition. The Dunnigan Hills AVA is 89,000 acres in size but has substantially more plantings, including 1,300 acres of estate vineyards belonging to R.H. Phillips Winery, the producers of Toasted Head Wine.

MADERA

Established in 1984 and amended in 1985 and 1987, the Madera ("wood" in Spanish) AVA covers 230,000 acres, with about 17 percent planted to grapes. Grape growing began here toward the end of the nineteenth century by transplants from Italy, France, and Armenia. Many of the grapes grown in this AVA are shipped elsewhere and used in inexpensive California appellation bottlings, but a handful of small wineries are gaining attention for small-batch, handcrafted wines.

THE WINERIES

BOGLE VINEYARDS

37783 County Road 144, Clarksburg, CA 95612
(916) 744-1139, www.boglewinery.com

Warren Bogle's family had farmed in the region since the mid-1800s, and he planted his first 20 acres of vines in Clarksburg in 1968. Bogle Vineyards is a large winery but remains family-run. Son, Warren W. Bogle, studied agriculture and returned in 1997 to the 1,500-acre ranch, where he serves as president. His sister Jody oversees customer relations and international sales, and his brother Ryan serves as vice president. The Bogle Vineyards Petite Sirah tastes of black cherry, blackberry, and spice. The Bogle Vineyards Old Vine Zinfandel boasts flavors of black cherry, blackberry, thyme, with a touch of milk chocolate on the finish. ❶

CAPAY VALLEY VINEYARDS

13757 Highway 16, Brooks, CA 95606
(530) 796-4110, www.capayvalleyvineyards.com

Tom Frederick, known for his earlier career building race cars, and Pam Welch founded Capay Valley Vineyards in 1998. Today they work alongside winemaker Terri Strain. The crisp and clean Capay Valley Vineyards Capay Valley Viognier has a bouquet of tropical fruits and melons. The fruit-forward Capay Valley Vineyards Capay Valley Tempranillo offers aromas of black cherry and smoked meats. ❷

CASEY FLAT RANCH

P.O. Box 1274, Tiburon, CA 94920
(415) 435-2225, www.caseyflatranch.com

Named for John Casey, one of Capay Valley's pioneer homesteaders, Casey Flat Ranch originally belonged to the Rancho Cañada de Capay in the historic 1846 Mexican Land Grant. Now owned by the Robert and Maura Morey family, the 6,000-acre ranch is home to Casey Flat Vineyards, Open Range wines, CFR, and a purebred longhorn cattle operation. The 24 acres of vineyards include Sauvignon Blanc, Bordeaux, and Rhône varieties. The Casey Flat Ranch Capay Valley Sauvignon Blanc offers flavors of peach and apricot with subtle herbaceous notes, ideal as an aperitif or paired with shellfish. The Casey Flat Ranch Capay Valley Estate Red Wine has a bouquet of black raspberry and black plum. ❸

CREW WINE COMPANY

12300 County Road 92B, Zamora, CA 95698
(530) 662-1032, www.crewwines.com

No strangers to the industry, John Giguiere, his wife, and brother Karl started RH Phillips Winery in 1983, sold the company to Vincor in 2000, and in August 2005 began Crew Wine Company with sister Lane. They make their wines under a variety of labels, including Mossback, Matchbook, Sawbuck, and Chasing Venus. The fruit-driven Matchbook Dunnigan Hills Tinto Rey offers aromas of espresso, dark chocolate, and dark fruits. The Mossback Russian River Valley Chalk Hill Cabernet Sauvignon has aromas of dried cherry and freshly grated white pepper with a big and balanced finish. ❹

DELICATO FAMILY VINEYARDS

12001 South Highway 99, Manteca, CA 95336
(877) 824-3600, www.dfvwines.com

Gaspare Indelicato first planted vines in 1924 and sold grapes to home winemakers during Prohibition. The company he started has become DFV, one of the leading family winegrowers in the country. Under the dutiful watch of Indelicato's sons and grandchildren, DFV grows grapes across California, from their Clay Station Vineyard in Lodi to the San Bernabe Vineyard in Monterey, producing wine under a variety of labels, including Noble, Gnarly Head, Twisted, Bota Box, Fog Head, HandCraft, and Irony. With full-on fruit flavors, the Noble Vines 337 Cabernet Sauvignon offers a bouquet of cassis, mocha, and black cherry. The Gnarly Head Authentic Red, with aromas of black cherry, black plum, and mocha, pairs well with a burger or ribs. The HandCraft Artisan Collection Inspiration Red Wine offers full flavors of cherry and red raspberry with just a touch of ripe fruit sweetness. 5

FIELDS FAMILY WINES

3803 East Woodbridge Road, Acampo, CA 95220
(209) 896-6012, www.fieldsfamilywines.com

Russ Fields and family bought their property in Lodi in 2005 and started building the winery and two homes right away. Business partner Ryan Sherman, the realtor who helped find the vineyard, is the Fields Family winemaker, working with estate-grown Syrah, Lodi Zinfandel, and Tempranillo, and Napa Valley Cabernet Sauvignon and Merlot. The winery offers tours and tastings, and the wine bar in downtown Lodi, which features art exhibits and live music, also does tastings. The Fields Family Wines Sherman Family Vineyards Lodi Old Vine Zinfandel has aromas and flavors of black plums, blueberry, cassis, and clove. 6

GALLO

600 Yosemite Boulevard, Modesto, CA 95354
(877) 687-9463, www.gallo.com

Brothers Ernest and Julio Gallo started Gallo Winery in 1933, and today the company is the world's largest family-owned winery, with multiple generations of the Gallo family working side by side to continue the legacy. Gallo headquarters are in Modesto, but the company makes wine from AVAs all over the state under more than sixty brands, including Apothic Red, Barefoot, Bella Sera, Ecco Domani, Frei Brothers, Gallo Signature Series, Indigo Hills, Mirassou, and Turning Leaf. The Gallo family continues to be the largest exporter of California wine to the world, serving more than ninety countries, and has multiple production facilities, including those in Modesto, St. Helena, and Dry Creek Valley. The fruit-forward yet restrained Gallo Signature Series Napa Valley Cabernet Sauvignon offers aromas of black currants, black raspberries, dark cherries, and powdered cocoa. The Gallo Signature Series Santa Lucia Highlands Pinot Noir is juicy on the palate with flavors of black currant, cherry vanilla, and pomegranate. 7

HARNEY LANE WINERY

9010 East Harney Lane, Lodi, CA 95240
(209) 365-1900, www.harneylane.com

The Harney Lane story began in 1907, when George Mettler's great-grandfather Fred Schnaidt bought land on Harney Lane and planted a vineyard. His descendants have farmed this land ever since. Joined by wife, Kathleen; daughter Jorja; and son-in-law, Kyle Lerner, Mettler bottles Tempranillo, Petite Sirah, Chardonnay, Zinfandel, and Albariño. Their Lizzy James Vineyard takes its name from Kyle and Jorja's two children, the sixth generation to live and work on the farm. The easy-drinking Harney Lane Winery Lodi Albariño presents an initial burst of lime sorbet followed by refreshing citrus flavors. 8

In her own words

CHERYL INDELICATO

Cheryl Indelicato became a registered nurse before returning to the family business in 1990. She runs Delicato Family Vineyards alongside her siblings and cousins, and in 2010 she launched her own brand, the HandCraft Artisan Collection. A member of Les Dames d'Escoffier, Cheryl is also the Monterey representative to the California Wine Institute.

You might say I have wine in my blood. I'm a third-generation vintner; my grandfather Gaspare Indelicato planted our first vineyards in 1924 and began making wine several years later. I grew up next door to the winery and always enjoyed being in the vineyards and in the cellar. My father and uncles, knowing how much I loved the family business, put me to work in the cellar when I was five years old.

I started working with traditional varietals such as Cabernet Sauvignon, Chardonnay, and Pinot Noir; however, I wanted to create distinctive wines that honored my Italian heritage, so I began experimenting with Italian varieties such as Malvasia Bianca and Sangiovese. I love to cook, and I find blending wine is similar, where small differences can change the flavor and aromatics. I kept on with the blending and created two signature wines: Inspiration White, which is a blend of Riesling, Moscato, Sauvignon Blanc, Viognier, and Pinot Grigio, and Inspiration Red, a food-friendly blend of Zinfandel, Merlot, Malbec, and Sangiovese.

I want to create wines that are approachable yet distinctive. My wines are fruit-forward and easy to pair with food. The distinctive aspect is the addition of Italian varieties not often seen in California wines, which makes my wines stand apart from a sensory perspective. If you provide consumers with the very best, if you overdeliver on quality, consumers will embrace your product and come back for more. Winemaking, and I emphasize, quality winemaking, should and will influence the market.

I love the Pinot Grigio grown in Monterey, at my family's San Bernabe Vineyard—it's full of flavor and bright acidity. My hope is to plant additional acreage of Pinot Grigio at San Bernabe and, fingers crossed, produce a HandCraft Pinot Grigio someday. Another area that means a lot to my family is Lodi. My grandfather settled in Lodi after making his way across the United States from Ellis Island. I would love to find a vineyard of old, gnarled head-trained Zinfandel in the Lodi area.

I live in Monterey, and I'm so pleased to see this region receiving the recognition it should as a world-class viticultural area. New AVAs are emerging with varietals we never thought would grow well here. The area is also becoming a wine destination, with many new tasting rooms opening in Carmel. When I first moved here over 10 years ago, many of the grapes grown here were shipped to other areas as blenders. It's great to see the growth of Monterey-labeled wines on wine lists and store shelves—both across the nation and abroad.

IRONSTONE VINEYARDS

1894 Six Mile Road, Murphys, CA 95247
(209) 728-1251, www.ironstonevineyards.com

Ironstone Vineyard boasts a seven-story winery and entertainment complex in a replica 1859 mill that includes a tasting room, delicatessen, aging cavern, conference center, museum, and jewelry store. The Ironstone Amphitheater hosts a summer concert series, and the winery offers lessons in panning for gold. In 1989, winemaker Steve Millier joined the Kautz family, fourth-generation grape growers who own more than 5,000 acres of vineyards in the Sierra Foothills and Lodi. Ironstone produces a variety of whites and reds, including Cabernet Franc, Cabernet Sauvignon, Malbec, Meritage blends, Muscat Canelli, Syrah, Verdelho, Viognier, and Zinfandel.

The Ironstone Reserve Lodi Malbec offers aromas of boysenberry with bright fruits-of-the-wood flavors in the persistent finish. 9

KIDDER FAMILY WINERY

17266 Hillside Drive, Lodi, CA 95240
(209) 727-0728, www.kidderwines.com

Aaron Kidder and wife, Linda Hauck Kidder, a Lodi native, were destined for stardom at an early age. Linda was the Lodi Kiddie Parade queen, and Aaron, his two brothers, and father performed as a barbershop quartet on *The Ed Sullivan Show*. Aaron and Linda met in Lodi and married in 1994, planted a vineyard, and started making wine in 2001. Their seven and a half acres of vineyards grow mainly Syrah and small amounts of Petite Sirah, Graciano, and Tempranillo. The Dutch-style barn on Kidder's labels depicts their winery and tasting room in Lodi's Clements Hills appellation. The Kidder Family Winery Duet offers flavors of blackberry and strawberry with a hint of milk chocolate. 10

KLINKER BRICK WINERY

15887 Alpine Road, Lodi, CA 95240
(209) 224-5156, www.klinkerbrickwinery.com

More than a century ago, the forebears of fifth-generation grape growers Steve and Lori Felten converted their watermelon fields to vineyards, including Zinfandel, Tokay, Carignane, and Alicante among their vines, and Klinker Brick's old-vine Zinfandel now ranges from 35 to more than 100 years old. Winemaker Barry Gnekow, a UC Davis graduate with more than 25 years' experience, is also a family member, as is Klinker Brick president Lynne White Barnard, who heads sales and marketing. After growing grapes for and selling bulk wine to other wineries, Klinker Brick, named for the style of heavy brick used in the area, was founded in 2000. The Klinker Brick Lodi Syrah boasts flavors of chocolate-covered cherries, cassis, star anise, and Szechuan pepper.

LANGE TWINS WINERY AND VINEYARDS

1525 East Jahant Road, Acampo, CA 95220
(209) 334-9780, www.langetwins.com

Johann and Maria Lange came to Lodi in the 1870s. After growing watermelons, they planted grapes in 1916. Great-grandson twins Brad and Randall farmed the family land, striking out on their own in 1974 and building a winery in 2006. Randall's wife, Charlene, and Brad's wife, Susan, actively participate in winery and vineyard operations, as do the couples' five children, Marissa, Aaron, Philip, Kendra, and Joe. Based outside Lodi, Lange Twins' grape-growing efforts spread across San Joaquin, Sacramento, Solano, and Yolo Counties, growing varieties including Albariño, Barbera, Cabernet Sauvignon, Chardonnay, Malbec, Petit Verdot, Pinot Noir, Sauvignon Blanc, Syrah, Viognier, and Zinfandel. The Lange Twins Winery Estate Grown Musqué Clone Lodi Sauvignon Blanc offers flavors of grapefruit and fresh pineapple.

In her own words

GINA GALLO

Gina Gallo is the granddaughter of California wine pioneer Julio Gallo. Her husband is Jean-Charles Boisset, president of the St. Helena–based Boisset Family Estates. She is the winemaker for Gallo Signature Series.

I developed a deep connection to the land at a very young age. As I child, I loved picking fruits and vegetables for my mother and grandmother to use in their recipes. I also spent a lot of time walking in the vineyards with my grandfather Julio. But my family history and my own love of the land didn't translate to a passion for winemaking until after college. I joined the sales division of E. & J. Gallo Winery and started taking coursework in winemaking at UC Davis. Right away, I knew I had found my calling. From that moment on, I wanted to be a winemaker.

I definitely look to the Old World for a historical foundation, but there is so much to be learned from so many different regions across the globe. I've spent significant time in New Zealand and the cool-climate regions of Australia, getting a different perspective on Pinot Noir. I also had the incredible opportunity of traveling with my father and brother through the oak forests of France and the United States. I gained such a depth of understanding about how the forests are maintained and how different types of oak can impact a wine. I also spent time with a cooper in Kentucky, diving into the process of crafting barrels and toasting the oak. Winemaking isn't just about the vineyards and the grapes. Oak plays such an integral role, so these experiences have been invaluable for me.

My family has always approached farming with a deep respect for the land and the environment—long before sustainability was fashionable. In the past decade, our industry has begun to understand that sustainable agriculture is essential for the preservation of our vineyards and the surrounding land. At Gallo, we have moved very quickly to bring all of our estate vineyards and wineries up to the highest standards of sustainability; in fact, we've been among the first to earn certification for sustainable practices.

There are certainly more women winemakers now. It's exciting, because we bring a different perspective to the craft. It's also fascinating to see how far we've come with Pinot Noir in California. I am what they call a die-hard Pinotphile, so I am enamored with the Pinot sites that have been developed in the Russian River Valley and the Santa Lucia Highlands over the years. We have such a greater understanding now of how Pinot Noir adapts to different clones and different microclimates.

I love to experiment with different winemaking techniques. Right now, for example, we are working with concrete egg fermenters for our Sonoma Coast Chardonnay. I am able to better control the temperature and oxidation during fermentation, which in turn allows the wine to develop more complex layers of flavor and a rounder mouthfeel. It's always a challenge to be able to express myself through my wines and honor the land in a way that feels true to me and to my family's legacy. It's a challenge, but I take it on wholeheartedly. My approach is to consider the land—the *terroir* of the vineyard, the grapes that are suited to that site—and convey the story of that specific place in a personal and meaningful way. Given my background, I certainly take a historical perspective, but I also aim to create wines that feel authentic to my own style and true to today's wine culture.

The wine world is a lot like the art world. Creating art for the sake of art has an intrinsic value, but the human connection to that art is just as important. As winemakers, we introduce the market to new varieties and new styles of wine, but ultimately we strive to create wines that people will enjoy. There is a healthy push and pull that creates significant influence in both directions—and that is a good thing. It keeps us all moving forward.

MACCHIA WINES

7099 East Peltier Road, Acampo, CA 95220
(209) 333-2600, www.macchiawines.com

Tim and Lani Holdener started Macchia in 2001 and source grapes for their Zinfandel from prime vineyards in Lodi and Amador County, making a range of wines, including some single-vineyard bottlings. They also produce Amador County Barbera and Sangiovese. Italian for "the spot," Macchia has a tasting room filled with visitors and wine club members every weekend. The Macchia Wines "Mischievous" Lodi Old Vine Zinfandel has prominent flavors of mixed-berry pie, vanilla, and baking spice.

METTLER FAMILY VINEYARDS

7889 East Harney Lane, Lodi CA 95240
(888) 509-5969, www.mettlerwine.com

The Mettler family has been making wine since the late eighteenth century and growing grapes in Lodi since the end of the nineteenth. Sixth-generation grape farmer Carl Mettler married Gladys Handel in the 1940s, joining the families and their vineyard holdings. Son Larry; his wife, Charlene; and their three grown children started making their own wine in 2001. In addition to Cabernet Sauvignon, their first bottling, they produce Zinfandel and Petite Sirah from their certified-organic vineyards. The Mettler Family Vineyards Estate Grown Cabernet Sauvignon offers smooth flavors of blackberry, strawberry confiture, air-cured Spanish ham, and chocolate-covered espresso bean. 11

MICHAEL DAVID WINERY

4580 Highway 12, Lodi, CA 95242
(209) 368-7384, www.michaeldavidwinery.com

Brothers Michael and David Phillips are the fifth generation of their family to grow grapes in Lodi, now joined by the sixth, Kevin Phillips and Melissa Phillips Stroud. Under the direction of winemaker Adam Mettler, also a member of a multigenerational Lodi grape-growing family, Michael David produces a variety of labels, including the well-known 7 Deadly Zins and 7 Heavenly Chards. In addition to estate-grown fruit from their Bare Ranch and Windmill Estate, grapes for specific bottlings are sourced from throughout Lodi and from Sonoma and Monterey. The Michael David Winery Inkblot Lodi Cabernet Franc offers flavors of strawberry preserves, black raspberry, and chocolate-covered cherries. 12

QUADY

13181 Road 24, Madera, CA 93637
(559) 673-8068, www.quadywinery.com

Andrew and Laurel Quady started Quady, known for its sweet wines, in 1975. In 1977 the couple built a small winery behind their home in Madera and began making port-style wines, but the brand took off in 1980 when they made a fortified dessert wine they called Essensia from Orange Muscat grapes. Big and viscous, the Quady Essensia has delightfully sweet flavors of orange, tangerine, and lime sherbet. The Quady Elysium Black Muscat boasts rich fruit flavors and a balanced crisp yet pleasantly sweet finish. 13

SORELLE WINERY

9599 North Highway 88, Stockton, CA 95212
(209) 931-4350, www.sorellewinery.com

Named for Kim and Melissa Scott, the sisters (*"sorelle"* in Italian) who oversee the daily operation of the family business, Sorelle produces wines from Italian grape varieties. Visitors can check out the Dodge House, named for Jonathan Holt Dodge, a gold miner who bought the property in 1857 and first planted grapevines here. The Scott sisters honored his heritage by replanting vines and building a winery in 2007. The Sorelle Winery Grazia Clarksburg Pinot Grigio offers aromas of Cavaillon melon, Mission fig, and cantaloupe and has a crisp, clean finish. The Sorelle Winery Troppo Bella Lodi Sangiovese has pronounced fruit flavors with a persistent finish.

UVAGGIO

P.O. Box 10708, Napa, CA 94581
(707) 224-2254, www.uvaggio.com

After a successful career that included crafting award-winning wines for Robert Mondavi, Jim Moore wanted to focus on his beloved Italian varieties, which makes sense given California's Mediterranean climate. Uvaggio's current lineup consists of Barbera, Moscato, Primitivo, Sangiovese, and Vermentino. In the Uvaggio Lodi Vermentino, a bright nose of fresh citrus gives way to refreshing flavors of citrus fruits, honeysuckle, and shale. (14)

11

2

9

VINTAGE 2010
BOGLE
VINEYARDS
As grape growers we hold high regard for the mindful tending of the soil and exacting knowledge of the cellar.
Petite Sirah
CALIFORNIA

1

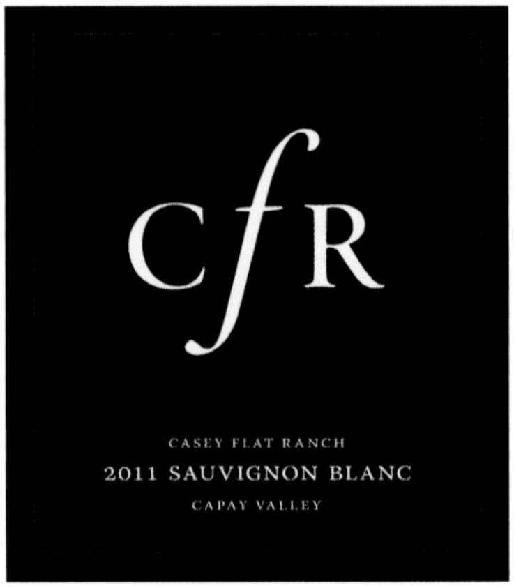
CfR
CASEY FLAT RANCH
2011 SAUVIGNON BLANC
CAPAY VALLEY

3

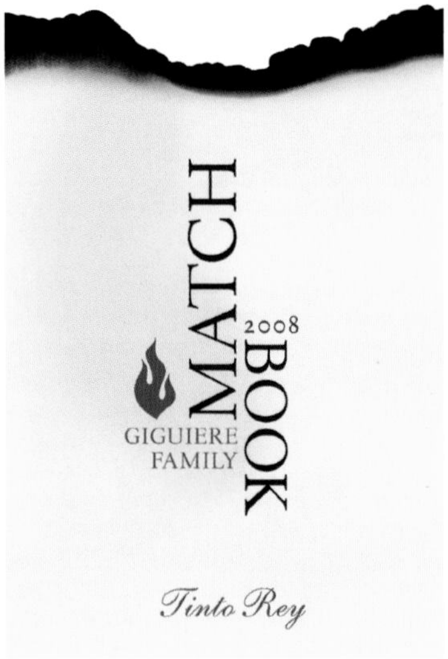
MATCH BOOK
2008
GIGUIERE FAMILY
Tinto Rey

4

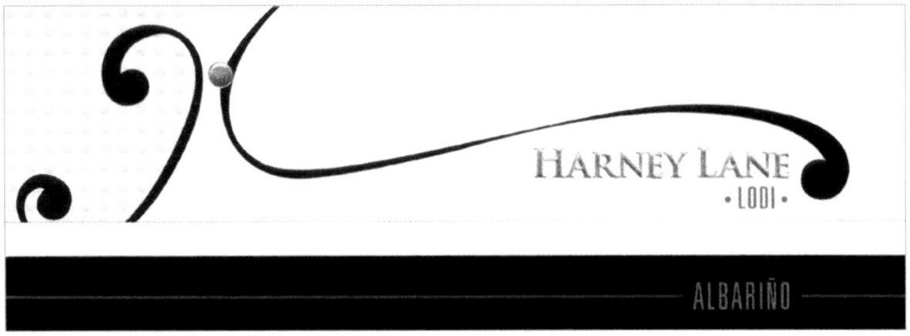
HARNEY LANE
• LODI •
ALBARIÑO

8

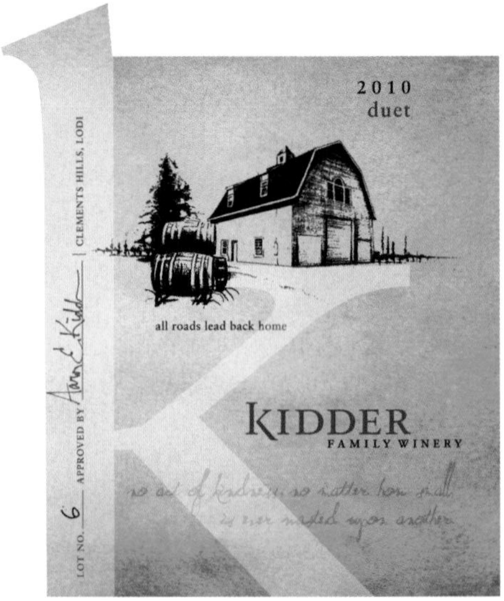
2010
duet
all roads lead back home
KIDDER
FAMILY WINERY
LOT NO. 6 APPROVED BY
CLEMENTS HILLS, LODI

10

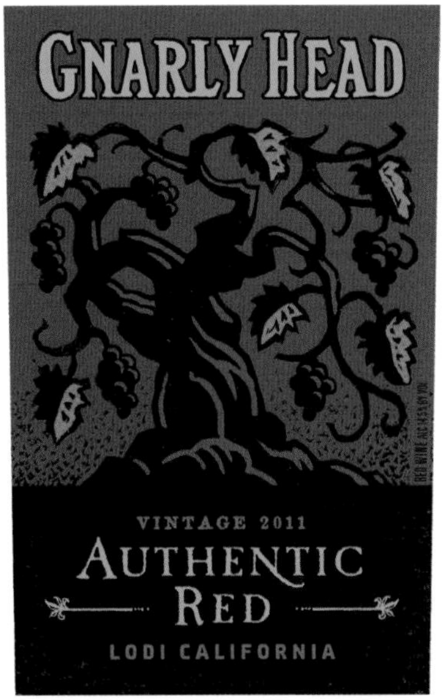
GNARLY HEAD
VINTAGE 2011
AUTHENTIC RED
LODI CALIFORNIA

5

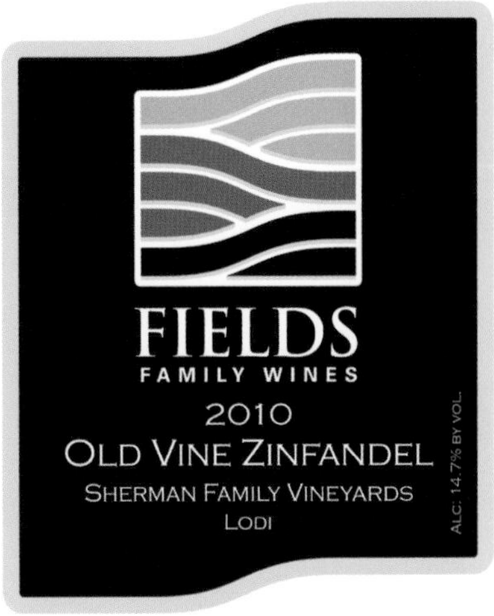
FIELDS
FAMILY WINES
2010
OLD VINE ZINFANDEL
SHERMAN FAMILY VINEYARDS
LODI
ALC. 14.7% BY VOL.

6

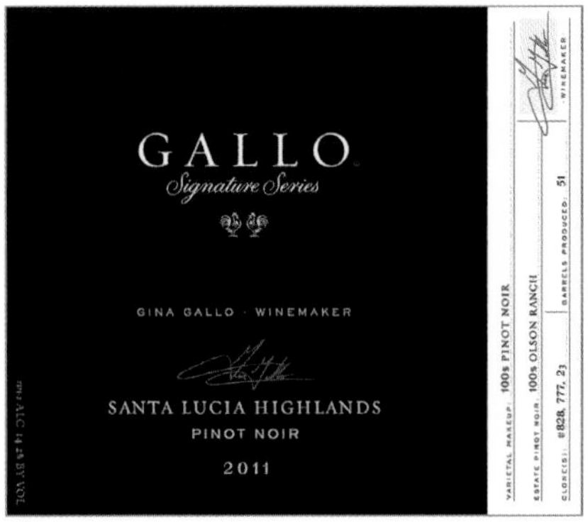
GALLO
Signature Series
GINA GALLO · WINEMAKER
SANTA LUCIA HIGHLANDS
PINOT NOIR
2011

7

Michael David
Inkblot
Lodi 2010 Cabernet Franc

12

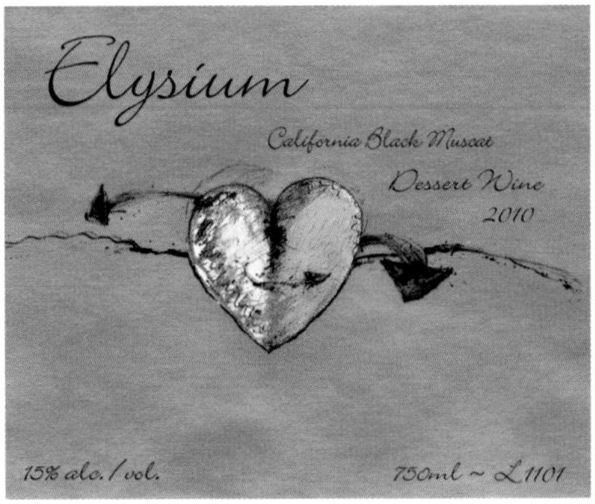
Elysium
California Black Muscat
Dessert Wine
2010
15% alc./vol.
750ml ~ L1101

13

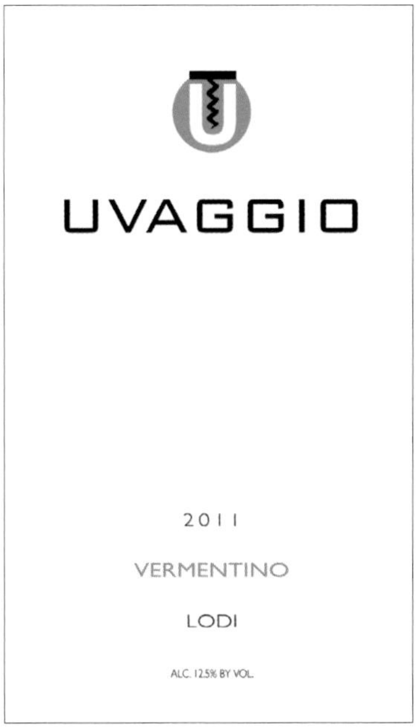
UVAGGIO
2011
VERMENTINO
LODI
ALC. 12.5% BY VOL.

14

SIX

MARIN COUNTY

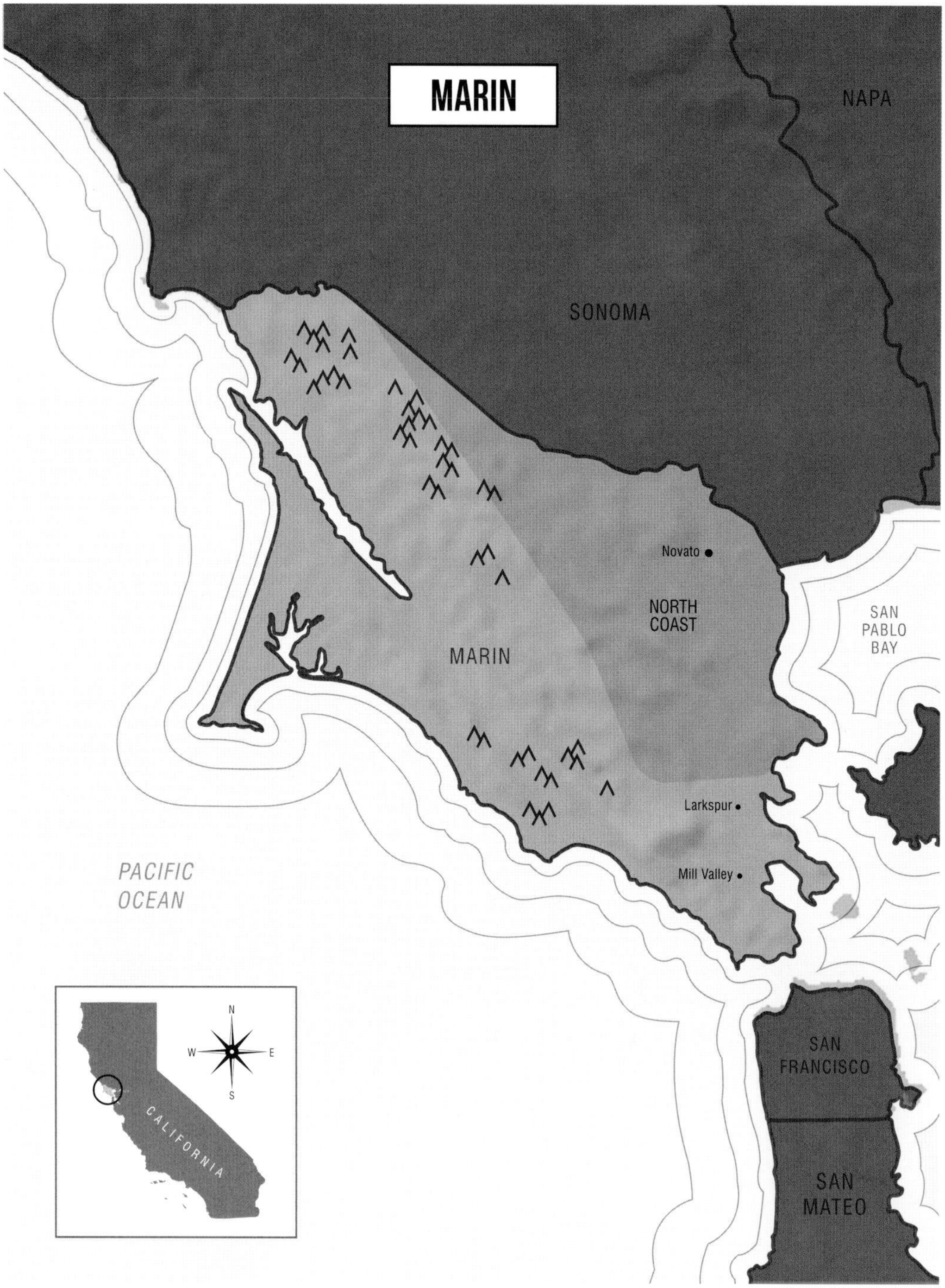
MARIN
NAPA
SONOMA
Novato
NORTH COAST
SAN PABLO BAY
MARIN
Larkspur
Mill Valley
PACIFIC OCEAN
N
W
E
S
CALIFORNIA
SAN FRANCISCO
SAN MATEO

Grapes came to Marin County with Spanish missionaries and were planted around the same time that Mission San Rafael was constructed in 1817. It's said that some of those vines were transplanted to General Mariano Vallejo's Sonoma County ranch about 20 years later. German immigrant Hermann Zopf, proprietor of a San Rafael grocery store and saloon, also planted grapes and made wine. French expatriate Jean Escalle, his original winery built in the 1890s, planted almost 25 acres of vines on his land in Larkspur.

Marin County is San Francisco's gateway to Sonoma and Napa. It has long been a dairy-farming area, and some of the best-known local cheese producers, a key component of the thriving farm-to-table movement, operate here. Located between the Pacific Ocean and San Pablo Bay, Marin has rainy winters and cool springs and benefits from the water's cooling effects, which protect grapes from harsh summer heat. The county's rolling hills, home to more acres of pasture than grapevines, have a multitude of soil types shaped by volcanic and alluvial influences, including gravelly loam that offers good drainage and silt-filled clay that holds moisture even in the driest season. Prohibition all but destroyed the hundreds of acres of vineyards that existed in the early part of the twentieth century, and today only about 200 acres of grapes are cultivated in Marin.

The handful of producers in Marin County work with a combination of locally sourced fruit, much of it coming from estate vineyards and small amounts of grapes from other regions. The primary varieties grown here are Pinot Noir and Chardonnay, with a smattering of Cabernet Sauvignon, Syrah, and Zinfandel. All the wineries in Marin are small, focusing on handcrafted artisanal wines.

THE WINERIES

KALIN CELLARS

61 Galli Drive, Novato, CA 94949
(415) 883-3543, www.kalincellars.com

Kalin Cellars uses traditional European techniques to create small-batch wines. Annual production is fewer than 7,000 cases, and both red and white wines ferment in oak with no fining or filtering. Kalin produces exclusively single-vineyard wines and ranks among the few wineries that cellar their wines for a long period—sometimes more than 10 years—before releasing them to the public. The powerful yet restrained Kalin Cellars Cuvée LV Chardonnay offers aromas of fresh citrus and candied orange peel. ❶

KENDRIC VINEYARDS

48 Tamalpais Avenue, San Anselmo, CA 94960
(415) 806-4944, www.kendricvineyards.com

Named in memory of Stewart Johnson's father, Kendric Vineyards produces Pinot Noir and Viognier from estate vineyards in Marin County. Johnson likes to tell people that he handles all aspects of the winemaking process: planting the vines, tending them, picking the grapes, crushing them, and making the wine. But wife Eileen Burke handles marketing as well as running a busy San Francisco law practice. The clean-finishing Kendric Vineyards Marin County Pinot Noir exhibits nice fruit flavors in the mouth.

PACHECO RANCH WINERY

235 Alameda Del Prado, Novato, CA 94949
(415) 883-5583, www.pachecoranchwinery.com

Situated on the land granted to Ignacio Pacheco in 1840, Pacheco Ranch Winery was replanted in 1970 by his descendants and their winery partners and has been making handcrafted wines for more than 30 years. Winemaking is under the direction of Jamie Meves, who cellars many of the wines for at least five years before release. Pacheco Ranch Winery Cabernet Sauvignon has aromas of dried black cherry and cassis with a top note of Indian spice.

PEY-MARIN VINEYARDS

P.O. Box 912, San Anselmo, CA 94960
(415) 455-9463, www.scenicrootwinegrowers.com

Jonathan and Susan Pey made wine for other vintners around the world and started Pey-Marin Vineyards in 1999. They currently specialize in small-lot, artisanally made Pinot Noir and dry Riesling with grapes grown on the western side of the county. The crisp and clean Pey-Marin Vineyards The Shell Mound, Marin County Riesling has aromas of Anjou pears, citrus, and candied lemon peel. The Pey-Marin Vineyards Trois Filles, Marin County Pinot Noir has juicy red fruit flavors and pleasant spice in the finish. ❷

POINT REYES VINEYARDS

12700 Highway 1, Point Reyes Station, CA 94956
(415) 663-1011, www.ptreyesvineyardinn.com

The Doughty family, which has been farming the land for three generations, receives credit for opening the first tasting room in Marin County since 1930. The family sources grapes from nearby growers and since 1990 has grown Pinot Noir on their own estate. The Point Reyes Vineyards Estate Pinot Noir offers aromas of black cherry and dried red cherries. ❸

SEAN THACKREY

240 Overlook Drive, Bolinas, CA 94924
(415) 868-9543, www.wine-maker.net

Art gallery owner turned winemaker, Sean Thackrey likes his grapes to rest under the stars before crushing. He claims that the Ancient Greeks used this technique and that Hesiod described the procedure in his early poems. Thackrey moved to Bolinas in 1964 and became a bonded winemaker in 1981. The medium-bodied Sean Thackrey Cassiopeia Wentzel Vineyard Anderson Valley Pinot Noir has a good expression of fruit and a touch of spice in the well-balanced finish.

STARRY NIGHT WINERY

359 Bel Marin Keys Boulevard, Suite 5, Novato, CA 94949
(415) 382-6200, www.starrynightwinery.com

Winemakers and friends Wayne Hansen, Bruce Walker, Skip Granger, and Mike Miller began making wine in Wayne's basement. Their first crush produced fifty cases of Zinfandel, Cabernet Sauvignon, and Chardonnay. Turning their hobby into a vocation, they became bonded as a winery a few weeks before the 1999 harvest. They strive for minimal intervention in their winemaking, use small open-top fermentation tanks, and employ manual punchdowns during fermentation. The rich and fruit-forward Starry Night Winery Moonhead Red Petite Sirah Zinfandel Blend offers aromas of black plums, black raspberries, and black cherries. The Starry Night Winery Lake County Terre Vermeille Vineyard Cabernet Franc has a rich bouquet of black currant, blueberry pie, freshly cut green pepper, and black raspberry.

1

2

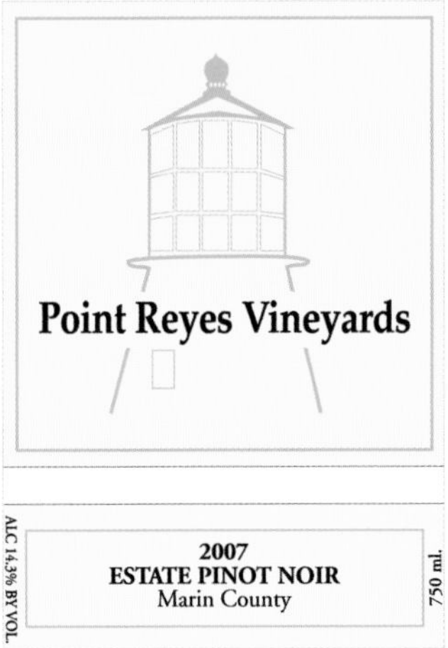

3

SEVEN

SAN FRANCISCO BAY AND THE SURROUNDING AREA

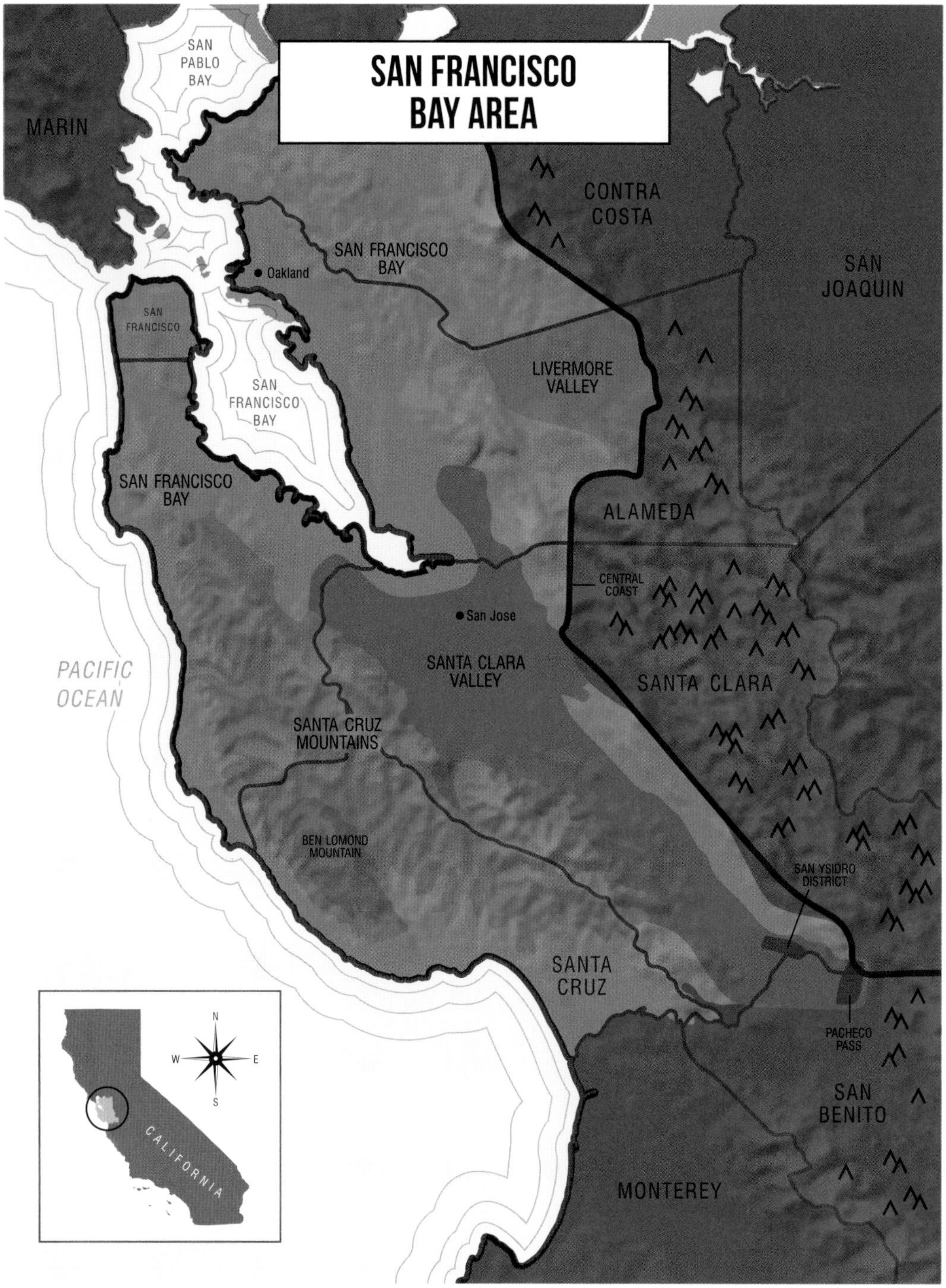
SAN FRANCISCO BAY AREA
SAN PABLO BAY
MARIN
CONTRA COSTA
SAN FRANCISCO BAY
Oakland
SAN JOAQUIN
SAN FRANCISCO
SAN FRANCISCO BAY
LIVERMORE VALLEY
SAN FRANCISCO BAY
ALAMEDA
CENTRAL COAST
San Jose
SANTA CLARA VALLEY
SANTA CLARA
PACIFIC OCEAN
SANTA CRUZ MOUNTAINS
BEN LOMOND MOUNTAIN
SAN YSIDRO DISTRICT
SANTA CRUZ
PACHECO PASS
N
W
E
S
SAN BENITO
CALIFORNIA
MONTEREY

About 6,500 acres of vines grow in the San Francisco Bay AVA, and more than a hundred wineries operate there, funky newcomers and the descendants of California wine industry notables alike. Established in 1999 and amended in 2006, the San Francisco Bay AVA encompasses the Santa Cruz Mountains AVA and the Ben Lomond Mountain AVA and contains the Pacheco Pass, San Ysidro District, and Santa Clara Valley sub-AVAs. Vineyards here tend to be rural, but a handful of small-scale urban winery operations and tasting rooms exists in San Francisco, Oakland, and Berkeley. The most prevalent grape is Chardonnay, followed by Cabernet Sauvignon and Merlot. Grapes planted in well-drained gravel soils benefit from hot days, cool nights, and coastal fog through the late morning.

In what is now Alameda County's Livermore Valley AVA, Spanish missionaries first planted grapes in the 1760s. About 80 years later, immigrant pioneers planted commercial vineyards, and in the 1880s the Wente, Concannon, and Wetmore families founded the region's first commercial wineries. In 1889 a wine from Livermore Valley brought acclaim to the California wine industry by winning a gold medal at the Paris Exhibition. Approved as an AVA in 1982, Livermore Valley now hosts about fifty wineries and has more than 4,000 acres of grapevines, mainly Petite Sirah, Sauvignon Blanc, Sémillon, and Merlot.

Ygnacio Martínez planted one of the first vineyards in Contra Costa County in the early nineteenth century, and vintners have produced wine here, mainly near Oakley, for more than a century. More than 3,000 acres of vines werre growing in Contra Costa in 1891, and double that number by 1897. Some 40 percent of the county's farmland was planted with grapes by 1919, but Prohibition pressed farmers either to abandon their vineyards or to convert to more salable crops. Today almost 2,000 acres of Oakley-area old-vine vineyards bear Zinfandel, Carignane, and Mourvèdre, many originally farmed by Valeriano Jacuzzi (of hot tub and spa fame). Jacuzzi's grandson Fred Cline still sources grapes from those family-owned vineyards for wine produced and bottled in his eponymous Sonoma winery.

The Santa Cruz Mountains AVA has some of the finest vineyards in the region that produce Cabernet Sauvignon, Chardonnay, and Pinot Noir. Elevations range from 400 to 800 feet, with some ridges reaching as high as 2,500 feet or more. Achieving AVA status in 1981, the AVA covers about 322,000 acres, 1,500 planted to vines, and has more than 200 mainly small vineyards.

THE WINERIES

BONNY DOON VINEYARD

328 Ingalls Street, Santa Cruz, CA 95060
(831) 425-3625, www.bonnydoonvineyard.com

In 1979 Randall Grahm set out to produce what he called "the great American Pinot Noir," but Pierce's disease decimated his Bonny Doon Estate Vineyard. He replanted to Syrah, Roussanne, Marsanne, and Viognier. The Bonny Doon Vin Gris de Cigare has aromas of peach, ripe strawberry, and citrus with waves of fresh fruit in the finish. Big, juicy, and fruit-driven, the Bonny Doon Le Pousseur Syrah has aromas of black plum, black raspberry, and air-cured meats. ❶

BROPHY CLARK CELLARS

P.O. Box 955, Nipomo, CA 93444
(805) 296-3017, www.brophyclarkcellars.com

Winemaker husband John Clark and viticulturist wife Kelley Brophy founded Brophy Clark Cellars in 1996. They focus on Zinfandel, Pinot Noir, Syrah, Chardonnay, and Sauvignon Blanc and limit their small-lot production to 2,500 cases per year. The Brophy Clark Santa Maria Valley Chardonnay offers aromas of pear, peach, papaya, guava, and buttered brioche. The Brophy Clark Santa Maria Valley Pinot Noir has notes of strawberries and cream, red cherry, and cherry cola. ❷

CLOS LACHANCE

1 Hummingbird Lane, San Martin, CA 95046
(800) 487-9463, www.clos.com

Bill Murphy and Brenda LaChance Murphy were looking to purchase vineyards and came across a suitable parcel of land in San Martin. They partnered with CordeValle Resort to plant 40,000 vines and build a new winery that could produce 60,000 cases per year. The winery was finished in 2001 in time for the harvest, and the visitor center opened in 2002. Today Stephen Tebb oversees winemaking from the estate's 150 acres, and Jason Robideaux joined him as associate winemaker in 2007. The crisp, clean Clos LaChance Estate Central Coast Sauvignon Blanc has aromas of lemon zest and a delightfully zingy finish. The Clos LaChance Estate Zinfandel has aromas of red and black fruits and a bright fruit finish. ❸

CONCANNON VINEYARD

4590 Tesla Road, Livermore, CA 94550
(800) 258-9866, www.concannonvineyard.com

James Concannon planted vineyards and built his winery in 1883, one of the first successful wineries founded by an Irish immigrant. The fourth-generation of the family takes credit as the first to bottle and label Petite Sirah as a variety; they also ranked among the first to have a female winemaker, Katherine Vajda, who joined the team in 1961. The Concannon Captain Joe's Reserve Petite Sirah, with aromas of Christmas baking spices, cassis, and black raspberry, is fruit-forward in the mouth. The Concannon Selected Vineyards Cabernet Sauvignon has aromas of black raspberry, black plum, and black olive tapenade, and the berry flavors transfer easily onto the palate. ❹

CUDA RIDGE WINES

2400 Arroyo Road, Livermore, CA 94550
(510) 304-0914, www.cudaridgewines.com

Founders Larry and Margie Dino make small-lot, artisanally produced wines. Cuda Ridge's new winery opened in 2013 and brought production capacity to about 1,600 cases of Bordeaux-style wines made from Sémillon, Cabernet Sauvignon, Merlot, Cabernet Franc, Sauvignon Blanc, Malbec, and Petit Verdot. The Cuda Ridge Livermore Valley Sauvignon Blanc, with aromas of Cavaillon melon, grapefruit, and citrus, pairs well with fish and shellfish. The Cuda Ridge Livermore Valley Merlot offers notes of freshly picked cherries, blueberry pie, and cranberry sauce.

DARCIE KENT VINEYARDS

7000 Tesla Road, Livermore, CA 94550
(925) 243-9040, www.darciekentvineyards.com

Darcie Kent founded her family-operated winery in 1996. In addition to estate-grown grapes, they source fruit from a variety of family-owned vineyards, including DeMayo Vineyards, Madden Ranch, Picazo Vineyard, Rava's Black Jack Vineyard, and West Pinnacle Vineyard. The Darcie Kent Vineyards Rava Blackjack Vineyard Pinot Noir offers flavors of strawberry, blackberry, and black cherries, and the Darcie Kent Vineyards DeMayo Vineyard Chardonnay tastes of caramelized pineapple, lemon-lime soda, anise, and mint.

DASHE CELLARS

55 4th Street, Oakland, CA 94607
(510) 452-1800, www.dashecellars.com

Michael and Anne Dashe founded Dashe Cellars also in 1996. Their winery sits in downtown Oakland, near Jack London Square. With 40 years of combined experience at Ridge Vineyards, Far Niente, Chappellet, and Château Lafite Rothschild, among others, they source fruit from a variety of California AVAs and produce about 10,000 cases per year. The Dashe Cellars Potter Valley McFadden Farms Dry Riesling has aromas of Anjou pear and generous fruit flavors. The Dashe Cellars Alexander Valley Todd Brothers Ranch Petite Sirah has rich fruit flavors and aromas of cassis, black raspberry, and black plum. 5

DONKEY & GOAT WINERY

1340 5th Street, Berkeley, CA 94710
(510) 868-9174, www.donkeyandgoat.com

Jared and Tracey Brandt learned natural winemaking in France and brought the technique back to downtown Berkeley to make wine from Chardonnay, Pinot Noir, and Rhône varieties. Their Donkey & Goat El Dorado Grenache Blanc offers aromas of Cavaillon melon and white peach and citrus flavor notes. The crisp, clean Donkey & Goat Improbable El Dorado Chardonnay has enticing aromas of white stone fruits. 6

HEART O' THE MOUNTAIN

No visitor facilities
Scotts Valley, CA 95066
(831) 406-1881, www.heartothemountain.com

Pierre and Sada Cornwall originally planted this property in 1880 and made wine until Prohibition. In 1940 Alfred Hitchcock bought the property, and in 1978 Bob and Judy Brassfield acquired it, replanted vines, and began preservation of the historic estate. The Brassfields have planted five different Dijon and Pommard clones of Pinot Noir. Heart O' The Mountain Estate Pinot Noir, with aromas of spice, cracked black pepper, fresh red cherries, and dried black cherry, is fruit-forward in the mouth. 7

JC CELLARS

55 4th Street, Oakland, CA 94607
(510) 465-5900, www.jccellars.com

Jeff Cohn's provenance includes Rosenblum Cellars, and he sources fruit for his wines from grape growers around the state, releasing his wines under twenty-one different labels. The JC Cellars Iron Hill Vineyard Zinfandel offers jammy flavors of dark fruits, anise, and white pepper. Crisp and clean, the JC Cellars Stagecoach Vineyard Marsanne has delightful aromas of white peaches. 8

1

2

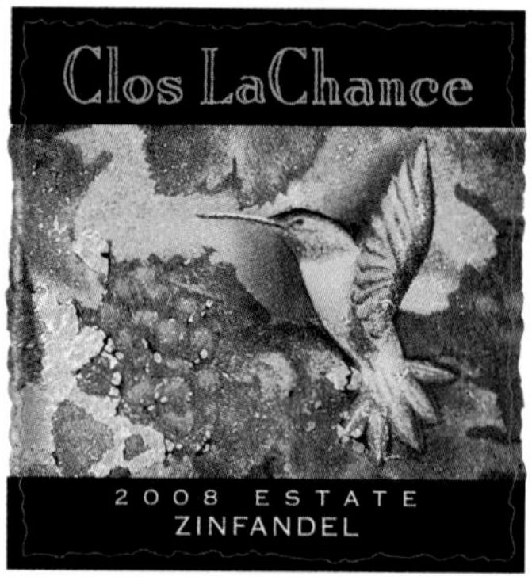

3

4

5

6

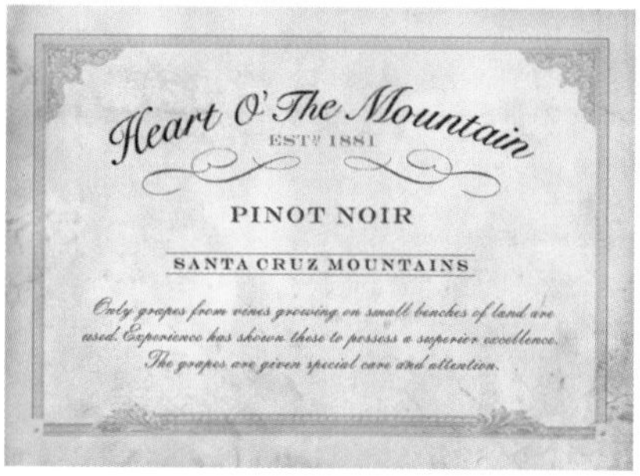

Heart O' The Mountain
ESTD 1881
PINOT NOIR
SANTA CRUZ MOUNTAINS
Only grapes from vines growing on small benches of land are used. Experience has shown these to possess a superior excellence. The grapes are given special care and attention.

7

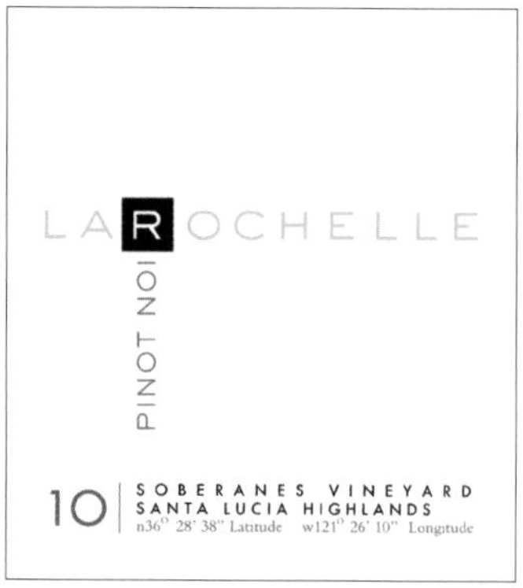

LA R OCHELLE
PINOT NOIR
10
SOBERANES VINEYARD
SANTA LUCIA HIGHLANDS
n36° 28' 38" Latitude w121° 26' 10" Longitude

9

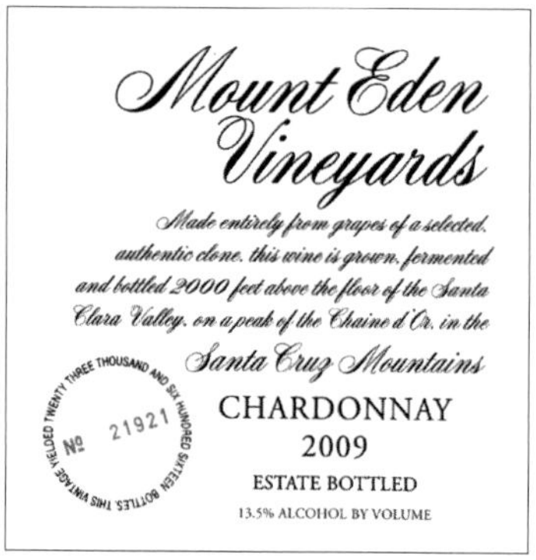

Mount Eden Vineyards
Made entirely from grapes of a selected, authentic clone, this wine is grown, fermented and bottled 2000 feet above the floor of the Santa Clara Valley, on a peak of the Chaine d'Or, in the Santa Cruz Mountains
THIS VINTAGE YIELDED TWENTY THREE THOUSAND AND SIX HUNDRED SIXTEEN BOTTLES
№ 21921
CHARDONNAY
2009
ESTATE BOTTLED
13.5% ALCOHOL BY VOLUME

10

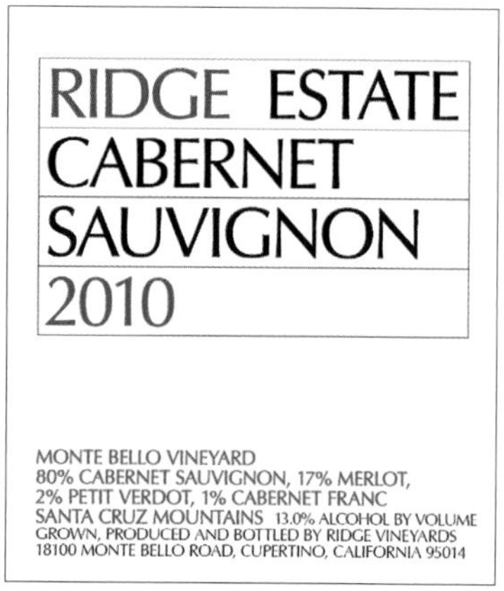

RIDGE ESTATE
CABERNET
SAUVIGNON
2010
MONTE BELLO VINEYARD
80% CABERNET SAUVIGNON, 17% MERLOT,
2% PETIT VERDOT, 1% CABERNET FRANC
SANTA CRUZ MOUNTAINS 13.0% ALCOHOL BY VOLUME
GROWN, PRODUCED AND BOTTLED BY RIDGE VINEYARDS
18100 MONTE BELLO ROAD, CUPERTINO, CALIFORNIA 95014

12

8

11

LA ROCHELLE WINERY

5433 Tesla Road, Livermore, CA 94550
(925) 243-6442, www.lrwine.com

Steven Kent Mirassou's great-great-great-grandfather departed France from the port of La Rochelle, hence the name of his winery, and his descendants planted Pinot Noir in California in the 1850s. Mirassou also makes wine under the Steven Kent and Lineage labels. At La Rochelle he remains committed to Pinot Noir, and together he and winemaker Tom Stutz make varietally correct Pinots. The La Rochelle Santa Lucia Highlands Soberanes Vineyard Pinot Noir has rich aromas of blackberry and dried black cherries and a touch of lifted cocoa powder. 9

MOUNT EDEN VINEYARDS

22020 Mount Eden Road, Saratoga, CA 95070
(888) 865-9463, www.mounteden.com

The legacy of Mount Eden Vineyards begins with Burgundian winemaker Paul Masson and Martin Ray, who purchased the Frenchman's Champagne Company after the repeal of Prohibition. Ray sold the property in 1943 and moved to Mount Eden, where he planted Pinot Noir and Chardonnay and brought in investors in the 1960s. Ray produced his last vintage in 1970, and today winemakers Jeffrey and Ellie Patterson run the winery as majority shareholders. They live with their two children, Sophie and Reid, in the original house that Ray built. The Mount Eden Vineyards Estate Santa Cruz Mountains Chardonnay offers aromas of lemon rind, fennel bulb, and Provençal herbs, while the Mount Eden Vineyards Estate Pinot Noir Santa Cruz Mountains Pinot Noir has aromas of Indian spice, black cherry, and red plum. Drink both now, or hold them for a few years. 10

MURRIETA'S WELL

3005 Mines Road, Livermore, CA 94550
(925) 456-2390, www.murrietaswell.com

Named for Joaquín Murrieta Carrillo, the infamous local bandit who frequented the artesian well on the property, Murrieta's Well's original winery was built by Louis Mel in the 1870s. Philip Wente and Sergio Traverso purchased the property in the 1990s, and today the Wente family owns the winery, with Sergio as consulting winemaker. Murrieta's Well produces approximately 12,000 cases of wine per year, and its 92 acres are planted with Cabernet Sauvignon, Sauvignon Blanc, Sémillon, Cabernet Franc, Merlot, Zinfandel, Petit Verdot, Tempranillo, Mourvèdre, Souzão, Touriga Nacional, and Touriga Francesa. The Murrieta's Well The Spur Livermore Valley offers aromas of dark cherry, blueberry pie, and mocha. 11

RHYS VINEYARDS

No visitor facilities
(650) 419-2050, www.rhysvineyards.com

Owner Kevin Harvey, winegrower Javier Meza, and winemaker Jeff Brinkman select grapes from five sites in the Santa Cruz Mountains to make their wines that concentrate on Chardonnay, Pinot Noir, and Syrah grapes grown using organic and biodynamic principles. The Rhys Family Farm Vineyard Pinot Noir has aromas of dried black cherries, ripe red cherries, and Mediterranean herbs and fruit sweetness on the palate. Drink it now, or age it for a few years.

RIDGE VINEYARDS

17100 Monte Bello Road, Cupertino, CA 95014
(408) 867-3233, www.ridgewine.com

Osea Perrone first planted terraced vines on 180 acres of land on Monte Bello Ridge in 1885. The vines were abandoned during Prohibition, and ownership changed hands a few times before Paul Draper joined the owners in 1969. In 1991 the group acquired Lytton Springs in Sonoma County. Although the original site lies on Monte Bello Road, Ridge makes wine in Cupertino as well as wine from a variety of California AVAs, including those grown, produced, and bottled by Ridge Vineyards at the Lytton Springs Road facility in Healdsburg. The rich Ridge Estate Santa Cruz Mountains Monte Bello Vineyard Cabernet Sauvignon has fruit flavors accented by dark chocolate and brown spice. With a crisp, clean, satisfying finish, the Ridge Estate Santa Cruz Mountains Monte Bello Estate Vineyard Chardonnay has great texture and flavors of ripe stone fruits. 12

ROSENBLUM CELLARS

2900 Main Street, Suite 1100, Alameda, CA 94501
(510) 995-4100, www.rosenblumcellars.com

Kent Rosenblum started Rosenblum Cellars among the docks and shipyards of Alameda in 1978. Boasting more than twenty different Zinfandel variations, including old-vine Zin, big-attitude Zin, and high-altitude Zin, Rosenblum sources its fruit from all over the state. The fruit-forward Rosenblum Cellars Sonoma Valley Monte Rosso Vineyard Reserve Zinfandel features flavors of fruit and black pepper. The big, bold Rosenblum Cellars Reserve Cullinane Zinfandel tastes of juicy fruit with secondary flavors of English toffee.

TESTAROSSA WINERY

300 College Avenue, Los Gatos, CA 95030
(408) 354-6150, www.testarossa.com

Seeking to fund Santa Clara College, Jesuits constructed Novitiate Winery in 1888. The priests enjoyed a 98-year run—even during Prohibition—until they closed the doors in 1986. Rob and Diana Jensen bought the property in 1997, making it the fourth oldest continuously operating winery in California. Today production is approximately 20,000 cases per year. The medium-bodied Testarossa Jensen Reserve Diana's Chardonnay has creamy fruit flavors and a long, clean finish. The Testarossa Rosella's Vineyard Santa Lucia Highlands Pinot Noir has enticing aromas of red fruits, dried black cherries, and brown spice.

THOMAS FOGARTY WINERY

19501 Skyline Boulevard, Woodside, CA 94062
(650) 851-6777, www.fogartywinery.com

Vascular surgeon Thomas Fogarty planted his first grapes in 1978, made wine in a small cabin, and established his commercial winery in 1981. The estate sits at an elevation of 2,000 feet and covers 325 acres, with 25 under grapes. Michael Martella has directed winemaking since the inception of the winery and is assisted by Nathan Kandler and cellarmaster Ryan Teeter. The Thomas Fogarty Skyline Riesling has flavors of stone fruits and crisp apple, and the Thomas Fogarty Santa Cruz Mountains Pinot Noir has notes of red cherries and brown spice in the complex bouquet.

WENTE VINEYARDS

5565 Tesla Road, Livermore, CA 94550
(925) 456-2300, www.wentevineyards.com

At more than 130 years old, Wente Vineyards is the country's oldest continuously operated family-owned winery. German immigrant C. H. Wente learned winemaking from Charles Krug and opened his own winery in 1883. His original vineyard spanned 48 acres, but today the fifth generation of Wente ownership maintains 2,800 acres. The Wente Estate Grown Riva Ranch Chardonnay offers flavors of tropical fruits with nuances of butter and toffee. The Wente Vineyards Nth Degree Cabernet Sauvignon has flavors of black cherry, Chinese black tea, and espresso.

EIGHT

MONTEREY AND SAN BENITO COUNTIES

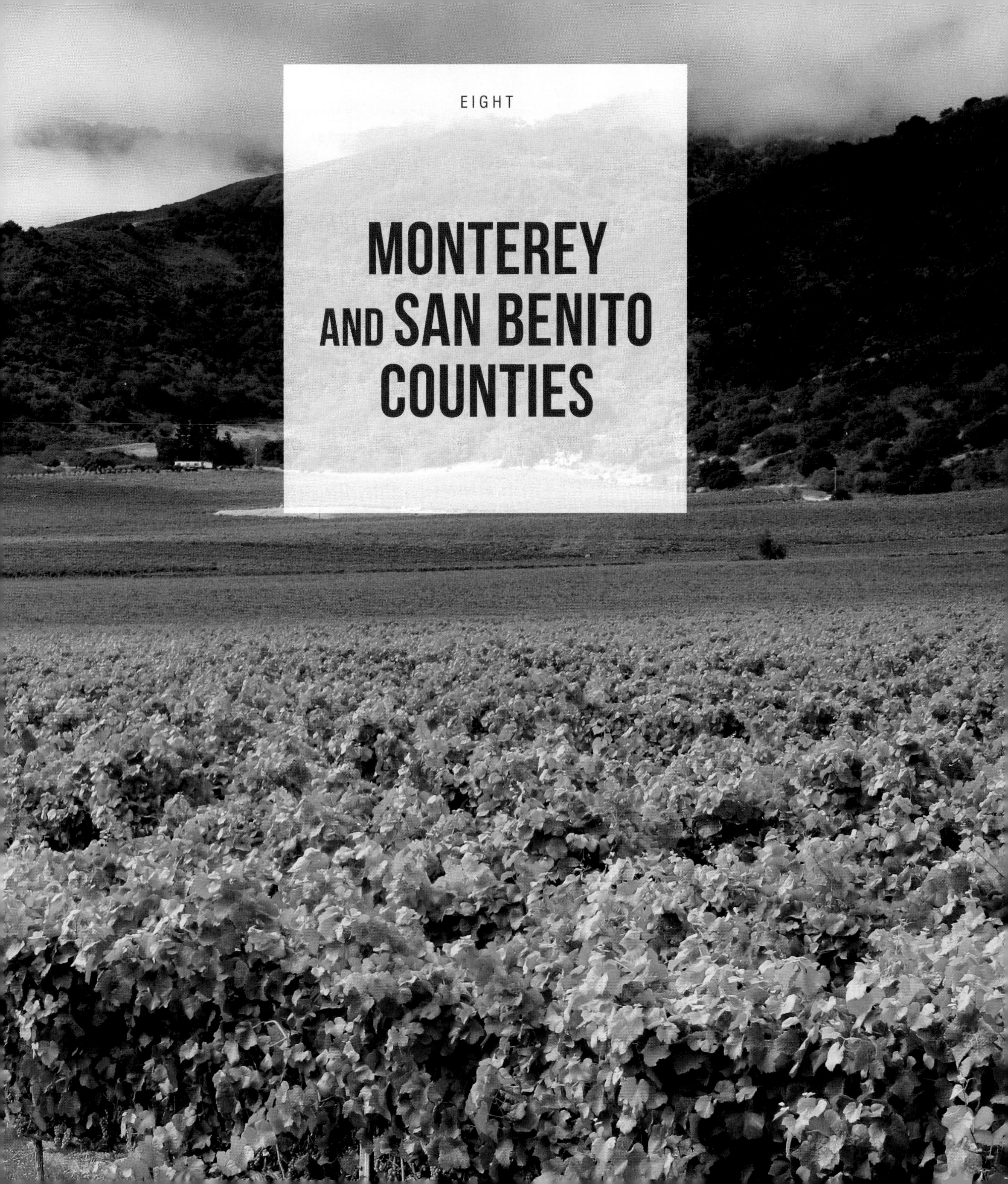

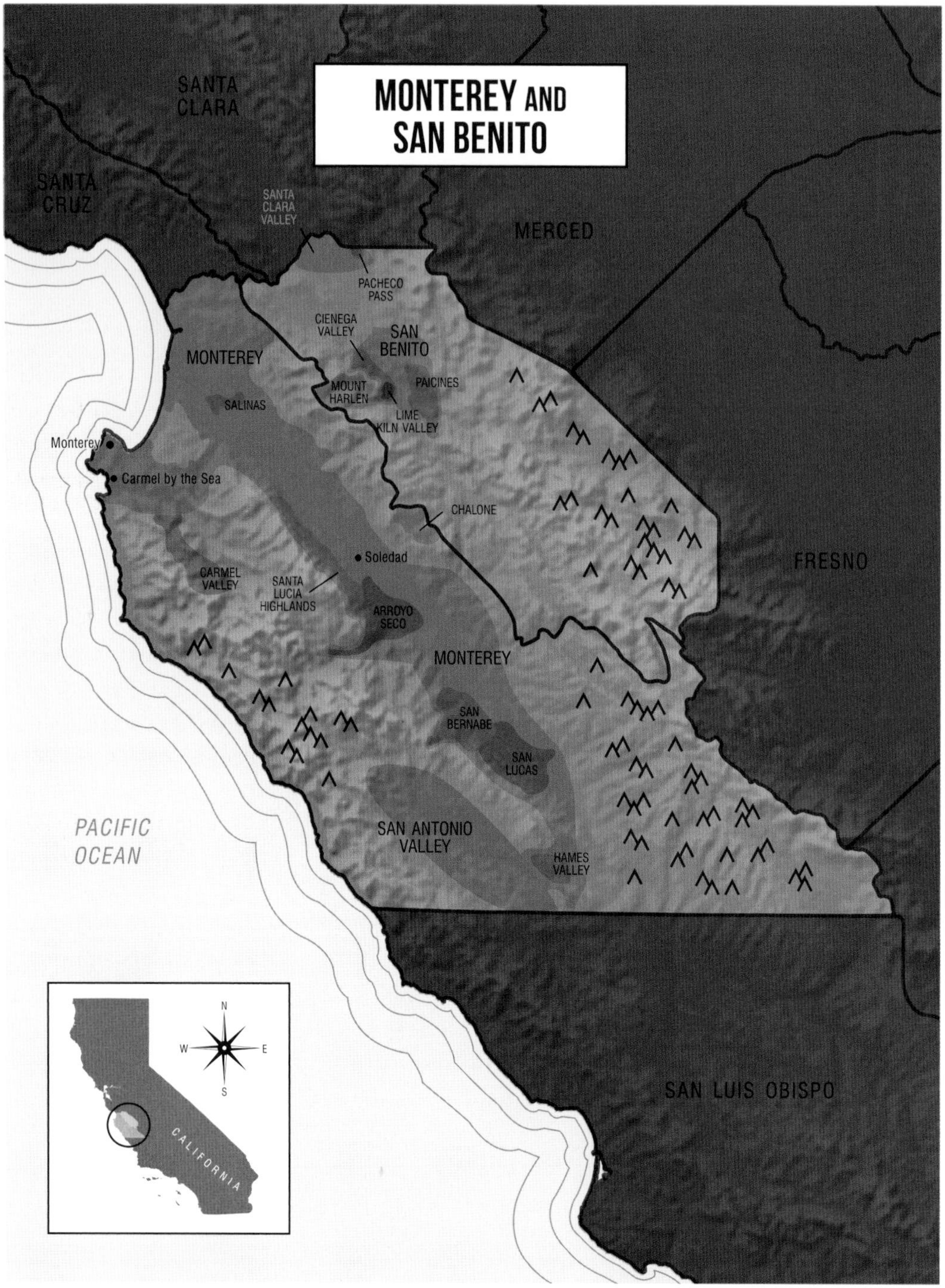

MONTEREY AND SAN BENITO
SANTA CLARA
SANTA CRUZ
SANTA CLARA VALLEY
MERCED
PACHECO PASS
CIENEGA VALLEY
SAN BENITO
MONTEREY
MOUNT HARLEN
PAICINES
SALINAS
LIME KILN VALLEY
Monterey
Carmel by the Sea
CHALONE
Soledad
FRESNO
CARMEL VALLEY
SANTA LUCIA HIGHLANDS
ARROYO SECO
MONTEREY
SAN BERNABE
SAN LUCAS
PACIFIC OCEAN
SAN ANTONIO VALLEY
HAMES VALLEY
N
W
E
S
SAN LUIS OBISPO
CALIFORNIA

Inland from Monterey County's rugged cliffs and sandy beaches lie more than 40,000 acres of wine grapes grown in nine AVAs and featured in more than a hundred wineries and tasting rooms. The Monterey AVA, established in 1984, runs the length of Monterey County, with widely varying growing conditions resulting from variations in temperature and soil. Monterey's other AVAs include Santa Lucia Highlands, Arroyo Seco, San Lucas, Carmel Valley, Chalone, Hames Valley, San Antonio Valley, and San Bernabe.

The Spanish mission Nuestra Señora de la Soledad, now the city of Soledad, founded in 1791, first grew grapes here. Modern-day growers looked to the soils of Monterey in the late 1960s, when well-known wineries began planting new vineyards and building new facilities. From about 5 acres in 1966, vineyard acreage grew to more than 2,000 by 1970. Since then, new plantings in Monterey have averaged 1,000 acres annually, and now all commercially viable grape varieties grow on its nearly 45,000 acres.

The Monterey AVA's proximity to the Pacific Ocean and Monterey Bay provides cool days throughout the long growing season. The somewhat cooler north is ideal for Chardonnay (the top grape here, at just over 40 percent of plantings), Pinot Noir, Pinot Gris, and Riesling; in the slightly warmer south, Bordeaux varieties such as Cabernet Sauvignon and Merlot grow alongside Syrah, Sangiovese, and Touriga Nacional. Sandy soils and an almost complete lack of rainfall during the growing season make irrigation a must in most of the region.

The 19,000-acre Carmel Valley AVA, established in 1983, has just 300 acres of grapevines planted at altitudes of 200 to 2,762 feet. Soils are mainly sandy loam, and the valley enjoys cool coastal influences. Higher-elevation vineyards above the fog line rely on altitude and daily summer temperature variations of up to 60 degrees Fahrenheit to retain freshness in the grapes. Bordeaux varieties are most prevalent, with Cabernet Sauvignon and Merlot accounting for more than 70 percent of the plantings and a few small plantings of Pinot Noir and Chardonnay as well.

The Santa Lucia Highlands AVA, first planted with Mission grapes at the end of the eighteenth century, experienced a planting boom starting in the early 1970s. Santa Lucia Highlands gained AVA status in 1991 and includes just over 6,000 acres of vineyards planted at altitudes of 100 to 2,350 feet. Morning sun aids in sugar and flavor development, and afternoon fog and strong winds off Monterey Bay delay ripening for two to three weeks beyond comparable regions in the state. Both Pinot Noir and Chardonnay thrive here, while Syrah and other Rhône varieties do well in sheltered canyons and slopes beyond the reach of chilling winds. Many Santa Lucia Highlands vineyards provide fruit for Pinot Noir–focused producers in other regions.

Arroyo Seco, Spanish for "dry riverbed," received AVA approval in 1983, about 20 years after the first commercial plantings in the area. The appellation covers 14,000 acres, with half under grapes. Soil is sand and loam, and vineyard elevations run from 266 to 1,670 feet. Canyons offer shelter from late-day winds, but vineyards on the valley floor benefit from cooling Pacific breezes. Soil types vary: Inhospitable canyon soils force vines to dig deep for water and nutrients, while in the valley fist-sized stones called Greenfield potatoes (after the nearby town of Greenfield) offer drainage and retain warmth from the sun, preventing overnight frost damage to delicate vines. Cooler areas of Arroyo Seco are home to Chardonnay and Riesling, and red Bordeaux and Rhône varieties and Zinfandel grow in the warmer areas.

Granted AVA status in 1982, Chalone has a grape-growing history that dates to before Prohibition. Its 300 vine acres include Chardonnay, Pinot Noir, Pinot Blanc, Chenin Blanc, and Syrah. Vineyards planted in the granite and limestone soils range in altitude from 1,200 to 2,323 feet, and the AVA has just two wineries. San Bernabe, which became an AVA in 2004, consists of the 11,000-acre San Bernabe Vineyard, where twenty varieties grow, including Merlot, Syrah, Pinot Noir, Chardonnay, and Riesling. The San Lucas AVA, previously home to grazing cattle, received official recognition in 1987. With 8,000 acres of grapes, mainly Cabernet Sauvignon, Merlot, Chardonnay, and Sauvignon Blanc, San Lucas is less affected by maritime breezes and provides grapes with a warmer climate than other AVAs in Monterey County. Grapes have been planted here in alluvial shale and sandstone since the 1970s.

The San Antonio Valley, established in 2006, is the most recent AVA in the county. The maritime influences of the nearby Pacific and lacustrine effects from Lake San Antonio moderate the area's warm days. More than 800 acres of grapes, mainly red Rhône and Bordeaux varieties, grow in the gravelly loam and clay soils.

Hames Valley, granted AVA designation in 1994, has the warmest daytime temperatures and reportedly has the largest day-to-night temperature variation in the region. Syrah and other red Rhône varieties predominate among the 2,000 vine acres. The Mount Harlan AVA, with one commercial winery, received AVA status in 1990. The soils here are almost all Pinot Noir–friendly limestone. Chardonnay, Aligoté, and Viognier also grow here at elevations between 1,800 and 2,200 feet.

Cienega Valley, Lime Kiln Valley, and Paicines received AVA status in 1982 (amended 1987). The 45,000-acre San Benito AVA, established in 1987, now contains those three sub-AVAs. Before 1984, Almaden acquired a large portion of its grapes from San Benito vineyards, specifically Cienega Valley and Paicines, but after Almaden's sale to Constellation in the mid-1980s plantings dwindled to fewer than 1,000 acres. A handful of small-scale wineries and a couple of larger operations have discovered San Benito, and the total planted area has increased to almost 3,000 acres. A wide array of grape varieties grow here, including Chardonnay, Pinot Noir, red Rhône varieties, Tempranillo, and Barbera.

7

THE WINERIES

BERNARDUS WINERY

5 West Carmel Valley Road, Carmel Valley, CA 93924
(831) 659-1900, www.bernardus.com

Dutch native Bernardus Pons was born into wine: His family owns the oldest wine distribution house in Holland. A lifelong sportsman, he has raced six times at Le Mans and competed in the 1972 Olympics as a skeet shooter. He and wife, Ingrid, settled in Carmel Valley, where they planted vines on 50 acres of their 220-acre estate. They grow primarily Bordeaux varieties, including Cabernet Franc, Cabernet Sauvignon, Petit Verdot, and Merlot. Dean DeKorth, who trained in Burgundy, directs winemaking and oversees the winery's daily operations. The Bernardus Winery Ingrid's Vineyard Estate Chardonnay offers aromas of Granny Smith apples, pear compote, and brown spice. The medium-bodied Bernardus Winery Ingrid's Vineyard Estate Pinot Noir has aromas of cherry preserves and fresh red raspberry.

CALERA WINES

11300 Cienega Road, Hollister, CA 95023
(831) 637-9170, www.calerawine.com

Josh Jensen returned to California from Burgundy in 1971 and began searching for a site to plant vines. He came across an old lime kiln in the Gabilan Mountains and found the limestone-rich *terroir* in which he wanted to plant Pinot Noir. In 1975 he planted 24 acres in three separate parcels. The Calera Mount Harlan Chardonnay has lovely flavors of Anjou pear, Granny Smith apple, and creamy lemon curd. The current vintage may be drunk now or in three to four years. The fruit-forward Calera Mount Harlan Jensen Vineyard Pinot Noir has a bouquet of black raspberry, red plum, and Provençal spice. ❶

CHALONE VINEYARD ESTATE

No visitor facilities
Soledad, CA 93960
(800) 407-9047, www.chalonevineyard.com

Charles Tamm planted the first grapevines on Chalone Peak in 1919, and in 1960 Philip Togni made the first wine to bear the Chalone label. In 1966 Dick Graff produced the first commercial vintage, and the 1970s through the 1990s saw extensive expansion. Today the estate has more than 1,000 acres, a quarter planted to vines, and Chalone is one of just two wineries in the Chalone AVA. The Chalone Vineyard Estate Chalone Appellation Chardonnay offers a bouquet of Anjou pear, white stone fruits, and citrus. The Chalone Vineyard Estate Chalone Appellation Pinot Noir features notes of ripe cherry, red raspberry, and sage.

HAHN FAMILY WINERY

37700 Foothill Road, Soledad, CA 93960
(866) 925-7994, www.hahnwinery.com

Swiss-born Nicolaus Hahn saw the potential of Monterey as a wine-growing region more than 30 years ago. Today, Greg Freeman performs the hands-on winemaking, which Paul Clifton directs. When you visit, take the ATV tour through the Santa Lucia Highlands and bring a picnic lunch. The medium-bodied Hahn Winery Monterey Chardonnay offers flavors of Bartlett pear and white peach and a crisp, clean finish. The Hahn Winery Exclusive Monterey GSM has aromas of red raspberry, red plum, and Mediterranean herbs.

MORGAN WINERY

590 Brunken Avenue, Salinas, CA 93901
(831) 751-7777, www.morganwinery.com

Dan Morgan Lee and Donna George made their first 2,000 cases of Monterey Chardonnay in 1982. Thirty-five years later, they opened Taste Morgan, their fun visitor center and tasting room at the Crossroads Shopping Village in Carmel. Gianni Abate, formerly of Woodbridge, Delicato, Robert Mondavi, and Bronco, is their winemaker. Full and creamy in the mouth, Morgan Winery Rosella's Vineyard Chardonnay has aromas of lemon curd, dried apricots, and white peach. The Morgan Winery Gary's Vineyard Pinot Noir has a nose of red raspberry and red cherry. 2

PARAISO VINEYARDS

38060 Paraiso Springs Road, Soledad, CA 93960
(831) 678-0300, www.paraisovineyards.com

Rich and Claudia Smith planted vines in 1973, and today their 400-acre estate has more than 150,000 of them in sixteen blocks. Parents, kids, and spouses own, operate, and manage this slice of paradise—along with their dogs. Besides making wine, the Smith family takes an active role in the community and charitable organizations, including Ag Against Hunger. The Paraiso Vineyards Santa Lucia Highlands Riesling has heady aromas of dried apricot, Anjou pear, and Christmas baking spices and pairs well with spicy Asian cuisine. The Paraiso Vineyards Faite Pinot Noir tastes of red raspberry and red cherry. 3

PISONI VINEYARDS

P.O. Box 908, Gonzales, CA 93926
(831) 675-7500, www.pisonivineyards.com

Farmers Eddie and Jane Pisoni used the profit from their 1979 celery crop as the down payment for the current vineyard site in the Santa Lucia Highlands. Son Gary planted vines in 1982, growing grapes for an array of wines. Gary's sons have joined the family enterprise: Mark manages the vineyards, and Jeff is winemaker. The full and rich Pisoni Santa Lucia Highlands Pinot Noir has flavors of red fruits, dried Mediterranean herbs, and a touch of mint. Full-bodied with luxurious texture, the Pisoni Santa Lucia Highlands Soberanes Chardonnay offers aromas of white stone fruits and caramelized pineapple.

ROAR WINES

32721 River Road, Soledad, CA 93960
(831) 675-1681, www.roarwines.com

Gary and Rosella Franscioni grew up in the Santa Lucia Highlands and recognized the grape-growing and winemaking potential early. In 1996 they planted their first vines in Rosella's Vineyard. Roar takes its name from the Monterey Bay winds that whip through their vineyard and keep the grapes cool at night. The Roar Wines Santa Lucia Highlands Pinot Noir offers fresh fruit flavors of red raspberry and ripe cherry. The Roar Wines Sierra Mar Vineyard Viognier tastes of white peach, anise bulb, and Christmas baking spices and is good either as an aperitif or with Asian cuisine. 4

SCHEID VINEYARDS

1972 Hobson Avenue, Greenfield, CA 93927
(831) 386 0316, www.scheidvineyards.com

Investment banker Al Scheid started Scheid Vineyards in 1972. Today he owns ten estate vineyards and farms 4,200 acres. In addition to a large high-capacity winery that produces custom-made wine for other brands—including GIFFT, created in partnership with daytime television host Kathy Lee Gifford—Scheid also has a smaller reserve winery, where the Scheid Vineyards wines are made. Clean and crisp, the GIFFT Estate Grown Monterey Chardonnay has flavors of peach and apple and a hint of toast; the GIFFT Estate Grown Monterey Red Blend offers a palate of black plum, cherry, and vanilla; and the Scheid Vineyards Pinot Noir tastes of black cherry with a touch of clove.

TALBOTT VINEYARDS

53 East Carmel Valley Road, Carmel Valley, CA 93924
(831) 659-3500, www.talbottvineyards.com

Robb Talbott grew up in Carmel Valley and attended college in Colorado, but in 1972 he returned and built a log cabin on the property that became his Diamond T Vineyards. He planted vines in 1982, enlisted the help of his wife and children, and today runs both Talbott Vineyards and his family's Robert Talbott Tie Company. The Talbott Vineyards Logan Sleepy Hollow Vineyard Chardonnay offers aromas of white peach and Granny Smith apples. Rich in the mouth, the Talbott Vineyards Diamond T Vineyard Monterey Pinot Noir proffers aromas of black cherry, red plum, and brown spice. 5

TONDRÉ WINES

P.O. Box 866, Gonzales, CA 93926
(831) 675-3214, www.tondrewines.com

Father-and-son team Tondré and Joe Alarid planted their first 6 acres in 1997, and today Tondré Wines has 80 acres of Pinot Noir vines and 21 acres of Chardonnay. Tondré Wines remains a passion project for both families. The Tondré Santa Lucia Highlands Pinot Noir 2010 has aromas of ripe red cherries and dried black cherry. Crisp yet creamy in the mouth, the Tondré Debut Vintage Chardonnay 2010 has bouquet notes of mango, guava, and pineapple. 6

VENTANA VINEYARDS

2999 Salinas Highway, Monterey, CA 93940
(831) 372-7415, www.ventanawines.com

Ventana Vineyards benefits from a cool climate and brisk evening winds perfect for cultivating Chardonnay, Riesling, and Pinot Noir. Steve McIntyre introduced sustainable farming practices and tends the 300 vineyard acres under the direction of Randy Pura. Ventana Vineyards Riesling, with flavors of white peach, orange zest, and dried sage, pairs well with spicy Thai or Vietnamese cuisine. The Ventana Vineyards Chardonnay has aromas of guava and pineapple upside-down cake and flavors of crisp apple and pear compote.

WRATH WINES

35801 Foothill Road, Soledad, CA 93960
(831) 678-2212, www.wrathwines.com

Inspired by the similarities between Salinas Valley and the Italian countryside, archaeologist Michael Thomas and his mother, Barbara Wrath, bought San Saba Vineyards in 2007. The smooth, medium-bodied Wrath San Saba Vineyard Monterey Chardonnay has flavors of vanilla, lemon curd, and hazelnuts, and the Wrath Boekenoogen Vineyard Santa Lucia Highlands Pinot Noir offers an initial burst of bright fruit and secondary flavors of black cherry, black raspberry, mint, oregano, and sage. 7

CALERA
2010
Thirty-Fifth Anniversary Vintage
JENSEN
VINEYARD
Pinot Noir
MT. HARLAN

1

MORGAN
Rosella's Vineyard
2011
Chardonnay
Santa Lucia Highlands

2

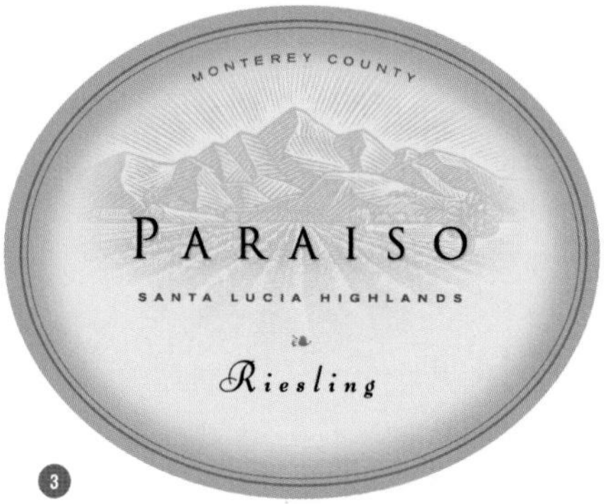
MONTEREY COUNTY
PARAISO
SANTA LUCIA HIGHLANDS
Riesling

3

VINTAGE 2011
ROAR
Viognier
APPELLATION SANTA LUCIA HIGHLANDS
SIERRA MAR VINEYARD

4

TALBOTT
LOGAN
2011
CHARDONNAY
SLEEPY HOLLOW VINEYARD
Estate Grown

5

TONDRÉ
2010
Pinot Noir
Santa Lucia Highlands
Tondré Grapefield
ALC. 14.1% BY VOL.

6

NINE

SAN LUIS OBISPO COUNTY AND PASO ROBLES

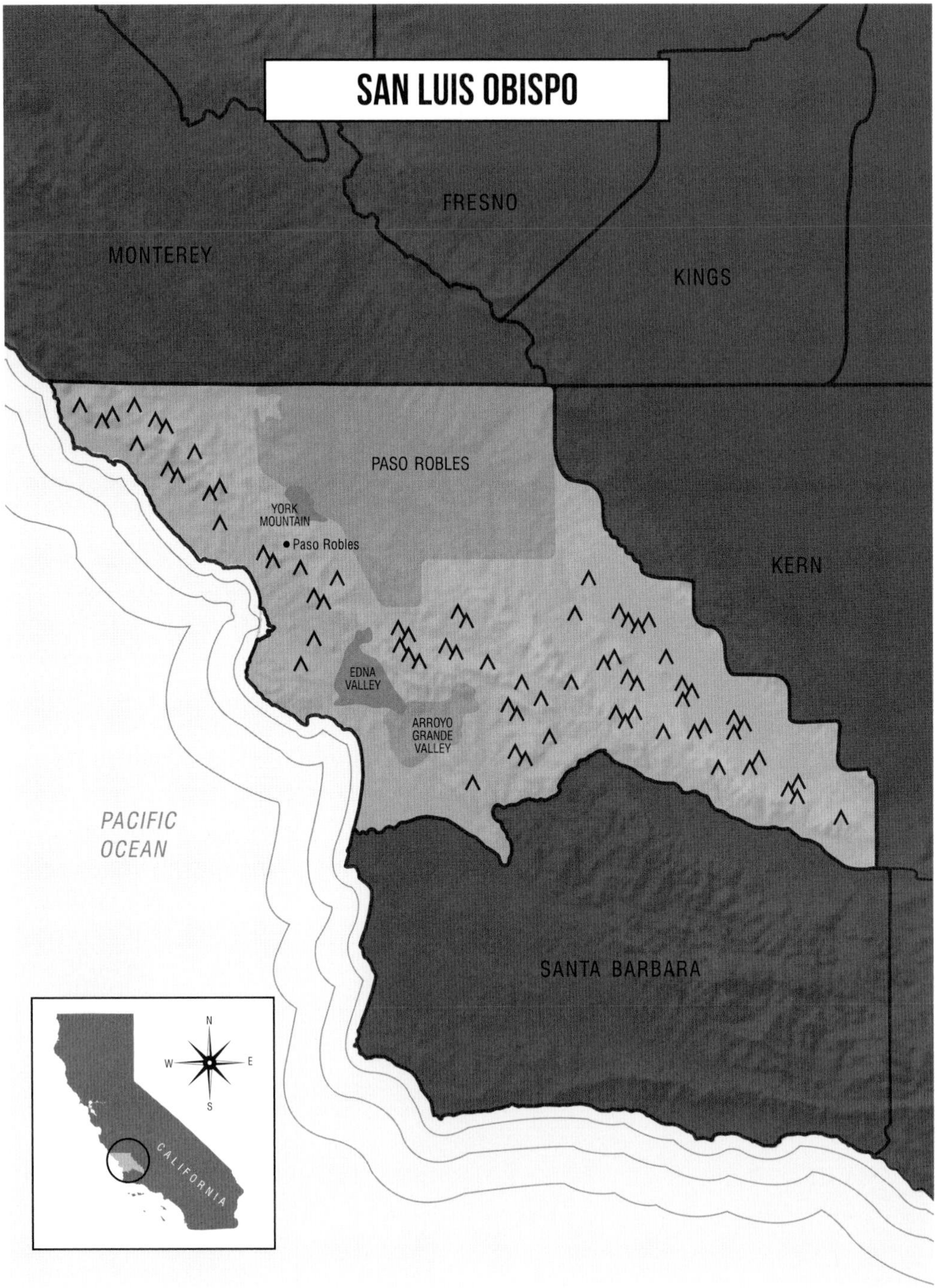
SAN LUIS OBISPO
FRESNO
MONTEREY
KINGS
PASO ROBLES
YORK MOUNTAIN
Paso Robles
KERN
EDNA VALLEY
ARROYO GRANDE VALLEY
PACIFIC OCEAN
SANTA BARBARA
N
W
E
S
CALIFORNIA

Farming families have lived in Paso Robles, the largest AVA in San Luis Obispo County, for generations. Cattle ranches sit alongside fertile vineyards. Ranchers and grape growers alike wear cowboy hats for protection rather than as fashion statements. Local food producers and restaurants have a strong farm-to-table ethos, and a number of restaurants in downtown Paso Robles serve locally grown food and locally made wine.

In an area once populated by the native Chumash people, San Luis Obispo gradually rose around Mission San Luis Obispo de Toloso and today has just under 50,000 residents. Founded by Father Junípero Serra in 1772, the mission honored Saint Louis of Anjou, bishop (*"obispo"* in Spanish) of Toulouse. The earliest known vineyards were planted in the late eighteenth century, near Santa Margarita Ranch's Asistencia Chapel. Around 1850, immigrants primarily from Italy and Germany planted wine grapes. Andrew York, a rancher from Indiana, founded the Ascension Winery in 1882, which later became the York Mountain Winery, purportedly the oldest winery operating in the region. More Italians arrived in the early twentieth century, and many of the oldest vineyards were planted during Prohibition, growing especially Zinfandel to be shipped east to home winemakers. At that time Polish prime minister and piano virtuoso Ignacy Paderewski came to Paso Robles to visit the area's hot springs and bought 2,000 acres, which he planted to Petite Sirah and Zinfandel. After Prohibition, Padarewski's grapes were vinified at York Mountain Winery. Stanley Hoffman established Hoffman Mountain Ranch Winery, the first modern large-scale winery, in 1964. He planted Pinot Noir, Chardonnay, and Cabernet Sauvignon in the Adelaida Hills, and within 10 years his wines had become a success. Development proceeded rapidly, and vineyards spread from west of the Salinas River to the flatter, warmer east side. Gary Eberle, one of the 1970s pioneers, receives credit for planting the first Syrah vines here, and today Cal Poly San Luis Obispo programs in viticulture, enology, and wine business provide a steady supply of well-trained graduates eager to join neighbors and family in the thriving wine industry.

Other AVAs exist within the Central Coast AVA, but when wine people talk about the Central Coast generally they mean San Luis Obispo County and the Paso Robles AVA. The county itself is an AVA, and besides Paso Robles it contains three smaller AVAs: York Mountain, Edna Valley, and Arroyo Grande Valley. The county has 29,000 acres of wine grapes, Cabernet Sauvignon covering about a third, followed by Merlot, Syrah, Zinfandel, Chardonnay, and Petite Sirah. Despite the predominance of Cabernet Sauvignon, Paso Robles has become known for Rhône varietals: Syrah, Grenache, and Mourvèdre for the reds and Viognier, Marsanne, and Roussanne for the whites. But Paso Robles produces many different types of grapes and wine, including Pinot Noir, Zinfandel, Albariño, Tempranillo, Sangiovese, Aglianico, and Nebbiolo.

The Paso Robles and York Mountain AVAs were established in 1983. Because of the wide variety of terrain and climate conditions in Paso Robles, the Alcohol and Tobacco Tax and Trade Bureau (TTB) approved the creation of eleven sub-AVAs within the larger AVA in November, 2014: Adelaida District, Creston District, El Pomar District, Paso Robles Estrella District, Paso Robles Geneseo District, Paso Robles Highlands District, San Juan Creek, San Miguel District, Santa Margarita Ranch, Paso Robles Willow Creek District, and Templeton Gap District.

Fault lines crisscross the area, most notably the San Andreas Fault, which created the hot springs that first brought many settlers to the region. Soils west of the Salinas River tend to consist of sedimentary clay and loam with calcareous and silicone elements. Soils to the east are alluvial, predominantly gravel, clay, and sand. Mineral content increases at higher altitudes. Diurnal temperature variations of up to 50 degrees Fahrenheit in the growing season aid proper sugar development and acid retention in the grapes. Areas closest to the Pacific receive the most rainfall and cooling fogs and breezes, whereas those farther east often require irrigation and aggressive canopy management.

Of the 22,400 acres in the Edna Valley AVA, established in 1982, just under 3,000 are planted with grapevines. The AVA is best known for Pinot Noir and Chardonnay, but Syrah is grown there too. The Arroyo Grande AVA, established in 1990, covers about 40,000 acres, with 1,200 under grapes. Pacific breezes and fog temper morning and midday temperatures, protecting grapes from the harsh sun. Chardonnay and Pinot Noir thrive in the cooler areas in the center of the valley, and Zinfandel, Petite Sirah, and red Rhône varieties grow near Lopez Lake.

36

19

10

2

THE WINERIES

ALTA COLINA

2725 Adelaida Road, Paso Robles, CA 93446
(805) 227-4191, www.altacolinawine.com

After 35 years in the business world, Bob Tillman started Alta Colina with wife, Lynn, in 2003. Consulting winemaker Jeff Cohn joined the team in 2011 and helps produce Rhône blends. The Alta Colina Estate GSM features flavors of black cherry, raspberry, and freshly ground black pepper, and the Alta Colina Old 900 Estate Syrah tastes of black cherry and crème brûlée. ❶

ANCIENT PEAKS WINERY

22720 El Camino Real, Santa Margarita, CA 93453
(805) 365-7045, www.ancientpeaks.com

Originally part of a Mexican land grant, Ancient Peaks Winery—including its can't-miss zipline—and the town of Santa Margarita sit in the middle of the Santa Margarita Ranch. Karl Wittstrom, Doug Filipponi, and Rob Rossi own Ancient Peaks, and Mike Sinor directs winemaking. The full-bodied Ancient Peaks Winery Paso Robles Renegade offers rich fruit flavors and a touch of milk chocolate in the finish. The Ancient Peaks Winery Paso Robles Oyster Ridge tastes of black cherry, cassis, and black plums with a touch of spice and espresso bean. ❷

ARONHILL VINEYARDS

3745 West Highway 46, Templeton, CA 93465
(805) 434-3066, www.aronhillvineyards.com

Judy Hill Aron planted AronHill Vineyards in 1996 and made her first vintage in 2004. Winemaker Michael Olsten and viticulturist Richard Sauret help AronHill produce 2,000 cases of wine, 1,300 from estate-grown fruit. The AronHill Vineyards Cabernet Sauvignon has flavors of cherry vanilla and ripe black cherry, while the AronHill Primitivo offers nuanced fruit flavors that change to smooth cherry vanilla before a creamy milk chocolate finish. ❸

BAILEYANA WINERY

5828 Orcutt Road, San Luis Obispo, CA 93401
(805) 269-8200, www.baileyana.com

A Niven Family wine estate, Baileyana Winery harks back to founder Catharine Niven's vision of crafting Old World wines sustainably grown and made with New World standards. Raised and educated in Burgundy, winemaker Christian Rougenant continues the family tradition in Burgundian style. The medium-bodied Baileyana Edna Valley Firepeak Vineyard Chardonnay offers a bouquet of white stone fruits, citrus, and lemon curd, and the Baileyana Edna Valley Firepeak Vineyard Pinot Noir has aromas of dried red cherries, ripe black cherries, and red raspberries.

BOOKER VINEYARD

2640 Anderson Road, Paso Robles, CA 93446
(805) 237-7367, www.bookerwines.com

Eric Jensen made wine with Stephan Asseo of L'Aventure Wines for two years and with Justin Smith of Saxum for five before venturing out on his own. In 2001, he and wife, Lisa, bought a 72-acre parcel of land from the 1,200-acre Booker Estate. The 2005 vintage was Booker's first release. The Booker Vineyard Ripper Grenache boasts intense fruit flavors with nuances of fine dark chocolate and cocoa powder. The Booker Vineyard Oublié has notes of fresh red fruits and dried herbs in the bouquet. Drink a current vintage now or in the next 15 years.

CALCAREOUS VINEYARD

3430 Peachy Canyon Road, Paso Robles, CA 93446
(805) 239-0289, www.calcareous.com

Both wine distributors from Iowa, Lloyd Messer and his daughter Dana Brown established Calcareous Vineyards in 2000. They named the 342-acre vineyard after the solid rock and soil on which it sits. The Calcareous Vineyard Tres Violet has flavors of fruits of the wood, licorice, and a touch of menthol, and the Calcareous Vineyard Moose offers flavors of black cherry, ripe black raspberry, and caramelized fennel bulb. 4

CAYUCOS CELLARS

131 North Ocean Avenue, Cayucos, CA 93430
(805) 995-3036, www.cayucoscellars.com

Located in an old dairy barn on a working coastal ranch, Cayucos Cellars is a family-owned winery. Winemaker Stuart Selkirk; his wife, Linda; his two sons, Clay and Ross; and his daughter, Paige, run all aspects of the business. They situated the tasting room in downtown Cayucos, famous for its beaches, because, as Stuart puts it, "We don't want anyone being flattened by a tractor." The Cayucos Cellars Chardonnay has flavors of baked apples and poached pears. The medium-bodied Cayucos Cellars Estate Barrel #2 Pinot Noir offers delightful flavors of fresh and cooked fruit and a pleasant finish. 5

CHAMISAL VINEYARDS

7525 Orcutt Road, San Luis Obispo, CA 93401
(805) 541-9463, www.chamisalvineyards.com

Named for the Chamise flowering shrub that grows wild in the vineyard, Chamisal was the first vineyard planted in the Edna Valley AVA, in 1973. The 80-acre property originally formed part of the Spanish land grant named Domaine Alfred and today is planted to Chardonnay, Pinot Noir, Grenache, Pinot Gris, and Syrah vines. New Zealander Fintan du Fresne has directed winemaking since 2006. The Chamisal Vineyards Central Coast Stainless Chardonnay offers flavors of lemon curd, pineapples, and citrus. The Chamisal Estate Pinot Noir has notes of red raspberry in the bouquet and bright fruit flavors. 6

CHATEAU MARGENE

4385 La Panza Road, Creston, CA 93432
(805) 238-2321, www.chateaumargene.com

Businessman-turned-winemaker Mike Mooney's family history in Paso Robles goes back seven generations to a soldier in the 1775 expedition led by Juan Batista de Anza, but Chateau Margene is named for Mooney's wife. The Chateau Margene Cabernet Franc has aromas of black raspberry and bell pepper with flavors of black cherry and cassis. The Chateau Margene Beau Mélange also has great black fruit flavors.

CHRONIC CELLARS

2020 Nacimiento Lake Drive, Paso Robles, CA 93446
(805) 237-7848, www.chroniccellars.com

Josh and Jake Beckett grew up in Paso Robles wine country. After college, they both did a stint at Peachy Canyon Winery, opening Chronic Cellars a few years later. When they're not making wine, Josh surfs, and Jake tears up the dirt on his cross-country motorcycle. Big and bold, the Chronic Cellars Sofa King Bueno tastes of black plum and Christmas baking spices. The Chronic Cellars Dead Nuts has aromas of fresh dark fruits and freshly chopped toasted nuts, with full mouthfeel and strong cherry flavor.

CLAUTIERE VINEYARD

1340 Penman Springs Road, Paso Robles, CA 93446
(805) 237-3789, www.clautiere.com

Winemaking and fun go hand in hand at Clautiere Vineyard, founded in 1999 by Claudine Blackwell and Terry Brady and known for its parties and concerts. The Clautiere Vineyards Estate BDX has aromas of blueberry pie and dried black cherries. The Clautiere Vineyards Syrah has a bouquet of ripe red cherry and blueberry preserves.

CLAYHOUSE WINES

849 13th Street, Paso Robles, CA 93446
(805) 238-7055, www.clayhousewines.com

Fourth-generation agriculturist Rick Middleton and his family founded Clayhouse Wines, naming it after the 150-year-old adobe structure in the middle of their vineyards. Ben Mello manages the vineyard, and Blake Kuhn oversees winemaking. The medium-bodied Clayhouse Estate Old Vine Petite Sirah offers dark fruit flavors, and in the Clayhouse Estate Cuvée Blanc Red Cedar Vineyard tropical fruit flavors come alive in a rich mouth presence.

CLOS SOLÈNE

2815 Live Oak Road, Paso Robles, CA 93446
(805) 296 0027, www.clossolene.com

When winemaker Guillaume Fabre met his future wife, Solène, in France, it felt, he says, like a *coup de foudre*—a lightning bolt. Now, in his new home, Guillaume crafts his wines using Bordeaux and Rhône varieties with the love of his life at his side. The Clos Solène L'Insolent offers fresh fruit flavors and a touch of brown spice. The big, bold Clos Solène Hommage à Nos Pairs Reserve has aromas and flavors of ripe dark fruit. 7

CROAD VINEYARDS

3550 Vinedo Robles Lane, Paso Robles, CA 93446
(805) 226-9899, www.croadvineyards.com

Kiwi Martin Croad makes wines with distinctive New Zealand flavor profiles from California vines planted in the early 1900s. He works with Zinfandel and Rhône varieties, including Syrah, Grenache, and Mourvèdre, as well as Sauvignon Blanc grapes. The crisp and clean Croad Vineyards Sauvignon Blanc has aromas of Granny Smith apple, and the Croad Vineyards Syrah offers abundant sweet fruit flavors and a pleasant fruit-filled finish.

CYPHER WINERY

3750 Highway 46 West, Templeton, CA 93465
(805) 237-0055, www.cypherwinery.com

After working together at the 140,000-cases-per-year Four Vines Winery, Christian Tietje and Susan Mahler longed to make small-batch artisanal wines and run a cozier winery. Thus Cypher Winery was born. The smooth and velvety Cypher Winery Freakshow ZinBitch Paso Robles Zinfandel offers flavors of blueberry pie and black raspberry. Broad and generous, the Cypher Winery Freakshow Anarchy tastes of red and black fruits with a touch of baking spices and Mediterranean herbs. 8

DERBY WINE ESTATES

5620 Highway 46 East, Paso Robles, CA 93447
(805) 238-6911, www.derbywineestates.com

Planning for their retirement, Ray and Pam Derby relocated to the Central Coast in the early 1990s. They bought their first vineyard in 1998 and another a few years later, abandoning any intentions of a sedentary lifestyle. They use 10 percent of the grapes that they grow to make Derby wines and sell the remaining 90 percent to neighboring wineries. The Derby Wine Estates Derbyshire Vineyard Pinot Gris features flavors of pear cobbler and lemon curd.

EBERLE WINERY

3810 California 46, Paso Robles, CA 93446
(805) 238-9607, www.eberlewinery.com

Gary Eberle started working at his family's Estrella River Winery in 1973. In 1980 he helped establish the Paso Robles AVA, and in 1983 he founded his own winery. A decade later, Eberle oversaw the excavation of a 17,000-square-foot underground cave in which to age his red wines. Eberle Winery produces wine from a large number of varieties, including Chardonnay, Viognier, Syrah, Sangiovese, Barbera, Zinfandel, and Cabernet Sauvignon in 25,000 cases of wine per year. The Eberle Winery Estate Cabernet Sauvignon has notes of blackberry and dried cherry, with great fruit in the finish, and the Estate Cabernet Sauvignon is amazingly fresh and young-tasting. 9

EPOCH ESTATE WINES

7505 York Mountain Road, Templeton, CA 93465
(805) 237-7575, www.epochwines.com

Bill and Liz Armstrong fell in love with the area and the Paderewski Vineyards, named after former owner Ignacy Paderewski, the famed Polish pianist and prime minister. Jordan Fiorentini is winemaker, Justin Smith of Saxum is consulting winemaker, and Tim and Diana Rovenstine manage the ranch. The Epoch Estate Wines Ingenuity has aromas of big fruit and seductive notes of brown spice and Mediterranean herbs, and the Epoch Estates Block B Syrah tastes of ripe fruit, black pepper, cherry, and blackberry. 10

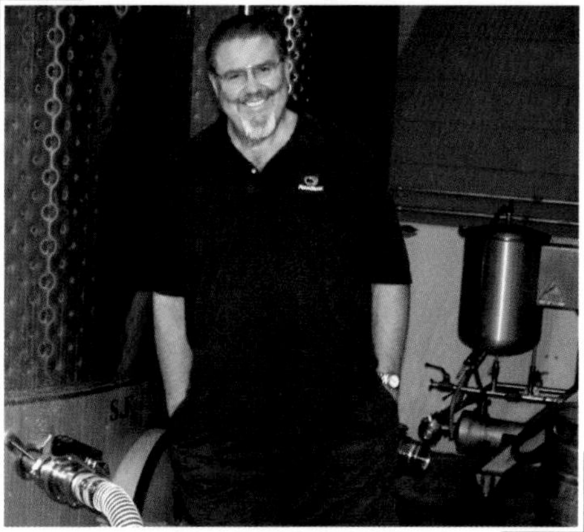

In his own words

GARY EBERLE

Winemaker Gary Eberle began his career in 1973 by heading his family's Estrella River Winery. He cofounded the Paso Robles appellation in 1980 and opened his eponymous winery in 1983.

In 1970s I was down in New Orleans working on a doctorate in genetics. One of my professors liked wine, so we'd get together and drink great French wines. I was trying to introduce him to the fine stuff I was drinking—you know, Mateus and Lancers. Turns out he was into wine of slightly higher quality, like Lynch-Bages and Ducru-Beaucaillou. I got the wine bug and I got it bad . . . so I made a trip to UC Davis and packed my U-Haul and old Pontiac and moved to California.

In 1976 I made wine with Ed Friedrich at San Martin in Gilroy. He was making delicate but delicious wines that came in at 7, 8, or 9 percent alcohol. I learned how to make softer, fruit-forward wines from him. Cabernet has always been my flagship. I planted the first Syrah vines since Prohibition. I love to work with Counoise, Viognier, Tempranillo, Sangiovese, and Barbera. I also make port with the five Portuguese varieties every few years. Our winemaker Ben Mayo is part Hobbit and part mad scientist. He's always coming to me and saying we should work with this grape that somebody just discovered under a rock in Slovenia. I make 25,000 cases of wine, and it's all wine that makes me happy.

GIORNATA WINES

3855 High Grove Road, Templeton, CA 93465
(805) 434-3075, www.giornatawines.com

Brian Terrizzi made wine at Rosenblum Cellars and Isole e Olena in Italy, and, fulfilling a lifelong dream, he and wife Stephanie now make their own wines at Giornata, many from Italian grape varieties. The Giornata Luna Matta Vineyard Paso Robles Nebbiolo has flavors of dark cherry, cranberry juice, and Indian spice, with an elegant finish. 11

HALTER RANCH VINEYARD

8910 Adelaida Road, Paso Robles, CA 93446
(805) 226-9455, www.halterranch.com

Founded by Hansjörg Wyss in 2000, Halter Ranch has grown from the original 40 vine acres to 280 planted amid a 1,000-acre ranch. More than twenty varieties grow in fifty-seven vineyard blocks, including most Bordeaux and Rhône varieties. Kevin Sass has directed winemaking since 2011. The velvety Halter Ranch Vineyard Cabernet Sauvignon has black fruit flavors, especially black plum, and the Halter Ranch Vineyard Côtes de Paso has bouquet notes of dark fruit, espresso, and oregano and dark fruit flavors on the palate. 12

HAMMERSKY VINEYARDS AND INN

7725 Vineyard Drive, Paso Robles, CA 93446
(949) 338-7813, www.hammersky.com

Dentist Douglas Hauck and wife, Kim, planted HammerSky Vineyards in 1997 and named it for their two young sons, Hamilton and Skyler. The family concentrates on Bordeaux varieties and takes pride in their Bordeaux-style blends. The HammerSky Vineyards Estate Grown Party of Four has flavors of black raspberry, black plum, anise, and vanilla, and the fruit-forward HammerSky Vineyards Estate Grown Red Handed proffers tastes of red plums, cloves, and red raspberry.

HEARST RANCH WINERY

442 SLO San Simeon Road, San Simeon, CA 93452
(805) 927-4100, www.hearstranchwinery.com

Publishing magnate Steve Hearst and Jim Saunders, his business partner, head up Hearst Ranch Winery. Grapes are sourced from Saunders Vineyard in Paso Robles, and the winery's tasting room lies inside the historic Sebastian's General Store, which caters to fishermen, campers, and tourists. The Hearst Ranch Winery Glacier Ridge Chardonnay offers flavors of caramelized pineapple, lemon curd, and bright lemon zest, and the Hearst Ranch Winery The Point has complex aromas of black raspberry, black currant, smoked meats, and brown baking spices. 13

HOPE FAMILY WINES

P.O. Box 3260, Paso Robles, CA 93447
(805) 238-6979, www.hopefamilywines.com

When the Hope family moved to Paso Robles more than 30 years ago, they planted grapevines and apple orchards. The apples are long gone, but the Hopes continue to make wines from Cabernet Sauvignon, Merlot, Syrah, Mourvèdre, and Grenache grapes. Austin Hope is president and heads winemaking; Jason Diefenderfer is the winemaker. Their portfolio contains five brands: Troublemaker, Austin Hope, Treana, Liberty School, and Candor. The fruit-driven Hope Family Wines Treana Red has aromas of red and black fruits and a touch of spice on the finish. The Hope Family Wines Liberty School Cabernet Sauvignon has fragrances of dark cherry and black fruit. 14

J. LOHR

6169 Airport Road, Paso Robles, CA 93446
(805) 239-8900, www.jlohr.com

Raised in a South Dakota farming family, Jerry Lohr began searching for potential vineyard sites in California in the late 1960s, acquiring his first vineyard in Monterey County in 1971. In 1986 he planted in Paso Robles, and today he has more than 2,000 acres of vineyards here, 900 in Monterey, and 33 in Napa Valley. The J. Lohr Paso Robles Wine Center opened its doors in 2001. Big in the mouth, the J. Lohr Estates Seven Oaks Paso Robles Cabernet Sauvignon features notes of ripe black raspberries and blueberries, and the fruit-forward J. Lohr Cuvée Paso Robles Cuvée Pau has aromas of black plums and black currant. 15

JACK CREEK CELLARS

5265 Jack Creek Road, Paso Robles, CA 93446
(805) 226-8283, www.jackcreekcellars.com

Doug and Sabrina Kruse bought their first 75 acres on Jack Creek Road in 1997 and planted Chardonnay, Pinot Noir, Grenache, and Syrah vines. Their vineyards sit on the southern end of the Santa Lucia Mountain Range, about seven miles from the coast, giving them a unique microclimate for growing. The Jack Creek Cellars Concrete Blond has aromas of tropical fruits and caramelized pineapple and pairs well with lighter cuisine and seafood. The Jack Creek Cellars Stained Pinot Noir has aromas of freshly picked red cherries and dried black cherry. 16

In his own words

JIM SAUNDERS

Wine grower Jim Saunders (right) began his career in wine by designing and building wineries. He partnered with Steve Hearst (left) of the Hearst publishing family to create delicious wines under the Hearst Ranch Winery label.

I have been a building contractor for many years. Early in my career, I helped design a small winery. I liked designing and building them so much that I created a niche for myself and became quite busy. I purchased a 100-acre ranch and asked one of my customers, if I planted grapes, would they purchase them. . . . The answer was "Yes," and I was committed. This worked well for many years, until the grape market became saturated and demand was no longer there. Winemakers would come into my vineyard and cherry pick rows of grapes they wanted and leave other rows to rot. It was not a good time for growers.

One winemaker and I were speaking of this dilemma, and it was suggested that, if I bought the tanks and equipment, they would simply buy the juice from me and I wouldn't have to put up with lunatic winemakers anymore. So I did just that. We then sold juice to many different wineries, using their protocol, and charged them to do so. This arrangement worked well for many years. By now we had planted out the entire ranch and had developed nine blocks of grape varieties. All of this came to an end when we entered into a partnership with Hearst, and now all of our production of grapes goes directly into our program.

Prima donna winemakers cannot drive the market, although they may think otherwise. I believe the consumer has redirected our winemaking in that we now find that it isn't just quantity, it must also be quality. The consumer is much more sophisticated now than in years past. If you get a good crop, you should be able to make great wine: "Overdeliver at an affordable price for the consumer."

1

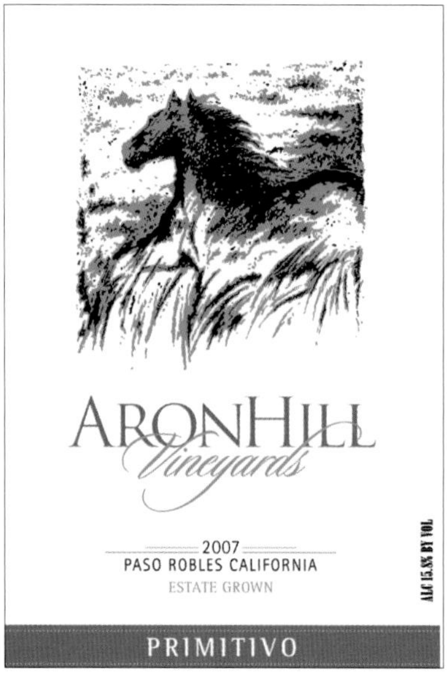

3

4

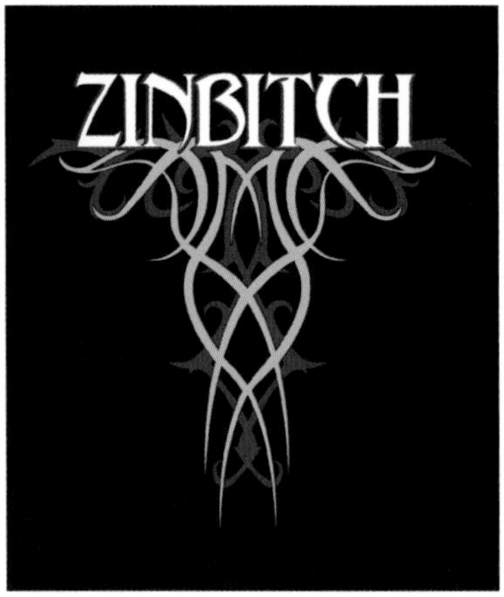

8

9

11

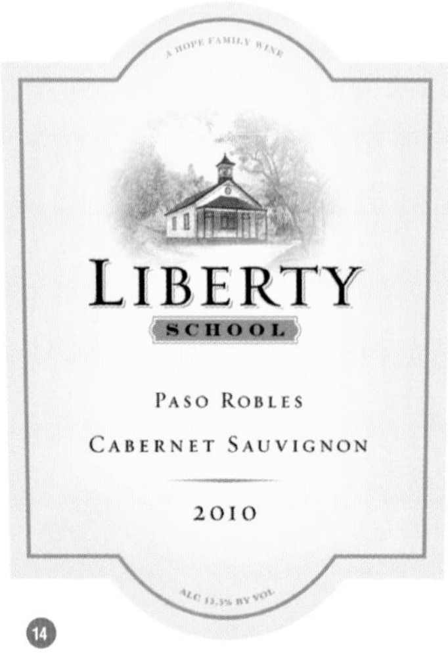

14

15

jack creek
cellars
Stained
Central Coast, California 2010 Pinot Noir

16

CAYUCOS
CELLARS
PINOT NOIR
2008 ESTATE

5

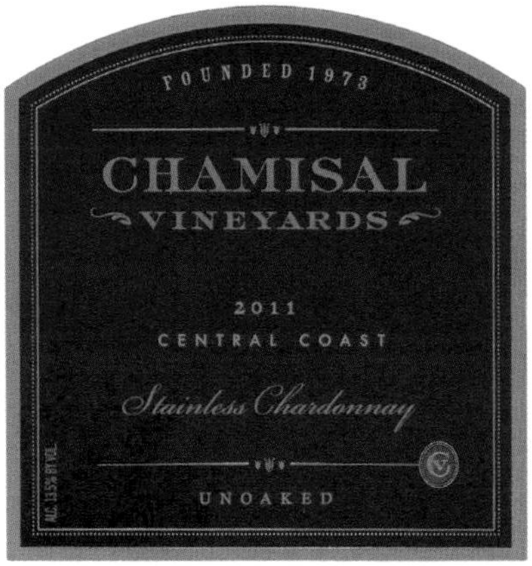
FOUNDED 1973
CHAMISAL
VINEYARDS
2011
CENTRAL COAST
Stainless Chardonnay
UNOAKED

6

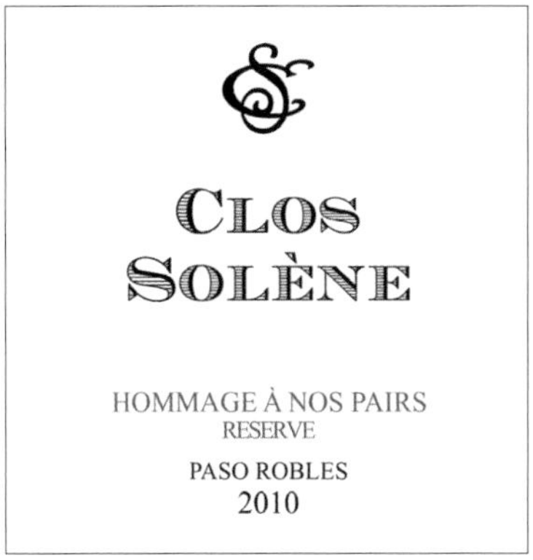
CLOS
SOLÈNE
HOMMAGE À NOS PAIRS
RESERVE
PASO ROBLES
2010

7

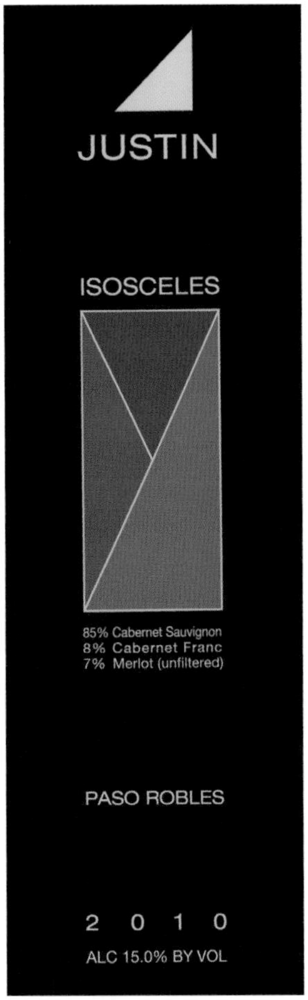
JUSTIN
ISOSCELES
85% Cabernet Sauvignon
8% Cabernet Franc
7% Merlot (unfiltered)
PASO ROBLES
2 0 1 0
ALC 15.0% BY VOL

17

HALTER RANCH
ESTABLISHED 1880
CÔTES DE PASO
2010
PASO ROBLES
ESTATE BOTTLED

12

EST. 1865
HEARST
RANCH
WINERY
"Glacier Ridge"
CHARDONNAY
2011
Monterey County
A LEGACY OF QUALITY™
ALC. 13.5% BY VOL.

13

Kenneth Volk
VINEYARDS
2010
TOURIGA NACIONAL
PASO ROBLES
POMAR JUNCTION VINEYARD

18

L'Aventure®
2010
PASO ROBLES
OPTIMUS
ESTATE

20

In his own words

AUSTIN HOPE

Austin Hope has made wine in Paso Robles since he was a teenager. He was named Winemaker of the Year in 2009 at the California Mid-State Fair and now serves on the board of the Paso Robles Wine Country Alliance.

I grew up helping in the vineyards, learning from my father and uncle. Later, during college, I studied crop science and was helping manage the family vineyard. When we decided to not just grow grapes and actually make wine, I ended up taking the lead role. It has been an amazing roller coaster. The filtration systems for the wine have come so far. In terms of making the wine taste better and allowing us to make more sound wines, they are amazing. Our job is to make a great wine that all will enjoy. . . . Trends and styles will continue to change as they have in the past, and we must be open-minded. We can always make a barrel of wine for ourselves to keep our palates happy.

The other change that was interesting to experience was the ramping up of alcohols, or the "Parkerization" of the wine world. We went from 13 to 16 percent alcohol pretty fast, and it was embraced by the public. With Paso Robles, it has been fun to see us become a global player in the wine world. When I was growing up, there were a handful of wineries here, and now people around America and even internationally know of Paso Robles as a wine region. The thing we love about Paso Robles is the diversity of the AVA. Not only in the varieties we can plant but the diverse microclimates in the area. We are continually finding new vineyards sites with different soils and weather that work great together.

JUSTIN VINEYARDS & WINERY

11680 Chimney Rock Road, Paso Robles, CA 93446
(805) 591-3200, www.justinwine.com

Justin Baldwin founded Justin Vineyards & Winery in 1981 and produces Central Coast wines from the major Bordeaux varieties. The property includes the Just Inn B&B and dining at The Restaurant at Justin. The Justin Vineyards & Winery Isosceles offers flavors of dark fruits, black currants, and mocha. Drink it now or in the next 10 years. (17)

KENNETH VOLK VINEYARDS

2485 Highway 46 West, Paso Robles, CA 93446
(805) 237-7896, www.volkwines.com

Ken Volk started making wine in the Central Coast in the 1970s and released his first commercial Pinot Noir for Wild Horse Winery in 1983. Well-known in Paso Robles and the Santa Maria Valley for crafting wines from Chardonnay and Pinot Noir grapes, he has begun releasing wines under his own name. Volk's winery lies in Santa Maria, but he maintains a tasting room in Paso Robles. The Kenneth Volk Vineyards Jaybird Chardonnay boasts flavors of tropical fruits, apple, and Anjou pear. The food-friendly Kenneth Volk Vineyards Touriga Nacional has aromas of dark fruit, black cherries, and lavender. (18)

KUKKULA WINERY

9515 Chimney Rock Road, Paso Robles, CA 93446
(805) 227-0111, www.kukkulawine.com

Owner Kevin Jussila fell in love with winemaking when he and two friends bought half a ton of Russian River Valley Pinot Noir in 1991, but a 1995 vacation in Provence sealed his fate as a winemaker. The Finnish word for "hill or high place," Kukkula consists of 80 acres of land, 34 with walnut trees, 29 under grapevines, and 8 with olive trees. The ultramodern Kukkula Winery was completed in 2010. The Kukkula Sisu has wonderful complexity in the mouth with flavors of black fruits. The Kukkula i.p.o. Paso Robles offers aromas of black cherry preserves, cassis, and anise. (19)

L'AVENTURE

2815 Live Oak Road, Paso Robles, CA 93446
(805) 227-1588, www.aventurewine.com

Stephan Asseo was educated in Macon, Burgundy, and in 1982 he and his family purchased Château Robin and Château Fleur Cardinale in Bordeaux. After honing his winemaking skills in France for 15 years, he fell in love with Paso Robles in 1996, began a new adventure in his life, and established L'Aventure Winery. L'Aventure Estate Rosé has aromas of fresh strawberry and strawberry conserves in the bouquet. L'Aventure Optimus offers fragrances of fresh red raspberries, black cherry, and cocoa powder. (20)

LAZARRE WINES

5678 Lone Pine Place, Paso Robles, CA 93446
(831) 402-1153, www.lazarrewines.com

A behind-the-scenes kind of guy, Adam LaZarre has 20 years of experience between making wine for Hahn Estates as well as for his own label. The LaZarre Albariño has aromas of Anjou pear, Granny Smith apple, and white stone fruits, with a touch of fruit sweetness before an elegant dry finish. The LaZarre Central Coast Pinot Noir offers frangrances of red raspberry, cherry cola, and dried black cherries and big fruit flavors. (21)

LINNE CALODO

3030 Vineyard Drive, Paso Robles, CA 93446
(805) 227-0797, www.linnecalodo.com

Matt and Maureen Trevisan founded Linne Calodo in 1998. The family lives among the vines, so no harmful chemicals are allowed. Matt is the grape grower and winemaker. The full-bodied Linne Calodo Cherry Red has aromas of rich ripe red and black fruits with a touch of dried herbs. Drink it now or in the next five years. The Linne Calodo Problem Child has aroma and flavor notes of black plums and dark fruits.

MIDNIGHT CELLARS WINERY & VINEYARD

2925 Anderson Road, Paso Robles, CA 93446
(805) 239-8904, www.midnightcellars.com

After a family vacation in 1995, three generations of the Hartenberger family traded Chicago's harsh winters for a 160-acre ranch in Paso Robles. Twenty-eight acres grow Cabernet Sauvignon, Petit Verdot, Merlot, Chardonnay, and Zinfandel vines. With aromas of dried tarragon, dried cherries, and dark chocolate, the Midnight Cellars Winery & Vineyard Estate Zinfandel, offers bright fruit flavors. The Midnight Cellars Winery & Vineyard Mare Nectaris Reserve Red Wine tastes of black fruit, black pepper, and dried thyme.

In his own words
KEN VOLK

Ken Volk and his family established Wild Horse Vineyard in 1981 and sold it to Jim Beam Brands in 2003. He opened Kenneth Volk Vineyards in 2004 and has been active in many associations, including the Paso Robles Grape Growers Association, the Central Coast Wine Growers Association, the Paso Robles Vintners and Growers Association, and the Santa Barbara County Vintners Association.

I came up to Cal Poly San Luis Obispo to study greenhouse production and fruit science. Cal Poly has student enterprise projects where teams of students farm various fruits and vegetables. I had the berry vine project, down the hill from the campus vineyard. I had some good friends on the grape project, and I bought a couple hundred pounds of Pinot Noir fruit, a new trash can, and I used my Louisville Slugger baseball bat to crush the fruit and then pulled the stems out by hand. The fruit fermented out cleanly, and I drained the free run and pressed the skins by ringing them out in cheesecloth, and I had a beer keg and a couple of five-gallon glass water bottles. All things considered the wine turned out fairly decent for a rookie walk-on.

This experience really sparked my interest, and I started reading all the wine books I could get my hands on and took extension classes from UC Davis and was fortunate to attend all the classes of the now-defunct Napa School of Cellaring. I started filling my garage with winemaking equipment and barrels, to the shock of my housemates. The epiphany I had was to realize, compared to so many crops I was familiar with, wine growing got you out of the perishability issues and flooded markets of agricultural commodities. It allows you to create your own unique branded creation.

I like northern Rhônes and Iberian varieties. I have been an advocate of heirloom grape varieties, and the Central Coast has been on the leading edge of plantings of the seldom seen. Visiting Australia made me appreciate Verdelho, visiting Campania and tasting from clean cellars gave me appreciation on how much fruit Aglianico can display, visiting Hungary got me fired up on Blaufrankisch.

The cork industry has made great strides from being a cottage industry to utilizing much better technology to vastly improve the quality control procedures from the forest to the winery. There are a number of screw cap companies that are working on permeable membranes on screw caps to mimic the oxygen ingress of a cork closure which I have in trialing. I have always believed wine is made in the vineyard and the greatest improvement in grape growing is applied canopy management. The work of Dr. Richard Smart and his concept of canopy management's impact on wine quality in his publication *Sunlight into Wine* has done more to improve global wine quality than anything else in my lifetime.

NINER WINE ESTATES

2400 Highway 46 West, Paso Robles, CA 93446
(805) 239-2233, www.ninerwine.com

Princeton and Harvard Business School graduate Dick Niner started Niner Wine Estates in 2001 by acquiring the 224-acre Bootjack Ranch and the 130-acre Heart Hill Vineyard two years later. Varieties planted include Petite Sirah, Cabernet Sauvignon, Merlot, Syrah, Sangiovese, Barbera, and Sauvignon Blanc. The Niner Wine Estate Bootjack Ranch Estate Bottled Sangiovese has flavors of black fruits, blackberry, brown spice, coffee, and mocha, while the Niner Wine Estates Bootjack Ranch Cabernet Sauvignon offers aromas of black cherry, sage, and cherry cola. 22

PEACHY CANYON WINERY

2025 Nacimiento Lake Drive, Paso Robles, CA 93446
(805) 237-1577, www.peachycanyon.com

Established in 1982 by Doug and Nancy Beckett, Peachy Canyon has 100 acres of estate vineyards and long-term contracts with more than twenty growers to source grapes for 64,000 cases of wine annually. One of the first wineries in the area, Peachy Canyon over the years has served as the proving ground for many up-and-coming winemakers to hone their craft. The Peachy Canyon Chardonnay offers flavors of caramelized pineapple and white stone fruits, and the Peachy Canyon Incredible Red Zinfandel has bouquet notes of fresh strawberry and dried black cherry. 23

PIPESTONE VINEYARDS

2040 Niderer Road, Paso Robles, CA 93446
(805) 227-6385, www.pipestonevineyards.com

Jeff Pipes left a career in environmental law and environmental engineering to grow grapes in Paso Robles and start Pipestone Vineyards with wife, Florence, a former fashion designer. Two draft horses plow the vineyards, which are laid out according to feng shui principles. The vineyard is a certified wildlife habitat, and the winery is solar-powered. With aromas of black fruits, the Pipestone Vineyards Estate Syrah is generous in the mouth, and the Pipestone Vineyards Reserve Chateauneuf du Pipe features flavors of blackberry, cassis, and smoked meats. 24

POMAR JUNCTION VINEYARD AND WINERY

5036 South El Pomar, Templeton, CA 93465
(805) 238-9940, www.pomarjunction.com

The Merrill family grew grapes for other wineries for more than 30 years before making and selling their own wines. Today Dana and Marsha direct the vineyards; son Matthew acts as general manager; and Jim Shumate handles winemaking. With aromas of freshly picked strawberries and ripe cherry juice, the Pomar Junction Vineyard and Winery Syrah Rosé tastes of cherry vanilla and soft Mediterranean herbs, and the Pomar Junction Vineyard and Winery Train Wreck offers flavors of black cherry, tart red cherry, and pomegranate. 25

RANCHERO CELLARS

No visitor facilities
(805) 423-3765, www.rancherocellars.com

Amy Jean Butler has made wine for venerated Napa wineries and new ventures in Paso Robles for more than 16 years. Ranchero Cellars La Vista Vineyard Chrome, her new blend, is delightful in the mouth, with superb roundness and balanced acidity.

ROBERT HALL WINERY

3443 Mill Road, Paso Robles, CA 93446
(805) 239-1616, www.roberthallwinery.com

Native Minnesotan Robert L. Hall fell in love with the idea of making wine on a family vacation to France in the 1970s, but not until 1995 did he find the perfect piece of land in Paso Robles. He bought the Home Ranch and then the Terrace and Bench vineyards. The Robert Hall Winery Merlot offers aromas of black raspberries and black currants, and the Robert Hall Winery Meritage boasts intense dark fruit flavors. 26

ROXO PORT CELLARS

6996 Peachy Canyon Road, Paso Robles, CA 93446
(805) 464-0922, www.roxocellars.com

Founded by Jeff and Kim Steele in 2005, Roxo Port Cellars produces only sweet port-style wines. They source fruit from Paso Robles, San Luis Obispo, and Cienega Valley and make the wines in the traditional Método Português. Roxo Port Cellars shares a tasting room with Chateau Margene and Limerock Orchards. The Roxo Ruby Tradicional Paso Robles offers lingering dark berry flavors, and the Roxo Magia Preta Paso Robles has fruit flavors framed by dark chocolate. 27

SAXUM VINEYARDS

2810 Willow Creek Road, Paso Robles, CA 93446
(805) 610-0363, www.saxumvineyards.com

Justin Smith founded Saxum, Latin for "stone," in 2002. He keeps production between 3,000 and 4,000 cases per year and uses grapes from his family's James Berry Vineyard as well as Paderewski, Heart Stone, Terry Hoage, and Booker vineyards. The Saxum James Berry Vineyard has sweet fruit flavors and a long finish.

SCULPTERRA WINERY

5015 Linne Road, Paso Robles, CA 93446
(888) 302-8881, www.sculpterra.com

Warren Frankel practiced medicine for years before moving to Paso Robles in 1979. He and his wife, Kathy, wanted a simpler life and planted pistachio trees and Cabernet Sauvignon vines. In 1997 they expanded their vineyards with 20 additional acres of Merlot and Zinfandel. They completed their winery in 2007, and a portion of the wine profits goes to the charity His Healing Hands. The smooth and velvety Sculpterra Winery and Sculpture Garden Paso Robles Cabernet Sauvignon has fruit flavors that mingle with chocolate and mocha, and the Sculpterra Statuesque offers flavors of black raspberries, espresso, black cherries, and dark chocolate. 28

SINOR-LAVALLEE WINES

P.O. Box 701, Arroyo Grande, CA 93421
(805) 801-2502, www.sinorlavallee.com

Mike Sinor and Cheri LaVallee-Sinor met in college in San Luis Obispo and worked together at local wineries. Their fanatical dedication to Pinot Noir prompted them to wed in Burgundy, land of their favorite grape. The Sinor-LaVallee Pinot Gris boasts heady aromas of white stone fruit and is generous in the mouth, and the Sinor-LaVallee Pinot Noir has delightful aromas of red cherries, red raspberries, and cocoa powder.

STARR RANCH VINEYARDS

9320 Chimney Rock Road, Paso Robles, CA 93446
(805) 227-0144, www.starr-ranch.com

Judy Starr pulled up her East Coast roots in 2000 and moved her family to the hills of Adelaida to grow grapes. Today they continue growing grapes and have started making their own wine. The Starr Ranch Vineyards Reserve Syrah tastes of black cherry, dried plums, and a touch of chocolate. The Starr Ranch Vineyards Marriage has rich flavors of ripe red and black fruits with a touch of anise and black pepper.

STEINBECK VINEYARDS AND WINERY

5940 Union Road, Paso Robles, CA 93446
(805) 238-1854, www.steinbeckwines.com

Howie Steinbeck and daughter, Cindy, run the show at their Steinbeck Vineyard, historic site of a 1956 B-26 plane crash that claimed the life of one airman while four others parachuted to safety. The Steinbeck Vineyards The Crash offers fruit flavors that mingle with mocha and dark chocolate, while the Steinbeck Vineyards and Winery Viognier has aromas of lemon zest and green apple. 29

TABLAS CREEK VINEYARD

9339 Adelaida Road, Paso Robles, CA 93446
(805) 237-1231, www.tablascreek.com

Robert Haas and the Perrin family of Château de Beaucastel founded Tablas Creek Vineyard in 1985. In 1989 they purchased 120 acres of West Paso Robles land with similarities to Châteaneuf-du-Pape. Today, Tablas Creek is known for its Grenache, Syrah, Mourvèdre, Counoise, Marsanne, Viognier, Grenache Blanc, and Roussanne vines. The Tablas Creek Vineyard Grenache Blanc has bouquet and flavor notes of licorice, green apple, and pear. A perfect companion for grilled meats and barbecue, the Tablas Creek Vineyard Counoise offers flavors of subdued citrus and cherry cola. 30

TERRY HOAGE VINEYARDS

870 Arbor Road, Paso Robles, CA 93446
(805) 238-2083, www.terryhoagevineyards.com

After playing for six teams in the NFL, Terry Hoage moved to Paso Robles to give his family a better life, which now includes producing wine. He and wife, Jennifer, share viticulturist and winemaker duties. The Hoages have 17 acres under vines, use organic farming principles, and produce about 2,500 cases per year. Terry and Jennifer take part in Must! Charities, and $1 from the sale of each bottle goes to the organization. The Terry Hoage Skins Grenache has aromas of black cherry, toast, and anise and big fruit flavors with nuances of cherry cola and dried herbs. The Terry Hoage The "46" offers big flavors of sweet red fruits and a long finish. 31

THACHER WINERY

8355 Vineyard Drive, Paso Robles, CA 93446
(805) 237-0087, www.thacherwinery.com

Sherman and Michelle Thacher fell in love with Paso Robles while attending a 2003 wedding at the Kentucky Ranch. When it came up for sale shortly thereafter, they bought it and relocated from Santa Cruz. A UC Davis graduate, Sherman worked as a beer brewmaster until his first grape harvest in 2004. The Thacher Winery Paso Robles Controlled Chaos offers flavors of red and black fruits with a sweet, soft tannic finish, and the Thacher Triumvirate Reserve Zinfandel has flavors of rich fruit, spice, and milk chocolate. 32

TOBIN JAMES CELLARS

8950 Union Road, Paso Robles, CA 93446
(805) 239-2204, www.tobinjames.com

Winemaker Toby James worked at Estrella, Eberle, and Peachy Canyon before building his own winery in 1993. In 1996 he formed a business partnership with Lance and Claire Silver and expanded the winery to what it is today. Evoking an Old West saloon, the winery is built on the site of a former stagecoach stop, and the mahogany bar dates to 1860. The Tobin James 5 Paso Robles offers rich aromas of dark fruits, ripe cherry, and red plum, and the Tobin James Ballistic Paso Robles Zinfandel has aromas of blackberry jam, black pepper, and brown spice and rich and lively black fruit flavors. 33

LAZARRE
2011
ALBARIÑO
EDNA VALLEY

21

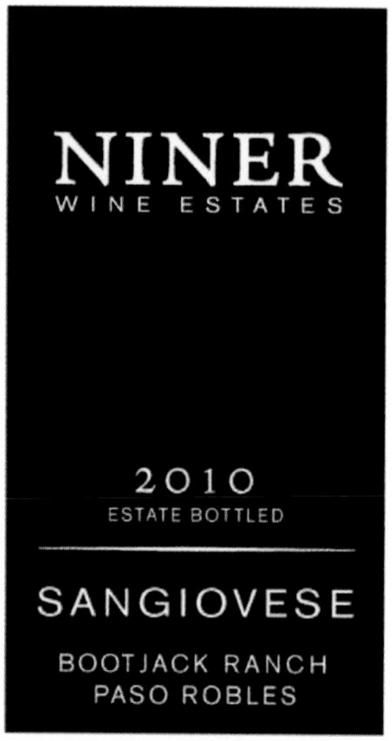
NINER
WINE ESTATES
2010
ESTATE BOTTLED
SANGIOVESE
BOOTJACK RANCH
PASO ROBLES

22

PEACHY
CANYON
Chardonnay
PASO ROBLES
2011

23

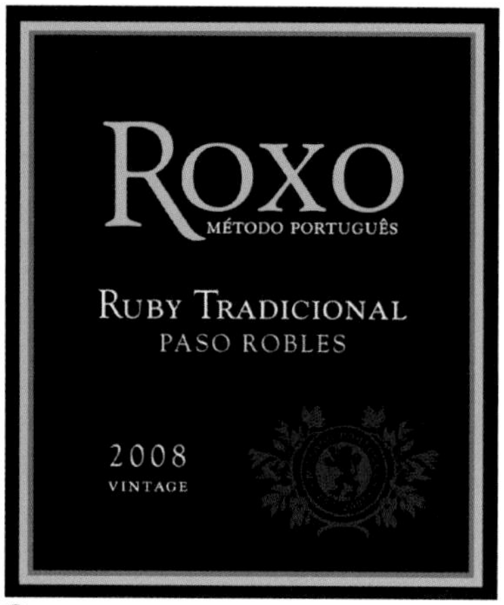
ROXO
MÉTODO PORTUGUÊS
RUBY TRADICIONAL
PASO ROBLES
2008
VINTAGE

27

Sculpterra
2008
PASO ROBLES
CABERNET
SAUVIGNON
ALC. 13.4% BY VOL.

28

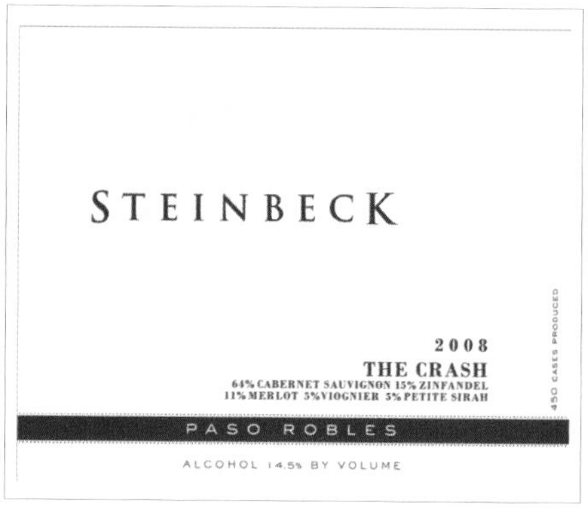
STEINBECK
2008
THE CRASH
64% CABERNET SAUVIGNON 15% ZINFANDEL
11% MERLOT 5% VIOGNIER 5% PETITE SIRAH
450 CASES PRODUCED
PASO ROBLES
ALCOHOL 14.5% BY VOLUME

29

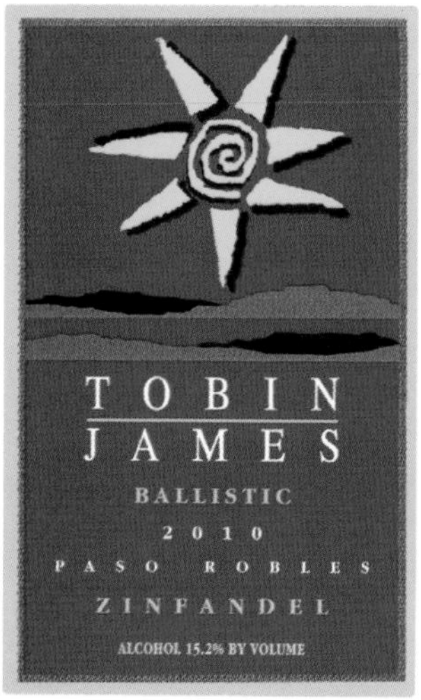
TOBIN
JAMES
BALLISTIC
2010
PASO ROBLES
ZINFANDEL
ALCOHOL 15.2% BY VOLUME

33

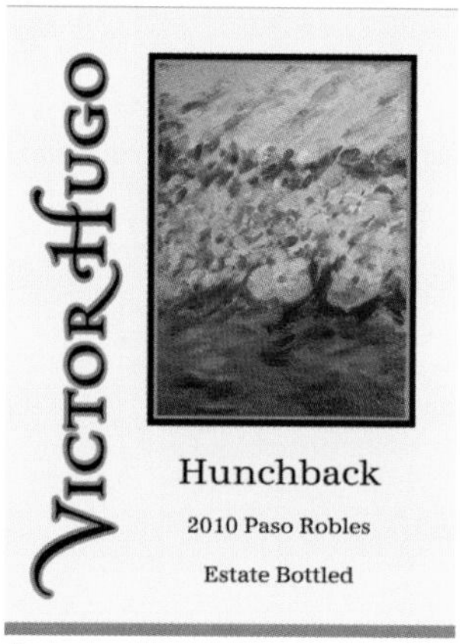
VICTOR HUGO
Hunchback
2010 Paso Robles
Estate Bottled

34

Villicana
estate grown
cabernet sauvignon
paso robles
2009

35

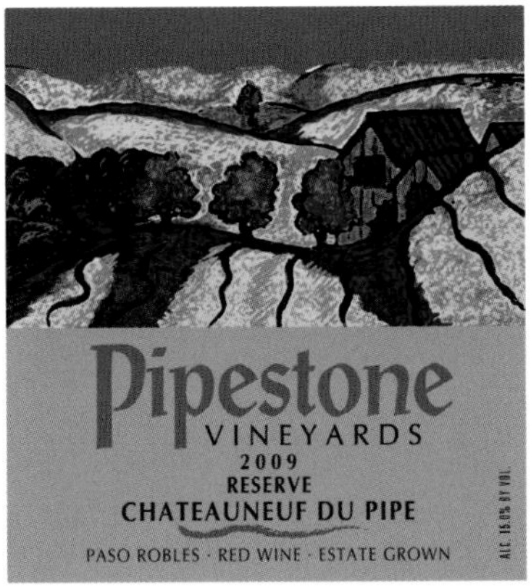

Pipestone
VINEYARDS
2009
RESERVE
CHATEAUNEUF DU PIPE
PASO ROBLES · RED WINE · ESTATE GROWN

24

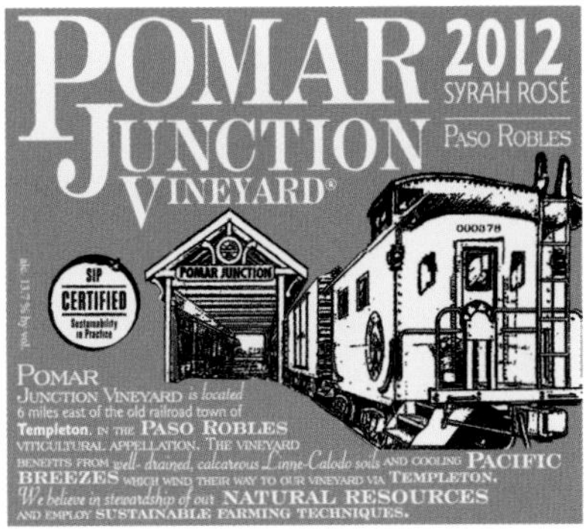

POMAR JUNCTION VINEYARD®
2012
SYRAH ROSÉ
PASO ROBLES
SIP CERTIFIED
POMAR JUNCTION
Pomar Junction Vineyard is located 6 miles east of the old railroad town of Templeton, in the Paso Robles viticultural appellation. The vineyard benefits from well-drained, calcareous Linne-Calodo soils and cooling Pacific breezes which wind their way to our vineyard via Templeton. We believe in stewardship of our natural resources and employ sustainable farming techniques.

25

26

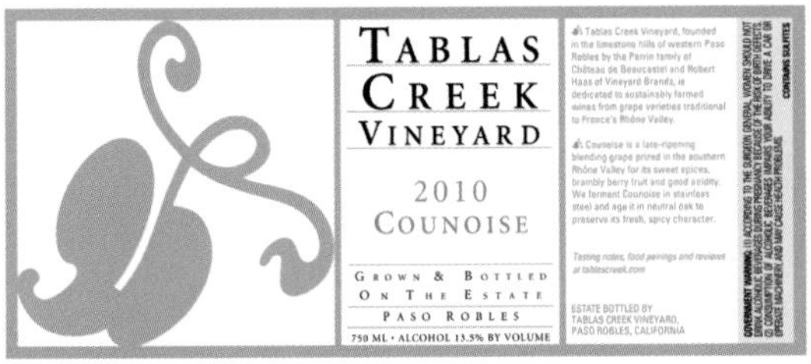

30

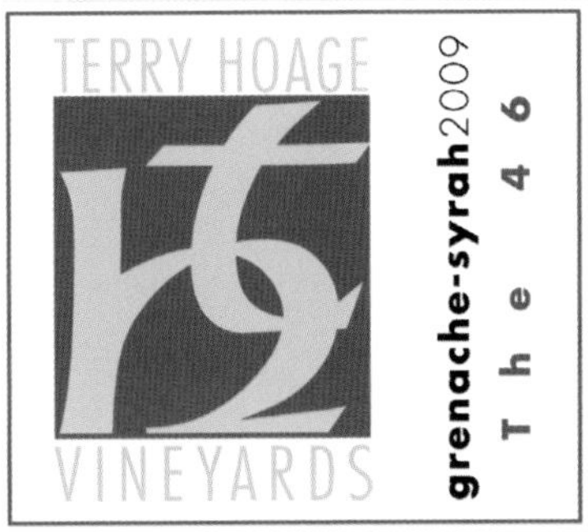

31

32

37

WINDWARD
VINEYARD
ESTATE BOTTLED
PINOT NOIR
APPELLATION PASO ROBLES :: ALCOHOL 14.3% BY VOL.

38

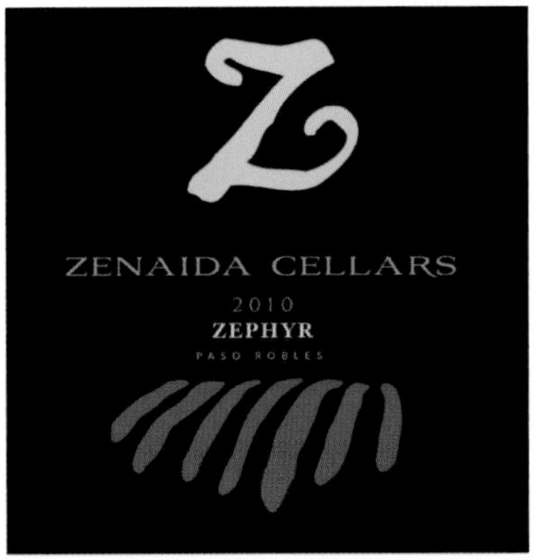

39

In his own words

TOBIN JAMES

From six tons of discarded Zinfandel grapes, Tobin James made his first award-winning wine. He opened his own winery in 1994, and today he enjoys talking to customers at the mahogany bar in his tasting room and chatting with wine club members on the deck of a winery-chartered cruise ship.

I grew up on a vineyard my brother started in Indiana 45 years ago. We were real rookies at grape growing, but I learned about farming, and early on I set my sights on the wine business.

If you really look at it, we've only made wine in this country in a concerted effort since Prohibition was repealed. Around the world, most countries have been doing it for hundreds of years. Twenty-five years ago, I would tell a wine buyer I had a winery in Paso Robles, and he would say, "Oh, you have a winery in Texas?" I would say, "No, that's El Paso." In the last 20 years Paso wines have reached world status. Paso Robles is now firmly on the wine map.

Zinfandel is our flagship, and every year we love to add a new variety at crush because it's fun and exciting! We make thirty different wines. You have to make what the public enjoys, but if we think we have a cool recipe or new variety we think they should try, we go for it. No matter how the wine turns out, that's the way we planned it.

VICTOR HUGO WINERY

2850 El Pomar Drive, Templeton, CA 93465
(805) 434-1128, www.victorhugowinery.com

Unrelated to the French literary great, Victor Hugo Roberts likes to create intrigue around the names of his wines. Roberts earned his enology degree from UC Davis in 1979 and now makes wine in a century-old converted barn that sits amid 78 acres of vines. The Victor Hugo Winery Paso Robles Estate Hunchback has flavors of black fruits and tart cherries, and the Victor Hugo Winery Paso Robles Estate Opulence tastes of black fruits, toasted espresso bean, and coffee. 34

VILLA SAN-JULIETTE

6385 Cross Canyons Road, San Miguel, CA 93451
(805) 467-0014, www.villasanjuliette.com

Villa San-Juliette, owned by Nigel Lythgoe and Ken Warwick, consists of 168 acres of vines and a 14,000-square-foot Tuscan-style estate complete with tasting room. The first estate-grown vintage was bottled in 2008. The Villa San-Juliette Reserve Albariño has a nose of white stone fruits, lemon zest, and Bartlett pears, and the Villa San-Juliette Reserve Malbec offers aromas of black fruits and fresh fruit flavors on the palate.

VILLICANA WINERY AND VINEYARD

2725 Adelaida Road, Paso Robles, CA 93446
(805) 239-9456, www.villicanawinery.com

Culinary student Alex Villicana fell in love with winemaking while working at Creston Vineyard, whose owners allowed him to hand-harvest and keep the grapes remaining after the mechanical harvest. In 1996 he and wife, Monica, bought 72 acres in Paso Robles and planted Cabernet Sauvignon, Cabernet Franc, Merlot, Zinfandel, Viognier, Grenache, Mourvèdre, and Syrah. The Villicanas began distilling vodka and gin under the Re:Find label in 2012. A natural match with grilled meats and ribs, the Villicana Estate Grown Paso Robles Cabernet Sauvignon has a bouquet of black currant, black cherry, and oregano. 35

VINA ROBLES

3700 Mill Road, Paso Robles, CA 93446
(805) 227-4812, www.vinarobles.com

Swiss-born Hans Nef became enchanted with the Pacific coastline and the cowboy culture of Paso Robles back in the mid-1990s. In 1996 he partnered with another Swiss expat, Hans R. Michael, and they hired Swiss native Matthias Guber as winemaker in 1999. Big and round in the mouth, the Vina Robles Estate Paso Robles Petite Sirah has aromas of black plums, black raspberries, and a touch of Christmas baking spices. The Vina Robles Suendero Meritage Paso Robles offers black fruit flavors with a touch of spice. 36

WILD HORSE WINERY AND VINEYARDS

1437 Wild Horse Winery Court, Templeton, CA 93465
(805) 788-6310, www.wildhorsewinery.com

Founded by Ken Volk in 1982, Wild Horse Winery was one of the first wineries in the region. The first crush came in 1983, and today Wild Horse continues making vineyard-designated wines from Cabernet Sauvignon, Syrah, Zinfandel, Chardonnay, and Pinot Noir. Other varieties in limited release include Grenache Blanc, Zinfandel, Syrah, Blaufrankisch, Malvasia Bianca, and Verdelho. Chrissy Wittmann directs winemaking, and Emerson Philpot manages the vineyards. The fruit-forward Wild Horse Winery and Vineyards Cheval Sauvage Santa Maria Valley Pinot Noir has notes of red fruits and Chinese five-spice powder in the complex bouquet. The Wild Horse Winery and Vineyards Central Coast Pinot Noir offers aromas of cranberry, black cherry, cherry cola, and a touch of nutmeg. 37

WINDWARD VINEYARD

1380 Live Oak Road, Paso Robles, CA 93446
(805) 239-2565, www.windwardvineyard.com

Husband and wife Marc Goldberg and Maggie D'Ambrosia planted Windward Vineyard in 1989 with the goal of producing single-vineyard "Monopole" Burgundian-style wines in Paso Robles. Their 15-acre vineyard has four different French Pinot Noir clones, and the couple produces wines made exclusively from the single variety. Their Windward Vineyard Pinot Noir has aromas of dried black cherries and cherry vanilla ice cream. 38

ZENAIDA CELLARS

1550 Highway 46 West, Paso Robles, CA 93446
(805) 227-0382, www.zenaidacellars.com

Biologist-turned-winemaker Eric Ogorsolka first worked with Ken Volk at Wild Horse Winery and began making wine under his Zenaida Cellars label in 1998. With the help of wife, Jill, he completed the winery in 2000. The property has 36 acres, 22 under vine. The Zenaida Cellars Wanderlust has flavors of freshly picked berries, espresso bean, and dark chocolate, and the fruit-forward Zenaida Cellars Zephyr offers flavors of black plum, blackberry, savory herbs, baking spices, and a touch of mocha. 39

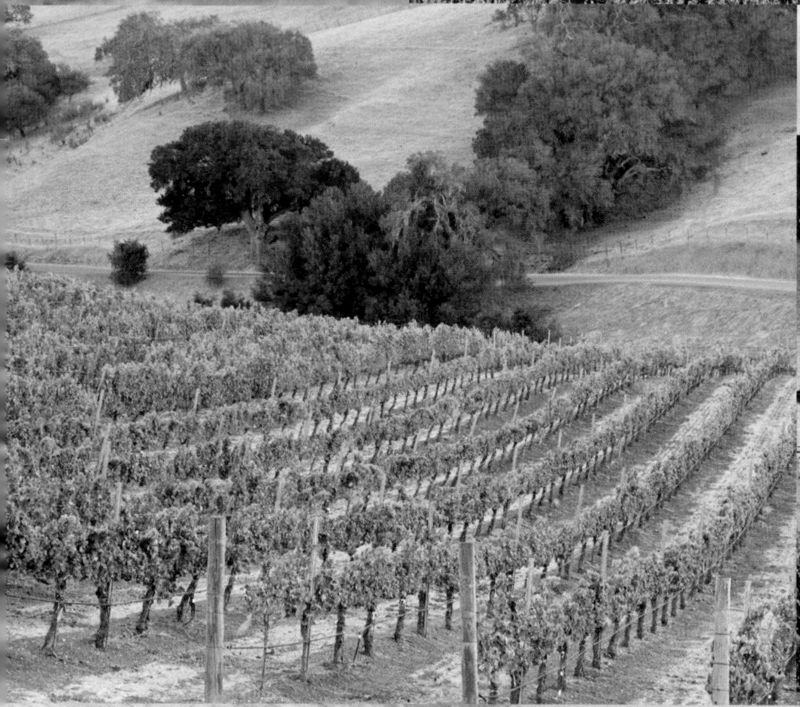

TEN

SANTA BARBARA

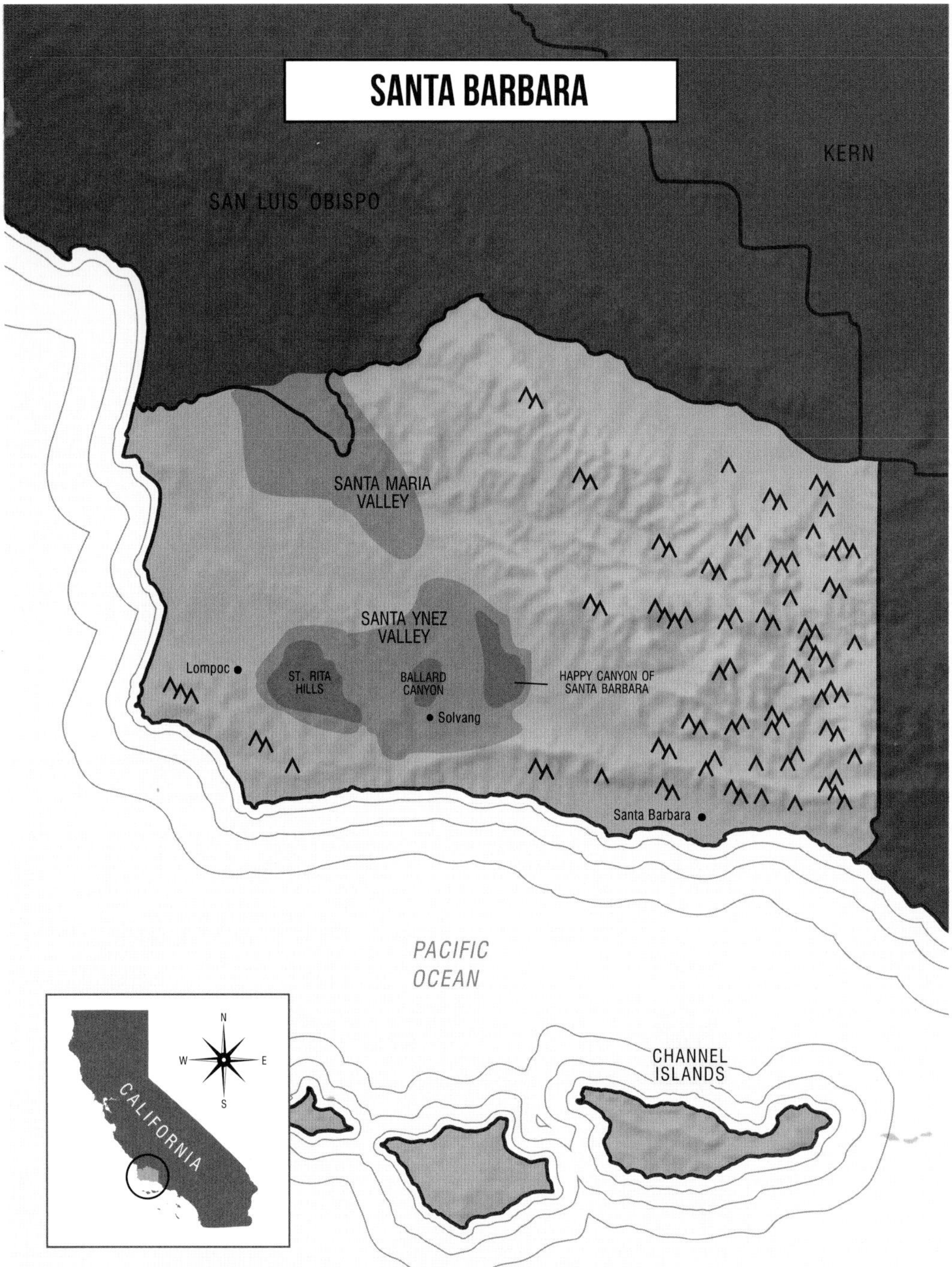

SANTA BARBARA
KERN
SAN LUIS OBISPO
SANTA MARIA VALLEY
SANTA YNEZ VALLEY
Lompoc
ST. RITA HILLS
BALLARD CANYON
HAPPY CANYON OF SANTA BARBARA
Solvang
Santa Barbara
PACIFIC OCEAN
CHANNEL ISLANDS
N
W
E
S
CALIFORNIA

Inhabited by the native Chumash people for more than 10,000 years, Santa Barbara received its name in 1602 from Spanish explorer Sebastián Vizcaíno, who survived a storm on the eve of the saint's feast day. Under the direction of Father Junípero Serra, Spanish colonists and missionaries arrived in 1769. Serra planted vines bearing Mission grapes here in 1782, and the Mission Santa Barbara was completed in 1786.

The San Jose Winery, now a county landmark, was built in the local adobe style in the early nineteenth century. The Lompoc Wine Ghetto, an industrial park turned winery and tasting room complex, was founded in 1874 as an alcohol-free temperance colony ironically called New Vineland. In 1884 Frenchman Justinian Caire, who ran a successful ranching operation, planted a large vineyard on nearby Santa Cruz Island, and by the end of the century forty-five vineyards operated on 260 acres in the area.

In the early twentieth century, Santa Barbara had a small but thriving wine industry. But as it did statewide, Prohibition took its toll on grape growing. Not until the 1960s did wine farming again take hold in Santa Barbara, specifically in Santa Maria Valley. At that time, large commercial growers produced grapes for big operations dominating the domestic wine industry, while family-owned wineries were developing the Santa Ynez Valley with an interest in the small-batch, handcrafted wines that remain the hallmark of the region. Local wineries, supplemented by a critical mass of tasting rooms and restaurants featuring local food and wine, and augmented by the popularity of the 2004 hit movie *Sideways*, have offered a serious draw for visitors to Santa Barbara wine country.

The Santa Maria Valley AVA attained official status in 1981, the first AVA in Santa Barbara and the third in the United States. Expanded in 2011, it now covers 116,273 acres. Pacific fog often blankets vines until midday, creating cool temperatures ideal for growing Pinot Noir and Chardonnay. Soils toward the north of the valley tend to include thin layers of earth over decomposed shale and limestone. Soils south of the Santa Maria River run deeper, containing alluvial qualities and sand brought inland over the years.

Uriel Nielson planted 100 acres of vines in 1964, the first modern large-scale vineyard. Originally planted to multiple varieties sold to large producers, the Uriel Nielson Vineyard now grows Pinot Noir and Chardonnay. In 1969 the Millers, a fifth-generation California farming family, bought the two large plots of land, and the next year brothers Stephen and Robert planted the Bien Nacido Vineyard. In the early 1970s the Sanford and Wild Horse wineries developed other area vineyards.

The Santa Ynez Valley AVA, established in 1983, has the highest concentration of wineries in the county. Santa Ynez Valley covers 77,000 acres, while Sta. Rita Hills, created in 2001, has 31,000 acres and Happy Canyon (established in 2009) has 24,000. Soils range from heavy clay to shale, gravel, and sand. The valleys of Santa Barbara receive cool Pacific breezes and fog during the day, protecting grapes from the sun's heat during the dry growing season.

The Santa Ynez Valley AVA contains three sub-AVAs: Sta. Rita Hills, expanded in 2013, Happy Canyon of Santa Barbara, and Ballard Canyon. Sta. Rita Hills, known as Santa Rita Hills from 2001 through 2006, now uses the Spanish abbreviation for "saint," after negotiations with Chilean wine producer Viña Santa Rita. Ballard Canyon features multiple twisting hills and canyons, unlike the more level landscape of the surrounding Santa Ynez Valley. The TTB is considering a petition for the establishment of the Los Olivos District AVA within Santa Ynez Valley.

Santa Barbara has more than a hundred wineries, which grow more than sixty grape varieties on more than 16,000 vine acres. The top variety is Chardonnay, followed by Pinot Noir, Syrah,

Cabernet Sauvignon, Sauvignon Blanc, and Grenache. Vineyards are divided almost equally between red and white grapes. Other varieties include Grenache, Viognier, Marsanne, Roussanne, Albariño, Merlot, Malbec, Petit Verdot, and Sangiovese. Many of the area's Chardonnay plantings date back to the 1970s, and Chardonnay is made here in a variety of styles, from steely sharp to oak tinged. Some 80 percent of Sta. Rita Hills' vines grow Pinot Noir grapes, which is vinified into different styles, from fresh and fruity to a deeper, more savory fashion. Syrah lags behind Chardonnay and Pinot Noir in production, but more wineries in the county produce it as a single variety than any other grape. It's blended with Grenache and Mourvèdre as well as with Cabernet Sauvignon or Zinfandel. Sauvignon Blanc makes up only 4 percent of total acreage here, thriving particularly in Happy Canyon, which is where the bulk of Cabernet Sauvignon grows, vinified as a single variety or in Bordeaux-style blends.

Santa Barbara's wine regions have a strong farm-to-table movement. Locals and visitors alike enjoy regional meat and produce alongside a bounty of area wine. Summertime festivals celebrate this ethos, and many wineries and tasting rooms offer music and other programs throughout the year.

23

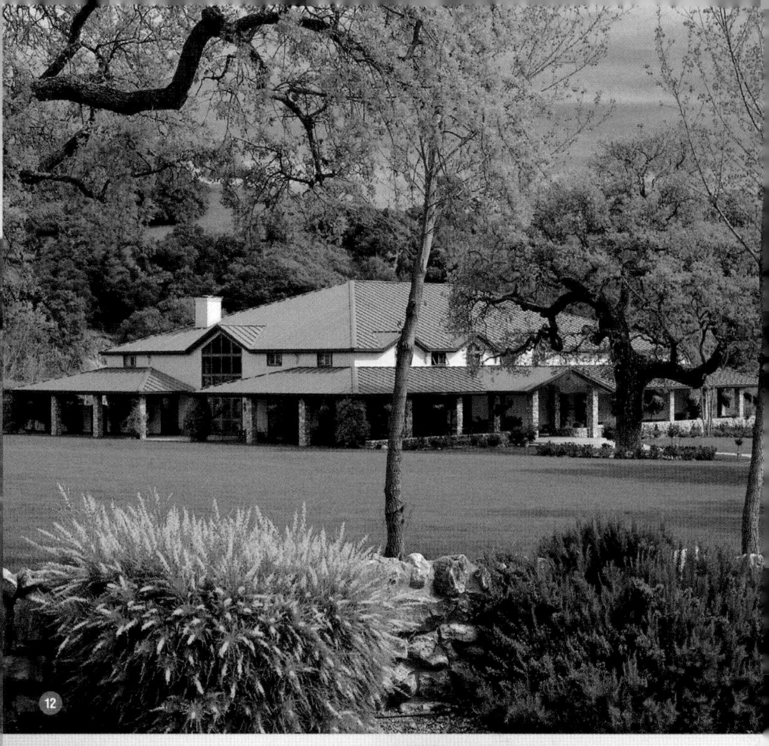
12

16

29
Sea Smoke
B
115
3309

THE WINERIES

ALMA ROSA WINERY & VINEYARDS

7250 Santa Rosa Road, Buellton, CA 93427
(805) 688-9090, www.almarosawinery.com

After returning home from the Vietnam War in 1968, Richard Sanford organized a partnership to buy a ranch and planted Pinot Noir—first in the Sta. Rita Hills—at Sanford & Benedict Vineyard in 1970. He married Thekla Brumder in 1978, and together they started Sanford Winery in 1981. In 2005 they founded Alma Rosa. Today they produce wine from 100 acres of certified-organic vineyards in the Sta. Rita Hills. The full-bodied Alma Rosa La Encantada Vineyard Sta. Rita Hills Pinot Noir has aromas of red raspberry, dried black cherry, and Christmas baking spices. The Alma Rosa El Jabalí Vineyard Sta. Rita Hills Chardonnay, with aromas of freshly cut Cavaillon melon, white stone fruits, and caramelized pineapple, is crisp on the palate. ❶

ALTA MARIA VINEYARDS

2933 Grand Avenue, Los Olivos, CA 93441
(805) 686-1144, www.altamaria.com

Winemaker Paul Wilkins and viticulturist James Ontiveros founded Alta Maria Vineyards and named it after the upper Santa Maria River. They make small-batch Chardonnay, Sauvignon Blanc, and Pinot Noir. The clean-finishing Alta Maria Vineyards Santa Barbara County Sauvignon Blanc offers flavors of tropical fruit. The medium-bodied Alta Maria Vineyards Santa Maria Valley Pinot Noir offers fruity aromas of dried red cherries and fresh strawberries.

ANDREW MURRAY VINEYARDS

2901-A Grand Avenue, Los Olivos, CA 93441
(805) 693-9644, www.andrewmurrayvineyards.com

Former paleontology student Andrew Murray—"one of the shining stars in the Santa Barbara firmament" according to Robert Parker—developed an infatuation with Rhône varieties in France in 1980 and subsequently moved to Australia. After earning his bachelor's in enology from UC Davis, he started his own winery. Big and bold yet restrained, the Andrew Murray Esperance Red Blend offers aromas of dark fruits, while the Andrew Murray RGB White Blend is generous in the mouth with rich fruit flavors.

AU BON CLIMAT

813 Anacapa Street, Santa Barbara, CA 93003
(805) 963-7999, www.aubonclimat.com

Aspiring lawyer Jim Clendenen visited France for his twenty-first birthday and on returning to the United States embarked on a career in wine. He became assistant winemaker at Zaca Mesa Winery in 1978, and in 1982 he started Au Bon Climat, which roughly translates from French as "a well-exposed vineyard." Perfect with food, the Au Bon Climat Santa Barbara County Pinot Noir, with aromas of cherry preserves, freshly picked strawberries, baking spices, and crushed coriander seeds, is big and full-bodied in the mouth. The Au Bon Climat La Bauge Au-dessus Pinot Noir is a raucous party of red fruit aromas laced with Chinese black tea infused with Asian spices. ❷

BECKMEN VINEYARDS

2670 Ontiveros Road, Los Olivos, CA 93441
(805) 688-8664, www.beckmenvineyards.com

A family affair since its start in 1994, Beckman Vineyards fulfills the vision of Tom and Steve Beckman. They began with 40 acres and subsequently purchased a 365-acre ranch in Santa Ynez Valley in 1996 which they named Purisima Mountain Vineyard and which has been farmed biodynamically since 2006. The Beckman Vineyards Purisima Mountain Vineyard Whole Cluster Grenache has notes of ripe cherry, pomegranate, and red raspberry in the complex bouquet. ❸

BIEN NACIDO VINEYARDS

4705 Santa Maria Mesa Road, Santa Maria, CA 93454
(805) 937-2506, www.biennacidovineyards.com

The original ranch here formed part of a Spanish land grant made to Tomas Olivera by the governor of Alta California, Juan Bautista Alvarado, in 1837. The Miller family bought two parcels of Rancho Tepusquet totaling more than 2,000 acres in 1969 and planted grapevines soon after. In Spanish, "*bien nacido*" means "well-born," a concept reflected in Bien Nacido's site selection and vineyard management. The medium-bodied Bien Nacido Vineyards Santa Maria Valley Chardonnay has pronounced citrus flavors and a clean finish. The Bien Nacido Vineyards Santa Maria Valley Pinot Noir has aromas and flavors of dark cherry, dried cranberry, and a touch of mint. 4

BLAIR FOX CELLARS

2902 San Marcos Avenue, Los Olivos, CA 93441
(805) 691-1678, www.blairfoxcellars.com

Blair Fox's travels in the Rhône Valley influenced his French winemaking style first at Fess Parker Winery and then at his own organically farmed vineyards. The zippy and zesty Blair Fox Cellars Paradise Road Vineyard Viognier has aromas of ripe white fruits and Indian spices. Rich and fruit-driven, the Blair Fox Cellars Thompson Vineyard Syrah offers flavors of black currant, black plum, and black raspberry.

BREWER-CLIFTON

329 North F Street, Lompoc, CA 93436
(805) 735-9184, www.brewerclifton.com

In their former lives Greg Brewer taught French and surfer Steve Clifton sang in a rock band—which isn't to say that Brewer doesn't still speak French and Clifton doesn't sing anymore. The duo crafts their wine together just yards from the Lompoc Wine Ghetto. The Brewer-Clifton Sta. Rita Hills Chardonnay has heady aromas of citrus, lemon zest, and crystallized ginger, and the Brewer-Clifton Ampelos Pinot Noir has flavors of rich red fruits, pomegranate, and black Chinese tea. 5

BYRON WINES

2367 Alamo Pintado Avenue, Los Olivos, CA 93441
(805) 938-7365, www.byronwines.com

Ken Brown founded Byron in 1984 to make Chardonnay and Pinot Noir wines, and in 2003 Jonathan Nagy took over winemaking duties. Production has moved to neighboring Cambria Estate, but Byron continues to focus on small-batch wines. The Byron Santa Maria Valley Chardonnay has flavors of ripe peach and dried apricot. The fruit-forward Byron Santa Maria Valley Pinot Noir offers aromas of dried black cherry, red raspberry, cherry cola, and a touch of brown spice in the bouquet. 6

CAMBRIA ESTATE WINERY

5475 Chardonnay Lane, Santa Maria, CA 93454
(805) 937-8901, www.cambriawines.com

In 1986, Barbara Banke of Jackson Family Wines acquired a large section of Rancho Tepusquet, a Mexican land grant, to serve as the site for Cambria Winery. Tepusquet Vineyard was originally planted in 1971 and over the subsequent years has been replanted and expanded. The Cambria Estate Winery Katherine's Vineyard Santa Maria Valley Chardonnay is rich in the mouth with aromas of Anjou pear and caramelized pineapple. The Cambria Estate Winery Julia's Vineyard Santa Maria Valley Pinot Noir offers notes of ripe cherry, red plum, and a touch of spice in the bouquet. 7

In their own words

SONJA MAGDEVSKI AND EMILIO ESTEVEZ

Winemaker Sonja Magdevski and fiancé, actor, and director Emilio Estevez, planted vines in their front yard and began making wine in their garage. Today the couple makes delicious world-class wines at a proper winery and can often be found at their Babi's Tasting Room in Los Alamos.

Emilio grew up visiting his grandfather Francisco's vineyard in Spain. To him as a child it was the most natural environment he had ever known. For me, I grew up running around my family's villages in Macedonia each summer when I'd visit with my family every year. There we had cattle, apple orchards, vineyards, beehives, walnut and chestnut trees, chickens, pigs, everything. The idea of working with the land was integral to our upbringing though not encouraged in school or home for success. And yet we kept coming back to it in various ways. Planting the vineyard was the first step to our ongoing education of a lifetime, though we didn't know it yet.

When we started, we didn't have a plan; we simply wanted to grow something and share it with our community. Now our goal is to create community while growing something to share—incredible fruit for delicious wine for the wonderful people we meet. When my grandmother, God rest her, came to visit us for the first time in Malibu and she saw the vineyard and the garden, the first words out of her mouth were, "I left the village 50 years ago, and you have come back to it." That is the driving force toward all we do. Trends are trends, and good wine is what remains.

Once I decided to take over the winemaking production, I began to take classes at the local Allan Hancock Community College in Santa Maria. Being in that program gave me the confidence and determination to continue forward. And it gave me the ability to share and debate everything I had learned with everything I was doing in the winery with Emilio, who is an absolute hands-on learner and a damn good one, too. Today we say that I am the winemaker and he is my assistant winemaker, while he is the farmer and I am his farmhand with our vineyard in Malibu.

We make Pinot Noir from our property in Malibu, which has proven to be the most challenging endeavor most years, and yet when it works, the fruit creates the most unique, velvety wine we have tasted. The issue is that there simply isn't that much of it even in good years. Our primary focus is on Rhône varieties—Viognier, Syrah, Grenache, Roussanne, a Syrah Rosé, and a Sparkling Syrah Rosé, which we call Sonja's Suds. And for good measure a Gewürztraminer that is 100 percent dry with a good portion of the fruit fermented cold on the skins for a few weeks. This is for my grandmother. I'd love to experiment more with skin-fermented whites and cofermentations and perhaps add another sparkling wine to the repertoire. Also with the use of various fermentation and aging vessels in the future. The possibilities are endless, and it is important to keep that playful experimentation alive.

[Our winemaking philosophy] is purity and authenticity achieved through attentiveness, which may mean babying to some or careful consideration to others. And also letting the fruit express itself—I call this wine independence—because it has its own energy and we need to work together to create a cohesive, "balanced" wine. I have to trust the process and the history of the process and remain open to every new idea while keeping grounded in the foundations of our style.

Winemaking should influence the market because I want to make wines that I want to make in the way that I want to make them. But that said, everyone needs input and we all need an open mind to understand our environment. Communication in all parts of life is vital to our growth. Though again, once you get people inside the tasting room tasting wines, whatever they believed outside changes once they start tasting. Good wine bucks all trends or marketplace fever.

CARGASACCHI

420 East Highway 246, Buellton, CA
(805) 691-1300, www.cargasacchi.com

Peter Cargasacchi planted his namesake vineyard in Sta. Rita Hills in 1998 and Jalama Vineyard the next year. He and Julia Manuela Cargasacchi produce estate-grown Pinot Noir under their own label and Syrah, Pinot Grigio, Chardonnay, and Pinot Noir from estate and purchased grapes under the Point Concepción label, all of which you can sip at their tasting room. The Cargasacchi Cargasacchi-Jalama Vineyard Santa Barbara County Pinot Noir offers aromas and flavors of red raspberry, red currants, and black raspberry with a touch of dried herbs. ❽

CASA DUMETZ

388 Bell Street, Los Alamos, CA 93440
(805) 344-1900, www.casadumetzwines.com

Winemaker Sonja Magdevski and fiancé, Emilio Estevez, recently dug up their Malibu front yard to plant Pinot Noir grapevines, and Sonja named her tasting room Babi's, for her Macedonian grandmother, Babi Ilinka. The fruit-forward Casa Dumetz Gewürztraminer, with delightful aromas of grapefruit peel, clementine, lemon juice, and vanilla, is perfect as an aperitif. The Casa Dumetz Tierra Alta Vineyard Grenache offers great fruit flavors with notes of anise, blackberry preserves, and cassis. ❾

COLD HEAVEN CELLARS

92 A Second Street, Buellton, CA 93427
(805) 686-1343, www.coldheavencellars.com

Started in 1996 by winemaker-owner Morgan Clendenen, Cold Heaven Cellars sources grapes for its Viognier from the Clendenen family–owned Le Bon Climat Vineyard in Santa Barbara County and Sanford and Benedict Vineyards in Sta. Rita Hills. Clenenden has been making Syrah since 2003, and in 2008 she added Pinot Noir to her portfolio. The Cold Heaven Cellars Le Bon Climat Viognier has aromas of citrus and white stone fruits and vivid fruit flavors.

DIERBERG VINEYARD

P.O. Box 217, Santa Ynez, CA 93460
(805) 697-1467, www.dierbergvineyard.com

Jim and Mary Dierberg bought Hermannhof Winery in Hermann, Missouri, in 1974, but their love of cool-climate grapes and wines brought them to Santa Barbara in 1996. The next year they planted Pinot Noir and Chardonnay in the Santa Maria Valley. Andy Alba joined as winemaker in 2001 for the first crush, and Tyler Thomas succeeded him. Light on the palate, the Dierberg Santa Maria Valley Dierberg Vineyard Chardonnay has flavors of green apple and candied orange peel. Fruity in the mouth, Dierberg Santa Maria Valley Dierberg Vineyard Pinot Noir offers aromas of black raspberry and black cherry. ❿

EVENING LAND VINEYARDS

1503 East Chestnut Avenue, Lompoc, CA 93436
(805) 736-9656, www.eveninglandvineyards.com

Film producer Mark Tarlov founded Evening Land Vineyards in 2005, and he and his team crafted wine there until 2012, when he left to make wine in Oregon, selling his Santa Barbara property to winemaker Sashi Moorman, sommelier Rajat Parr, and their partners. The medium-bodied Evening Land Bloom's Field Vineyard Sta. Rita Hills Pinot Noir offers aromas of dried black cherry, red raspberry, and a touch of Indian spice. The Evening Land Estate Sta. Rita Hills Pinot Noir has notes of red plum, red cherry, and freshly ground black pepper in the bouquet and rich fruit flavors on the palate. ⓫

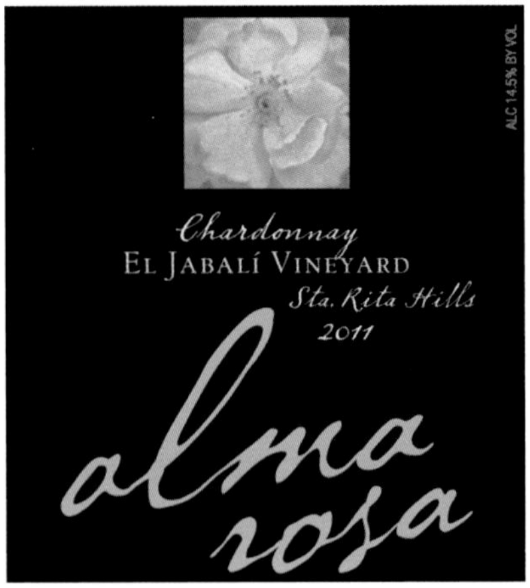

1

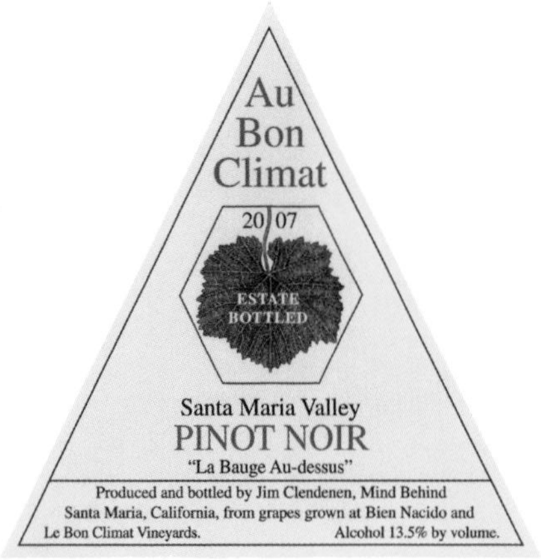

Au Bon Climat
2007
ESTATE BOTTLED
Santa Maria Valley
PINOT NOIR
"La Bauge Au-dessus"
Produced and bottled by Jim Clendenen, Mind Behind
Santa Maria, California, from grapes grown at Bien Nacido and
Le Bon Climat Vineyards.
Alcohol 13.5% by volume.

2

3

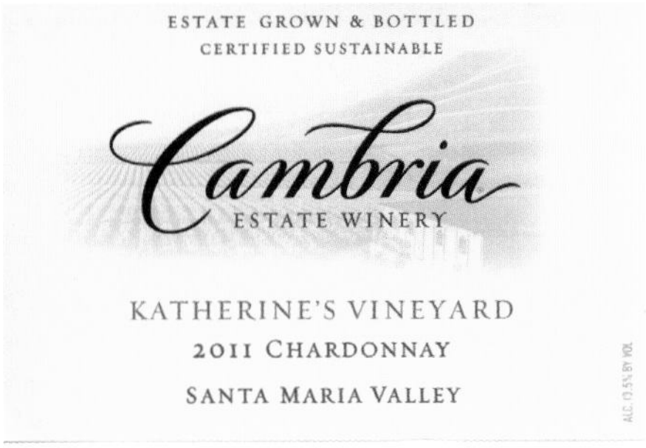

7

Winemaker Peter Cargasacchi is the fifth generation of his family in
California, but the first born in the New World. His great-great grandfather
2010
came from Italy, but then disappeared. His great grandfather founded a
restaurant and hotel in San Francisco, the Saint Gotthard, which was
CARGASACCHI
destroyed in the earthquake and fire of 1906. Subsequent generations,
though born in Italy, farmed and made wine in California's Central Coast.
PINOT NOIR
Paintings of Saint Gotthard often show him hanging his cloak on a sunbeam.

8

9

14

15

17

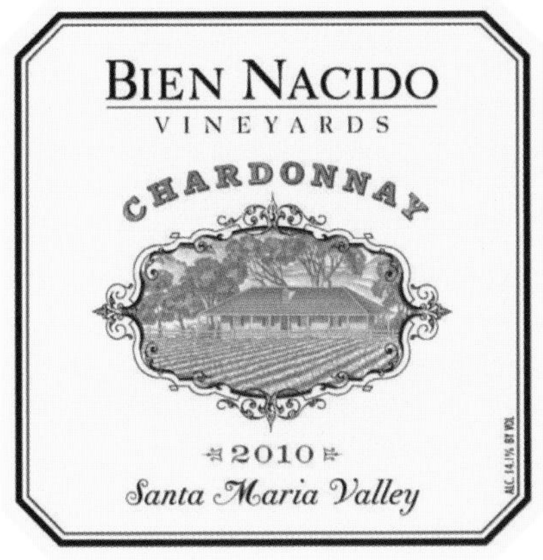
BIEN NACIDO
VINEYARDS
CHARDONNAY
2010
Santa Maria Valley

4

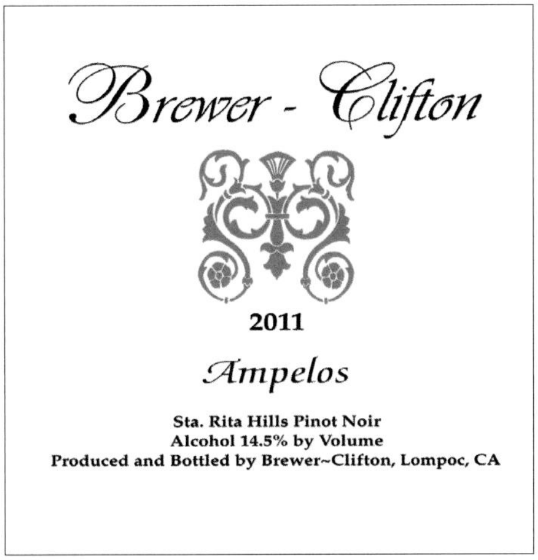
Brewer - Clifton
2011
Ampelos
Sta. Rita Hills Pinot Noir
Alcohol 14.5% by Volume
Produced and Bottled by Brewer~Clifton, Lompoc, CA

5

BYRON
2011
PINOT NOIR
Santa Maria Valley
FIRST COMMERCIAL VINEYARD PLANTED IN SANTA BARBARA COUNTY, 1964

6

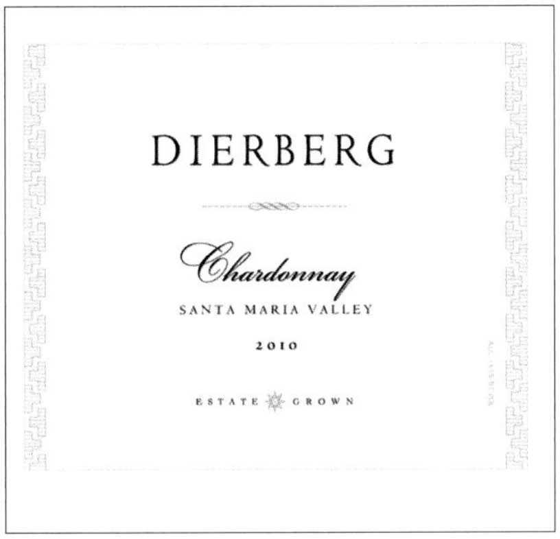
DIERBERG
Chardonnay
SANTA MARIA VALLEY
2010
ESTATE GROWN

10

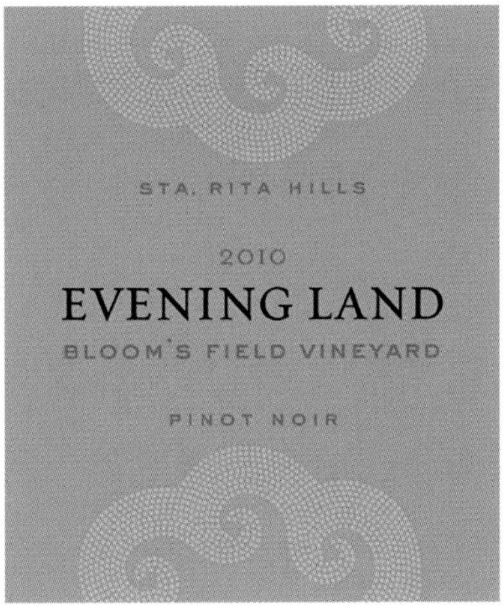
STA. RITA HILLS
2010
EVENING LAND
BLOOM'S FIELD VINEYARD
PINOT NOIR

11

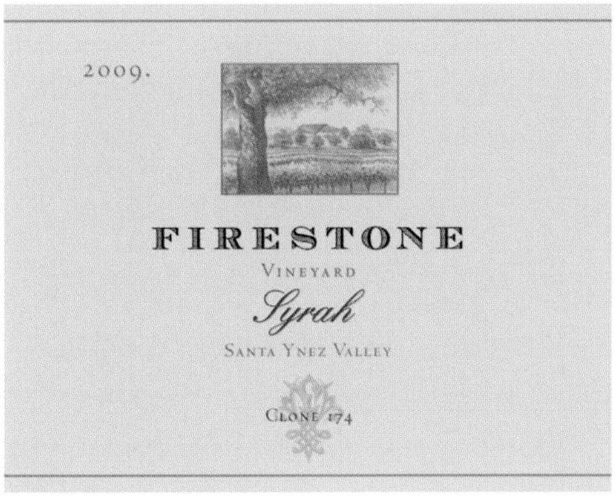
2009.
FIRESTONE
VINEYARD
Syrah
SANTA YNEZ VALLEY
CLONE 174

13

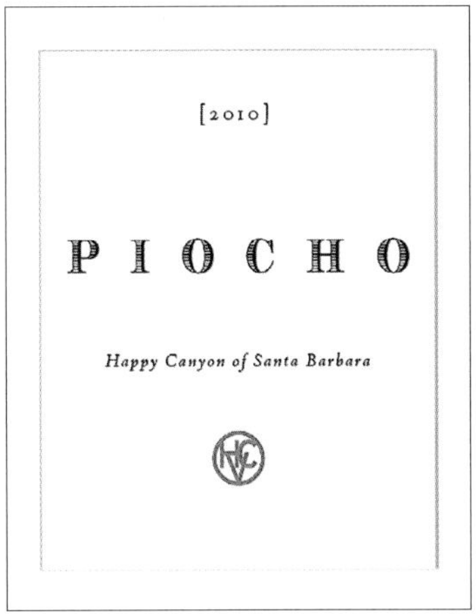
[2010]
PIOCHO
Happy Canyon of Santa Barbara

18

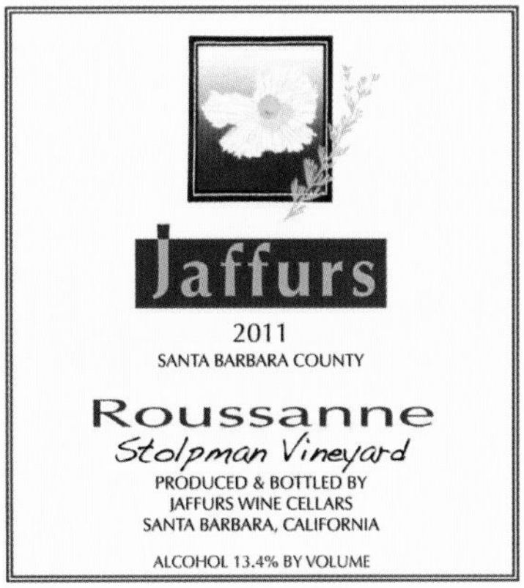
Jaffurs
2011
SANTA BARBARA COUNTY
Roussanne
Stolpman Vineyard
PRODUCED & BOTTLED BY
JAFFURS WINE CELLARS
SANTA BARBARA, CALIFORNIA
ALCOHOL 13.4% BY VOLUME

19

FESS PARKER WINERY AND VINEYARD

6200 Foxen Canyon Road, Los Olivos, CA 93441
(805) 688-1545, www.fessparkerwines.com

Better known as Daniel Boone or Davy Crockett, actor Fess Parker bought a 714-acre ranch in the Santa Ynez Valley in 1987. He purchased the Grand Hotel in Los Olivos in 1998 and converted the twenty-one-room Victorian-style inn to what now is Fess Parker's Wine Country Inn and Spa. He died in 2010, but his son Eli still directs winemaking and vineyard operations, and his daughter Ashley serves as vice president of marketing and sales. The clean, crisp Fess Parker Winery and Vineyard Santa Barbara County Riesling has notes of fresh fruit and jammy flavors on the palate, and the Fess Parker Winery and Vineyard Bien Nacido Pinot Noir has aromas of fresh red cherries, dried black cherries, and peppermint and features flavors of sweet fruit. 12

FIRESTONE VINEYARDS

5017 Zaca Station Road, Los Olivos, CA 93441
(805) 688-3940, www.firestonewine.com

Leonard Firestone and son Brooks started Firestone Vineyards in 1972 and made wine for more than 35 years before they sold their holdings to Santa Barbara vintner Bill Foley in order to concentrate on their Curtis Winery and eponymous brewery. Foley and his team oversee all aspects of the production of fine wines from Chardonnay, Merlot, Cabernet Sauvignon, Syrah, and Sauvignon Blanc grapes grown on the estate's 400 acres. The fruit-forward Firestone Vineyards Ambassador Meritage has aromas of black currant, red plum, and black raspberry with top notes of Christmas baking spice, and the Firestone Vineyard Clone 174 Syrah tastes of ripe black fruits with nuances of smoked meat and vanilla. 13

FLYING GOAT CELLARS

1520 East Chestnut Court, Unit A, Lompoc, CA 93436
(805) 736-9032, www.flyinggoatcellars.com

Winemaker Norm Yost and wife, Kate Griffith, wanted a fun name for their serious wines, taking it from their acrobatic pygmy pets, Never and Epernay. Known for their Pinot Gris, Pinot Noir, and sparkling wines, the couple sources grapes from a variety of vineyards, including Bien Nacido, Clos Pepe, Dierberg, Rancho Santa Rosa, Rio Vista, Salisbury, Solomon Hills, and Sierra Madre. The Flying Goat Cellars Pinot Gris proffers flavors of candied orange peel, pineapple upside-down cake, and baking spices. The Goat Bubbles Blanc de Blancs Sierra Madre Vineyard has aromas of citrus and freshly baked brioche. 14

FOLEY ESTATES VINEYARD & WINERY

6121 East Highway 246, Lompoc, CA 93436
(805) 737-6222, www.foleywines.com

Bill Foley realized his dream to produce cool-climate wines from Pinot Noir and Chardonnay grapes grown in Santa Barbara County when he established Foley Estates Vineyard & Winery. In 1998 he planted 230 acres of Pinot Noir, Chardonnay, and Syrah into fifty-nine blocks on Rancho Santa Rosa. Leslie Mead Renaud is the winemaker, assisted by Lorna Kreutz Duggan. The Foley Estates Vineyard & Winery Two Sisters Courtney's Vineyard Sta. Rita Hills Chardonnay offers aromas of toasted almonds, citrus, and a touch of cinnamon. Vibrant and bright in the mouth, the Foley Estates Vineyard & Winery JA Ranch Pinot Noir offers flavors of blueberries, red raspberries, and red cherries. 15

FOXEN WINERY AND VINEYARDS

7600 Foxen Canyon Road, Santa Maria, CA 93454
(805) 937-4251, www.foxenvineyard.com

Dick Doré and Bill Wathen have been making wine together since 1985, when the duo started Foxen, named for Dick's great-great-grandfather William Benjamin Foxen, who owned 9,000 acres in what is now Foxen Canyon. Today the family owns the 2,000-acre Tinaquaic Ranch on which Foxen Winery operates. The Foxen Winery and Vineyard Cuvée Jeanne Marie Williamson Doré Vineyard Santa Ynez Valley has aromas and flavors of fresh red raspberry and cherry jam. 16

GAINEY VINEYARD

3950 East Highway 246, Santa Ynez, CA 93460
(805) 688-0558, www.gaineyvineyard.com

The 100-acre Gainey Vineyard sits on the 1,800-acre Gainey Home Ranch in Santa Ynez Valley, and the rest of the land fosters Arabian horses, cattle, and organically grown fruits and vegetables. The family also owns two other vineyards, Rancho Esperanza and Evan's Ranch, in the Sta. Rita Hills AVA. Dan J. Gainey and son, Dan H., planted 50 acres of vines in 1983 and opened their winery in 1984. Today Gainey Vineyard produces 18,000 cases of wine per year. The full-bodied Gainey Vineyard Limited Selection Riesling has aromas of green apple and dried apricot, and the Gainey Vineyard Limited Selection Merlot, with aromas of black plum, cassis, and bittersweet chocolate, is round in the mouth with pronounced fruit flavors.

GYPSY CANYON

2753 Gypsy Canyon Drive, Lompoc, CA 93436
(805) 737-0204, www.gypsycanyon.com

Deborah Hall and husband, Bill, bought a ramshackle farmhouse on an old lima bean farm in Santa Barbara as their early retirement home. While clearing the property, they discovered gnarled grapevines that had belonged to Marcelina Felix Dominguez, reportedly the first female grape grower in California. Bill died shortly after their purchase, and Deborah plunged headfirst into restoring the vineyards and a new career as a winemaker. In addition to using her Mission grapes to make small-batch handcrafted Angelica, a traditional style of fortified dessert wine, Deborah produces Pinot Noir and offers a limited number of special-order 300- to 400-year-old collectors bottles each year. Her vineyards are believed to be the oldest extant in Santa Barbara County, and she makes Gypsy Canyon Angelica using a late-nineteenth-century formula. The Gypsy Canyon Ancient Vine Angelica NV offers mouth-pleasing flavors of dried fig, apricots, and toasted almond. 17

HAPPY CANYON VINEYARD

813 Anacapa Street, Santa Barbara, CA 93101
(805) 966-9463, www.happycanyonvineyard.com

According to owner Thomas Barrack, "*piocho*" means "where the two rivers meet and go to heaven" in the indigenous Chumash language. Barrack bought Piocho Ranch in 1992 partly for his love of vineyards and partly for his love of polo. The land has two regulation-sized polo fields, and late summer brings polo teams from around the world. Doug Margerum directs winemaking. The fruit-forward but restrained Happy Canyon Vineyard Ten Goal offers aromas of black fruits and black licorice, and the Happy Canyon Vineyards Piocho Santa Ynez Valley has flavors of black raspberries, black currant, and black cherries. 18

HARTLEY OSTINI HITCHING POST WINES

P.O. Box 2009, 406 East Highway 246, Buellton, CA 93427
(805) 688-0676, www.hitchingpostwines.com

In the movie *Sideways*, protagonist Miles falls hopelessly in love with waitress Maya at the Hitching Post restaurant in Buellton. There's no waitress named Maya, but Buellton has a restaurant called the Hitching Post, owned by larger-than-life chef Frank Ostini. He and his good friend fisherman Gray Hartley started making homemade wine in 1979 before moving their operation to local wineries, including Au Bon Climat and Qupé. Hartley Ostini Hitching Post Wines are currently made at the Terravant Winery, just a short distance from the restaurant. Clean-finishing Hartley Ostini Hitching Post Pinks Dry Rosé has aromas of strawberries and cream, crushed red raspberry, and citrus. The Hartley Ostini Hitching Post Highliner Pinot Noir offers flavors of red raspberries, red cherries, and a touch of Christmas baking spices.

JAFFURS WINE CELLARS

819 E. Montecito Street, Santa Barbara, CA 93103
(805) 962-7003, www.jaffurswine.com

Craig Jaffurs produced his first wine in 1994, and today he releases around 3,500 cases of small-lot wines. Known in Santa Barbara for his Rhône variety wines, Jaffurs sources Syrah, Grenache, Petite Sirah, Viognier, and Roussanne grapes from growers in Santa Ynez, Santa Rita, Los Alamos, and Santa Maria. The crisp and clean Jaffurs Wine Cellars Stolpman Vineyard Santa Barbara County Roussanne has intoxicating aromas of lemon zest, lime juice, and white pepper. The fruit-forward Jaffurs Wine Cellars Santa Barbara County Syrah offers big flavors of cassis, black raspberry conserves, and dried black cherries; drink it now, or store it for a few years. (19)

LARNER VINEYARD

955 Ballard Canyon Road, Solvang, CA 93463
(805) 350-1435, www.larnervineyard.com

Founded by Stevan and Christine Larner in 1997, Larner Vineyard consists of 34 acres of vines—including Grenache, Mourvèdre, Syrah, and Viognier—on 134 acres of land. Make sure to visit the compact tasting room on Grand Avenue in Los Olivos. The fruit-forward Larner Vineyard Estate Grown Santa Ynez Valley Syrah offers aromas and flavors of cassis, black plum, and black raspberry. (20)

LINCOURT

1711 Alamo Pintado Road, Solvang, CA 93464
(805) 688-8554, www.lincourtwines.com

Named for Bill Foley's daughters Lindsay and Courtney, Lincourt sources grapes from its own estate vineyards in Santa Barbara County: Rancho Las Hermanas and Rancho Santa Rosa in the Sta. Rita Hills for Chardonnay, Pinot Noir, and Syrah; Santa Ynez's Alamo Pintado for Sauvignon Blanc; and La Cuesta for Cabernet and Merlot. The fruit-forward Lincourt Carol Ann Chardonnay has aromas of Granny Smith apples, citrus, and a touch of cinnamon in the mouth while the Lincourt Bouchaine Estate Block 43 Pinot Noir offers a nose of cherry cola, black currants, and dried black cherries. (21)

LONGORIA WINES

2935 Grand Avenue, Los Olivos, CA 93441
(805) 688-0305, www.longoriawine.com

Rick Longoria was winemaker for J. Carey Cellars. With a loan from his father he started his own business in 1982, producing 500 cases of Chardonnay and Pinot Noir from vineyards in the Santa Maria Valley. He worked as winemaker for Gainey Vineyards in 1985, and in 1998 he moved his equipment into a 5,400-square-foot building in what has since become the Lompoc Wine Ghetto. He continues to produce small-lot handcrafted wines in annual productions of only 3,000 cases. The Longoria Sta. Rita Hills Fe Ciega Vineyard Pinot Noir has aromas of red cherries and dried Mediterranean herbs. The Longoria Santa Ynez Valley Clover Creek Vineyard Tempranillo features flavors of red raspberries and red cherries with black peppercorns in the bouquet. 22

MARGERUM WINE COMPANY

813 Anacapa Street, Santa Barbara, CA 93003
(805) 845-8435, www.margerumwinecompany.com

Doug Margerum began his food and wine career in 1981 when his family bought the Wine Cask, a local wine store, and expanded it first to a bistro and then into a restaurant. He started his wine company in 2001 and now produces 6,000 cases of wine annually under four labels: Sybarite, Über, M5, and Klickitat. The Margerum Wine Company M5 Santa Barbara County offers aromas of black licorice and black plum, and the refreshing and pleasant Margerum Wine Company Klickitat Pinot Gris offers a touch of residual sugar on the finish, a perfect match for spicy cuisine. 23

MELVILLE WINERY

5185 Highway 246, Lompoc, CA 93436
(805) 735-7030, www.melvillewinery.com

Ron Melville's passion for the wines of Burgundy brought him to Lompoc, and in 1996 he planted four different clones of Chardonnay and fourteen different clones of Pinot Noir on 82 acres of land. He subsequently purchased an additional 100 acres in Cat Canyon, north of Los Alamos in Santa Barbara County. Sons Brent and Chad take part in the family business, and Greg Brewer directs winemaking. With aromas of white peach, Cavaillon melon, and citrus, the Melville Winery Sta. Rita Hills Estate Chardonnay has bright fruit flavors with a touch of creaminess. The Melville Winery Block M Estate Pinot Noir offers aromas of candied orange peel, red fruits, and cherry cola. 24

OJAI VINEYARD

109 South Montgomery Street, Ojai, CA 93023
(805) 798-3947, www.ojaivineyard.com

Adam Tolmach studied enology and viticulture at UC Davis, graduating in 1976. He started his career at Zaca Mesa Winery and partnered with coworker Jim Clendenen in 1982 to start Au Bon Climat. In 1991 the pair separated; Clendenen bought Tolmach's interest in the company, and Tolmach focused his efforts on his Ojai vineyards. Today Tolmach works closely with his wife, Helen, and they produce approximately 6,500 cases of wine per year. The Ojai Vineyards Bien Nacido Vineyard Chardonnay proffers aromas of citrus, white flowers, and white stone fruits. Big and fruit-forward, the Ojai Vineyard Kick On Pinot Noir offers aromas and flavors of ripe black cherry. 25

PALMINA

1520 East Chestnut Court, Lompoc, CA 93436
(805) 735-2030, www.palminawines.com

Steve Clifton honored his good friend and surrogate grandmother, Palmina, by naming his winery in her memory. His whites include Arneis, Malvasia Bianca, Pinot Grigio, Tocai Friulano, and Traminer, and his reds include Barbera and Nebbiolo. The food-friendly and full-bodied Palmina Santa Barbara County Barbera has aromas of black raspberries, cassis, and orange zest. The light and crisp Palmina Santa Barbara County Malvasia Bianca, with flavors of citrus and green olives, pairs well with oysters and shellfish. 26

20

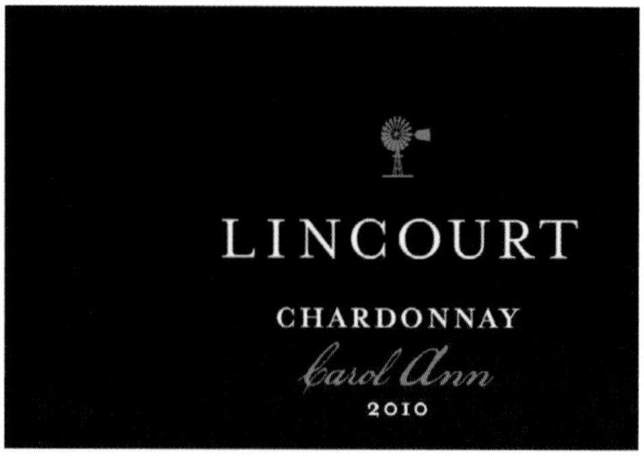

21

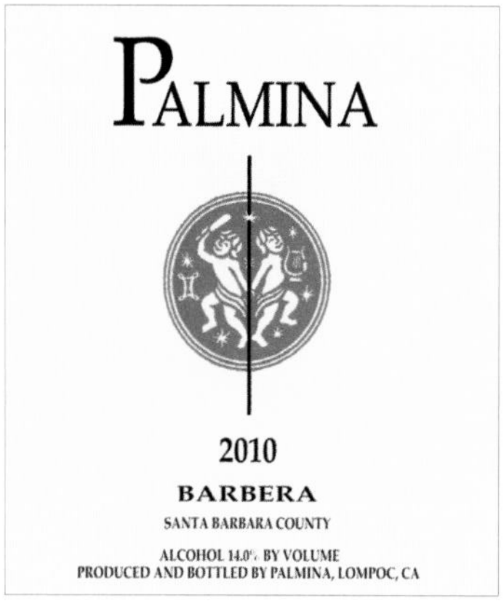

26

27

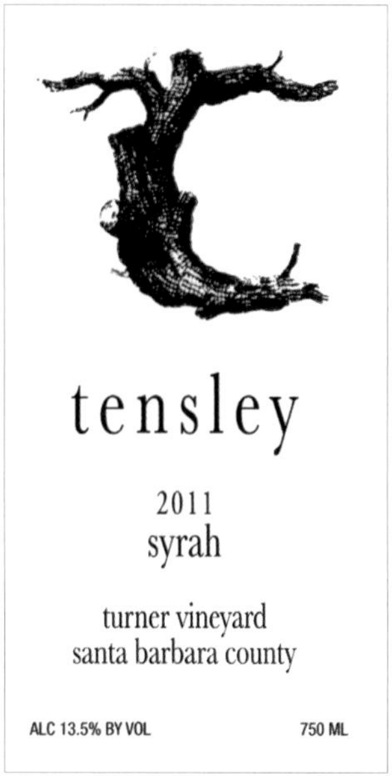

31

32

22

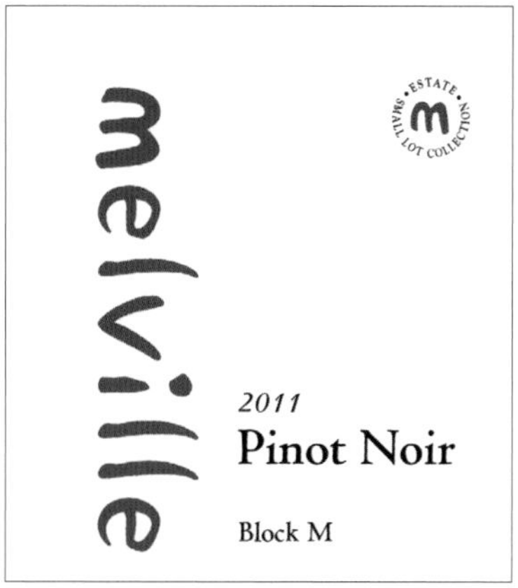

24

25

28

30

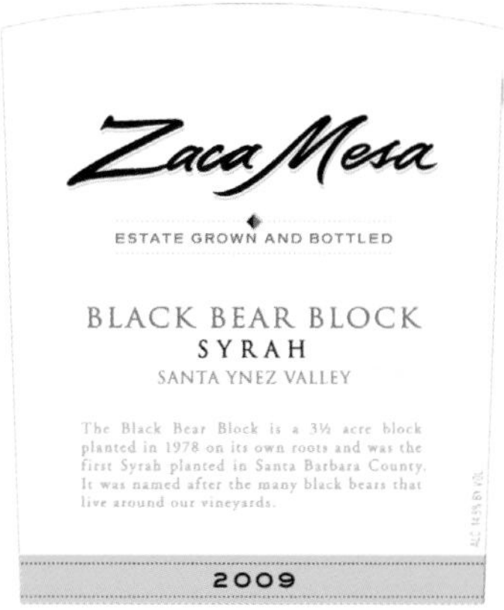

33

QUPÉ WINE CELLARS

2963 Grand Avenue, Los Olivos, CA 93441
(805) 686-4200, www.qupe.com

Bob Lindquist named his winery for the indigenous Chumash word for "poppy," California's state flower. Lindquist began his wine career at Zaca Mesa Winery, trading his services for the use of the winery's equipment. His first commercial release was 900 cases of Chardonnay, Syrah, and Pinot Noir Rosé in 1982. In 1989 he partnered with Jim Clendenen, and they produced wine in conjunction with Bien Nacido Vineyards. In 2013 investor Charles Banks purchased a majority share in Qupé, with Lindquist remaining as winemaker and partner. The full-bodied Qupé Wine Cellars Sawyer Lindquist Vineyard Viognier has aromas of Anjou pears, white stone fruits, and citrus. The Qupé Wine Cellars Edna Valley Sawyer Lindquist Vineyard Grenache has aromas of freshly picked red cherry and dried Mediterranean herbs and is fruity on the palate. 27

SANFORD WINERY AND VINEYARDS

5010 Santa Rosa Road, Lompoc, CA 93436
(800) 426-9463, www.sanfordwinery.com

Founded in 1971, Sanford Winery and Vineyards first planted Pinot Noir vines in its Sanford & Benedict Vineyard. Today Anthony Terlato and his sons are the majority owners. With the work of winemaker Steve Fennel, Sanford continues to produce cool-climate Pinot Noirs and Chardonnays. The Sanford Winery Sta. Rita Hills Pinot Noir offers flavors of red raspberries and dark cherries, and the Sanford Winery Sanford & Benedict Vineyard Pinot Noir has notes of red raspberry, Chinese five-spice powder, and dried cherry in the bouquet. 28

SEA SMOKE CELLARS

No visitor facilities
(805) 737-1600, www.seasmokecellars.com

In 1999 Bob Davids acquired the land that became Sea Smoke Cellars. His belief in *terroir* is the reason that Sea Smoke makes wine only from estate fruit grown in their vineyard in the Sta. Rita Hills AVA. Sea Smoke is a small operation: Only six people work here to produce these wines. The full-bodied Sea Smoke Chardonnay has flavors of Anjou pear and lemon curd. The Sea Smoke Southing Pinot Noir offers aromas of cherry cola and red raspberries and is complex in the mouth. Hold it for a few years to develop the flavors. 29

SINE QUA NON

No visitor facilities. P.O. Box 1048, Oak View, CA 93022
(805) 640-8901, www.sinequanon.com

What started as a hobby in 1994 for Manfred and Elaine Krankl soon became their dream. Latin for "without which [there's] nothing," the winery sources Rhône variety grapes—including Syrah, Grenache, Mourvèdre, Roussanne, and Viognier—from the couple's four estate vineyards: Eleven Confessions, Cumulus, Third Twin, and Molly Aida. Fruit-forward yet restrained, the Sine Qua Non Five Shooter Grenache offers aromas of black and red fruits and a touch of spice in the enticing palate.

STOLPMAN VINEYARDS

2434 Alamo Pintado Avenue, Los Olivos, CA 93441
(805) 688-0400, www.stolpmanvineyards.com

Tom and Marilyn Stolpman founded their vineyards in 1990, sold grapes for years, and began making their own wine in 1997. Ruben Solorzano handles vineyard management, and Sashi Moorman joined as winemaker in 2001. The Stolpman

Vineyards L'Avion has a strong presence of white stone fruits with a top note of peppermint. The Stolpman Vineyards Syrah offers ripe fruit flavors and a balanced sweet tannic finish. (30)

TANTARA WINERY

2330 Westgate Road, Santa Maria, CA 93456
(805) 938-5051, www.tantarawines.com

Named for owner Bill Cate's horse, Tantara has been producing wine since 1997 from grapes sourced from Solomon Hills, Sanford & Benedict, Bien Nacido, Silacci, Pisoni, Tondre, and Brousseau, among other vineyards. The full-bodied Tantara Winery Bien Nacido Vineyard Chardonnay offers aromas of caramelized pineapple and white stone fruits, and the Tantara Winery Bien Nacido Adobe Pinot Noir has balanced acidity and flavors of red fruits accented by a fine dusting of cocoa powder.

TENSLEY WINES

2900 Grand Avenue, Los Olivos, CA 93441
(805) 688-6761, www.tensleywines.com

Joey Tensley began his winemaking career as a "cellar rat" at Fess Parker Winery in 1993, and in 1998 he launched his own label while maintaining his position as assistant winemaker at Beckmen Vineyards. Today he produces more than 3,000 cases per year of vineyard-designated Syrah while maintaining his artisanal approach to winemaking. The Tensley Winery Camp 4 Vineyard Blanc has aromas of Granny Smith apples and Anjou pears and a smooth, round mouthfeel. The Tensley Winery Turner Vineyard Syrah has flavors of blueberry and black plum. Drink it now, or keep it for 10 years. (31)

TRANSCENDENCE WINES

313 N. F Street, Lompoc, CA 93436
(805) 689-5258, www.transcendwines.com

Kenneth "Joey" Gummere has been making wine in Santa Barbara County since 1997. He and wife, Sarah, make cool-climate, small-production wine from Syrah, Pinot Noir, and Chardonnay grapes and take part in several nonprofit organizations, including Hope through Opportunity, Fallbrook Healthcare Foundation, and Project Transcend. The Transcendence Zotovich Vineyard Chardonnay, with aromas of tropical fruits, Anjou pear, and lemon blossoms, is full in the mouth, while the Transcendence Lafond Vineyard Pinot Noir offers notes of dried black cherry in the bouquet. (32)

ZACA MESA WINERY & VINEYARDS

6905 Foxen Canyon Road, Los Olivos, CA 93441
(805) 688-9339, www.zacamesa.com

Started in 1973 by a group of friends, Zaca Mesa Winery & Vineyards takes credit for first planting Syrah in Santa Barbara County. The team also planted Grenache, Mourvèdre, Viognier, and Roussanne, allowing the winemakers to create Rhône-style blends. The Zaca Mesa Estate Black Bear Block Santa Ynez Valley Syrah has elegant, mouth-filling flavors of dark fruits, and the fruit-forward Zaca Mesa Z has delightful aromas of black raspberry and fresh-picked blueberries with prominent flavors of dark fruits. (33)

ELEVEN

SOUTHERN CALIFORNIA AND THE SOUTH COAST AVA

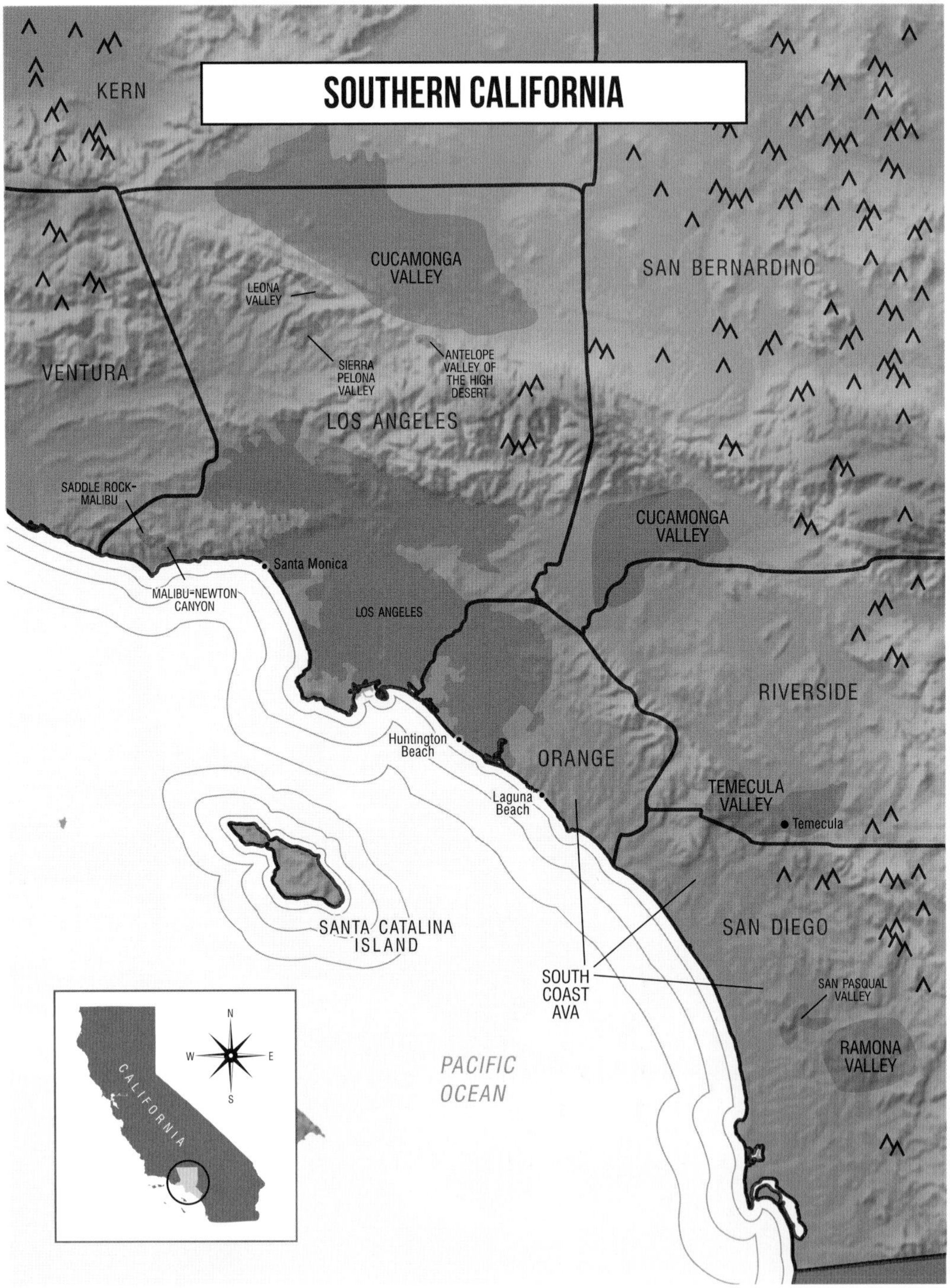
SOUTHERN CALIFORNIA
KERN
VENTURA
CUCAMONGA VALLEY
LEONA VALLEY
SIERRA PELONA VALLEY
ANTELOPE VALLEY OF THE HIGH DESERT
LOS ANGELES
SAN BERNARDINO
SADDLE ROCK-MALIBU
MALIBU-NEWTON CANYON
Santa Monica
LOS ANGELES
CUCAMONGA VALLEY
RIVERSIDE
Huntington Beach
ORANGE
Laguna Beach
TEMECULA VALLEY
Temecula
SANTA CATALINA ISLAND
SAN DIEGO
SOUTH COAST AVA
SAN PASQUAL VALLEY
RAMONA VALLEY
PACIFIC OCEAN
CALIFORNIA
N
W
E
S

You might not think of wine when considering the southern part of the state, but grape growing and winemaking in California started here. Father Junípero Serra planted California's first successful vineyard for winemaking in 1779 near modern-day San Diego at Mission Basilica San Diego de Alcalá. A rudimentary winery to process the exclusively Mission grapes was built on the site a year later.

In 1833, Jean-Louis Vignes imported Cabernet Sauvignon and Sauvignon Blanc cuttings from his native Bordeaux. Vignes may have been the first in California to age his wine in wood, using barrels made of lumber forested from his San Bernardino Mountains property. Ten years later, he was shipping wine to Santa Barbara, Monterey, and San Francisco, and by 1850 he was producing more than 150,000 bottles of wine each year.

The Antelope Valley of the High Desert AVA covers 665 square miles and has fourteen growers and six wineries. Two smaller AVAs, Leona Valley and Sierra Pelona Valley, are nearby. To the south, on the coast, lie two Malibu AVAs: Malibu-Newton Canyon and Saddle Rock-Malibu, both within the Malibu Coast AVA, recently approved by the TTB. The Malibu-Newton Canyon AVA owes its existence to real estate and hotel mogul George Rosenthal; the majority of the AVA's vineyards grow on his private estate. Because of regulations limiting industry within municipal limits, however, grapes grown in Malibu generally are vinified elsewhere.

Cucamonga Valley, about 15 miles from San Bernardino, has a history of grape growing that began in 1838, and at one time the valley's annual grape production exceeded that of Napa and Sonoma counties combined. But Cucamonga Valley grape growing came to an abrupt halt with Prohibition in 1920. Grapes are still grown today in this hot, dry valley with alluvial soils, but urban sprawl from Los Angeles and its environs has encroached on vineyard land. The 109,400-acre Cucamonga Valley AVA, established in 1985, has about 1,000 acres of vineyards, primarily Bordeaux and Rhône varieties, and some of the state's finest old-vine Zinfandel vineyards, production of which generally is sold to winemakers elsewhere in the state.

The South Coast AVA encompasses 115,200 acres and several other AVAs within its limits: Temecula Valley, Ramona Valley, and San Pasqual Valley. The most densely planted and best known of these is Temecula Valley, its first commercial vineyard established in 1968. The Temecula AVA achieved recognition in 1984 and became the Temecula Valley AVA in 2004. Named after the native Temecula people, the word roughly means translates as "the place where the sun breaks through the mist," and that meteorological occurrence over the valley's sedimentary soils, filled with decomposed granite, makes the area perfect for cultivating grapes. The well-drained soil and warm year-round temperatures also provide an ideal environment for Pierce's disease, caused by the *Xylella fastidiosa* bacterium and spread by the glassy-winged sharpshooter. Over the last 15 years, the state has made a concerted effort to eradicate the disease.

Average vineyard elevation in the AVA is around 1,500 feet, which, when combined with the cold Pacific air infiltrating the valley, helps cool the grapes and keep finished wine from tasting cooked or stewed. Large day-night temperature swings help retain acidity in the grapes. The Temecula Valley Winegrowers Association has thirty-five member wineries, and the AVA produces several different styles of wine, including Zinfandel, Cabernet Sauvignon, and Bordeaux-style blends, both white and red Rhône Valley blends, Italian varieties such as Sangiovese and Nebbiolo, and white wines such as Chardonnay and Sauvignon Blanc.

THE WINERIES

BAILY VINEYARD & WINERY

33440 La Serena Way, Temecula, CA 92591
(951) 676-9463, www.bailywinery.com

Phil and Carol Baily started growing grapes more than 25 years ago, making this one of Temecula's oldest wineries. Visitors can dine at the onsite restaurant or try their other locations, Baily's Fine Dining and Front Street Bar and Grill, in the town center. The Baily Vineyard & Winery Estate Bottled Meritage offers rich flavors of fresh cherry and black raspberry along with notes of freshly ground white pepper and brown spices. ❶

CALLAWAY VINEYARD & WINERY

32720 Rancho California Road, Temecula, CA 92591
(951) 676-4001, www.callawaywinery.com

Golf icon Ely Reeves Callaway founded Callaway Winery & Winery more than 40 years ago, and the Hiram Walker Company and then Allied Domecq owned it until 2005. Today the Lin family of San Diego owns it, and the wines are available only at the winery. The Callaway Vineyard & Winery Winemaker's Reserve Chardonnay has flavors of honeydew melon, buttered toast, and guava, while the Callaway Vineyard & Winery Winemaker's Reserve Calliope Red has abundant red and black fruits with nuances of oregano, black pepper, and cremini mushrooms. ❷

DOFFO VINEYARDS

36083 Summitville Street, Temecula, CA 92592
(951) 676-6989, www.doffowines.com

The Doffo family's hearty and heartfelt Argentine-Italian hospitality welcomes visitors again and again. Built on the site of a historic schoolhouse, the winery encompasses 15 acres of planted vines. Motorcycle enthusiasts will love the family's private collection of more than 100 vintage and racing motorcycles at its onsite museum, MotoDoffo. The Doffo Vineyards Reserve Syrah has flavors of dark plum, black cherry, tart cherry, and mocha with a refreshing fruit splash in the finish.

FALKNER WINERY

40620 Calle Contento, Temecula, CA 92591
(951) 676-8231, www.falknerwinery.com

Ray and Loretta Falkner left jobs in technology and retail to open Falkner Winery in 2000. The winery sits atop a 1,500-foot hill, and visitors can enjoy lunch at their Pinnacle restaurant. Steve Hagata heads winemaking. The Falkner Winery Estate Grown Viognier offers flavors of white peach and Cavaillon melon, and the Falkner Winery Special Selection Amante has flavors of cherry cola, mocha, and espresso. ❸

HART WINERY

41300 Avenida Biona, Temecula, CA 92591
(951) 676-6300, www.hartfamilywinery.com

Joe and Nancy Hart planted their first Cabernet Sauvignon, Cabernet Franc, Merlot, Sauvignon Blanc, Syrah, and Viognier vines in 1974 and in 1980 built their winery and produced their first wines. Today, with son Jim, they produce about 5,000 cases annually. The Hart Family Winery Sangiovese has black cherry and dark plum flavors and a touch of spice in the finish. Crisp and refreshing, the Hart Family Winery Roussanne offers notes of citrus blossom and grapefruit. ❹

LEONESS CELLARS

38311 De Portola Road, Temecula, CA 92592
(951) 302-7601, www.leonesscellars.com

Both Gary Winder and Mike Rennie had been involved in Temecula Valley agriculture for years, so the decision to open Leoness Cellars in 2003 came naturally. They produce wine from Cabernet Sauvignon, Cinsault, Grenache, Merlot, Cabernet Franc, Syrah, Chardonnay, Muscat Canelli, and Viognier varieties. The Leoness Cellars Curry Vineyard Syrah has flavors of licorice root and black plum and a splash of bright fruit that lingers on the palate. The Leoness Cellars Mélange de Rêves has flavors of sweet black fruits, dried black cherry, fennel, and Mission fig. 5

MIRAMONTE WINERY

33410 Rancho California Road, Temecula, CA 92591
(951) 506-5500, www.miramontewinery.com

In 2000, Cane Vanderhoof founded Miramonte, which has been entertaining regulars with live music every Friday and Saturday night since 2001. Vanderhoof bought a neighboring piece of property in 2008 and sources grapes from 44 acres of vineyards in Temecula that he owns, manages, or maintains long-standing contracts with. The Miramonte Winery Tempranillo has flavors of cranberry, boysenberry, smoked meats, and grilled Portobello mushrooms. Smooth and sensual, the Miramonte Winery Opulente offers flavors of cherry and mint. 6

MONTE DE ORO

35820 Rancho California Road, Temecula, CA 92591
(951) 491-6551, www.montedeoro.com

Sixty-eight family owners from the United States, the United Kingdom, and South Africa came together in 2002 and started OGB ("One Great Blend"). Their guiding principle: "Vines, Wine, and People." Monte de Oro's first vineyard, Vista del Monte, was planted that year with 18 acres of Cabernet Sauvignon and Syrah. Their second vineyards, DePortola and Galway, planted in 2003, consist of 18 acres and 23 acres respectively and are planted with Cabernet Franc, Viognier, Zinfandel, Merlot, Pinot Gris, Sauvignon Blanc, Muscat Canelli, and Chardonnay. Today the group owns 72 acres and produces wine only from its estate-sourced grapes. The Monte De Oro Estate Grown Nostimo has pure grapefruit and citrus flavors with a crisp, clean, and refreshing finish, ideal as an aperitif or paired with seafood. The Monte De Oro Vista Del Monte Estate Grown Syrah is smooth and silky, with a burst of fruit flavors. 7

MORAGA VINEYARDS

650 North Sepulveda Boulevard, Los Angeles, CA 90049
(310) 471-8560, www.moragavineyards.com

In 1959, Tom Jones, former Northrop Grumman CEO, and wife, Ruth, purchased and developed the horse ranch once owned by Hollywood director Victor Fleming and the couple lived on the estate for many years. In 2013, media mogul Rupert Murdoch bought the property, which includes seven-plus acres of vines, including Cabernet Sauvignon, Merlot, Sauvignon Blanc, Petit Verdot, and Cabernet Franc. Moraga was the first commercial winery to become bonded in Los Angeles after the repeal of Prohibition. Winemaker Tony Soter began working here in 1987 and later brought in Scott Rich. The Moraga Estate White is fresh and lively in the mouth with persistent flavors of tropical fruits, while the Moraga Estate Red has aromas and flavors of black fruits.

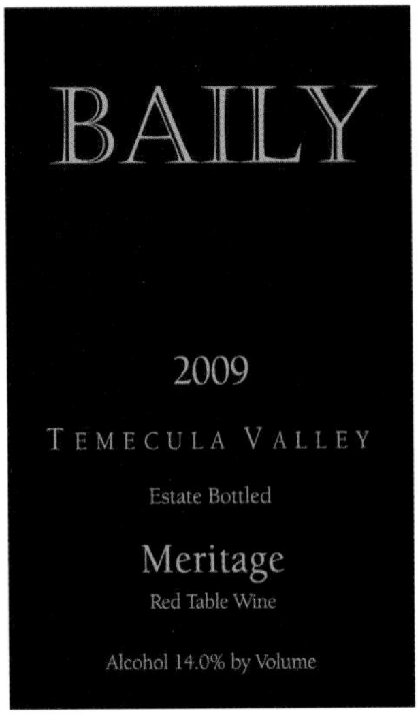
BAILY
2009
TEMECULA VALLEY
Estate Bottled
Meritage
Red Table Wine
Alcohol 14.0% by Volume

1

CALLAWAY
VINEYARD & WINERY
"Where the sun shines through the mist"
2009
Winemaker's Reserve
CALLIOPE RED
TEMECULA VALLEY
BOTTLE # OF 6200
ALC. 14.8% BY VOL.

2

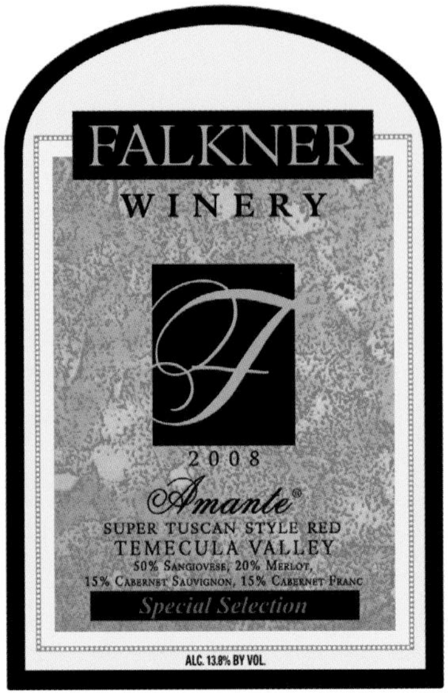
FALKNER
WINERY
F
2008
Amante®
SUPER TUSCAN STYLE RED
TEMECULA VALLEY
50% SANGIOVESE, 20% MERLOT,
15% CABERNET SAUVIGNON, 15% CABERNET FRANC
Special Selection
ALC. 13.8% BY VOL.

3

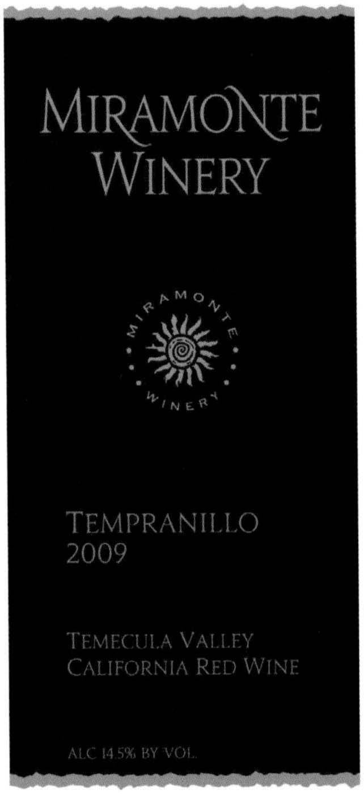
MIRAMONTE
WINERY
MIRAMONTE
WINERY
TEMPRANILLO
2009
TEMECULA VALLEY
CALIFORNIA RED WINE
ALC 14.5% BY VOL.

6

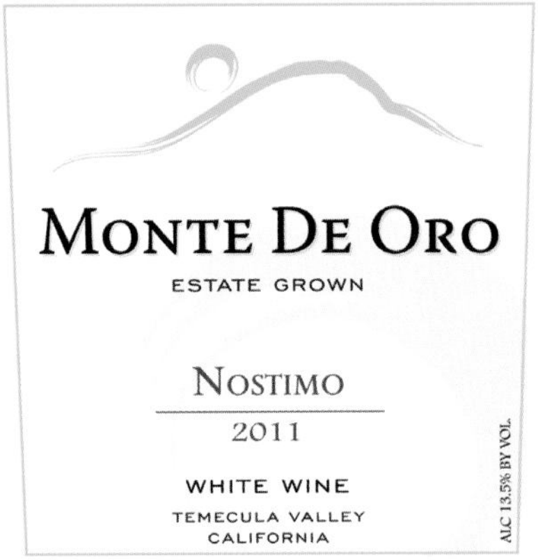
MONTE DE ORO
ESTATE GROWN
NOSTIMO
2011
WHITE WINE
TEMECULA VALLEY
CALIFORNIA
ALC 13.5% BY VOL.

7

Robert Renzoni
VINEYARDS
2011
barile
CHARDONNAY
TEMECULA VALLEY
ALC. 13.8% BY VOL.

9

LIMITED RELEASE
HART
ESTATE GROWN
Roussanne
2011
TEMECULA VALLEY · HART FAMILY VINEYARD

4

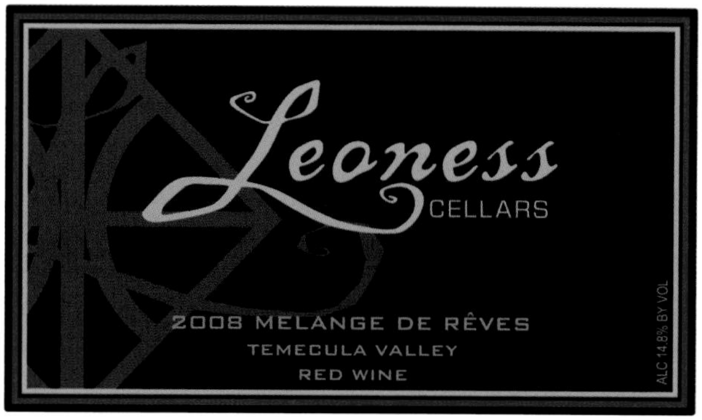
Leoness
CELLARS
2008 MELANGE DE RÊVES
TEMECULA VALLEY
RED WINE
ALC 14.8% BY VOL

5

Rosenthal
The Malibu Estate
2008
Malibu Newton Canyon
Cabernet Franc
ALC. 14.5% BY VOL.

10

Carter Estate
Carter Estate
MALBEC
PRIVATE RESERVE
SOUTH COAST
LOT NO
0001
VINTAGE
2009

11

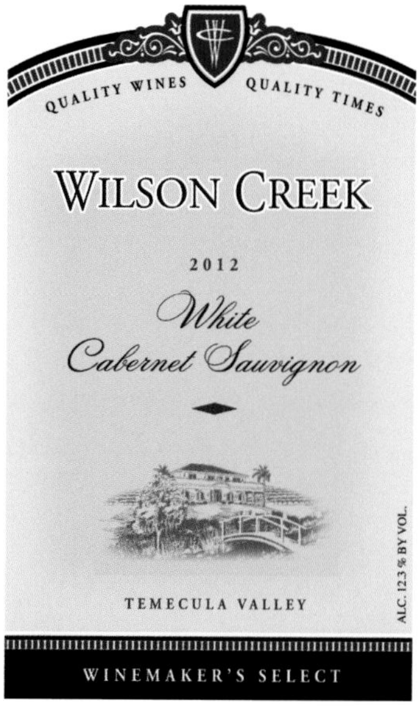
QUALITY WINES
QUALITY TIMES
WILSON CREEK
2012
White
Cabernet Sauvignon
TEMECULA VALLEY
ALC. 12.3 % BY VOL.
WINEMAKER'S SELECT

12

In his own words

GEORGE ROSENTHAL

George Rosenthal began his career as a real estate developer in 1955, and today his company, Raleigh Enterprises, owns fifteen subsidiaries, including the Raleigh Film and Television Studios, the Sunset Marquis hotel in West Hollywood, and the Malibu Estate, where he grows grapes to make his fine wines.

To be able to enjoy a fine glass of wine in either a formal or a very casual setting of an exotic restaurant or on the beaches of Saint-Tropez is a wondrous experience, making any day or meal more complete. After intensive study with a preeminent viticulturist from Napa and studies in conjunction with the University of California, Davis, we determined that the Malibu area could produce fine wines. Although there were many who doubted our ability to create a high-quality wine, our weather studies, soil studies, and temperate climate six miles inland from the Pacific Coast proved to be ideal. In 1987, Rosenthal The Malibu Estate was the first vineyard to be created in the Malibu area. Since our beginning there are now seventeen or eighteen vineyards in Malibu producing wines of various varieties.

We are not trying to emulate any given specific area but are always attempting to produce the finest quality wine from what the *terroir* and climactic conditions provide in Malibu. We will maintain our discipline with respect to alcohol levels and continually maintain a high standard of production quality with very specific and direct attention to the vineyard on a daily basis. This while also working extensively with our winemakers to determine which grapes from each vineyard will produce the best wines without consideration to quantity but maintaining only quality.

Over the years we have seen an increase in the level of alcohol content, which to my mind masks the differential in varieties. I also believe that having high levels of tannin to enhance the long-term quality of the wines in the general marketplace is extremely difficult to be accepted. For the most part, people drink wines within 24 hours of purchase, and therefore it is a balance between creating a wine that is drinkable within a year of its release and still maintaining its ability to lay down for multiple years.

There is no question that there is a romance around cork closures in wine bottles. The very act of removing the cork, the sound of it leaving the bottle, and the psychological aspect of a cork and foil equals fine wines. In truth, I have no objection to a screw cap—we have in fact used them on some of our wines, and I believe that screw caps are coming more into acceptance. There is also the aspect that irrespective of the price one pays for their corks, there is always the opportunity to wind up with bottles "corked." The difficulty is that many people do not know the musty "off " flavor that a cork can create in a fine wine and oftentimes they are put off by a brand simply because they thought that the wine represented something different than that which was actually placed in the bottle and spoiled by the cork. After a bottle of wine is placed in an ice bucket, carafe, etc., the fact that it had a cork in it or was a screw cap becomes rather irrelevant.

The greatest challenge ahead is to create an acceptance of wines from Malibu. We have had reasonable success throughout various states in the country and to some degree internationally. However, it has been extremely difficult to get acknowledgment in locales outside of Southern California as to the quality of our wines. We do, however, maintain a very significant wine club with extremely loyal wine club members. We look forward to the continuation and the development of wines in Malibu as more people become familiar with the ability to enjoy the great viticultural area.

PALUMBO FAMILY VINEYARDS & WINERY

40150 Barksdale Circle, Temecula, CA 92592
(951) 676-7900, www.palumbofamilyvineyards.com

Nick Palumbo's career in food and wine began when he lived in Williamsburg, Brooklyn, and signed up for culinary courses at the New School. He returned to San Diego in 1997, and the next year he bought seven acres of vineyards and began growing grapes. Soon after, he purchased additional vineyards and today produces limited-production wine from grapes grown on his estate's 13 acres. The Palumbo Family Vineyards & Winery Tre Fratelli Meritage offers flavors of cherry cola, cassis, baking spices, and mint. Drink it now or in the next few years. Fruit-driven but restrained, the Palumbo Family Vineyards & Winery Shiraz/Cabernet Sauvignon offers flavors of red raspberry, charcuterie, thyme, and sage. 8

PONTE FAMILY ESTATE WINERY

35053 Rancho California Road, Temecula, CA 92592
(877) 314-9463, www.pontewinery.com

The Ponte family has farmed their vineyards since 1984, and in 2003 they opened their winery, surrounded by 300 acres of gardens and vineyards. Visitors can dine at the signature restaurant and stay at the Ponte Vineyard Inn. The crisp and clean Ponte Family Estate Arneis entices with aromas of Bartlett pear, white stone fruits, and grapefruit. The Ponte Family Estate Moscato has aromas of white peaches, and its pleasant sweetness makes it ideal as a summer aperitif.

ROBERT RENZONI VINEYARDS

37350 De Portola Road, Temecula, CA 92592
(951) 302-8466, www.robertrenzonivineyards.com

Federico Renzoni came to the United States in 1912 and began a wine and cordial business with his brother-in-law, Romeo Battistoni, but Prohibition soon ended their venture. In 1954 Federico's sons Dominic and Romero formed an alliance with Canandaigua Wine Company (now Constellation Brands) to become the first US distributor for Richards Wild Irish Rose. The family business was eventually sold in 1994, but Federico's great-grandson Robert has continued the family's passion for making wine since 2008. The Robert Renzoni Vineyards Barile Chardonnay has aromas of buttered brioche and lemon curd and flavors of canned apricots, toffee, and peach pie. The Robert Renzoni Vineyards Cabernet Sauvignon tastes of cassis and black cherry preserves with a touch of mint and spice. 9

ROSENTHAL MALIBU ESTATE

18741 Pacific Coast Highway, Malibu, CA 90265
(310) 456-1392, www.rosenthalestatewines.com

Los Angeles businessman George Rosenthal planted vines on his 250-acre Malibu estate in 1987 and started making wine soon after. Winemaker Christian Roguenant crafts them in a decidedly French style. The Rosenthal Malibu Estate Viognier has aromas of white stone fruits in the bouquet and flavors of Granny Smith green apple and white peach on the palate, while the Rosenthal Malibu Estate Malibu Newton Canyon Cabernet Franc has flavors of dark plums, black cherries, freshly ground black pepper, and brown spices. 10

SOUTH COAST WINERY RESORT & SPA

34843 Rancho California Road, Temecula, CA 92591
(951) 587-9463, www.wineresort.com

Jim Carter bought 400 acres of land in the Temecula Valley in 1981 and eventually put 38 of them under vine. Today his resort, winery, and spa sit in the middle of those vineyards. The South Coast Winery GVR has flavors of white stone fruits, white peach, and freshly baked brioche, and the South Coast Winery Carter Estate Private Reserve Malbec offers restrained fruit flavors and bold spice. 11

WILSON CREEK WINERY

35960 Rancho California Road, Temecula, CA 92591
(951) 699-9463, www.wilsoncreekwinery.com

Gerry and Rosie Wilson had little winemaking experience, except for attempts at making rhubarb and dandelion wine in their Minnesota basement, when they bought their 20-acre winery in 1996. The Wilson Creek White Cabernet Sauvignon offers flavors of canned peaches in sugar syrup, candied apricots, and toasted pineapple, with residual sugar that pairs well with Asian cuisine. The Wilson Creek Distinction Vineyard Family Reserve Petite Sirah has flavors of dark chocolate, cherry conserves, fresh red cherry, brown spice, and licorice. 12

8

ACKNOWLEDGMENTS

We're lucky to have friends and family who live in the great state of California, and we're even luckier to visit them when winter descends on New York City. We thank those generous souls who opened their cellars, kitchens, and hearts to us and helped make this book possible.

We thank Carlo DeVito for his friendship and support. His guidance and vision shaped this book. We can't thank Diane Abrams enough for her steady grip on the rudder and keeping *Wines of California* on course. We also thank Scott Amerman for his eagle eyes and amazing organizational skills, Brita Vallens for wrangling the artwork, and Christine Heun, Jo Obarowski, Amy Trombat, and Stacey Stambaugh for their stunning art and design skills. We are thrilled and eternally grateful that Theresa Thompson, Marilyn Kretzer, and James Jayo had the vision to re-release this book as a "special deluxe edition." We can't thank them enough for their advocacy and support. We'd also like to recognize the amazing efforts of Sari Lampert and Blanca Oliviery in bringing this book to our readers.

No expression of gratitude would be complete without thanking our manager and friend, Peter Miller, for his undying support, his staunch respect for the written word, and his defense of authors' rights.

We extend heartfelt gratitude to Michael Mondavi and Kevin Zraly for their kind words in our foreword and preface. We have the utmost admiration for these two innovative geniuses in the ever-changing world of wine.

We thank the various state, regional, and county winemaker and grape grower associations that provided us with assistance. Let's start with thanking the statewide California Association of Wine Grape Growers for their generous help and continue our deep appreciation in alphabetical order. We thank Alexander Valley Winegrowers, Amador County Grape Growers Association, Amador Vintners Association, Anderson Valley Winegrowers Association, Calaveras Winegrape Alliance, Carneros Wine Alliance, Central Coast Wine Growers Association, Clarksburg Wine Growers and Vintners Association, El Dorado Wine Grape Growers Association, El Dorado Winery Association, Hospitality de Los Carneros, Humboldt Wine Association, Lake County Winegrape Commission, Lake County Winery Association, Livermore Valley Winegrowers Association, Lodi District Grape Growers Association, Lodi Grower Vintner Alliance, Lodi Winegrape Commission, Madera Vintners Association, Mendocino Winegrowers, Monterey County Vintners and Growers Association, Mount Veeder Appellation Council, Napa Valley Grape Growers, Napa Valley Vintners, Oakville Winegrowers, Paso Robles Wine Country Alliance, Placer County Vintners Association, Placer County Wine and Grape Association, Ramona Vineyard Association, Russian River Valley Winegrowers, Rutherford Dust Society, San Diego County Vintners Association, San Joaquin Valley Winegrowers Association, San Luis Obispo Vintners Association, Santa Barbara County Vintners Association, Santa Cruz Mountains

Winegrowers Association, Santa Maria Valley Wine Country Association, Sierra Grape Growers Association, Sierra Vintners, Silverado Trail Wineries Association, Sonoma County Winegrape Commission, Sonoma County Vintners, Sonoma Valley Vintners and Growers Alliance, Stag's Leap District Winegrowers Association, Sta. Rita Hills Winegrowers Alliance, Suisun Valley Vintners and Grape Growers Association, Temecula Valley Winegrowers Association, Ventura County Winery Association, West Sonoma Coast Vintners, Wine Artisans of Santa Lucia Highlands, Wine Growers of Dry Creek Valley, Wine Growers of Napa County, Wine Road of Northern Sonoma County and Wineries of Santa Clara Valley. If by accident we have omitted a specific association, please accept our heartfelt apologies.

We thank all of the wonderful people who allowed us to interview them "In Their Own Words," including Barbara Banke, Bo Barrett, Heidi Barrett, Mike Benziger, Mark Beringer, Jean-Charles Boisset, Eileen Crane, Stéphane Derenoncourt, Gary Eberle, Gina Gallo, Mike Grgich, Steve Hearst, Austin Hope, Agustin F. Huneeus Jr., Cheryl Indelicato, Tobin James, Zelma Long, Sonja Magdevski and Emilio Estevez, Philippe Melka, Michael Mondavi, Peter Mondavi Sr., Rob Mondavi Jr., Joel Peterson, Jon Priest, George Rosenthal, Jim Saunders, Pierre Seillan, Tom Tiburzi, Michael Trujillo, and Ken Volk.

Heartfelt thanks go to all of the winemakers, winery owners, and marketing professionals who made sure that we received the samples and information that we needed to compile this book.

So many people assisted us on every level, and most of them are named here, but if we've missed a few, it's only because there's not enough paper and ink in the world to list them all. We thank Virginie Boone, Kathie Lee Gifford, Jennifer Simonetti-Bryan, Peter Mondavi Jr., Mary Beth Bentwood, Isabel Mondavi, Kristin Green, Chris Taranto, Jennifer Porter, Melissa McAvoy, Mark McWilliams, Skye Morgan, Sienna Spencer, Camron King, Kimberly Charles, Jennifer Chin, Bob DeRoose, Katarina Maloney, Suzie Kukaj, Robin Kelley O'Connor, Susan Kostrzewa, Allison Langhoff, Joe Magliocco, David Drucker, Rebecca Hopkins, Michelle Woodruff, Kristina Kelley, Anna Miranda, Katie Calhoun, Sonia Meyer, Kara Hoffman, Holly Evans, Pat Burns, Erika Michelis, Kate Regan, Lisa Klinck-Shea, Amelia Weir, Michelle Flores, Helen Gregory, Mary Anne Sullivan, Kanchan Kinkade, Ken Morris, Randy Martinsen, Elaine Mellis, Natalie Gerke, Keely Garibaldi, Amy Miranov Janish, Helene Mingot, Claire and Lance Silver, Korinne Munson, Colleen Chen, Jannis Swerman, Chris Silva, Phil Baily, Farley Green, Jessica Blanco, Heather Muhleman, Jetty Jane Connor, Andrea Werbel, Carole MacDonal, Tim McDonald, Liam Mayclem, Lea Wilson, Mimi Huggins, Kirsten Hampton, and Terri Stark.

Finally, we thank all of our friends and colleagues in the wonderful world of wine. Without your support, this book would not have been possible.

Thank you all so much!

CREDITS

Images courtesy of the wineries with the following additions:

Alamy
© Design Pics Inc: 170 top center

Jeremy Ball of Bottle Branding
253

© Brassfield Estate Winery 2013
28

California State Library
Isaiah West Taber: 3

© Rocco Ceselin
100 bottom left

© Kaitlin Childers
47 center left

Corbis
© Yadid Levy/Robert Harding World Imagery: 170 top left, 171

© Kevin Cruff/Courtesy the Antinori Family
100 top right

Depositphotos
© alancrosthwaite: 256 bottom center, 267 bottom right; © amanalang: 88 top center; © Jeffrey Banke: 160 top center & right, bottom & center left; © Sergey Borisov: xiv center right (ocean); © Francesco Carucci: 88 center left; © Andy Dean: 76 bottom left, 186 bottom right; © Grafvision: xiv center right (flag); © londondeposit: 256 bottom & center right, 257; © James F. Mattil: 212 top left; © nikitos1977: 236 top left; © David M. Schrader: 236 bottom center; © slickspics: viii center, 14 bottom left; © Sopotnicki: 240 top; © Konstantin Sutyagin: 14 top left; © tigerfilm: 212 bottom center, 216 bottom; © ulkan: 88 bottom right, 207 bottom left, 236 bottom right, 267 top left; © Jeff Whyte: xiv top center; © woodkern: 212 bottom left

Forest Doud
228

Dreamstime
© Jeffrey Banke: 160 bottom right

E&J Gallo CS Photography
180

© Timm Eubanks
47 top right

© Alex Farnum
143 bottom right

Getty Images
© Panoramic Images: 193

© Adrian Gregorutti
vii bottom right, 77 center left

© Alanna Hale
23 bottom right

© Marie Hirsch
46 bottom left

Intrepid Production
63

Kirk Irwin
241 bottom left

iStockphoto
© aimintang: 186 bottom left & top right, 192 bottom right; © alacatr: 88 bottom center, 192 center left, 192 top left; © John Alves: vi top center, 94; © Bartfett: xiv center; © Bdyksen: 22 bottom left; © Keith Binns: x-xi, 32 bottom right, 76 center right, 163, 169 bottom left; © Maciej Bledowski: xiv bottom center; © bmdesign: vi bottom center; © Denice Breaux: 14 bottom right; © Ken W Brown: xiv bottom left; © canbalci: 88 center right; © CIAPIX: 32 bottom center, 97 bottom; © compassandcamera: vi bottom left, viii top & center right, 32 bottom left, 77 center right, 97 top, 202 bottom right, 236 top center & right, center, 237, 240 bottom; © Creativeye99: xiv center left, 88 bottom right; © donald_gruener: 32 center right, 33, vii bottom center; © Vasileios Economou: 266 bottom; © ejs9: viii bottom left, 170 bottom right; © Star Foreman: xiv top left; © franckreporter: 8 top left; © Agnieszka Gaul: 8 bottom left; © Cristie Guevara: 32 top left; © IBlum: 256 top left; © Jacek_Sopotnicki: 202 top center; © jedphoto: center left & top right, 39; © Jim_David: 216 center; © kanonsky: 192 bottom center; © kevinruss: 267 bottom right; © lenta: 170 top right; © LICreate: 212 bottom right; © lynnbcreative: 202 center left; © malija: 182 bottom; © marslasarphotos: 14 top right; © matsf: 170 center right; © Jerry Moorman: 187; © Aleksandar Nakic: xiv top right; © patagonia20: 170 bottom left; © pawel.gaul: vi top left; © Alexander Raths: vii top right, 8 bottom right, 182 top, 216 top; © Steve Rosset: 192 top right; © Rostislav Sedlacek: 14 center left; © Sparky2000: 186 center left; © stevezmak: 202 top & bottom left; © StinkyJess: 175; © Stroeby: 192 bottom left; © swalls: 8 top right, 186 bottom center, 212 center right; © texasmile: 31; © Ron Thomas: 256 center left; © Ron and Patty Thomas: xii-xiii; © tobiasjo: xiv bottom right; © Gary C Tognoni: 32 top center; © tschuma417: 170 center left, 266 top; © valentinrussanov: 207 bottom right; © YinYang: viii top & center left, 89, 186 top left, 202 top right

© Moanalani Jeffrey
48

© Andy Katz
143 top right

© Michael Kelley
207 top

© Chris Leschinsky
88 top left, 142 center right

Library of Congress
2

LiFT Photos
267

© Andrew Macpherson/Macfly Corp
244

© Map Resources
California state maps

© Briana Marie
104

© Damon Matson
77 top left

© Caitlin McCaffrey 2008
46 top left

© Bob McClenahan
241 bottom right

© Matthew Millman
101 bottom left

© Cathy O'hagain
43 center right

© Rien van Rijthoven
101 bottom right

© Steven Rothfeld
112

Shutterstock
© aspen rock: vii top left, 212 center right; © Danielle Balderas: 202 center right; © Jeffrey Banke: 160 center right; © Brandon Bourdages: 14 center right; © Richard Coencas: viii bottom right; © Deyan Georgiev: ii-iii; © Gserban: 199 bottom left; © kaband: vi top right, 199 top right; © Radoslaw Lecyk: 186 center right; © N. F. Photography: vii top center, 15; © David M. Schrader: 236 bottom left; © Hank Shiffman: 192 center right; © Richard Thornton: 160 top left, 161 top left; © Tupungato: 189; © Lynn Watson: 212 top left; © welcomia: 256 top right

© Derek Skalko
217 top right

Keith Sutter
143 center left

Thinkstock
© Daniel McCarthy: 213; © Henry Turner: 212 top center; © Steve Zmak: 203

© Jamey Thomas
22 bottom right

Jason Tinacci
135, 138

© Matt Wallac
217 bottom right

© M. J. Wickham
76 center left, 101 center left

Courtesy Wikimedia Foundation
Eadweard Muybridge: 4

© Brent Winebrenner
47 top left

INDEX

Note: Page ranges in parentheses, such as (17–28) indicate non-contiguous/intermittent references. Page numbers in **bold** indicate main discussions of grape varieties. Page numbers in *italics* indicate photos/illustrations related to wineries.

D

E

F

G

H

M

O

P

S

T

U

V

Korrine Munson

ABOUT THE AUTHORS

MIKE DESIMONE and JEFF JENSSEN, known as the World Wine Guys, are wine, spirits, food, and travel writers, educators, and hosts. They have been featured guests on a variety of national television programs. They are the entertaining and lifestyle editors at *Wine Enthusiast* magazine, and their articles and photographs have appeared in numerous other publications. DeSimone and Jenssen are the authors of *Wines of the Southern Hemisphere: The Complete Guide*, which won the 2012 Gourmand International Award for Best Wine Book, and *The Fire Island Cookbook*. The duo regularly host wine tastings and educational seminars around the world, and they are members of the International Food, Wine & Travel Writers Association, the Society of Wine Educators, and the James Beard Foundation. They have received the prestigious Golden Pen Award for food, wine, and travel journalism and have been inducted into the Confrérie des Chevaliers du Tastevin at the Château du Clos de Vougeot in Burgundy. Visit them at www.worldwineguys.com.